P9-EDM-291

Praise for I'LL BE WATCHING YOU

"This tale skillfully balances a victim's story against that of an arrogant killer as it reveals a deviant mind intent on topping the world's most dangerous criminals. Phelps has an unrelenting sense for detail that affirms his place, book by book, as one of our most engaging crime journalists."

—Dr. Katherine Ramsland, author of *The Human Predator*

Praise for MURDER IN THE HEARTLAND

"Drawing on interviews with law officers and relatives, *Murder in the Heartland* will interest anyone who has followed the Stinnett case. The author has done significant research and—demonstrating how modern forensics and the Internet played critical, even unexpected roles in the investigation—his facile writing pulls the reader along."

—*St. Louis Post-Dispatch*

"Phelps uses a unique combination of investigative skills and narrative insight to give readers an exclusive, insider's look into the events surrounding this incredible, high-profile American tragedy. . . . He has written a compassionate, riveting true crime masterpiece."

—Anne Bremner, op-ed columnist and legal analyst on Court TV, MSNBC, *Nancy Grace,* FOX News Channel, *The O'Reilly Factor,* CNN, Good Morning America, and *The Early Show*

"When unimaginable horror strikes, it is certain to cause monstrous sufferings, regardless of its locale. In *Murder in the Heartland,* M. William Phelps expertly reminds us that when the darkest form of evil invades the quiet and safe outposts of rural America, the tragedy is greatly magnified. Get ready for some sleepless nights."

—Carlton Stowers, Edgar Award–winning author of *Careless Whispers, Scream at the Sky,* and *To the Last Breath*

"This is the most disturbing and moving look at murder in rural America since Capote's *In Cold Blood.*"

—Gregg Olsen, *New York Times* bestselling author of *Abandoned Prayers*

"A crisp, no-nonsense account . . . masterful."

—*Bucks County Courier Times*

"An unflinching investigation . . . Phelps explores this tragedy with courage, insight, and compassion."

—*Lima News* (Lima, OH)

Praise for SLEEP IN HEAVENLY PEACE

"An exceptional book by an exceptional true crime writer. In *Sleep in Heavenly Peace,* M. William Phelps exposes long-hidden secrets and reveals disquieting truths. Page by page, Phelps skillfully probes the disturbed mind of a mother guilty of the ultimate betrayal."

—Kathryn Casey, author of *She Wanted It All* and *A Warrant to Kill*

Praise for EVERY MOVE YOU MAKE

"An insightful and fast-paced examination of the inner workings of a good cop and his bad informant culminating in an unforgettable truth-is-stranger-than-fiction climax."

—Michael M. Baden, M.D., author of *Unnatural Death*

"M. William Phelps is the rising star of the nonfiction crime genre, and his true tales of murderers and mayhem are scary-as-hell thrill rides into the dark heart of the inhuman condition."

—Douglas Clegg, author of *The Lady of Serpents*

Praise for LETHAL GUARDIAN

"An intense roller-coaster of a crime story. Matt Phelps' book *Lethal Guardian* is at once complex, with a plethora of twists and turns worthy of any great detective mystery, and yet so well-laid out, so crisply written with such detail to character and place that it reads more like a novel than your standard non-fiction crime book."

—*New York Times* bestselling author Steve Jackson

Praise for PERFECT POISON

"*Perfect Poison* is a horrific tale of nurse Kristen Gilbert's insatiable desire to kill the most helpless of victims—her own patients. A stunner from beginning to end, Phelps renders the story expertly, with flawless research and an explosive narrative. Phelps unravels the devastating case against nurse Kristen Gilbert and shockingly reveals that unimaginable evil sometimes comes in pretty packages."

> —Gregg Olsen, bestselling author of *Abandoned Players,*
> *Mockingbird,* and *If Loving You Is Wrong*

"M. William Phelps's *Perfect Poison* is true crime at its best—compelling, gripping, an edge-of-the-seat thriller. All the way through, Phelps packs wallops of delight with his skillful ability to narrate a suspenseful story and his encyclopedic knowledge of police procedures. *Perfect Poison* is the perfect antidote for a dreary night!"

> —Harvey Rachlin, author of *The Making of a Detective*
> and *The Making of a Cop*

"A compelling account of terror that only comes when the author dedicates himself to unmasking the psychopath with facts, insight and the other proven methods of journalistic leg work."

> —Lowell Cauffiel, bestselling author of *House of Secrets*

"A blood-curdling page turner and a meticulously researched study of the inner recesses of the mind of a psychopathic narcissist."

> —Sam Vaknin, author of *Malignant Self Love—*
> *Narcissism Revisited*

Other books by M. William Phelps

PERFECT POISON

LETHAL GUARDIAN

EVERY MOVE YOU MAKE

SLEEP IN HEAVENLY PEACE

MURDER IN THE HEARTLAND

BECAUSE YOU LOVE ME

IF LOOKS COULD KILL

I'LL BE WATCHING YOU

M. WILLIAM PHELPS

PINNACLE BOOKS
Kensington Publishing Corp.
http://www.kensingtonbooks.com

Some names have been changed to protect the privacy of
individuals connected to this story.

PINNACLE BOOKS are published by

Kensington Publishing Corp.
850 Third Avenue
New York, NY 10022

Copyright © 2008 by M. William Phelps

All Kensington Titles, Imprints, and Distributed Lines are available at special quantity discounts for bulk purchases for sales
promotions, premiums, fund-raising, and educational or institu-
tional use. Special book excerpts or customized printings can
also be created to fit specific needs. For details, write or phone
the office of the Kensington special sales manager: Kensington
Publishing Corp., 850 Third Avenue, New York, NY 10022, attn:
Special Sales Department, Phone: 1-800-221-2647.

Pinnacle and the P logo Reg. U.S. Pat. & TM Off.

ISBN-13: 978-0-7860-1930-4
ISBN-10: 0-7860-1930-1

First Printing: July 2008

10 9 8 7 6 5 4 3 2

Printed in the United States of America

For my readers, old and new

AUTHOR'S NOTE

I

Is the boogeyman real? Generations of children would say, *Yes, of course he is*. There, hiding in the closet, amid boxes of toys and smelly socks, creeps that mysterious, unseen monster; that demon underneath the bed; that ghostly image, transparent and ominous, tucked behind the curtains gently drifting in the wind of an open window; that shadowy figure, who comes out at night when the lights are off and Mom and Dad are shouting from the next room, "It's your imagination. Go to sleep."

The boogeyman is there. Any child who has ever sat awake at night with a flashlight underneath his or her covers has seen or heard him.

Truth be told, however, popular culture rarely compares fictional boogeymen—i.e., Michael Myers, Freddy Krueger, and the like—to those predators out there right now blending into society, working with us, standing behind us in line at the bank, waving to our children as they pass by their houses on bikes, watching and waiting for the perfect opportunity to snatch one of us off the street to use as a prop in some sort of unimaginable game of God knows what. Think BTK: an outwardly normal, churchgoing animal control officer who tormented and tortured women for years under the nose of law enforcement. To be clear, this is a book about a *real* boogeyman (like BTK, Gacy, Dahmer, Bundy). A true monster.

A calculating maniac.

Twisted and despicable.

And yet contrary to what you might think, the boogeyman in this true story is not a disturbing-looking, vile creature—an attribute of his character that makes him even that much more dangerous. He doesn't have a scar, like a bead of weld, running the length of his face. Nor does he wear a hockey mask. Or a creepy Halloween costume. He doesn't sport big, pointy ears like a bat. Or have sharp, salivating fangs like a demon.

He does not dress up like a clown.

Or sport a tattoo of a swastika on his forehead.

He's not dirty and sweaty, like every bad guy, in every thriller, in every Stephen King novel and movie.

He's not stupid.

Or mentally challenged.

In fact, our boogeyman speaks quite charmingly.

Smartly. Intelligently. Even elegantly.

He's charismatic and good-looking. A Rutgers graduate. Honor student.

Fun to be around.

"The kind of guy your mother," a former female acquaintance told me, "would want you to marry."

Indeed. Right up until the moment he places his cold and clammy hands around the throats of those women he *chooses* to kill and squeezes the life out of them before penetrating the blade of his favorite knife into their chest, he is the *perfect* gentleman.

The all-American boy next door.

You see, every one of these ingredients—and there are plenty more in the pages that follow—are what make this boogeyman even more dangerous than that creature from your childhood dreams. The one all of us have *thought* we've seen. Yes, the features displayed by our boogeyman will make you *think* twice about those people you think you know—and, likely, when you're in bed some night and you hear a bump in the closet, you'll either get up and run out of the house as fast as you can, or, quite courageously, face your fears and open the door.

II

There are those stories that get under your skin and just sit there, tugging at your soul. For me, this is one of those cases. Having the opportunity to interview a serial killer—a guy who fashioned himself after Ted Bundy and later became obsessed with Bundy's killing strategy—only heightened the intensity of writing this book. Just when you think you've seen and heard it all, along comes a story that changes everything, and for a moment, you think, *Is there a human being capable of such madness?* And then you begin a dialogue with this person and a new understanding of brutality emerges alongside a rather voyeuristic need to know what makes a guy like this tick. From where do these terrible thoughts of harming women come?

I don't know why, but some stories never receive the national attention of, say, a Natalee Holloway, John Mark Karr, Jeffrey Dahmer, or any other high-profile crime story you want to insert here. Some stories are just designed for the 24-7 stimulus of roun'-the-clock news coverage the cable networks have adapted to over the years. While others, like the one I am about to tell, fall below that commercial radar.

Still, I love these stories—the ones we've never heard of. The ones that seem to embody the clichéd spirit of "truth is stranger than fiction." The truth is, we may never know what goes on inside the mind of a maniac. Yet, for the first time in my career, I believe I've come close. In this story, the killer speaks.

Loud and clear.

III

Hundreds of hours of interviews made this book possible: with prosecutors and crime victims, family members of victims, detectives, patrol officers, investigators of all types, forensic specialists, profilers, and, of course, a killer and jailhouse snitch. In no other book I've written, however, have I used more inside (anonymous) sources who have helped me, through their courage, get to the truth and put every piece of this complex crime story together. I cannot thank those courageous people enough for coming forward and making this book what it is.

IV

There may be a question as to why I refer to Ned Snelgrove as a serial killer. I questioned this myself. I've written two books about serial killers before this one. I understand the motives and thinking behind their crimes and, of course, the clinical definition. In talking with one of the top forensic psychologists in the United States, it was explained to me that Snelgrove could, easily, be considered a serial killer. He had killed in different states, years apart, and attempted to kill in between. His motives are clear in his own handwriting: he would continue to kill if he had the opportunity. Add to that the additional murders that sources claim he's responsible for, and a classic serial murderer emerges.

M. William Phelps
January 2008
Vernon, CT

If anyone kills a person, the murderer shall be put to death at the evidence of witnesses, but no person shall be put to death on the testimony of one witness. Moreover, you shall not take ransom for the life of a murderer who is guilty of death, but he shall surely be put to death.

—"Cities of Refuge," New American Standard Bible, Numbers (laws) 35: 30–31

BOOK I

MR. HYDE

1

I

Outside, the stars in the night sky are a brilliant shade of silver, flashing dimly against a dark plum-purple canvas. A vestibule, really. An inviting end-of-the-summer evening. Cool. But also crisp and refreshing, especially after what has been a long summer of fiery temperatures and stagnant, choking air.

This beautiful night doesn't seem to have an effect on this one man sitting, watching the Red Sox game on a big-screen television, inside Kenney's Restaurant and Bar, in downtown Hartford, Connecticut. To him, well, to this man it is just another night—consequently perfect in so many different ways, none of which having much to do with the weather.

Before we get too far, however, you must consider that "he" or "him" are relative terms. There are some who see this man as a predator. Nothing more.

Certainly nothing less.

Yes, when you clear away the residual variations of him being just another middle-aged man sitting at a bar, having a beer, it is a persistent evil inside his soul, behind his eyes, of which he can't seem to refuse or rid himself. Those thoughts of harming women and rendering them unconscious. Then grabbing their throats.

He cannot stop these random images—no, urges. Of squeezing and killing. Even as he sits calmly and watches a simple baseball game. There they are. Impulses. They come to him in waves.

I'm dying to know what causes this turmoil . . . inside of me, he once wrote, questioning it all himself.

II

Sitting with his chest against the edge of the bar, he switches his focus from the television—the Red Sox are likely losing, anyway—to her. Staring, he is quite infatuated tonight by her not-so-flawless figure: the bumpy, hourglass curves of her hips, her long legs, velvety dark hair, and large breasts—yes, double Ds, which are, surely, of great importance to him, not to mention a *necessary* part of his plan and basis for the illicit fantasy.

Although she is a bit rough around the edges, she looks good, all dolled up with dark red lipstick, rosy red cheeks of powdery blush, and a sultry, inviting smile. Tonight, for some reason, he can't seem to resist or turn away from her. She holds a sort of candid, arresting, magnetic attractiveness, like, say, for example, the urge some of us have to maybe slow down and have a quick peep at a fatal accident on the side of the interstate.

He doesn't want to look, but he does.

He doesn't want to give in to his impulses, but he will.

He's studied her for a few weeks. Even spoken to her. "I'm a maintenance worker in town," she had told him one night.

"Yeah, OK," he probably answered, not believing her for a minute.

Analyzing her every move, watching her closely, and getting to know her personally, however, aren't things he's done for the sake of love, companionship, or even obsession. He wants nothing to do with her in any of those ways. His motive tonight, so say law enforcement, is clear: she fits perfectly into an assortment of prey he's collecting, a mold he created while incarcerated from 1988 to 1999.

Tonight she is the Chosen One. She plays a role. Nothing more.

Tonight she is, simply, the Victim.

III

It took him some time to dredge up the nerve to talk to her. Before he had even opened his mouth, he watched as she schmoozed with other patrons, finagled free drinks out of the college kids, and, twisting her hair, prowled the bar for God knows what else. He's heard stories about her. Even offered her money for sex. With a voice gravelly from nicotine, she made idle chitchat with him one night, likely about the weather and baseball, as if she actually gave a damn about either.

He knows she doesn't.

But then, truthfully, if we're being honest, neither does he.

She tries to sit with him on occasion. In public, he shoos her away, same as the homeless he sometimes passes near Bushnell Park on his way into the bar; after all, to his fellow barflies, those sitting next to him night after night, he's a clean-cut businessman, a well-groomed and well-mannered professional. Yes, a working stiff like the rest of them.

During the day, he's a "food counselor"—a lavish industry term for a plain old-fashioned salesman—for a frozen-food company with a satellite office in Wethersfield. He travels alone all over the state of Connecticut and the Northeast. It's been quite a professional drop on the vocational ladder for a man with a bachelor's degree in business science from Rutgers—someone who had once lived in New Jersey and worked for

Hewlett-Packard (HP), traveling all over the country, making 40K a year, when the base annual income for Americans was half that. Indeed, selling boxed meats, frozen pizzas, and vegetables out of your trunk to the middle class of Connecticut, Rhode Island, and Massachusetts is a slap in the face.

And he knows it.

A job is a job, he might have told someone who cared to ask. To me, in a letter, he writes, *I am simply referred to as . . . a door-to-door meat salesman. Ha! [My company did] not sell frozen foods door-to-door. We made appointments.*

As if it actually matters.

He has no friends, perhaps as a result of having an enormous growth erupting from his neck. And never—that anyone who ever knew him could recall—has he kept a girlfriend longer than the time it takes her to figure out how perverted and abnormal he is. And even then, the only girlfriend on record he's had was later found murdered—stabbed and strangled, her body posed—in her apartment.

But what is an ex-con supposed to do with his life after prison? Where can a convicted felon—a man who has admitted strangling and stabbing a woman to death, and strangling and stabbing another who survived to identify him—go for a job? He is lucky that after he came clean with his boss about his past, the guy hired him anyway.

None of that matters at the moment, though. Right now, he sits and he stares. Thinking about *her.* Waiting for her to leave.

Yes. Waiting for her to walk out the door so he can follow.

Tonight, he's decided, it feels right.

Tonight, most definitely, it's *her* turn.

2

I

After that stretch in a New Jersey prison—nine years short of his sentence, mind you—he moved into a motel down the street from his childhood home for a few months, and then, in August 1999, he knocked on Mom and Dad's door in Berlin, Connecticut, some ten miles south of the bar he hangs out at in Hartford.

He had grown up in Berlin. The suburbs. The sticks. It was strange and humiliating, he claims, being back in the same house where it all began forty-something years ago, living once again with *them.* How pathetic, he thought one night, tossing and turning, contemplating suicide. How disappointing.

No wife. No kids. Mooching off his elderly parents.

But what else can he do?

There is a bedroom available upstairs, but he opts for—some later say *insists* on—the room in the basement. "He *wants* to live in the basement," says the prosecutor who soon goes after him. "He *wants* to live . . . in that little workshop—that little sexual fantasy den."

It seems weird and, all at the same time, wonderful—that is, his choice to live in an unfinished, musty basement and sleep on an old ragged couch (simply because for ten years he got used to sleeping on an iron mattress in prison). Stranger still, considering there are four bars within a mile radius of his parents' home, is that he frequents this particular bar in Hartford. Does he need a second DUI (to go with the one he got last year after hitting a parked car) on his rap sheet? What about his job? It depends on keeping an active driver's license.

And yet, according to some, for him, the pros of trolling downtown Hartford far outweigh the cons. It's something he *must* do. He cannot help himself. He has a few regular prostitutes he meets at the bar. He likes to treat himself once in a while. He likes to get rough with them, too, several later report. Put his hands around their necks and squeeze. Call them filthy names.

Bitch. Whore.

Maybe even make idle threats to their lives.

Some wonder if this is why he drives into Hartford on such a regular basis—to maintain that control over females? To make sure that no one in his hometown sees him. Or to simply frequent the seedier bars, trolling . . . searching for that perfect victim. He had once said the perfect woman, in his eyes, was a blonde, good-looking, big-breasted, laid out and posed, topless, dead, there for him to do as he wished. So this *must* be why he travels into Hartford. But then, it can't be. Because within earshot of his home in Berlin are three strip joints and a few underground clubs with an "anything goes" policy if you can swing the cover charge. In fact, if you know where the clubs are, you can walk in and set the rules, tell the ladies what you want, and they'll oblige.

Regardless, it's Hartford he chooses: night after night after night.

And so Hartford it is.

II

He has no family or friends in Hartford. No work contacts. But here he is, bellied up to the bar at Kenney's, on Capitol Avenue, mixing it up with the regulars, watching his favorite baseball team on the big screen, playing pool, eating his favorite meal (tuna salad with extra Russian dressing), and cracking jokes—not to mention talking to the prostitutes as if they are below him.

Imagine that: a convicted, admitted killer who looks *down* on hookers.

In the bar, he feels superior. Suddenly *he* is the more respected member of society. He's cocky that way; there isn't a law enforcement officer or former peer who later says different. Still, in a certain way, he's an enigma. Because for every person that says he's strange, weird, or even scary and dangerous, there's someone out there who says he's smart. Bright. Articulate. Borderline brilliant.

The Hartford prosecutor who will soon make him a priority, however, views him differently: "The embodiment of pure evil," Assistant State's Attorney (ASA) David Zagaja says. "A persistent dangerous felony offender," Zagaja's boss, State's Attorney (SA) James Thomas, adds.

Others put it more simply. More direct: "Scariest person I've ever met."

"The Devil incarnate."

"Even his cell mates thought he was weird," a prison source says. "And these are guys who've murdered and maimed people."

Nonetheless, to those around him inside Kenney's on this night—especially her, the one he has his eye on—he comes across as the friendly salesman who looks like a cross between a high-school math teacher and a professional golfer. His kinky, dirty blond hair is cut Wall Street short, his eyes comforting and sad. He likes to wear ties. Nice sweaters.

Mildly expensive shoes and slacks. In a way, he seems to fall in somewhere between the peculiar and the unconventionally charming. He appears gentle, laid-back.

Quiet. Unassuming.

Dare we say it . . . harmless.

III

The fact of the matter is, no one really knows him, or the compulsions bouncing off the dark walls of his soul. He harbors secrets. Sick thoughts, he himself later admits, that have penetrated, pervaded, and perverted his mind in waves, like motion picture slides, since the second and third grade. One secret he admitted while in prison was an innate—teetering on an uncontrollable jealous—fascination with sexually sadistic serial killers. He likes to cut out articles about them— Gacy and Dahmer and the "Green River"—from newspapers and magazines and store them in files in his basement bedroom. One of the most infamous serial killers of all time, however, is unquestionably his favorite. For the sake of argument, let's call this killer his mentor.

Born in 1946, inside a home for unwed mothers in Vermont, Theodore Robert Cowell soon took his stepfather's name, Bundy, and in 1968, while a student at the University of Washington, he was said to have been devastated after his first real girlfriend, a woman he fell deeply for, ended the relationship unexpectedly, shortly before graduation. This was said to have set Bundy on a path toward evil.

"He continually talks about Bundy," David Zagaja says of the man who adores the famous serial killer. "He continually talks about Bundy's prior experiences: what went right and what went wrong." He criticizes Bundy. Critiques him. "That's where you have the evolution of a killer—that's where you have his true and sincere reflections of what he did in the past and how he will improve his conduct in the present."

IV

Without a doubt, as he sits on that bar stool, staring at her, surely undressing her with his eyes, sipping from his favorite beer (Moosehead, which the bar, for his convenience alone, keeps a case on hand per his request), there is a violent monkey on his back that *no one*—especially this woman and the patrons passing by him night after night, or the bartender serving him those skunky beers—can see or feel: a sexually cruel past that includes one homicide, an aggravated sexual assault and attempted murder, and, well, another that is indisputably, undeniably, in the works.

3

I

It is the fall of 2001, the time of year when that refreshing air rushes down from Canada and pushes the summer humidity hovering in and around lower New England—Hartford, in particular—out to sea for another six months. Soon the leaves will turn. The trees will become skeletal. The air will have a bite to it. And the snows of November and December will bring in the icy freeze of winter and send people hibernating inside their homes.

Tonight, though, it is a relatively warm late-summer evening. As he sits inside Kenney's and continues watching her, he is no doubt posing her in his mind: unconscious and naked from the waist up. You see, that's his gig. His *fetish*. Strangle them until the white light approaches. Tear off their tops and bras. Expose their large breasts. Pose them. Then, of course, pleasure the sexual demons by doing whatever it is he *does*.

If they awake, well, that's their loss.

Out come the knives.

II

As she walks out the front door, he takes one final sip of his beer, grabs his car keys from the top of the bar, and follows, nodding to the bartender.

"See you tomorrow."

"Take it easy," the bartender says.

The one he's been watching pushes the door open, steps onto Capitol Avenue, and hooks a sharp right, clutching her pocketbook closely to her side, while walking a few steps north. Her nephew and a guy they call "John the Security Guard" are outside the bar by the entrance.

She sees them. Stops. Chats.

Meanwhile, he walks out of the bar and turns left toward his car. It is late—and very dark. Although Hartford is at once a bustling city during the workweek's daytime hours, being the birthplace of insurance, the creatures come out at night: dope dealers and addicts, urban crack-cocaine consumers and the suburban white middle-class junkies, carjackers and gangbangers. It is a virtual den of thieves and predators.

Tonight, of course, he is among them—but also *one* of them.

Those words he wrote years before, those words of confusion and regret for getting caught, they mean nothing to him right now. Instead, the need to quench that thirst supersedes any rational thinking on his part.

Satisfy Mr. Hyde.

It is the *only* way.

Satisfy Mr. Hyde.

I've ruined my life . . . , he wrote, *[I need to] get help to change my thinking towards women.*

III

In one of his letters from prison, he explains what is, essentially, a natural, even spiritual, connection he has with Bundy.

The two of them share many attributes, he feels. He can state "with confidence," he wrote, what Bundy was "feeling"—it is a "sexual thrill"—when he held the life of his victims in his hands and, staring coldly into their eyes (something he likes to do, too), took that life at the precise moment of his choosing. It is the last breath, that sudden rush—or, should we say, hush—of air from the lungs when the soul leaves the body.

It is the defining moment for the killer. Total control. It's what most of them crave.

Our guy, the one following the woman from the bar, gets off on it. He's stimulated by it. "He told me," one of his cell mates later says, "that the moment before the woman dies, that is the moment he lives for—when he has the authority to allow her to live or die."

Certainly there is a sexual thrill to it also.

"The erection he gets," says that same inmate, "is so profound that he orgasms from it."

Whatever you want to call it, though, don't call it a power trip. Because it isn't. It's a way to sustain a craving, he admits in those same letters, that can *never* be completely satisfied. He relates to those feelings Bundy experienced, because when *he* kills women, it is that same burn that Bundy felt that tears through *his* body, too: the racing heart, the adrenaline rush, the sweaty palms, and, yes, the growing desire—always too much to take—to feed into the sexual fantasies that come along with it all. There they are: those thoughts of violent sex driving every move.

Every decision.

Every thought.

He can walk away from Kenney's at this moment and find a hooker. He can offer her money. The same way he has in the past. He has money. He can give her a Ben Franklin and she'll no doubt do whatever the heck he tells her.

But that has nothing to do with rewarding the demons. Feeding the beast.

It *has* to be this way. It has to be *her*. The one he saw in the bar. The one he knows. Follows.

The one he *chose*.

A substitute won't do.

IV

While in prison, he compulsively studied Bundy's modus operandi (MO), Teddy Boy's signature way of killing. In a sense, although he would never admit it, he looks up to the famous serial killer, learns from him, especially admiring his *choice* of prey: college students. For him, perhaps the most vitally important part of it all was (unlike Bundy) choosing the vulnerable. The forgotten. Those women in society he believes *won't* be missed. (Prostitutes, of course, are a favorite among some of those serial killers he's read about.)

Not only that, but Hartford has a serial killer lurking, skulking its streets, killing hookers. (It's not him, by the way. Definitely not him. Don't jump to that conclusion this early in our story. He's much, much smarter than the other guy.) Almost two dozen so far. They call him the "Asylum Hill Killer." He beats his women into an unrecognizable pulp of blood and tissue, masturbates on them, then leaves their bodies out in the open.

Naked. Bruised and dead.

Bundy would never have done that.

Our guy would never do that.

Still, he scolds himself: *Bundy's way . . . ,* he wrote, *is a textbook for what I* should have *done. . . .* If he had just followed Bundy's plan in the past, he says, it would have helped him to "avoid arrest." *Bundy,* he wrote, planned *his crimes.* It would be a Friday night. Bundy would leave work and drive one hundred miles to *another town, where he would just settle in at a bar until he met a girl.* He views Bundy's life of killing as a "hobby." A way to pass the time and, all at once, satisfy what he himself, since childhood, has been trying to complete: the supreme craving. It is akin to the same itch an addict feels when he wakes in the morning and begins thinking about that first bag of dope. He knows feeding his addiction with one bag won't cure it—but it will certainly sustain him until the next time.

Our guy is no different.

As he wrote those letters sitting in his prison cell during the mid-1990s, he got down on himself for the way he had gone about it in the 1980s—behavior, in fact, that had put him in prison to begin with. He realizes now that he has never allowed himself to "actually sit down and *plan* something" in the same methodical way Bundy had.

And that, well, that is the one mistake—a mistake he vows *never* to make again—that he believes put him away the first time.

But he's out of prison now. Out and about and prowling the streets of Hartford. "I'm surprised he couldn't plan the perfect murder," someone close to him says. "He is so smart and intelligent. It's shocking that he couldn't do it."

Comparing himself to Bundy, he is positively angered by the notion that he has not learned from Bundy's few faults. He hates the fact that some damn prosecutor, the state's attorney, David Zagaja, a name no one can pronounce *(Za-guy-a)* —it's all his fault—will call him a Bundy "wannabe." In truth, he *did* get away with that first killing, strangling, and stabbing her to death. It took cops four years to catch him. He left no fingerprints. No hairs. No fibers.

Nothing.

He was even questioned by the police shortly after the crime. He took a polygraph, one source says, and passed.

So, in the sense of a hunt, the cops never actually *caught* him.

Yet, that second woman, she lived to tell her story. He'd made one mistake—allowing her to live.

Damn her!

It was a crime, he wrote, he had totally "botched."

Why? Because, he scolded himself, *she* didn't *die*. If she had, he is convinced, his *name wouldn't have even made the suspect list. . . .*

And he's right. It wasn't until they caught him for the second crime that he admitted to the first and copped himself the plea bargain deal of a lifetime: ten to twenty. So, in a way, he *has* fooled them. All of them. He gave them the first crime to avoid a longer sentence on the second.

Quid pro quo.

V

As he trolls through the streets of Hartford, however, he's walking around with over a decade's worth of thinking about what he did wrong—and, for that matter, what *Bundy* did wrong. He's read every one of those books written about Bundy. He boasts about studying the movie starring Mark Harmon. He has notes: a student of murder—a pupil of Bundy's predatory tactics.

And now, he believes, he is the *perfect murderer.* Surpassing even Bundy. He writes how in the end, Bundy was *stupid after the act. He kept maps, schedules & pamphlets of the hotels, beaches & ski resorts he visited. . . .*

Not him. He vows *never* to do that.

Not now. Not after all he has learned.

Bundy: *Stupid, stupid, stupid.*

Out of prison now, given this second chance, he is determined to prove himself worthy of the title he would never admit he so desperately wants.

Better than Bundy.

Yes. It's perfect.

It has a ring to it.

4

I

As he walks toward Capitol Avenue, he can see her out of the corner of his eye. She's in front of the bar. Talking. Walking sexily along the sidewalk. She's working it, too: back and forth. Her hair bounces. Heels click against the sidewalk like wooden blocks. Her breasts, the most significant part of all of this, are moving up and down gracefully—he can hardly take it—as she loiters down the runway toward the end of her life.

He needs her to leave. To walk away from them. Her nephew. That security guard. Walk away from the entrance to the bar.

Come on.

Streetlights. Other cars. The stars. The moon.

None of it matters.

His eyes are on the Target.

He needs to get her alone, out into the gloom of the city.

This must be fun for him: the hunt, the stalking part of it. It has to be like buying the dope and preparing it in a spoon. The high before the high. Heating it up. Sucking it in through a piece of cotton with the syringe.

He walks up closer to her, likely picturing the outcome. That scene running through his mind since, in his own words, "the second or third grade": strangling a woman until life departs from her body (while staring into her eyes, of course).

He starts to sweat. His hands shake. Heart. Racing.

Turn around and walk away.

No. There she is.

Leave.

No.

Take a breath.

II

On this night in early September 2001—days before the terrorist attacks—forty-two-year-old Christina Mallon (pseudonym) stands outside Kenney's Restaurant on Capitol Avenue while our forty-one-year-old predator acts as if he is heading for his car around the corner. Christina has no idea a killer, right at that moment, is staring at her. Neither does she have any idea that, of course, he has *chosen* her.

In a way, Christina knows better. Capitol Avenue at night is not a place for a woman with Tina Turner legs, and a walk that would make any man shudder, to be hanging around.

Turning, he approaches her. This close to it all, he can't help himself. Quite casually, as if he is speaking to a child, he says, "Get in the car." His tan Ford Escort is beside them.

She tells him to take a hike. Not tonight. And then turns.

He grabs her by the arm.

"Damn it, let go of me," she says. Christina is startled. She recognizes him from the bar. He's a regular at Kenney's. Not only that, but she's helped him get customers for his stupid frozen-food business. She's sat and talked with him. She knows him.

What are you doing? Christina thinks.

The security guard and her nephew, now watching from

afar, begin to suspect she is in trouble. As he tries to grab her more firmly by the arm and force her into his car, she jerks her shoulder and gives him a solid smack across the face.

He winces. *Ouch!*

"We tussled," Christina later tells the court.

So she gets away and she runs as fast as she can as her nephew walks hurriedly toward her. She's been through a lot in life, but she's terrified. It was that look on his face. In his eyes. He seemed "different."

Scared somebody has seen him, or that the security guard and her nephew will do something, he hops into his vehicle and pulls up, quickly, alongside Christina, as she registers what is going on. "Get in the car, bitch, or I'll hurt you," he yells from his window.

By now, she is standing directly in front of Kenney's, almost near the entrance.

"What's going on?" asks the nephew.

"You OK?" the security guard wonders.

There is a bottle in the gutter of the street. She picks it up and tosses it at his car, hitting the side of it.

Clank.

"Bitch!" he says before speeding off, looking in his rearview mirror.

5

I

Four months later, Christina is reading the newspaper one morning. Dead of winter. Frost on the windows. Snow on the ground. Outside, you can see your breath like cigarette smoke.

She had decided not to report the incident. What good would it do? The cops know her. She doesn't have a good standing with them. Although she's no hooker, she does have a few pockmarks on her record.

In any event, there's an article about a woman, a beloved local girl, Carmen Rodriguez, staring back at her. Christina knows Carmen. She has seen her at Kenney's. Carmen had been reported missing near the same time Christina had that run-in with the man on the street.

What's his name?

Then it clicks. Christina is horrified. Carmen was last seen leaving Kenney's with the *same* guy. No one has seen her since.

Christina picks up the telephone and calls the Hartford Police Department (HPD).

6

I

And so it appears he has made one more mistake—a vital mistake, which, unbeknownst to him at the moment, will open up a Pandora's box of possibilities for investigators looking into the disappearance of Carmen Rodriguez. All of which will, of course, lead back to him.

II

"This guy, the one you're writing the book about," one criminal profiler, who has studied him for the past twenty years, tells me as we are discussing serial killers over the telephone, "could have left bodies all over New England. He is one of the most dangerous people I've ever tracked."

"Everyone says that," I respond. "I don't know."

"Believe them," he offers.

Indeed, in the days of researching and writing this book, I come to learn that they are all spot on with their judgments of my guy. He is, as David Zagaja has said, the *embodiment* of pure evil.

Satan himself.

To get to the juxtaposition of Carmen and Christina's stories, however, we need to start at the beginning: in New Jersey, where the end of our serial killer's path began with the biggest mistake of his murder career, when he met a woman one night at a bar—a woman he underestimated.

BOOK II

MARY ELLEN

7

I

Mary Ellen Renard made it through what for many might have been the most volatile part of adulthood, and somehow managed to escape with her life. Sure, divorce, physical and emotional abuse, a witness to the sickness of alcoholism and its repercussions, weren't things to celebrate. There was likely going to be a lifetime of therapy in her future.

Contemplation. Medication. Nightmares.

Yes. Midnight screams. Awake, asleep.

Up and down.

Tossing and turning.

But for the most part, Mary Ellen—along with her two daughters, after seventeen years of living with a man she described as "intermittently violent"—had left him and made it out into the world on her own. That was something to commemorate, indeed. A major accomplishment. She wasn't running. Or hiding. Mary Ellen was *leaving*.

That first apartment, Mary Ellen said, after living in Ringwood, New Jersey, with *him,* had been an old construction office shanty at one time, she found out months after moving in. There had been a drought in New Jersey when she and the kids rented it. When the drought ended and the rains came, so did the water. Leaking directly above her bed.

But looking back, Mary Ellen agreed it was nothing compared to the violence and chaos she and the girls had left behind.

Walking out of that house wasn't easy. After all, it was two months after she was married, in 1963, that he had started hitting her, and didn't stop until 1980 when she left. After two kids and more beatings, she believed she could tame him. Love was going to get them through, she convinced herself. "I never considered," she said, "leaving. It wasn't something you did then. I truly believed that when you loved someone enough, you could overcome any problem."

Growing up Catholic didn't help, Mary Ellen insisted. Having a priest for a brother made divorce sacrilegious. "Yes, we went to church religiously," she said, laughing at the pun.

In fact, when Mary Ellen went to see her mother one night after her husband hit the kids for the first time, pleading with her, telling her the only option she had was to get rid of the bastard, Mary Ellen's mother looked at her with conviction and said, "You're a Catholic. There is no divorce."

Mary Ellen understood, but it didn't make it any easier. She thought maybe that if she confided in her mother, the woman might feel differently. But instead, "That is your cross to bear," her mother said. "And you bear it."

Mary Ellen accepted her mother's answer. "Look at my mother's crosses to bear," she recalled. "She was like the Rock of Gibraltar. I mean, nothing would stop her."

II

During the 1950s, north of Newark, west of White Plains, Fair Lawn, New Jersey, enjoyed one of its greatest periods of growth. By the 1960s, Fair Lawn would soar fourfold, from a meager nine thousand residents to almost forty thousand, in twenty years.

Working farms dominated the landscape. "We were like farm kids," Mary Ellen said. By example, Mary Ellen's parents taught their four children that living through hard times was never an excuse for a life of poverty. The American dream was theirs, if only they wanted it bad enough. Her dad, who hadn't made it past the eighth grade, went on to become an industrial engineer.

Mary Ellen was born in 1942. The first house she recalled living in with her three siblings was a modest cape-style ranch. She grew up as a tomboy in one sense, but a girly girl in another. With Mom home all day, she fell into the same reclusive life her mother had known for decades. "My mom was always home. Today it might be called agoraphobia. She never left the house."

It wasn't only the confines of being a wife and mother molded from the 1950s social class of stay-at-home moms that kept Mom cooped up. The family had a rare disease, which saddled most of them. Mom was a bleeder, not a hemophiliac, but had a disease of the veins known as hereditary hemorrhagic telangiectasia (HHT), which, according to the University of Michigan, is "a disorder of the small and medium sized arteries of the body." Primarily affecting four organ systems of the body—lungs, brain, nose, and gastrointestinal (stomach, intestines, or bowel) system—the "affected arteries either have an abnormal structure causing increased thinness or an abnormal direct connection with veins (arteriovenous malformation)." It was not uncommon for Mary Ellen to return from school and find her mother on the kitchen floor in a pool of blood. Her oldest memory of her mother, in fact, contains ghastly images of walking in the door with her book bag in one hand and a smile on her face, only to find her mom struggling to get up off the floor after the veins in her legs had burst open like a dry-rotted garden hose.

"All of my siblings have the symptoms." Luckily, the gene skipped over Mary Ellen. "No one knew what was wrong with my mother until many years later. Doctors actually took photographs of her for medical books."

8

I

As Mary Ellen's marriage fell into an abyss of alcoholism and violence, she had no one to whom she could turn. She had grown up in a reclusive household, cut off from a social world of any kind. It wasn't a stressful childhood, she insisted. They lived off the farm and ate, mostly, off the land. Mary Ellen's mother and father had lived in orphanages throughout their childhood. They met while working at a New Jersey silk mill. They were thirteen. Mary Ellen said the household was loving and caring.

Mary Ellen's dad was the stereotypical 1950s male provider. All through her years of school, Mary Ellen never had a boyfriend. She was intimidated by boys and had no time for them. Mom had surgery to repair a herniated disc when Mary Ellen was five and the doctors severed a nerve, which paralyzed one of her legs. "She came home in leg braces," Mary Ellen recalled. The old type: leather and steel, like Forrest Gump's. She also wore a back brace and had to walk with crutches. It lasted a year. Even though she was young, Mary Ellen helped her mother around the house. "What got my mother through all those tough times," Mary Ellen added, "was her faith in God. I asked her later, 'Why did you never get hopelessly depressed?' She said, 'I didn't have time for that. I had four little kids who needed me.' She was just amazing. Her faith is what got her through."

II

Mary Ellen described herself as a "painfully shy" high-school student. But it wasn't necessarily growing up in such an isolated environment at home that turned Mary Ellen into such an introvert. At thirteen, she learned she suffered from a form of scoliosis, which, in high school, began to curve her small vertebrae. Because of it, she started high school in a full-body brace. Luckily, "the brace prevented me from becoming a full hunchback"—yet it also prevented her from being active socially. "It added to my shyness. . . . If you have a mother who rarely leaves the house, you don't learn social skills. You don't know how to behave in the world."

What made matters worse was that Mary Ellen's father was on the road, traveling for work. He'd be gone a month and home for a weekend and gone again. Mary Ellen's high-school English teacher encouraged her to write. Her teacher suggested college, majoring in creative writing. But, Mary Ellen said, it was a time when the men went out into the world, educated themselves, and took care of the family financially, while the women stayed at home with the kids. So she enrolled in Seton Hall University and figured she'd pursue her dream in small doses. Tragedy struck, however, and derailed even that modest ambition. Her father was involved in an auto accident that had almost killed him. Then he had a stroke. He was forty-eight. For two years he was recovering at home, unable to work.

By the time her father got back on his feet, college was no longer an option for Mary Ellen. The money was gone. Plus, she had what was considered then to be a fairly good job for a girl as a service rep for the local telephone company, a job she had taken after high school to help out with the bills around the house.

Still, things were OK. Mary Ellen believed that helping her family was more important. Her Catholic education had taught her that life was worth living *only* when you helped others.

Be a servant of the Lord. It was the only way. The Catholic way.

"Even though I loved to write, I saw myself as a mother and a homemaker, just like *my* mother."

Be grateful for what you have, not what you don't. God had chosen Mary Ellen's path. She was fine with it.

III

Her parents kept a short leash on Mary Ellen when it came to dating. "Wrapped in tissue paper," she described that time frame, from the first day she left the house for kindergarten until she graduated. Even after high school, she wasn't one to go out looking for boys to date or even hang around with friends. She lived under a system: work, home.

Home, work. Five days a week. Chores and errands on Saturday. Church Sunday.

It wasn't that her parents—and Mary Ellen was quick to point this out—were shielding her from a profane life, sheltering her from opportunity or "devils," demanding she not date anyone. "Both of them had had such hardship in their childhood, they just wanted to protect their children."

9

I

It was one night at a Catholic social dance, Mary Ellen later explained, when she met her future husband, the alcoholic. He was three years older, six feet three inches tall, slender, good-looking.

Blond hair, blue eyes. What was there not to like, she thought. "I was swept off my feet. Here I was, this shy little country girl, and he had grown up in New York City and had already been in the service."

Kids came quickly. Within a few years, Mary Ellen was a stay-at-home mom, just like her mother, with two to take care of and, according to her and the girls, a husband who liked to drink, pop pills, and abuse all three of them.

II

After seventeen years of chaos, Mary Ellen dredged up the courage to leave. Out on her own now, with two kids, Mary Ellen was determined to make it. After all she had been through, Mary Ellen was ready to put it all behind her and start over.

Living with an alcoholic all those years, Mary Ellen said, it might have seemed as if she were a masochist. Most would ask, "Why not just leave?" But it wasn't simple, Mary Ellen insisted. He wasn't violent all the time. "It wasn't like you got your beating every Saturday night. Six months would go by without him becoming violent. People don't understand that you go from one nightmare to another—that when you leave, you're thrown into poverty immediately. And then your children are subjected to all kinds of *additional* horrors."

III

Mary Ellen had never been on her own. To leave meant setting out into the world by herself with two children and a husband, she feared, could come after them and maybe "kill us." On top of that, "I was childlike when I got married and in many ways still childlike when I left seventeen years later."

Those horrors Mary Ellen suffered, coupled with a childhood wrought with disappointment and heartache, even though there were plenty of good times, was nothing compared to what Mary Ellen was about to face in the coming days on her own. If she thought she had lived through the toughest days of her life, Mary Ellen had thought wrong.

10

I

One of Mary Ellen's daughters recalls those years of living with her alcoholic father and "bipolar" mother as turbulent and disordered—and also, she later told me, "a bit different from what my mom might tell you. It's been an ongoing chaotic life. Never-ending."

Diana was the younger of the two. She loves her mother and they speak every day. But the way Diana describes her life with Mary Ellen is quite a bit different from the way Mary Ellen remembered it. "My mother," Diana said, "believes what she believes." Mary Ellen had always tried to protect her kids from her husband's abusive hand. Yet Diana left the house when she was sixteen. But not, she said, "by my own choice." The house was an extreme environment.

Diana recalled punishment as being put in the corner for not a time-out, but for several hours. No dinner. No talking. No going to the bathroom. No television.

Mary Ellen, on the other hand, was trapped. Terrified. She couldn't rescue the kids for fear of retaliation.

There was one time when Diana's dad was cleaning his shotgun in the living room—or was he?—and it went off and buckshot destroyed one of the walls. A vivid memory for Diana was having to repanel the wall so no one would see it. "Everyday life was like that. Who knows if he was trying to kill my mother?"

When Mary Ellen finally got the courage to leave, it wasn't, Diana said, as if she decided one day, *That's it. I can't take this anymore.* "We were literally running down the street in our pajamas away from him to the police two blocks away. She thought he was going to shoot us."

11

I

Living on her own with the two kids hadn't turned out so bad for Mary Ellen Renard. After moving out of the construction shanty, she found a cozy little apartment for herself and embraced her new independence. And, at first, things went well.

She found a good job. Friends. Although they'd had some trouble of their own, her daughters were alive.

Life had gone on.

Soon, though, bouts of loneliness and depression crept up on Mary Ellen and she began to crave companionship. For most of her adult life, she had been around people. She'd had a man—for lack of a better way to describe the abuser she lived with—in her life for almost two decades. But now, she was alone. And she didn't want to be. So one night, Mary Ellen went to a church dance and met a man, a Catholic widower who met with her family's approval. Despite a few nagging doubts, she married him. Yet, during the early days of her new marriage, she began to wonder if there was some sort of bull's-eye on her back that attracted alcoholics and abusers.

It was as if she had advertised for them. This new man turned out to be no different from her first husband.

"I would have divorced him sooner than nine months," she said later, "but I was scared to leave him alone with *his* two daughters. Shortly after I left him, he burned the house down." Luckily, it was a few days after the man's daughter turned eighteen and had moved out with her sister.

II

Soon after the second chapter of her married life ended, Mary Ellen found what seemed like the perfect apartment. It was a two-family house in Elmwood Park, New Jersey, just outside Hackensack and Paterson, an area close to where she had grown up. It was the first apartment she had rented since her second divorce that felt even remotely like a home. It was in a rural neighborhood.

Nice people. Nice homes. Green grass. Picket fences.

Start fresh, Mary Ellen told herself, moving boxes up the stairs. *Learn from the past.*

After getting settled, Mary Ellen realized that it wasn't necessarily the men in her past that had made her life a living hell—but the fact that she had *chosen* them. She resolved now to be more cautious. If she had picked two alcoholics and abusers, there was a reason. Now it was time to take an inventory and go back out into the world a smarter, more self-assured woman.

12

I

Two major Hollywood films set the romantic tone for the year 1987: *Moonstruck* and *Fatal Attraction*. One showed how a hardworking woman learns to love and trust again while the other explored the darker side of the one-night stand, which had become fairly popular by the mid-1980s. *Fatal Attraction* proved that although you thought you felt a magnetism toward someone you had just met, you didn't really *know* the person. Heading out to a bar, hooking up with someone you shared a drink with, and then heading back home for a romp in the water bed could turn violent and even deadly.

Mary Ellen was forty-four. She had just started a new job at MediPhysics Corporation that April. Elmwood Park was not a bastion of crime. For the most part, Mary Ellen had little to worry about—save for living alone as a single woman. She lived on the second floor, and her landlady lived below. She didn't know the woman well. But Mary Ellen said the lady was a curmudgeon, an old hag who was paranoid about everything and everyone. "She was really eccentric," recalled Mary Ellen. "She'd do strange things. When it was cold out, she'd remind me to leave the upstairs bathtub water running as a trickle," which wasn't so odd, "but she would leave me a note to do it every single night."

There was no reasoning with the woman. She had her rules and that was it. Keys were a fascination. The entryway (the main door) to the house, because it was a two-family, was to the left of the landlady's first-floor apartment. When you entered the building, whether you were heading up to Mary Ellen's second-floor apartment or the landlady's first-floor apartment, you had to first go through a main door and either head up the stairs in front of you to Mary Ellen's, or take a quick left and walk into the landlady's. This front door, leading into the building, was not supposed to be left unlocked.

Unlike most dead-bolted doors, however, the door didn't have a latch on the inside; it had a key lock, same as it did on the outside. The landlady was firm about this door being locked at all times, whether you were inside or out. "Always lock it, Mary Ellen," she'd bark. "Never leave or return home without locking the dead bolt."

Not only was the lock illegal, but it posed a great danger if you were inside and couldn't find your keys. There were no windows in the hallway leading up to Mary Ellen's apartment, or downstairs near the entrance to the landlady's apartment. "While my daughter came to visit with her baby once," Mary Ellen said, "I ran out to the store. I came back, and she explained that she had wanted to get something from her car while I was gone, but couldn't get out of the house."

It was a strange way to live. However, Mary Ellen overlooked the woman's odd behavior because, compared to where she had come from, it was like living in a castle. What were a few rules? Even if she didn't agree with them.

13

I

On Saturday night, August 1, 1987, Mary Ellen decided to get back into the swing of being single and head out on the town. She left her apartment around 7:00 P.M. and went to a singles dance. Dances were held in hotels and restaurants. A singles dance was a way, Mary Ellen always believed, to meet and schmooze with other people in the same position. It was safe. She wouldn't have to go from bar to bar to meet new people. She could show up and feel a sense of empowerment that everyone at the dance was there for the same reason: to hook up.

It had been a year since she last went out or even thought about attending a singles function. Two marriages down the drain. Her parents and, especially, her pious brother, the priest, were not happy about the way her life had turned out. But Mary Ellen trudged on in the face of such discouragement. It felt right going out to a dance. She was her own woman. This particular event was being held at a bar she liked: Kracker's in Clifton, not too far from her apartment.

To her amazement, when she walked in, she noticed there were about eighty people standing around, dancing, chatting, getting to know one another. Quite a large crowd to work her way through. As the night wore on, Mary Ellen talked with and danced—"I love to dance," she said—with about four different men, none of whom seemed all that interesting. All was well, regardless. It wasn't a total loss. She had a drink. It was a good time.

And then she walked into the cocktail lounge to contemplate leaving. It was well after midnight. Standing in the doorway between the bar entrance and the ballroom, where the dance had been held, Mary Ellen thought it had been a fun night. Maybe she'd get back into the singles-dance scene again. Maybe not wait a year this time to start dating.

Just as she was preparing to leave, a "very clean-cut, blond . . . very well-dressed, suit and tie, very neat" man made a gesture toward her. He was sitting at the bar and had just happened to turn around as she was about to walk out.

"He was a wholesome-appearing person," she said later.

The music was loud. People were talking all around them. He had turned around on his bar stool and whispered, "Hello," making a funny face.

Mary Ellen noticed him right away.

She laughed. He seemed charming, even from so far away. He was working for her attention—and she liked it.

So she walked over to where he was sitting and sat down. "I'm a computer salesman," he said, sticking out his hand. "Hewlett-Packard."

"I'm learning the computer now," she said. ("We had quite a long conversation about computers," Mary Ellen recalled. "How everything was computerized back then, and if you're not learning computers, you're not going to get too far.")

He asked her if she wanted a drink.

She thought about it. "Sure." She had nursed the drinks she'd had, not even finishing one. Another wouldn't hurt.

"I'd like to see you again," the man said after about a half hour of the two of them sitting and talking.

Mary Ellen smiled coyly. "I think you're much too young," she said over the loud music. She didn't know how old he was, but she could tell he was maybe thirty at the most. He had a boyish way about him. A fragility. He reminded her of her son-in-law, who had just turned thirty. Mary Ellen wasn't looking for a boy toy. If she was going to date someone—and she wasn't necessarily looking for a long-term relationship—she wanted a man.

Not that she would insult the guy, but dating somebody as young as her son-in-law was not something she was at all interested in. (He never told her, but he was actually twenty-six, about to turn twenty-seven in eight days.)

"And how old are *you*?" he asked smugly, not insulting, as if he really wanted to know.

"Forty-four," Mary Ellen said without hesitating.

"You should get some points for being honest about your age."

She found this statement quite appealing. He wasn't taken aback by her age, but complimented her for being honest. It wasn't every day you met someone, she thought, who was frank, open, and even likeable. He seemed sincere.

"Watch my drink," Mary Ellen said after they went back and forth for a time, joking about her age.

When she returned from the restroom a moment later, the man stood up from his stool, stuck out his hand like a prince, reaching for hers, and asked, "How 'bout a dance?"

"Sure," she said—and they hit the dance floor and then returned to the bar.

Taking one last sip of her drink, Mary Ellen said, "It was nice to meet you. But it's getting late. I have to go."

He accepted that and said his good-byes.

She turned and left the bar.

14

I

Walking out of the bar and into the parking lot, Mary Ellen was trying to recall exactly where it was she had parked her car. It was approaching 2:00 A.M. The night sky was dark. With all the cars from the dance, it was hard to maneuver around the lot and see each vehicle. Finding her 1981 Olds Cutlass was posing to be quite the adventure.

"What kind of car do you have?" a voice said from in back. It startled her. She didn't think that the man had followed her out of the bar. She hadn't seen him. It was as if he had just appeared there behind her. Still, when she saw who it was, Mary Ellen felt relieved. She sort of knew him. At least he wasn't a stranger who had come up on her.

As Mary Ellen explained what kind of car she was looking for, they walked around the parking lot searching for it.

"There it is," Mary Ellen said, spying her car to the left of the bar door.

The man pointed to his car, which was parked just a row behind hers.

"I'm not sure how to get on the highway," Mary Ellen said as she opened her door and got in.

He pointed down the road. "You have to take a U-turn down there to get back on the other side of the road and head east."

"OK," Mary Ellen said thankfully. Then she got into her car without paying too much attention to where the man was standing. ("I thought he was leaving too," she said later.)

On the way to the dance, Mary Ellen's Olds had stalled. It had been running rough for a while. She'd just had some repairs done because she knew she was starting a new job and needed a dependable vehicle. When she tried starting it that night as the man stood by and watched, it wouldn't turn over.

So she tried again.

Nothing.

"You're going to wear the battery down," he said. "Maybe it's flooded. Leave it alone for a few minutes and try it again, it might turn over. Sometimes that happens."

Mary Ellen had the window down. She was still sitting in her car. He was standing by her window, leaning down. At some point (Mary Ellen couldn't recall exactly when) the man left her, got into his car, and pulled up alongside. Their cars faced opposite directions, but they were parked side by side to each other. He, too, sat in his car with the window rolled down. Waiting for the carburetor to flush itself out and dry up, so she could try to restart her car, they talked some more about how she would get on the highway. The man wanted to be sure she knew where she was going.

After waiting for what was about ten minutes, she tried to start her car again. Turning the key and allowing the ignition to crank and crank, the engine finally fired. But it was bumpy, sputtering and backfiring. She was nervous about driving it home.

"It stalled on the way over here," Mary Ellen yelled out her window as the engine groaned and hiccupped.

"I can show you how to get on the highway if you follow

me," the man yelled back. "Maybe I ought to follow you after that, because your car doesn't sound right."

"That would be nice," Mary Ellen said to the man. "Thank you."

Mary Ellen followed the man onto the highway and then pulled ahead of him so she could show him the way to her apartment.

II

Inside about twenty minutes, Mary Ellen pulled up in front of her apartment and parked her car on the street in front of the lawn.

The man parked directly behind her.

Before Mary Ellen could even get out of her car, the man was, as she later put it, "right up by my car door." He had startled her. As she opened the door, he said, "I didn't realize it was so far. I have to use the bathroom."

She didn't see the harm. He had helped her. He had demonstrated his thoughtfulness by following her home. The least she could do was allow him to use her bathroom.

"Sure, let me open the door."

15

I

Mary Ellen Renard had lived in fear for so many years after she left her first husband that she had become blind to its most outward signs. In some ways, she was an absolute whiz when it pertained to certain things. Her job was to transcribe doctors' notes. No one else could understand the Asian and other foreign language–speaking doctors who spoke with broken-English accents. But Mary Ellen picked it up with ease.

Where it pertained to judging males and their intentions, however, Mary Ellen later admitted that she was a bit naïve. She was cautious, but maybe just a bit inexperienced and trustworthy. It was 1987. What woman didn't watch the news? What woman didn't know that it wasn't such a smart move to invite a man you had just met into the privacy of your home? For all she knew, this man had taken her gratitude as a open sign for a nightcap and some good lovin'.

Still, if there was one attribute that separated Mary Ellen from most, it was that she gave people the benefit of the doubt. She wanted to believe in people.

II

After Mary Ellen unlocked the dead bolt and let him into the hallway leading up to her apartment, she turned around and, with her key, locked the dead bolt to the entrance door behind her, per her meddlesome landlady's orders. It was a safe bet, in fact, the nosey old woman was on the opposite side of her door as Mary Ellen and her friend were in the hallway, peering through the peephole, watching them.

A moment later, Mary Ellen and her new friend walked up the stairs to her apartment; within a moment, they were inside. "The bathroom," Mary Ellen said, putting her pocketbook down on the counter in the kitchen and pointing to the hallway just beyond where they were standing in the living room, "is right down there."

"Thanks," he said, looking around, adding, "nice apartment."

Mary Ellen took off her shoes and placed them by the door. After that, she walked into the kitchen and placed her keys inside her pocketbook. Then she went into the refrigerator and looked for a block of cheese she always kept on hand. "I always eat cheese when I got home," she explained, "because I have hypoglycemia and I need to eat frequently."

It was nearly 3:00 A.M. She hadn't eaten all night. With her condition, doctors suggested a small meal of protein every two hours. With a block of cheese on a plate, Mary Ellen took a knife out of the drawer below and carved the cheese into several slices. When she finished, she got herself a diet Slice ("my favorite"), grabbed the plate of cheese, and headed for the living room.

Just then, as she sat down on the couch, she heard the toilet flush. *He must be on his way. . . .*

Several minutes went by before he came out of the bathroom, however. It was odd that he was taking so long.

What is he doing?

When he finally returned, Mary Ellen asked, "Would you like a soda?"

"No," he said. Then, "Are those your kids on the wall over there?" He was standing by the door. Mary Ellen sat on the couch in front of him a few yards away.

Mary Ellen smiled. Everyone asked about the kids. She explained to him that she had grandkids. She was a grandmother. Imagine that.

"Your daughters are very pretty," he said. He was standing in front of Mary Ellen now. Closer. He seemed different. He even *sounded* different. Something was wrong.

"Thank you," Mary Ellen said.

As she went to speak again, he approached her and, bending down, tried kissing her on the lips. But she backed away immediately.

"I don't want you to do that. I really don't know you. It makes me uncomfortable."

On the mantel by her television set was a photograph of her brother. After backing away, he turned his attention toward the picture. "Is your brother a priest?"

Mary Ellen got up. She wanted him to leave. He was acting a bit squirrelly, as if he had taken some sort of drug (he hadn't) when he was in the bathroom. Mary Ellen had to cross paths with him to get to the door. She'd heard enough. The kiss scared her. She wanted to see him out and lock the door. But as she walked past him, he grabbed her by the shoulders and tried kissing her again.

She backed away instantly. ("I was alarmed," she recalled, "I mean, it was *not* the same type of kiss.")

Not only the kiss, but his entire demeanor had changed. He was totally out of it. Completely inside his own head, as if he were drifting away somewhere. Earlier that night, Mary Ellen was in awe of his good looks. But now he didn't even *look* the same.

He didn't speak. ("He just stared at me, stared into my eyes," she later remembered.)

Looking *through* her, the man grabbed Mary Ellen by the shoulders once again. Mary Ellen could feel his grasp this time. He was hurting her. "Stop it," she said loudly.

He began kissing her again, forcefully. She hated it. When she denied his advances repeatedly, he became enraged and threw her backward onto the couch. ("I was trying to break away," she recalled, "but I lost my balance.")

On top of her, down on the couch, he grabbed at her right breast. "Stop," she pleaded, "you're *hurting* me."

Without saying a word, he continued clutching her by the breasts. He was fascinated and, at the same time, aroused by the violence he was perpetrating while touching her breasts. Just the sight of them as he opened her blouse, ripping her bra off and exposing them, did something to change him, Mary Ellen knew.

She was large. C cup. Her breasts had changed him. After he was finished fondling Mary Ellen's breasts, he looked up. "He didn't say anything. He stared—just stared into my eyes."

16

I

This man in Mary Ellen's living room, the one on top of her, sexually assaulting her, planning in his head how he was going to kill her, profoundly hated his given name, Edwin Fales Snelgrove Jr. His distaste was so much that he had whittled it down years ago. "Call me 'Ned'," he'd tell new friends. Edwin sounded so Gilded Age. So dated and traditional. So, Ned it had been.

Ned had pushed-back kinky hair of a brownish blond persuasion, cut conservatively. He wasn't overweight by any means. He had a chiseled body (not through weight lifting, though, but genetics, one of those "you can eat whatever you want and never gain an ounce" bodies that some are lucky enough to be born with). Being a fan of wrestling, he could get you in a hold that, former college friends said, he could keep for hours. Beyond this penchant for pain, Ned had serious psychological issues. He hated women. Not that he hated being around them, or the sight of them, but something inside of him was wired so that he viewed the female—the good-looking ones with large breasts—as some sort of object that, in a certain position, provided, in his words, "*enormous* sexual arousement." Yes, they had to be in a particular situation. This was important to Ned. They had to submit. Appear helpless. Powerless. And there was only one way to get them there, Ned believed: strangulation.

If that didn't work . . . well . . . out came the knives.

These thoughts and urges began during Ned's childhood, as far back as the second and third grade. *For unknown reasons*, he wrote later, *he had never thought it was a problem* until years after it started. The pleasure, he explained to a friend in a letter, came from seeing a *good-looking female become helpless.* The woman could be "asleep," but he had to be standing over her "in person." Watching "a girl faint," too, did something for him. And yet, seeing a girl "killed in a movie or TV show" seemed to offer the most satisfaction—that is, beyond the real thing.

I cannot even come close to describing the feelings I get, he once wrote, talking about seeing a woman in a movie incapacitated. When he watched women in those situations, his heart rate increased to a point, he wrote, *until I think [it] is in my mouth.* Ned became "dizzy" and his "hands sweat." He also got an erection like never before. Back in grade school, Ned explained, he had these same feelings about his teachers. *Every time I see a girl I am attracted to,* he wrote, and it didn't matter if it was in person, on television, or in photographs, instead of "undressing" the woman with his "eyes," Ned *always imagine[d] strangling her or hitting her over the head* and carrying her *limp body onto a bed.* Once she was unconscious, he would undress her and arrange *her arms and legs in some kind of seductive pose.* Maybe position her like a doll. If she came to, well, that was *her* problem: he'd have to resort to other means.

II

The man who liked to be called Ned, or even "Neddy," whom Mary Ellen had met at the singles dance and allowed in to use the bathroom, was now on top of her, forcefully grabbing and clutching her breasts and holding her down with all his might. As Mary Ellen struggled with him, he put both of his hands "up onto her throat." And then he squeezed as hard as he could.

Mary Ellen started to say, "What are you doing?" but could not finish because her airway was closing. With that, he placed both of his thumbs together and dug them into the middle of her throat. He had obviously studied the human anatomy and knew exactly what he was doing.

"I almost wanted to think he was kidding," Mary Ellen said later, "but he *wasn't* kidding. . . . He was staring straight at me and he just squeezed my throat."

She could barely move. He wasn't much taller than Mary Ellen, but he was much more powerful. Looking at her, it wasn't hard to see what Ned had found so attractive earlier that night when it seemed he was interested in getting to know her. She had shoulder-length, wavy-cut dark brown hair, emerald green eyes (quite alluring and inviting), a comforting "Mary Tyler Moore" smile, and porcelain, blemish-free skin. Mary Ellen was plainly attractive, kept her figure slim, and had a charisma that drew men toward her.

Ned wasn't interested in any of those positive qualities, however: he was focused on rendering her unconscious so he could finish fulfilling his fantasy. As he squeezed her throat harder and Mary Ellen began to slip into unconsciousness, a notion occurred to her: *I never thought my life was going to end like this.* And then a white light, she recalled, approached . . . and here it was—after all she had been through. All she had put up with throughout her life. Here, things were beginning to get back on track and she had attracted another animal, a rapist this time, who was obviously going to kill her.

Has it really come to this?

She felt herself losing consciousness . . . and so she began to pray. The white light soon disappeared, Mary Ellen recalled. Then she saw total darkness. "I said my prayers—

I said *all* of my prayers . . . and the room was spinning, and it was getting black, and I knew, I knew I was dying."

"Our Father, who art in Heaven, hallowed be Thy name. . . ."

"Hail Mary, full of grace, the Lord is with thee. . . ."

What Mary Ellen didn't know was that as she slipped further into unconsciousness, he was undressing her from her waist up, refusing to strip off any of her clothing below the belt. He wasn't concerned with her vaginal area. It was her breasts. To complete his fantasy, he needed to have her breasts fully exposed. Her bra couldn't be hanging off her shoulder. This was important. He needed to stare at them as he straddled her like a horse and choked her.

"I remember," she said later, "as I was slipping into unconsciousness, him staring into my eyes, directly staring into my eyes. He never spoke a word. I realized later that he was watching me die. He was *fascinated* by this. Losing consciousness, it felt like I had died. . . . I knew I was dying."

III

Mary Ellen didn't know how long it was that she had been out. But it was quite some time later when she came to and realized that he was gone. *Where is he? He left? I'm alive?* Waking up, she looked around and figured out that she was on her bed—not the couch. He must have carried her into her room and posed her on the bed. She was at an angle on her bed, positioned in a certain way.

His way.

As Mary Ellen came to and began to get her bearings back, he realized she was moving as he walked back into the room. "He was coming back into the room, and I was on the bed, I was very dizzy," Mary Ellen said. "The next thing I knew, he was on top of me again." And that's when she felt "something cold" in the middle of her stomach. It was here when Mary Ellen first saw that, as she put it, "my clothes wre torn off down to my waist, but nothing from my waist down had been disturbed."

Looking toward her ribs, Mary Ellen noticed his fist going up and down and wondered what he was doing. She felt that "cold" feeling again—it was steel—on her ribs. It didn't hurt. Not then. She was still groggy. Dizzy. The room was spinning. She didn't have the strength to scream.

Realizing she still had a chance to survive, Mary Ellen made a decision to fight back. "I remembered that I had read an article about self-defense," she said. It was there, in her room, as the man called Ned, whom she had just met, began stabbing her in the chest that Mary Ellen decided not to be a victim any longer. Suddenly two lines from that self-defense article came back to her: *"Hurt the attacker in his eyes. Try to blind him for a moment."*

Without even thinking about it, totally involuntary, Mary Ellen reached up and raked her long fingernails across his face. ("I gouged his eyes as hard as I could.") It was as if her arm had moved on its own. ("I didn't even have to will it—it just happened.")

Mary Ellen never yelled or screamed. It was something she had learned not to do: "Usually when I'm frightened, I'm very quiet. . . . I kind of freeze."

Not this time, though. This time, Mary Ellen reacted in a violent way toward the man who was trying to kill her: "I knew I was fighting for my life. I tell people now," Mary Ellen said, "you have no idea of the strength you have and how quickly your mind can work when it's about your survival."

17

I

No sooner had Mary Ellen managed to gouge Ned in the eyes and rip the skin on his face open, when he jumped off her and ran out of the room.

The entrance door to the building was still dead-bolted.

As she got off the bed, Mary Ellen fell on the floor. Pulling herself up, she ran as fast as she could out of her apartment. She was weak. Sluggish. She had blood all over her skirt and blouse (which was torn and hanging down below her waist), but she didn't realize she was bleeding. When she reached the bottom of the stairs, Mary Ellen went straight for her landlady's door. She was definitely home.

Her keys to safety were still upstairs in her pocketbook.

Near the bottom of the stairs, with several steps to go, Mary Ellen fell and tumbled down the last few stairs. Bleeding and bruised, she basically fell onto the landlady's doorstep. ("My mind obviously couldn't deal with the pain at that time; I was too busy staying alive.")

Now Mary Ellen started yelling: "Come on . . . open the door," she screamed as loud as she could.

By this point, after hearing the commotion going on above

her, Mary Ellen's landlady had already made the trip to her door to see what was going on. Unbeknownst to Mary Ellen, or Ned, the landlady had called the police. Waiting for them to arrive, she was standing on the opposite side of the door to Mary Ellen, asking, "What is it?" Her words were muffled through the solid oak door. "What's happening out there? Go away!"

"Please, please," Mary Ellen said, "open the door. Please open the door. He's killing me. *Please* open the door."

This was the first time Mary Ellen saw the blood. She looked down toward her abdomen and blood was streaming out of two slits in her midsection. It was gushing, she remembered, so she put her hand over the wounds and continued pleading with the landlady to unlock the door. "Please . . . hurry. . . ."

Mary Ellen was trapped. She couldn't return to her own apartment. For all she knew, he was still inside, regrouping, gathering his strength after being seriously injured in the eyes—and getting ready to finish the job he had started. It wasn't hard to figure out that he *had* to kill her now. She was a witness. If she lived, he was going to jail.

II

Standing at the door, jiggling the doorknob, was a strange feeling for Mary Ellen. After getting no response from the landlady, Mary Ellen stepped a few feet back and then threw herself against the door.

But it wouldn't budge.

After that, she pummeled her shoulder against the door, but her strength was dwindling. At this point, her landlady screamed, "Who is it? What's going on out there? What's happening? Who's there?"

"Please . . . open the . . . door," Mary Ellen said, her words falling short. She was out of breath. Losing blood. Weak. Everything slowing down.

Then she'd get a bit of energy back and become frantic, pleading with her landlady.

During this moment, she had her back turned toward the stairs leading up to her apartment. She had no idea where Ned was or if he was still in the apartment. But as she continued pleading with the landlady, she felt a hand come from around her back and cover her mouth. And then he spoke for what was the first time since the ordeal had begun.

"Be quiet," Ned whispered in Mary Ellen's ear. "We have to go back upstairs."

Mary Ellen's eyes widened. She couldn't believe it. Hearing Ned whisper in her ear like that was one of the weirdest feelings Mary Ellen said she'd ever had in her life. Ned had said it in a way that made her think he believed she was a willing participant in it all. She felt as though he was playing a game and he believed that she liked it.

"Let's go. Don't say anything," he said.

III

It wasn't once or twice that Ned had violent thoughts of rendering females unconscious in order to sexually arouse and stimulate himself. He admitted later that it was "every time I look at or talk to a female."

Every time.

Living inside his head for thirty years or more, Ned added later, were these images of women disabled by the violence he had perpetrated for the sole purpose of sexual gratification. He wrote how he would *mentally rehearse* this scenario *dozens of times a day.* He'd sit and think about how to do it. 'd drive around in his car and go through it, over and over. ull up to a stoplight, see a nice-looking female in a car 'm, and imagine that she was lying naked from the waist up on a bed or couch, unconscious, indisposed, there for his pleasure. It was such an inherent part of his consciousness that, by one point in his teens and college years, he would *go out of his way,* he wrote, miss a party, stay up until the wee hours of the night, *to see a movie like* Psycho *(the shower scene),* Frenzy, No Way to Treat a Lady . . . The Boston Strangler, or any James Bond film where *at least one beautiful spy is killed. . . .*

Beauty and death. For Ned, they were like chocolate and peanut butter.

Ned was not an uneducated man. He wasn't incapable of knowing that these thoughts were abnormal. These fantasies he had, he hadn't told anyone about them.

Nor had he sought treatment.

In a way, I guess we can say, Ned liked these thoughts.

In one letter to a judge, Ned wondered what it would be like to have *an EKG machine monitoring [his] heart rate* while he sat and viewed some of the films in which women were killed. Alone with a female, he admitted, these thoughts were all that consumed his mind. *Ninety-nine out of a hundred times,* he wrote, he could contain himself. But it was that one time, he said, when he couldn't manage the urge, that usually got him into trouble. Unfortunately for Mary Ellen, tonight she was that 1 percent.

IV

After demanding that she be quiet, Ned tried pulling Mary Ellen up the stairs back toward her apartment. He needed to finish the job. She could identify him. She knew where he worked. His name. What he looked like. If she lived, there was no getting out of this.

Mary Ellen wasn't about to give up now, not after all she had done to survive. Her landlady wasn't going to open the door, however. She was possibly too scared or just didn't want to get involved. The old woman had no idea, of course, that a maniac was on the opposite side of the door trying to kill her tenant.

Or maybe she did.

Either way, as Ned tried forcing Mary Ellen up the stairs, she managed to scratch him in the eyes again.

He winced. Went down. Put his hands over his face.

"Who's there with you?" the landlady asked.

Mary Ellen yelled, "Help me . . . open the door!"

"Be quiet," she heard Ned say again.

"Help me . . . open the door."

"Who's there with you?"

Ned kept grabbing at Mary Ellen, but he kept losing his grip because of all the blood.

When he realized he wasn't going to be able to pull her up the stairs, Ned ran up the stairs by himself back into the apartment.

A moment later, he was gone.

18

I

Mary Ellen was able to stand and grab the doorknob to her landlady's apartment and rattle it. Her hand, however, kept slipping off the handle because they were "all wet."

Full of blood.

I really must have gotten his eyes good, she thought.

Then, standing there, with only a door to safety between her and the landlady, everything went quiet. Mary Ellen didn't hear the landlady and realized that Ned was gone. An eerie silence. It was just Mary Ellen. Alone. She could feel herself getting weaker and her body drooping. She looked down. Her dress was all "crumpled around her waist and full of blood." She then saw the holes in her body once again with "blood [still] spurting out of them." Her legs started to give out. Her knees buckled. She began to slide down against the door.

This is really crazy, she thought. *This only happens in movies. I'm inches away from safety and I'm going to die right here.*

Her life had come down to a door. A woman scared of

letting her in. She was going to die because she couldn't get through a damn wooden door.

II

The landlady must have seen the cops pull up, because she finally opened the door as two cruisers arrived out front. When she heard the door open, Mary Ellen pushed her way inside and said, "Call the police. Close the door right away. He's still up there."

When the landlady didn't respond, Mary Ellen closed and locked the door.

"The police are coming," the landlady said as Mary Ellen, bloodied, topless, and hysterical, fell into the landlady's apartment and started stumbling around from room to room. Dizzy and unsteady. Totally out of it. Fading in and out.

Pulling herself up off the floor, Mary Ellen found her way into her landlady's kitchen and collapsed on the linoleum floor. What seemed like only moments later, a policeman appeared over Mary Ellen and began asking questions. Seeing a silhouette of the policeman standing over her, Mary Ellen later recalled, was a relief. She had won.

She survived.

III

Just before police arrived, Ned ran back upstairs and grabbed Mary Ellen's keys—a souvenir, perhaps, which was something he had done in the past—pushed a window open and, swinging from the upper windowsill like a monkey, jumped from the roof, over the asphalt walkway. He landed on his feet, like a cat, on the grass out front—as luck would have it, right near his car. Within a few moments, Ned was on his way out of the neighborhood as more police were arriving from the opposite direction.

IV

Mary Ellen was hurt more severely than she knew. Survival wasn't a given. When Officer Gary Van Loon approached her as she lay on her landlady's kitchen floor, he and his partner noticed that her dress, "laying across her genital area," was covered with blood. The area of the floor around Mary Ellen was one large pool. *There was also a great deal of blood on her hands,* Van Loon later wrote in his report.

Noticing the two puncture wounds below her breasts, Van Loon immediately applied pressure in order to stop the bleeding.

Van Loon's partner, Officer Kayne, came into the kitchen with a first-aid kit and wrapped the wounds until an ambulance arrived. Another officer dashed upstairs to see if Mary Ellen's attacker was still inside the apartment. After a careful, gun-drawn search, it was clear he had slipped out a window and taken off. The drifting curtain in the open window was the only sign of his departure.

Mary Ellen was transported to Kennedy Memorial Hospital in Saddle Brook. Upstairs, inside her apartment, detectives working the scene noticed several things that caught their attention immediately. Mary Ellen's black bra was on the floor, but it was *unknown*, Van Loon wrote, *if it was torn off or taken off.* The telephone jack in the kitchen was ripped from the wall. Mary Ellen's bed was "open," the bedspread on the floor. The nightstand and lamp Mary Ellen had next to her bed had been knocked over, *as other pieces of furniture were spewn* [sic] *around.*

And no weapon was located.

19

I

As she struggled to stay conscious in the emergency room, doctors secured Mary Ellen's wounds and gave her a sedative so she could fall asleep and get some rest. This, while they figured out if they could save her life.

Several moments later, as Mary Ellen started coming to, she saw a man heading into her room. His hair was cut in a fashion similar to Ned's. Mary Ellen, groggy and drunk from the sedative, believed he was even the same height, that he looked like Ned.

Oh, my God . . . ("I was terrified it was him.")

Whenever Mary Ellen became frightened, she held her breath. It was part of being consumed by fear and anxiety that she had lived with most of her adult life.

There was another man behind the man who looked like Ned; they were heading for her. Holding her breath, Mary Ellen realized they were detectives and she started to cry, pleading, "Please find him. He's going to kill somebody. He tried to kill me."

Ned was like a snapshot in her mind. Doped up and suffering post-traumatic stress, she rattled off a description: "A blue paisley design on a red tie . . . white oxford cloth, button-down shirt. A navy blue suit." He had "California good looks," she said later. "Blond hair and blue eyes."

Doctors weren't going to allow such nonsense: cops questioning Mary Ellen so soon. She was in no condition to talk. "You must leave this room right now," her doctor said.

II

The way he felt, it was like running up a flight of stairs. Or taking an entire bottle, he explained, of "pep pills." A combination of "an electric shock and having someone sneak up behind you" and startle "the daylights out of you." That was how Ned explained it—that sensation when "I felt her throat in my hands." He wasn't talking about Mary Ellen. He was speaking of another woman—a woman he had killed four years before he met Mary Ellen. Like a hunter, he claimed it was his first kill. But cops, investigators, and profilers in the years to come would beg to differ.

As he later wrote to a judge and described these feelings, Ned said he could barely contain himself while writing the words. He could *feel that adrenaline* once again just writing about it, *racing through [his] heart, hands and legs.*

Words on a page had done it for him. He was picturing it all as he sat in his cell and wrote. Doing the actual deed of murder, Ned explained, was another thing entirely. Actually strangling a woman, he said, was nothing like it was portrayed in films. It was *practically impossible to kill someone with your bare hands,* he wrote. Sure, he continued, a football player could probably do it because he had "huge hands." But Ned was certainly no football player.

He had killed a woman and gotten away with it for several years before he met and attacked Mary Ellen. He had floated the notion in his head of getting "professional help," but it had been, for him, such a "terrible experience," and he was "so thankful" not to be arrested, that although he still had those crazy, violent, sexual "urges," he had "convinced" himself that he would "never allow" a situation to develop where the potential was there for him to "lose control ever again."

That was, of course, until he met Mary Ellen.

III

As he pulled into his driveway after attacking Mary Ellen, Ned had to hope that she would die in the hospital. Because if Mary Ellen Renard lived, Ned Snelgrove was going to jail.

IV

It was four in the morning when Diana Jansen, Mary Ellen's youngest daughter, heard what had happened to her mother. The hospital called. "Your mom's been attacked," a nurse said.

Diana had a nine-month-old child and was pregnant with her second. She didn't need drama. Not now. Her first child had been born premature—one would have to think it was because of all the stress she had been under her entire life, which had already been, as Dianna described it, "unbelievable."

So this is how it's going to end, Diana thought after hanging up the phone.

How scripted. How perfect, really. It was as if their entire lives had led up to this one moment. After everything, here was Mom, killed by an attacker.

V

When the fog left and Diana realized that her mother had been stabbed by a stranger and could die, she frantically began looking for a way to get from her home in Pennsylvania, where she lived with her husband and child, to New Jersey. She needed a babysitter. *Oh, my God,* she thought, *oh, my God. How am I going to get there fast enough?*

Then the spasms of guilt washed over Diana. *I shouldn't have left her alone down there. . . . Why did I not take her up here with me?* ("I've been guilt-ridden my whole life," Diana said later. "This just escalated that feeling.")

Diana called the hospital. She didn't know what else to do. Her mother needed her. In many ways, Diana felt as if she had taken care of Mary Ellen.

Now her mother was in the hospital after being violently attacked, and no one was with her.

"Mom?" Diana said when she heard a voice on the line. "That you?"

Mary Ellen was crying. She didn't know what to say. Perhaps she couldn't speak.

"Mom, I love you. I'm on my way down there. I'll be there as soon as I can."

20

I

The Elmwood Park Police Department (EPPD) had a potential serial rapist/murderer on their hands, a man who had just attacked a woman in her home and taken off with her keys. It was clear from the way in which Mary Ellen had described the attack that the guy was no novice. He had possibly done it before.

And would probably do it again.

As the investigation got under way back at her apartment, Mary Ellen wasn't going to be much help. She was in and out of consciousness.

Ned had victimized a woman who was already a victim, which was perhaps his plan from the moment he had met Mary Ellen. He picked up on her vulnerability. Sensed it. Exploited it. For a guy like Ned, who could be smooth and deliberate without ever giving himself away, Mary Ellen was easy prey. He didn't need to know that she had been mistreated her entire married life. It was written on her face. There in every word she spoke. Every mannerism.

II

When Diana showed up later that morning, she was told her mother was in surgery. There had been a problem. They were trying to save her life. She had been stabbed pretty badly. One of the wounds was deep.

Diana wondered what she could do.

Pray.

While Diana was waiting for her mom to come out of surgery, her uncle, Mary Ellen's brother, showed up. ("He started right in," Diana recalled, "with blaming her. 'Who was she out with? What is she doing now?'")

Diana couldn't take it. Here was a man of the cloth talking as if Mary Ellen was the one to blame for being attacked by some animal. It was disrespectful, and Mary Ellen could be dead.

Listening to her uncle, Diana snapped. "Shut the f*** up," she screamed. *"Enough!"*

She had heard it all before. Condemnation for the way Mary Ellen dressed or the way she walked or the way she talked. It was sickening for Diana. No matter what, even if her mother had invited the guy into the apartment and presented herself to him for sex, once she said *no,* once she said *stop,* that was it.

How in the heck could it be *her* fault? ("I lost it," Diana remembered. "I went at him full force.")

III

The doctors came out. They explained that Mary Ellen's heart had stopped once during the operation. But they had stabilized her and she was doing "OK."

"Will she make it?"

They were sure she would.

IV

Later on that same morning, detectives asked Diana if she would take a ride with them over to the apartment and answer a few questions. "Sure," she said.

Mary Ellen was recovering from surgery. Diana wasn't going to get a chance to see her until later on that day.

One of the detectives led Diana into the apartment entrance—and it was there where Diana saw the immensity and violence of the attack. Blood was everywhere. On the walls. The floor. The doorknob. Going up the stairs, leading into Mary Ellen's apartment. It was a wonder she was still alive.

Diana gasped. "I'm kind of hysterical," she said later, crying while recalling the memory. "The blood. It was all over the place."

There was blood on the bed, Diana said. The sheets and blankets and other items in the room were scattered. Cops were walking around. Taking photographs. Searching through drawers. Looking everything over.

"Do you see anything that might be missing?" one of the detectives asked Diana.

"No," Diana said.

"Nothing?"

"I have no idea."

"Do you know where your mom was heading out to last night?"

"No."

"Maybe who she's been hanging around with?"

"No."

Diana had a full plate of family life back home. She had been to the hospital during her current pregnancy regarding a few complications she had been experiencing. It was all she could do to keep her own life on track, let alone keep tabs on her mother. She spoke to her mother quite often, but Mary Ellen wasn't one to give Diana a rundown of what she was doing.

"Well," the detective said, "we greatly appreciate you coming out here. We know how hard this must be. I'll have someone take you back to the hospital."

V

Mary Ellen was just coming out of anesthesia when Diana got a chance to visit her. She was crying and looked, understandably, as if she had been left for dead. "It was awful," Diana said, recalling that moment. "About as awful as it gets."

The doctors had explained to Diana that Mary Ellen was going to be fine, at least physically. With some rest and recovery, her body would mend. The hospital that Mary Ellen was in, Diana believed, was not a nice place. She thought it was seedy and run-down. She felt odd about leaving her mother there. She couldn't speak to Mary Ellen at any real length as of yet, simply because Mary Ellen was out of it. ("I was not happy with the hospital and wanted her to be moved," Diana said.)

When she spoke to her mother about it the following day, Mary Ellen said she wanted to stay. There was no reason to be transferred. They had saved her life. That was good enough for her. Within a few days, Mary Ellen was able to get up and walk around.

Looking at her, Diana could only think of getting her out of there as soon as she could.

Leaving the hospital that night, Diana resolved to do something. "I have to get her home . . . soon."

21

I

A few days after the attack, Mary Ellen indicated that she was well enough to speak with police again. They had interviewed her hours after the attack and she had provided a bit of information. But they needed more.

Senior investigator Dennis Textor, from the Bergen County Prosecutor's Office (Sex Crimes and Child Abuse Unit), and Detective Robert Kassai, from the EPPD, sat with Mary Ellen. Looking at her, they could see bruises on her neck, where Ned had placed his hands—a ring of yellow and purple, a blurry collage of colors representing the nasty reminder of the violence she had survived.

The detectives were told that one of the knife wounds had just missed Mary Ellen's aorta.

After explaining where she lived and how she met Ned, Mary Ellen went straight into what she could recall from the night. She remembered things in detail. The episode was fresh in her mind.

"Describe Ned to me," said one of the detectives.

"Um . . . ," Mary Ellen started to say before breaking down in tears.

"Take it easy . . . his approximate height, weight, and age?" Detective Kassai asked, trying to ease her into it.

"He's five-nine . . . um"—she started crying again—"um . . . he weighs . . . I'm sorry, I would say, maybe one hundred and eighty pounds."

"How old?"

"I'd say thirty," Mary Ellen said. They had talked about her age, she recalled, but not his. She felt a bit more comfortable. Ned would do it again, she was convinced. And how would she ever be able to sit at home alone again with him on the street? He had her keys.

"How did you find out—I mean, how did you know his name was Ned?"

"Through conversation." Ned had asked her what her name was and said he had an "unusual name." Then he told her his name and she asked what Ned was short for, perhaps Edward?

"No, he told me," Mary Ellen explained. "He said Ned was short for Edwin."

"Did it appear to you that he knew anybody else at that club, whether it was employees or customers? Was he friendly with anybody?"

Mary Ellen thought about it. "A bartender," she said a moment later, "who he called 'Jimmy.' He had dark hair."

As the interview progressed, Mary Ellen explained how she and Ned ended up in the parking lot together. It was unclear whether Ned could have fixed Mary Ellen's car so it wouldn't start when she left the bar. She had used the restroom before she left. She couldn't recall if she had told Ned what kind of car she drove before leaving him.

The investigators were in an odd position. There were questions they had to ask. If Mary Ellen had made a move on Ned and casual sex had turned violent, it was still a crime, but the attack would have to be investigated—and later prosecuted—differently.

"When you came into your apartment," Kassai asked, "did you take any clothes off?"

Mary Ellen didn't hesitate. "I took my shoes off. I always take my shoes off when I get home, so I won't disturb my landlady."

After they went through the next five minutes inside Mary Ellen's apartment, one of the detectives asked her when the situation turned uncomfortable.

Mary Ellen pulled back a bit and tears welled up. "He grabbed my throat with both hands and both his thumbs on my Adam's apple and his fingers [wrapped] around the back of my neck and he was staring into my eyes."

It was obvious to Mary Ellen—as it would be to investigators in the coming years—that this procedure Ned had used, if it could be called such, had been something he had practiced. He knew exactly what he was doing. He was prepared. He hadn't randomly grabbed her throat, she believed. He strategically grabbed it in a specific area.

Ned never expected Mary Ellen to survive. He had chosen a victim and what was obvious in the way he acted, and the information he shared with her, was that he never thought she would be sitting, talking to the police about the attack. Either that, or he never intended Mary Ellen as a victim in the first place, but he was overcome by those feelings of not being able to control himself around females and acted out.

Near the conclusion of the interview, Detective Kassai asked, "During the night, did Ned tell you anything about himself, where he lived or where he worked?"

"A few blocks from Kracker's," she said. "He stopped there after attending a friend's wedding. I mentioned to him that I had just started a new job in Paramus, and he said that he worked in Paramus, on Century Road, for Hewlett-Packard."

"Prior to meeting Ned, have you ever seen him before?"

"I never saw him in my life before that."

Investigator Textor spoke up as the interview wound down.

"Did he say anything that he wanted to go to bed with you or have any type of sex with you?"

"No!" Mary Ellen said, lashing out. She was offended by the question, but understood its validity. "When I mentioned that I was going to have cheese, because I am hypoglycemic and I have a high protein diet and I have to eat frequently . . . he said, 'I don't want you to have cheese. . . .'" It was the last thing Ned had ever said to Mary Ellen—save for "be quiet," as he put his hand over her mouth at the bottom of the stairs.

After thanking Mary Ellen for her time and cooperation, they asked her if there was anything else she wanted to add.

Mary Ellen thought about it. "Yes," she said, "just that I believed that I was dead, except for the fact that I fought as hard . . . as hard"—she stumbled, obviously reliving that moment—"as hard as I possibly could."

Finding a guy named Edwin who worked at Hewlett-Packard, one of the biggest employers in the immediate area, was not going to be too difficult.

22

I

According to Ned years later, the attack on Mary Ellen was never supposed to happen. It was something inside him, he wrote, he couldn't control, which proved to him that it was not a premeditated event. As he explained it (or, rather, *justified* it), Mary Ellen invited him back to her apartment. He mentioned nothing of her car ever breaking down and his Good Samaritan work. Ned wrote that Mary Ellen had *undone the top half of her dress and taken her bra off* after they entered her apartment, which, he claimed, was too much for his sexually tangled mind to wrap itself around. Once he saw her breasts being offered up, he couldn't help himself. It was something inside him that took over.

A demon. Devil. Different personality.

At some point, Ned explained, he and Mary Ellen were on the couch. He was on top of her. She was enjoying herself. But then, out of nowhere, he wrote, *I could not stop my hands from squeezing her throat as hard as I could.*

An uncontrollable impulse.

An involuntary act.

Ned's mind equated sex with violence. There could be

many causes for this. The vectors stirring inside the mind of a violent sexual offender are seated deeply in the brain's behavioral wiring. In this instance, the offender, for some reason, enters into a state of blackout—much like an alcoholic—as he becomes aroused in the presence, or even photographs, of a female. When Ned saw Mary Ellen's breasts, he was out of his mind. He wasn't thinking with the same set of morals and values as he might have been moments before. This sexual arousal then becomes intertwined with a sense of pleasure that only violence mixed with some sort of sexual act can satisfy.

Stabbing Mary Ellen.

The blood, though, Ned explained later, was not part of the fantasy. The blood was a deal breaker.

A turnoff.

Saltpeter.

Still, to Ned, seeing Mary Ellen unclothed and in a vulnerable position was an invitation to fulfill his sexual fantasies. He blames Mary Ellen because, in his mind, it is her fault for being, essentially, in the wrong place at the wrong time and making herself available to him. This enables Ned to rationalize the crime in his warped sense of reality. Whether she invited him into her apartment and—for the sake of argument—took off her clothes voluntarily, or Ned ripped them off, is irrelevant to the end result. But in mitigating his behavior, Ned obviously felt the need to place the blame on Mary Ellen for putting herself in this position and offering her body to him.

A sacrificial lamb.

II

Talking about the crime itself, Ned later stated that Mary Ellen passed out "a few seconds" after he started strangling her. When that happened, he wrote, *he dragged her into her bedroom, half-naked.* It was at this moment, *these feelings completely took over* and there was no turning back.

In explaining that the act was never premeditated, Ned wrote that if he had planned it, *I wouldn't have allowed myself to be seen leaving with this lady. . . .* He would have, he added, *also brought a weapon into the bedroom with him.*

Likely, as Ned began to masturbate, "the lady," as he explained it, woke up and began struggling with him. As that happened, he wrote, *I ran back into the living room . . . in a panic, picked up a stupid . . . knife.*

"Stupid" was an interesting adjective; it implied that if he had chosen a better weapon, he could have killed Mary Ellen.

In any event, Ned wrote that he had *stabbed her, remembering how that worked to quiet things down* years before when he had committed the same crime—but had instead killed the woman. *[B]ut this time it did not work,* he wrote.

He claimed Mary Ellen then began to scream and the phone started ringing. *[I]t was the landlady calling from downstairs,* he guessed in his letter.

He tried to leave at that point, but, of course, he was locked in. So he jumped out the window.

As the letter continued, Ned blamed Mary Ellen over and again, saying that she was "obviously embarrassed" by what had happened and the fact that, according to him, she had *invited* him back to her apartment for sex. Moreover, he said, he never fixed her car or helped her with it because it had started right up.

Ned agreed that he needed help with his problem—that there was "something inside of" him that he could not "handle by" himself.

III

If there was one thing Ned had not embellished in describing the attack on Mary Ellen, it was that he had no criminal record and had not tried to hide his identity from Mary Ellen.

Then again, Ned admitted that he had never expected Mary Ellen to survive the attack. *I botched it . . . ,* he wrote to a friend years later, this merely months after claiming he needed help for his condition. *She didn't die!*

IV

Elmwood Park police detectives had little trouble locating Ned. Mary Ellen had described his build, recalled his first name—Edwin, which, to begin with, was rare—and remembered that he worked for Hewlett-Packard.

Detectives searched the immediate area around Mary Ellen's apartment and didn't find the knife or her keys. They photographed bloodstains running down the stairs by the landlady's door, up the stairs into Mary Ellen's bedroom. The sheets on her bed looked like old painting rags smeared with redwood stain. Bloodstains littered the door into her apartment, while spatter was all over the floor and walls.

On the top of the windowsill inside Mary Ellen's living room, detectives located a few latent fingerprints, all of which were in perfect condition.

V

At around 10:30 P.M. on August 3, 1987, detectives spoke to several employees at Kracker's, all of whom identified Ned as a "regular customer" who, Jimmy the bartender said, "liked to play golf and was employed by Hewlett-Packard."

Investigator Textor took a ride over to Hewlett the following morning and spoke to the personnel director. "Ned? Sure," he said, "I know Ned. His name is Edwin Fales Snelgrove."

Ned was described as a model employee: a salesman who produced results while out on the road and worked hard when he was transferred to a desk job. The company, in fact, had high hopes for Ned. The white shirts saw Ned as a leader one day, someone who was going to run his own department. In addition, Ned's fellow employees said he was an all-around "great guy," captain of the company softball team, a genius when it came to stock market tips, even "charming," a sort of "ladies' man, good-looking" and a brilliant intellectual. In fact, there wasn't an employee Ned knew who didn't like him or have not good—but great—things to say about him.

He was pleasant. Funny. Calm and delightful. Always fun to be around. A regular jokester. No one could understand how Ned had gotten mixed up in any trouble. He'd worked at Hewlett for four years, lived in the area for eight. There must be some sort of terrible misunderstanding.

VI

Investigator Textor found Ned at the plant doing some paperwork at his desk. After reading him his rights, Textor explained that he would have to take a ride downtown.

As some of his fellow employees looked on with curiosity, Ned said, "No problem. Anything I can do to help."

Once, Textor had Ned inside the confines of the police department, however, Ned was a different person. All of a sudden, he wasn't so congenial and willing to talk.

"I want a lawyer."

The detective explained the details of the case, while Ned sat and listened for what was three hours. Textor later wrote in his report how Ned *refused to make any statements*.

"Do you know the victim?" the investigator asked.

Ned shook his head.

"You're going to be charged with attempted murder, aggravated sexual assault, and sexual contact," Textor explained, looking up at Ned's blank expression.

VII

Near 3:00 A.M., after being processed, Ned was placed in a cell, his bond set at $100,000, and the case referred to the first assistant prosecutor Dennis Calo. In the due course of New Jersey law, Calo would have to present the charges against Ned to a grand jury.

Textor sped over to the hospital and had Mary Ellen, who had just undergone yet another surgery, take a look at a photo lineup, which included a shot of Ned.

Mary Ellen was groggy and stoned. In and out of it. "That's him," she said through tears. Just the sight of his face was enough to bring her back to the moment. "That's *definitely* him." How could she forget that stare? The way he looked into her eyes, waiting, watching her die.

Ned's car, a 1987 gray Ford sedan, was towed from Hewlett's parking lot as a throng of Ned's peers watched through the window blinds. It was brought to the EPPD, where forensics would have a go at it. Two investigators sped over to Ned's apartment, taped it off, and began a search.

Within a few days, the FBI called Detective Robert Kassai and related some important information. The fingerprints Ned had given to Investigator Textor matched those found on Mary Ellen's windowsill. It was clear that Ned had been inside her apartment and had jumped from her living-room window.

23

I

The first assistant prosecutor in Passaic County, Dennis Calo, was in charge of indicting Ned Snelgrove. From a prosecutorial standpoint, the case against Ned appeared to be ironclad. Talking to the press after Ned's arrest, Calo said, "He helped her start her car and then agreed to follow her home to make sure she got home OK. He then asked if he could come in and clean up [and] tried to rape her and she struggled. He stabbed her twice in the chest with a knife."

The Passaic County Prosecutor's Office, in which Calo was also the chief of the investigation unit, had photographs, Calo explained to reporters, of Mary Ellen's—a name they were not releasing at this time—neck and the injuries she had sustained from the knife wounds. Calo had secured Mary Ellen's medical records. She had identified Ned in a photo lineup. They had a latent fingerprint matching Ned's. Even if the argument came down to whether Mary Ellen invited Ned in for sex, there was no doubt Ned had stabbed and strangled her.

And then there was Ned's past. Four years ago. That *other* case haunting investigators who believed Ned was their guy.

Ned had been questioned. Cops had him on radar. They had always believed he had committed the crime, but they didn't have enough evidence to arrest him. Maybe now they did.

II

EPPD Detective Robert Kassai was a street-smart cop with seventeen years on the job when he met up with Mary Ellen Renard—a job that would span several decades by the time he retired in 2000 to run a successful campaign for town council. He had dealt with guys like Ned throughout his career. For a number of years, Kassai had worked with the Crimes Against Women and Children Unit, where, he said, his passion for law enforcement was deeply rooted. There was something about Ned that struck Kassai right away, he re-called. It was a feeling he had about him that led the veteran cop to believe Ned fit into a certain, rare category of serial sex offenders. Kassai relayed that he had a "sixth sense that we had a predator on our hands. Somebody that's capable of doing it again and again."

While going through Ned's personal possessions shortly after his arrest, Kassai found a business card in Ned's wallet. It was from a detective in Woodbridge, New Jersey, near Mid-dlesex County, south of Bergen County, where Ned was living at present. Although it wasn't a far drive for Ned, De-tective Kassai wondered why he had the business card to begin with. So he picked up the phone and dialed the detec-tive's number.

"We're looking at him for a murder down here," the de-tective said.

Kassai sat back in his chair, shook his head. He knew it. Had sensed it. Ned was not some sort of random attacker.

She was a Rutgers student. Ned's age. She had been stran-gled. Stabbed. And posed.

This victim in Middlesex County, like Mary Ellen, fit into

Ned's preferred victim pool perfectly. More than that, Kassai was onto something. Getting the investigating officer on the phone shortly after finding the card in Ned's wallet, Kassai asked him why they never arrested Ned.

"We couldn't tie him to the murder scene," the cop said. They had questioned Ned. Followed him. Pestered him. But they couldn't find any physical evidence to link him to the crime. In 1983, when the woman was killed, and even in 1987, as investigators began digging into the crime scene at Mary Ellen's, DNA was not a major part of the investigator's toolbox. "You had to do footwork," Kassai recalled. "You didn't have science the way you have science today." So even if Ned had left a hair, skin tissue, or bodily fluids behind in 1983, there was no way to tie him to the crime scene.

This new information sent Kassai back out to speak with Ned's coworkers and friends at HP. "All I heard," Kassai told me years later, "as I began to try to get some background information on the guy was that he was a 'lovely man,' 'nice guy,' et cetera. His coworkers called him a 'polite guy,' 'a gentle, kind person.' It was almost as if you were dealing with Dr. Jekyll and Mr. Hyde."

III

Kassai began asking questions back at Kracker's, where Ned and Mary Ellen had met. He was trying to find out all he could about Ned. He had heard Ned liked to brag about playing golf. That he'd talk to people in the bar about his swing, his handicap, boast to the females about how good an athlete he was. "The thing is," Kassai said, "he had never golfed a day in his life. Ned was cool. Smooth. But when you started to push Ned's buttons, *boy,* did he get annoyed."

When Kassai and Textor interviewed Ned, he was careful about saying anything that was going to come back to him. But when Kassai made an accusation, Ned became a bit heated, like he wanted to say something, but he thought it better to control his emotions. For Kassai, this meant something. "He struck me as a [chronic BSer], but not in . . . how can I say this, not in [a] liar's sense. He was a con artist. Smart. Very intelligent."

In Ned, he saw a predatory nature. He could tell Ned worked hard at what he did. It wasn't a random crime or something that happened on the spur of the moment (as Ned himself later said).

Ned was a hunter. He preyed on a certain type of female. He thought things through carefully, deciding on the best way to carry out his plans. "Ned reminded me of a serial sex offender I had just arrested," Kassai recalled. "Staturewise, anybody pushed to a point can overpower anybody." Ned was five feet nine inches tall. He weighed in at about 170 pounds, had blond hair then, and kept up an outward appearance of a pretty boy. Ned presented himself to the world as a clean-cut intellectual who cared about his hygiene and appearance. This was clear from his colleagues at Hewlett, who spoke admiringly of him.

"And yet, when we searched his apartment in Passaic," Kassai remarked, "it was a s***house." He lived like a slob. Stuff all over the place. A pack rat. "He gave the impression and dressed and maintained an appearance as if he was running a million-dollar operation, like you'd walk into his apartment and see thirty or forty expensive suits." But Ned had hardly any clothes. His apartment looked as though a burglar had ransacked the joint looking for something specific.

The search of Ned's apartment told Kassai a lot about who Ned was in his private life. But also, while digging through Ned's things, Kassai found what was possibly the weapon Ned had used to stab Mary Ellen. It wasn't a knife. Inside the apartment, they found an "awl," Kassai said later, "like a seaman's pocketknife—a knife that sailors carried, with a blade on one side and a pick of some sort on the other."

IV

When word got back to Ned about the investigation, he went silent. He said he wasn't going to talk to *anyone*. He demanded cops speak to him through his new attorney, John Bruno, a man Ned's parents in Connecticut—including his father, a seafaring man who liked to tie knots and collect sailor's tools—had recently hired and, according to one source, "had spent a *ton* of money on."

24

I

Diana Jansen was overwhelmed by what had happened to her mother. When she went back to see Mary Ellen a few days after her second surgery, there were tubes protruding from her mother's mouth and nose, IV lines sticking out of her arms. Diana was not happy about the care her mother was receiving at the hospital. Seeing her up and walking, she thought Mary Ellen was making great progress; but walking in that second time and seeing Mary Ellen bedridden was disturbing to Diana. She put both hands over her mouth and gasped. The bruises Mary Ellen had sustained during the attack had become more pronounced. Her mother looked beat up. There was one point when Mary Ellen's oldest daughter—Diana's sister—was in the room and Mary Ellen began falling in and out of consciousness, moaning in pain.

"Can't she have more medicine?" her daughter asked the nurse.

"Absolutely not," the nurse said.

Any more sedation and Mary Ellen's slow heart rate might stop, the nurse explained. Yet, moments later, when the nurse left, all the alarms suddenly went off. Mary Ellen stopped breathing. The code blue team pushed their way into the room with the crash cart and, after a few tries, brought her back to life.

II

Mary Ellen later explained those first hours at the hospital when she didn't know if she was going to survive. Arriving at the hospital after the attack, on her way into surgery, she believed it was over. "Black and white," she called that period. "Some of this is as clear as a photograph and some is as dark as night. That was me going in and out."

"Am I going to die?" Mary Ellen asked the doctor as they prepped her for surgery.

"Can I get anyone for you?" the doctor asked. "Can we call anyone?"

Mary Ellen thought of calling her brother. Maybe he could perform last rites over the phone, just in case she didn't make it.

Making matters worse, Mary Ellen's family blamed her. She began to sense their reproach as the days passed. She shouldn't have been at a singles dance. It was ungodly. A good Catholic wouldn't be out and about, trolling the town for men. Family members routinely asked: *What were you doing there? How could you be so stupid?* "My father especially," Mary Ellen said. "This is a family who thought that I should have spent time with the church, doing service, after my first divorce, which was actually an annulment. They were very angry with me for dating at all. My father would call me a couple times a week. If I wasn't home, he wanted to know where I was."

From the family's pious point of view, a divorced man was not an eligible candidate for Mary Ellen. The men she dated were supposed to be widowed or bachelors. When it came to divorce, "they insisted on an annulment."

It was three days before her parents even showed up at the

hospital for a visit. Apparently, they just couldn't deal with what had happened, or disagreed with her social behavior.

III

Mary Ellen's liver had been lacerated. She had an incision running the entire length of her abdomen, from the upper part of her chest all the way down to her belly button. Surgeons had conducted exploratory surgery. "This man knew anatomy," one of the doctors told Mary Ellen. "Your clothes had been ripped down to your waist. These were carefully aimed wounds. Very clean. This person knew what he was aiming for."

Despite it all, Mary Ellen was alive. And she believed she had learned something from the attack. Until that day, she had always thought of herself as a weak person. "I had this violent husband who had terrorized me for years, and I thought I was weak because of that. But I know I fought Ned Snelgrove on that night—and, at least in part, I know that my actions saved my life."

25

I

As Ned's attorney, John Bruno's job was to present the best defense he could manage, or cut his client a deal the prosecution was willing to offer and Ned was willing to accept. It sounded simple. But for a defense attorney with a conscience, it was harder than most people thought. There were clients and cases that made Bruno ill to think about—every defense attorney has them. In Ned, Bruno saw a well-liked man with a respectable job, whose parents were spending a fortune to prove his innocence, but were willing to do that in order to defend a son they could in no way believe committed the crimes of which he was accused.

Meanwhile, Ned initiated a campaign to push the blame onto Mary Ellen's shoulders, saying that she had invited him into her apartment for sex. He claimed all he wanted to do was wash his hands and use the restroom, but instead, Mary Ellen came on to him as soon as he walked out of the bathroom. As far as the wounds Mary Ellen sustained, Ned said they occurred only after he "refused" her pushy sexual advances. Being the advocate, the diligent soldier, Bruno spoke for Ned, telling the same story to anyone in the press who would listen. During a superior court hearing in Hackensack, during the first week of August, Bruno stood in the courtroom and said his client "was invited into the woman's apartment after the two met" at a local bar. When they got inside, Bruno explained, she "locked" Ned in the apartment and "tried to engage him in some rough activity."

Assistant county prosecutor Fred L. Schwanwede had taken over the case from Dennis Calo. Schwanwede stood in the courtroom listening, dropped his head, disgusted with Bruno's blame-the-victim mentality.

"The facts are not as they may have first appeared in the prosecutor's report," Bruno continued, explaining to Judge Charles R. DiGisi. The hearing was designed to discuss a reduction in Ned's bail, which had been set at $100,000. Bruno wanted it reduced to $25,000. After hearing arguments on both sides, Judge DiGisi decided on $50,000.

Schwanwede was appalled. Here was a dangerous man, obviously capable of extreme violence. He had almost killed a woman. And now he was being allowed to walk away from the courtroom on $50,000?

Unheard of.

What helped Ned was the fact that he had no criminal record and had, Bruno argued, "close ties in the community." Moreover, Ned's fellow coworkers at HP were in total support of him. No one who personally knew Ned believed Mary Ellen. Many of Ned's coworkers said he couldn't have attacked her, as she described. He was *not* that type of person.

Schwanwede stood and faced the judge, saying, "In stabbing this woman twice in the chest, his purpose was clear: he was unable to do what he wanted to do sexually, and there was only one way out."

In lowering his bail, the judge told Bruno that Ned was to have no contact with Mary Ellen.

Bruno was optimistic. He felt he could present a strong case on Ned's behalf. In fact, Bruno told reporters outside the courtroom that Ned's friends and coworkers from HP were in the process of "setting up a fund for his defense. . . . His friends and family are completely shocked by this accusation. Everybody is just outraged. We have witnesses who know that this would be totally out of character. There has to be more to it than what the state claims," Bruno said to the throng of people.

One reporter asked about the life-threatening injuries "the victim" had sustained. How was Bruno going to explain those injuries? How was Ned going to defend himself against what he had done? Self-defense? A man versus a woman? It didn't add up.

Bruno painted a picture of Mary Ellen preparing a cheese plate for her and Ned as he used the bathroom. And when Ned came out and saw Mary Ellen with her top down, being as shy as he was, he immediately told her that he wanted no part of it. That was when, Bruno insisted, she "lunged at [my client] with the cheese knife, when he refused to participate in 'rough' sexual activity."

II

Mary Ellen was terrified to hear that her attacker, whom she now knew to be a twenty-six-year-old Berlin, Connecticut, native named Edwin Snelgrove, was out of jail on a $50,000 bond. When Mary Ellen left the hospital after ten days, Diana insisted her mother stay with her until she could get back on her feet again. Being with her daughter and grandchild in the Pocono Mountains of Pennsylvania would help Mary Ellen cope. What frightened her more than anything was Ned. She had no idea if she'd return home one night, only to find Ned lurking in the bushes, waiting to get rid of, essentially, the only witness against his alleged crimes.

After about five weeks in the Pocono Mountains, Mary Ellen decided she wanted to go back home and return to work. Getting back into the routine of everyday life would help her cope and perhaps act as a precursor for what a normal life could be like down the road. It wasn't going to be easy, but she would force herself to do it.

"I want to drive you back home, Mom," Diana said when Mary Ellen told her she was leaving.

"You're pregnant," Mary Ellen said. "It's too long of a ride. I'll be OK."

Diana didn't want to see her leave. She believed her mother was unprepared for life back out on her own. When she spoke to Mary Ellen about her feelings, it was like talking to someone in another language, Diana said later. "She refused to believe the reality of the situation, or see what's going on."

"I need to be on my own," Mary Ellen told Diana.

What else could Diana do?

"In some ways," Diana later told me, looking back on that time in her life, "I was relieved. I couldn't handle it any longer myself."

When Mary Ellen left, Diana said a prayer. What else could she do?

III

Walking through the door that first time after not being inside her apartment since the attack only increased the anxiety Mary Ellen already felt. What she found upon her return was not only shocking, but alarming and quite unexplainable at first. It was the atmosphere. She'd had a dozen or so lively, colorful plants, which she had always taken pride in taking care of, in the large windowsill holder. They were all dried up and dead now.

More victims of the attack.

Beyond that, throughout the apartment, all over the place, as if it had fallen from the ceiling, was a metallic blue powder investigators had used to find fingerprints. Forensic scientists spread the talcumlike substance over an area and brushed away the excess, hoping to come up with a latent print or two. Upon seeing it all, Mary Ellen understood why it was there, but she was overwhelmed by the sheer amount of it. Not to mention the fact that no one had cleaned it up.

"My bedroom was torn apart, too," Mary Ellen said. "To come home and find this, I mean, it really threw me into a horrible sense of reality."

An emotional tailspin was more like it. Here she was, trying to recover from the most devastating time of her life, sustaining injuries that almost killed her, and it was back in her face, when all she wanted to do was try her best to carry on with life. She knew a trial was possibly in the future and could deal with testifying, but that was months away. She just wanted to get back into the swing of her life and return to her job.

IV

As she settled back in, within a day or two, Mary Ellen's landlady knocked on the door with some bad news. "I think it's best you leave," the old woman said.

Mary Ellen was shocked. How heartless. Thoughtless. Did the woman have an ounce of compassion?

"I cannot move right now," Mary Ellen said. "Where would I go? I'm not even physically recovered."

"Nope. I think it's best. I think it's best that you move from here."

And then the notes started again. Mary Ellen would find them on her door, on the windshield of her car, in the hallway: *I think it's best you leave.*

Caving to the pressure, Mary Ellen started looking for a new apartment, but couldn't find anything right away. "The way I like to describe this period of my life," Mary Ellen said, looking back, trying to make sense of how she made it, "it's like when an animal is wounded, it likes to crawl into its hole to recover. You're wounded. You want to be in your home and what's familiar to you in order to recover."

Her landlady was denying her that one comfort: recovery.

A friend ultimately stored Mary Ellen's belongings for her while she moved back in with her parents, which became a situation that only added to a growing list of problems. Her father wouldn't even look at her or speak to her. She'd walk into a room and "start shaking from head to foot. I didn't know how to deal with it."

Or Dad.

As stories about her attack started circulating in the newspapers, Mary Ellen's parents began hiding the papers from her so she couldn't see what was being written and what Ned and his supporters were saying.

V

Getting back to work provided a bit of social comfort from the toil of being home with Mom and Dad, but as time went on, Mary Ellen began to suffer from post-traumatic stress. It started when she'd answer the telephone and speak to a client. As soon as she hung up, she'd forget who called and what he or she wanted. She couldn't understand what was going on. She'd be at her desk, doing paperwork, or just sitting, and suddenly burst into tears. She'd drive down what was once a familiar road and not know where she was. ("I just cried and cried and cried. I could not stop crying.")

Then the flashbacks started. There was Ned in her face, staring into her eyes again, his hands around her throat, watching the life drain from her. It got to a point where after moving into her own place she'd have friends bring her home and they'd walk into the new apartment before her, checking underneath the bed, in the closets, and in back of the curtains to make sure the coast was clear. All at once, it was eerie and surreal: she could see the events take place step-by-step in her head, and it seemed like it was happening all over again. On some nights, she'd lie in bed wide awake, lights out, and hear Ned breathing in her ear. "I mean, it was, I swear, it felt as if he was right there. . . . I would freeze. I could feel him get on the bed behind me (just as he had). I could hear him, breathing and breathing."

And she would turn around and there he was: watching her.

26

I

Ned had always challenged himself to be the best at whatever he did. Sales. Studying stocks and bonds. Tracking the statistics of the Boston Red Sox. Or, of course, studying killers. Whatever Ned did, he prided himself that he was the absolute best. Writing to a friend years after attacking Mary Ellen, Ned could talk about himself—his letters were always about Ned—and encourage his friend not to buy a certain stock in one breath and, in another, describe killing as if it were like clipping hedges or washing his car. In one letter, after warning his friend that GM wasn't a good buy that month, Ned explained how he had umpired Little League games for six or seven years. He enjoyed being around baseball, he wrote, even on such a young level of play. The money wasn't all that good ($30 per month), but if he couldn't play the game himself (he had a bum ankle), being around it satisfied the need to be involved. And yet, after talking about Little League baseball and helping kids, in the next sentence, he mentioned reading all of the books about Bundy he could get his hands on and watching (studying) the movie about Bundy starring Mark Harmon. Ned didn't see the resemblance between Harmon and Bundy. He said Harmon looked like Lee Harvey Oswald—that is, before launching a detailed description of killing and how to avoid being caught.

Ned wrote that he *was always thinking about it.*

"It" being killing a woman.

His point was that although it was always on his mind, he didn't necessarily drive around town like Bundy and prowl for victims or, as he put it, "find a situation."

What was clear from the letters was that Ned enjoyed the art involved in getting away with a crime as evil as murder. It was something he aspired to. Not a goal, per se, but more than a game. He liked playing. With his victims first. Cops second. Meeting Mary Ellen that night, he wrote, fooling her into inviting him upstairs into her apartment, *was* a perfect situation. When it was over, however, and he realized Mary Ellen had survived, Ned said he knew he was going to get caught. But even when the cops came and he was arrested— he beamed later when remembering the time period in his letter—he was thrilled how everyone the cops spoke to about him couldn't say anything bad. No one really knew him. They talked of the man they *thought* they knew. But Ned had fooled them. And there they were, like fools, supporting him, when he knew damn well that his goal that night, the game he had played with Mary Ellen Renard, involved murder.

Ned loved it: the thrill of fooling all of them. It was part of crime itself.

27

I

By April 1988, Ned's attorney, John Bruno, knew more about his client than he had perhaps wanted to know. An attorney from Middlesex County had visited Bruno's office one afternoon, bringing with him information that didn't bode all too well for his client. "The method of attack," the prosecutor explained to Bruno, talking about Mary Ellen's case, "is strikingly similar to an unsolved murder at Rutgers."

There was that case again, hovering in Ned's past. Even if he hadn't committed the crime, the way in which the murder had been carried out, was almost identical to that of the attack on Mary Ellen. With that, Bruno wondered how he was going to get around explaining the case away. Ned was in trouble down the road when his case went to court. And yet, Bruno realized, Ned's network of supporters seemed to grow with each passing week. People were coming forward to support him. Promising to walk into court and explain that he wasn't some psychopath who could kill people and attack them with knives. It just wasn't in his character.

II

What was it about that Rutgers murder that made investigators certain Ned had been involved? "He could be a like-able guy—piano player, salesman, captain of the softball team, a guy's guy," Bruno explained to me years later. "He was always organizing the parties, the softball games. He seemed like somebody who always wanted to have a company picnic. Not some quiet little nerd who sits in the corner and is afraid to face people socially."

According to the women Bruno spoke to, Ned was "charming" and always "polite." Bruno had to go to Ned with the allegations from Middlesex, explaining to him that the Middlesex murder had the parallels of a repeat offender, and was intrinsically similar in signature to the attack on Mary Ellen. Bruno explained that Ned had been on Middlesex's radar for some time, but they had no evidence to arrest him. They had even questioned Ned a few times, but they had to release him due to the fact that they had nothing with which to charge him.

After Bruno went to Ned and explained the situation, Ned thought about it. The bottom line was this: What if, while he was in jail awaiting trial on the Mary Ellen Renard charge, Middlesex came up with some sort of new evidence? Ned knew he had killed the woman in Middlesex. He thought he had gotten away with it. He believed he left no evidence. But what if something surfaced?

Murder one. The death penalty. Add the Mary Ellen Renard attack to the Middlesex case and he would face death if a jury found him guilty.

"It's something to think about," Bruno told Ned.

On the other hand, with the right plea bargain, Ned realized, he could avoid a murder charge in Middlesex and walk out of prison one day—if only he admitted to it and accepted a lesser charge.

And so Ned came clean. He admitted to Bruno that he committed the murder, but, of course, it was the same old story: self-defense. The Rutgers woman had come on to him, and when he refused *her* advances, he had no other choice but to strangle and stab her to death.

But she had forced him to do it, of course. What was he supposed to do?

The murder had occurred in 1983. Same set of circumstances.

"He looks like a Boy Scout," Fred Schwanwede told the court during one of Ned's plea hearings. "He doesn't look at all dangerous. He looks like he could be the boy next door."

Wasn't that what made Ned even more dangerous—that he looked like and could portray the friendly neighbor?

The Good Samaritan.

The salesman.

Softball player.

Life of the party.

Ned didn't have that evil look of a serial killer, or the rough look of a multiple murderer. In public, he was warm and funny and forthcoming. Just a pleasure to be around.

Ted Bundy redux, in other words. Bundy, who chose mostly college girls and worked his way into their good graces with his all-American pretty-boy looks and charming demeanor, liked to sexually mutilate his victims. In one case, he broke into the dorm room of Lynda Ann Healy, a university student, knocked her unconscious, dressed her in jeans and a T-shirt, wrapped her in a sheet, and tossed her into his car without anyone seeing. Healy's body was found about a year later—she had been decapitated and dismembered.

28

I

Fred Schwanwede—a name, he professes, that he shares with no one else in the United States—was chief of sex crimes with the Bergen County Prosecutor's Office. He knew from looking over the file that Mary Ellen Renard was, he said, "extremely lucky to be alive." Most of the cases resulting in the injuries she had sustained hadn't turned out so well. "Had Miss Renard not been so lucky," Schwanwede speculated, "this case probably would have gone on unsolved. If he had killed her, chances are that unless he did something else subsequent to that and left a print or some other identifying forensic evidence somewhere else, Miss Renard's homicide, if it had become that, would have never been solved."

Ned had never been arrested. There was absolutely no connection between him and Mary Ellen until that night when they met at the singles dance. Aside from Ned and Mary Ellen's chance meeting at Kracker's, there would have been no way to tie them together. Even the print Ned left on Mary Ellen's windowsill wouldn't have done any good. There would have been nothing to compare it with.

Looking at the case, Schwanwede was fortunate, he knew,

that Mary Ellen lived to tell her story. Going after a homicidal maniac and, with any luck, putting him away was what Schwanwede got up in the morning to do. If there was one prosecutor who could go after Ned, and pull in that Middlesex County case to make sure Ned's jury knew the type of fanatic for blood he was, it was Fred Schwanwede.

As Schwanwede sat one morning and read the file on Mary Ellen, he was appalled by the sheer intimidation and manipulation Ned had obviously used to gain her confidence and trust.

II

To Mary Ellen Renard, allowing her attacker to skate on a plea of twenty years—suffice it to say after she was told he had also murdered a woman five years before in a strikingly similar fashion—made her sick to her stomach. The fact that Ned could be out in eleven years made her body ache, her mind race.

Mary Ellen later said the prosecutor's office came to her and told her it was going to allow Ned to plead out his case. "At first, I was upset. It was *not* OK with me," Mary Ellen later insisted.

She had explained to the prosecutor's office that she was fully prepared to face Ned in court and testify. She knew the consequences to her already shattered emotional state, understood how tough it would be, but she was resolved to put him in prison, where he belonged. "They told me I had no choice in it—that it wasn't up to me. But they did talk to me about it before they went ahead."

Prior to the plea deal, Fred Schwanwede called Mary Ellen with a request. "Snelgrove's attorney wants to meet you," he said.

It seemed like an odd demand. "It's very unusual," Schwanwede said, "but I will allow it. I have to be present, and he won't be allowed to ask you anything about the case."

Ned's attorney John Bruno's strategy was to find out what type of witness Mary Ellen would make during trial. He wanted to see how she'd react on the witness stand, even though he had to keep his questions formal: *Where'd you grow up? Where'd you go to school?*

Mary Ellen decided to do it. Why not? She could show Bruno—and Ned—that she wasn't about to back down and curl up like a scared little girl and essentially be victimized all over *again*. Ned had violated her once. She wanted that control back. As it was, there were times when Mary Ellen would be forced to park her car as close to her building as possible and, after checking left and right, looking for Ned, jump from her car and race into the building as fast as she could. When alone, she was scared he was going to dash out from around a corner and grab her. Facing him, facing off *against* him, she would be able to take that fear back.

As they sat in Bruno's office, Mary Ellen recalled later, Schwanwede and Bruno talked about the town of Newark, where the courthouse was located, and how beautiful the nearby cathedral was, which was when Mary Ellen spoke up, saying, "That's where my brother was ordained."

"Your brother's a priest?" Bruno asked with shock.

"Yeah," she said.

At another point in the conversation, Schwanwede asked Mary Ellen how her weekend was. "I went to visit my grand-children," she said casually.

"You're a grandmother?" Bruno interrupted, again quite astonished by the admission.

At forty-five, Mary Ellen was better-looking than a lot of women half her age. She had an innocent beauty that went far beyond her stunning looks and shapely figure. Bruno couldn't believe what he was hearing. Even more, he knew Mary Ellen had an ironclad reputation of attending church and living at home, added to a perfect professional work record, a brother who was a priest, and many friends who could vouch for her. Plus, she was strong-willed and spoke with authority.

The perfect witness.

Leaving, Fred Schwanwede said, "Everything you talked about in there said you were going to make an excellent witness."

The jury would have bonded with Mary Ellen inside five minutes of her direct testimony. Bruno was a smart enough lawyer to know that although he would take a few shots at her while she was on the stand, he could alienate the jury by attacking Mary Ellen and her terrifying ordeal. Branding her in the newspapers as the instigator was one thing, but doing it in court would blow up in his face. They'd hate him—and his client—for it. He couldn't blame Mary Ellen.

In the parking lot, showing Mary Ellen to her car, Schwanwede said, "Look, I have a hunch Bruno knows his client is guilty."

Weeks later, when Schwanwede met with Mary Ellen again, he felt bad about having to plead the case out, but he explained to her that juries were funny. "You never know what they're going to do. This way, we get him off the street."

Mary Ellen was unhappy, but she understood.

Although most of the professionals involved knew Ned was a danger to society—and if he had the chance, he would act out on his perverted sexual fantasies again—Mary Ellen had no idea she would, some twenty years after that conversation with Schwanwede, be once again confronted by Ned and his sadistic behavior.

29

I

During a hearing before Superior Court Judge James Madden, Ned addressed the court. Standing in front of the bench, he looked like an eighteen-year-old high-school senior. With his blond hair and blue eyes, small frame and baby face, he embodied an innocence that showed how easily Mary Ellen could have fallen into his web.

Ned said he understood the charges against him, but didn't "know why [he] assaulted the women." He had no explanation. It was something that had come over him, he seemed to say. Some sort of change.

Mary Ellen had seen it. Ned had gone into her bathroom one person and had come out another.

Those in the courtroom were unaware that during the past week Ned and his lawyer had made a plea agreement with the Bergen County Prosecutor's Office. But that's not what had stunned everyone in the courtroom that day. It was the word "women." The plural form Ned had used while addressing the court.

Wasn't it only one—Mary Ellen Renard?

Women? What is he talking about?

Ned said he had no words to describe his actions. No excuse.

But clearly, in saying so, he had admitted to both crimes.

Fred Schwanwede asked the court to order a psychiatric evaluation before Ned's sentencing date, which was scheduled for May 13, 1988.

II

Under the plea agreement offered to Bruno, Ned faced a maximum of twenty years, minimum of ten, a sentence that, of course, shocked both Mary Ellen and family members of Ned's first victim. Even more outrageous to both was that with good behavior, Ned could be eligible for release—not parole—inside eleven years.

Eleven years.

A little over a decade behind bars for murdering one woman and savagely, cruelly, attacking a second, nearly killing her, too.

Fred Schwanwede and the Middlesex County people wanted to close the Middlesex murder they believed Ned was responsible for. The problem with charging Ned with the crime—he had never been indicted for it—was that he knew the victim. He had dated her months before the crime took place. That meant, Schwanwede perceptively pointed out, that any trace evidence connecting Ned to the murder would ultimately be thrown out of court. Ned had every reason to be with the woman. All he had to say—and he was an expert at manipulating people and situations—was that he and the victim had reunited. They were talking about getting back together.

All that being said, there wasn't a lot of evidence against Ned. Thus, the best way out of it all was to offer a plea. Having him admit to the crime would be a major coup.

"The family had suspected him all along, but they never

had what they needed to close the book on it," Schwanwede said. "To have him admit that he did that was helpful to them. For us, it wasn't so much about closing out a cold case, but bringing some peace to the family."

The thing that surprised Schwanwede most was that Bruno had allowed Ned to plead the case out the way it had been written: aggravated manslaughter. Generally speaking, as time goes on, a case against a suspect grows colder. The Middlesex case was already pushing five years. Ned was likely never going to be arrested for it. That was clear. Yet, he admitted to killing the woman, stabbing her to death. Why wouldn't he fight for a lesser charge instead of signing the plea the way it was written?

This baffled everyone.

What no one knew, of course, was that Ned Snelgrove had a plan himself.

30

I

Most defendants who plead out their cases sign on the dotted line, face a judge for sentencing, keep their mouths shut, and fall into prison life best they can, hoping to one day sit in front of the parole board and argue for early release. Ned Snelgrove, the Bergen County court was about to learn, was quite a bit different than most defendants it had seen pass through its walnut-and-maple doors.

Ned had been told that it was a good idea for him to write to the judge before his sentencing and, in perhaps a compassionate way, apologize for his actions. He should relay a feeling that he was willing to accept punishment, whatever that may be, move on, and get some help while incarcerated. The thought was that Ned could begin his sentence on a powerful, positive note. Although the judge was unlikely to lower Ned's sentence, the letter might prove that Ned knew what he did was wrong and understood that he had hurt many people.

As everyone was about to learn, however, Ned Snelgrove was not your average criminal.

II

On Thursday, April 14, 1988, Ned sat down in his cell and began drafting a letter to the judge. He opened by saying he was writing to "describe what happened" in both his crimes. Ned claimed both "incidents" were generated by chronic sexual urges he had developed in grade school for "unknown reasons," which later grew into an uncontrollable penchant he had for perpetrating violence against women.

The letter, all at once, was shocking, disturbing, and chilling. Some later said, it was perhaps a plea on Ned's part for help. He described his life leading up to both crimes as being tormented by these unmanageable feelings of attacking women and putting them into a state of not being able to defend themselves. He got off on it, he said in not so many words. He agonized over what was an "<u>enormous</u>"—he underlined the word—"sexual arousement" he would get when seeing women, the good-looking ones with large breasts, rendered unconscious and incapable of defense.

He wrote about being able to restrain himself, most of the time, *although there have been a few very close calls*.

He said he knew it was all wrong, but he couldn't do anything about it. He tried. He really did. But it was "difficult," he added, just to "control" his own "hands," as if they had a life of their own.

He expected that this sickness—which he hadn't told anyone about—was one of the reasons why his friends and coworkers had such a tough time believing that he had committed these crimes. He had easily fooled them all. Same as Mary Ellen and his first victim.

Over the next several pages—in powerful, frightening detail—Ned described how he had killed the woman in Middlesex and attacked Mary Ellen years later. It was almost as if in writing it out, Ned got the same cathartic sense of fulfillment all over again that he had gotten while committing the actual crimes. *I held [her] throat,* he wrote of the woman in Middlesex, *pressing down with my thumbs, for as long as I could. . . .*

When they had a chance to read the letter, the judge, along with Fred Schwanwede and even Ned's attorney, John Bruno, couldn't believe Ned had put such incredibly vile words on a page.

The passion.

The gall.

The elements of murder.

A confession?

Why? For what purpose?

Ned wanted everyone to believe that the letter was a new beginning for him: a point at which he could start to heal his perverse mind. The violent feelings he had, Ned explained, defied "logic." He knew they did. He wasn't naïve. He understood that not everyone thought this way. Still, he wrote, *Fred Schwanwede* was likely going to argue that he was a *cold-blooded, heartless killer,* but he wanted the court to know that he wasn't. If he had been that type of murderer, Ned justified in the letter, why, then, would he have chosen the victims he had? He wasn't some sort of "Green River Killer." Some lunatic who prowled the streets for victims. His victims, Ned argued, were "unlucky."

Wrong place, wrong time.

That's all. If they hadn't been near him, he insisted, they wouldn't have been attacked.

III

Ned's letter was nothing more than a narcissistic rant, unlike anything the court had ever seen. It was all about Ned and why he had acted on his violent thoughts. There was little remorse. No apology. But he did "hate" himself, and he was upset that he "had it made" at the time of his arrest.

Great job.

Great friends.

Good family.

He couldn't understand why he had chosen this specific time to act out. It made no sense to him. He had let everyone down: *I cry every time I think of my parents . . . ,* he wrote.

In all that he had said, Ned encouraged the court not to worry about him in the future. Why, as long as he wasn't allowed, he wrote, *to be alone with a female,* well—lo and behold—he was *not a threat to society.*

Imagine that.

His friends, he ended the letter, would *back [him] up on this point.*

The words of an admitted killer. A man whom society didn't have to worry about for at least a decade or more. In fact, the only way Ned would see freedom again inside a decade was if he complied with *every* single standard that the system had set in place for rehabilitation. If Ned met *every* single recommendation, he could be a free man by the year 1999—and not a day before.

IV

What about that woman Ned had murdered in Middlesex County—the one he had squeezed the life from, then stabbed repeatedly in the chest and face as she, he explained in his letter to the court, "sputtered" back to life after his efforts to choke her to death failed? After she expired, he had posed her so he could sexually gratify himself. That beautiful woman, whom he had met and dated at Rutgers, had a family and friends. There were people who loved her and adored the way she had dedicated her short life in many respects to the welfare of animals. Anyone who knew her could never forget her smile, or the way she had of making everyone around her feel comfortable and cared for.

Indeed, that *woman* Ned had killed, well, she had a name.

BOOK III

KAREN

31

I

Looking at photos of Karen Osmun from high school and college, with her light skin, curly blond hair, thin smile, large, all-encompassing eyes, and checkmark eyebrows, one could easily tell she embodied the image—no, the *spirit*—of a young woman from Nordic descent. Karen's mother, Elizabeth Anne Asmund—yes, Asmund—married Ralph Osmun in 1954. Elizabeth went to Clifford J. Scott High School in East Orange, New Jersey, with Ralph, and they graduated together in 1945. In high school, though, Ralph and Elizabeth Anne never hooked up. Some years later, when both were in their twenties, Ralph got a job delivering flowers. Elizabeth Anne, the one with the Icelandic roots and an immediate family the size of a symphony, had spent the morning one day many years after high school at the funeral of an uncle. Later on, back at the house, Ralph showed up to deliver a bouquet of flowers and they locked eyes.

I remember you from high school. . . .
Yes, and I remember you.
Destiny?
Perhaps.

Either way, they made a date and . . . after a small but lovely wedding, Ralph and Elizabeth Anne set up a home in Cedar Grove, New Jersey. It was "a cute little town," Barbara Delaney, Karen Osmun's sister, Ralph and Elizabeth's first child, later said. Cedar Grove wasn't quite Reykjavik, but it fit the needs of the Osmun family when they all lived together in one house during what were the happy days of the 1960s and 1970s.

II

The opposite side of that marital bliss the Osmuns so much enjoyed early in their lives was that Ralph had had polio since he was three years old, an incapacitating disease of the spine that started, for Mr. Osmun, when he ended up with meningitis as a small child. For the most part, polio has been wiped out in the United States. But during the mid-twentieth century, the disease had set its hooks firmly in place, affecting a wide variety of people from all social classes. And yet Ralph was such an optimistic person, such a grateful human being and marvelous father and husband, he didn't allow the disease to disturb his daily life, or those precious lives he loved so much that were around him now. "A polio victim," Barbara told me later, "[the disease] made him a tremendous person. Some people can have those diseases and it makes them, I don't know, *bitter*. But Dad was the kind of person who *embraced* life."

The kids, Karen and Barbara, never thought of their dad as having limitations: To them, he was as normal as any other dad. "It wasn't until people pointed them—his limitations—out to us, that we really noticed," Barbara said. "He was definitely instrumental in my life and our core religious values."

III

North of Verona, west of Clifton, Cedar Grove, New Jersey, of the 1970s, was a working-class town, like many of New

Jersey's northern boroughs were back then. For some, it was a place where men went to work in the morning with black lunch boxes in hand, hard hats, and robotic smiles.

Blue-collar.

No doubt about it.

For others, like Ralph, who picked up the bus down the block and commuted into Manhattan, Cedar Grove was an eclectic mix of white-collar, second-generation immigrants who had taken their parents' dreams and, slowly, turned them into their own reality. Barbara and Karen were the Osmuns' only children. Barbara was born in 1957, Karen a few years later, in 1960. From the earliest years of their lives together, Karen and Barbara might have seemed different, but they were as close as sisters could be, building a venerable bond throughout their adolescent years. They might not have agreed on everything, and viewed life in vastly different ways, but they got along and loved each other.

Elizabeth Anne was the one to crack the whip in the house. Always the demanding wife and mother, she had that hard-nosed Icelandic toughness about her that only foreigners, generally Europeans, can lay claim to. And she wasn't, Barbara said, afraid to show it around the house. "She had a really domineering personality and he—my dad—could kind of blow her off. She'd be ranting and yelling. . . ." Sometimes stomping through the house. Complaining about something. Something minuscule. Something unimportant. Something that didn't seem to be *that* big of a deal.

Spilled milk.

When she did, Ralph—not one to be negative at all, a rather patient man by all accounts—would shake his head and jokingly utter, "Nag. Nag. Nag." (Barbara laughed when she later told me this story: the memory giving her a moment of pleasant recall.)

This would always seem to calm Elizabeth down.

In many ways, when the kids were young, Barbara and

Karen and Ralph were, Barbara said, "the Three Musketeers." They spent time together. Every night, Mr. Osmun would come into the children's bedroom before bedtime and sit and tell stories of his past, or read books, or recite Bible passages. "They were all fascinating," Barbara recalled. "Very fond memories of the three of us kind of laying in bed with the lights out, telling stories . . . talking."

Innocent times, when the world spun on an axis of purity and hope and wholesomeness.

IV

There came a time when Karen decided that she loved animals. All sorts of animals.

Didn't matter: cats, pigs, goats, dogs, squirrels.

Later, during her college years, Karen would aspire to be a veterinarian, but it was Barbara, really, who had the passion for animals when they were kids. Barbara kept snakes in the family pool. Lizards in her bedroom.

Fish. Turtles. Ducks. Gerbils.

A regular old animal farm.

Karen, though, had what a relative later called was a "sensitive and gentle" way with animals. It was Karen's "touch," which, this same relative shared, brought "healing and caring to animals . . . especially [Karen's] pet poodle, Charlie."

It seemed that beyond an innate love for animals, Karen enjoyed everything life in the outdoors had to offer: swimming, sailing, camping, skiing. "She smelled the aromas of living," said a friend, "the fragrance of flowers, and [she] frequently brought her mother a rose to express her love and share feelings of closeness."

Taking after Ralph, who was a magician during his younger years, Karen liked to perform magic tricks for the family. "She delighted in the fun," the friend added, ". . . as her hand moved faster than our eyes, bringing laughter and joy to those who watched her perform."

32

I

Ralph Osmun worked for the insurance industry in New York City. It was hard work, especially for a guy with polio. Ralph had never gone to college. But he hit the industry at a time when all you needed was a high-school diploma, a strong work ethic, and an appreciation for just having a job to begin with. When the girls, growing up, ever mentioned going to college after high school, Ralph was adamant. Like so many men from his generation, Ralph had never gotten the chance to do it himself. So, in some respects, living through his children, he would not only encourage them to place college on the top of their list of future goals, but insist on it: "You are *both* going to college."

End of discussion.

It didn't matter what they had to do, he said. Or how they were going to get in. But Karen and Barbara both, regardless of what they wanted or even thought, were going to get a college diploma.

It would be a Monday—the only night the bank in town was open—and any money the kids had been given for birthdays, or just for being good girls, would be on its way into a

college fund they had set up. "This is for your school," Ralph
would tell the kids as they trotted down to the bank to make
their Monday-night deposits.

II

As the kids grew, church became a way of life.
Sunday school.
Bible study.
Mass.
They enjoyed the sanctity of the wholeness the church embraced and loved the communal aspect of it all. Ruth Smith,
who ran the Sunday school, later talked about Karen's open
display of loving life: "She had a winning smile and sparkling
eyes, and whenever I think of Karen, I'll think of that beautiful face."

Karen was one of those kids, Ruth explained, that neighborhood parents always welcomed into their homes with open
arms. She was quiet among the adults, generally, but when left
with a group of kids her own age, she would "bubble over. . . ."

One thing that every one of Karen's relatives and friends
later beamed about was her Christian values. "She was not
judgmental," Ruth insisted. "What a quality—that is Christ-
like. I never heard Karen say anything against anyone."

III

Ralph Osmun had done such a good job with investing the
family's savings that, by the time the girls were eight and
eleven, in 1968, he had enough money saved to treat everyone to a trip to Iceland.

Elizabeth Anne was thrilled: *Home. I'm going to see my
family.*

What a wonderful surprise.

The kids, too, would get a chance to see where their grandmother grew up, where a majority of their ancestors were from and many family members still lived.

And so it was off to Newark, New Jersey.

The airport.

Then a short plane ride.

Touchdown.

Then cold.

And wet.

"Welcome to the middle of nowhere."

The kids were in awe. Everything around them was new. Iceland was a place categorically different from the smokestacks and oil barges and honking horns and tall buildings and smell left behind in certain parts of New Jersey. They were too young to realize it, but Iceland was a culture shock. Everything was so fresh and, well, interesting. At the time, Karen and Barbara's grandmother had seventy-two living first cousins on the island. Karen and Barbara loved the country. They ate fresh bread with bananas and sugar. They swam in the public pools—all fed naturally by hot springs. They took long rides into the countryside in a relative's Volkswagen. They were introduced to the metric system.

They danced.

Sang.

Took it all in.

And loved every minute of it.

IV

In seventh grade, Karen took an interest in—of all things—carpentry. In her day, said Barbara, the girls cooked and cleaned and did all those things little girls are supposed to do. This, of course, while the boys built things and played in the mud.

But not Karen. Like a little boy who strapped on his tool belt and felt the heaviness of that steel hammer in his hand, pencil in his small ear, Karen would hit the shop to create something from a few planks of wood.

In high school, Karen seemed to run with the conservative crowd. "We were definitely not the cheerleader type," said Barbara. "We were more . . . well, joiners. We did a lot of activities. The drama club. Newspaper."

Brownies.

And Girl Scouts.

Church youth groups.

Barbara and Karen even had a few boyfriends in high school. The two sisters were "average," Barbara recalled. "Just your average kids. We did a lot of things with the other kids. Very social."

V

When Barbara was a senior, Karen a sophomore, tragedy struck. There it was—that ringing phone in the early-morning hours no one wants to hear. The bells of death. That solemn rush of life that sneaks up on everybody when things seem to be running on autopilot.

When life seems perfect.

For Karen and Barbara, it was something neither one of them had ever expected, nor could have prepared for, in all their years.

33

I

Even though he suffered from polio, Ralph Osmun was expected to live a full life. Sure, there were always going to be doctor's visits. Trips to the emergency room. Pills. Exercises. Joint pain. Sleepless nights.

Lots of discomfort.

But Ralph was a fighter. He fought off the ill effects of the disease—because what else could he do? The guy had a family that depended on him. Complaining about pain wouldn't do anybody any good.

But then . . . it happened.

He was forty-seven.

Ralph had been in the hospital undergoing a few routine procedures, suffering from the residual effects, Barbara said later, of a heart attack three years earlier. His family expected him to take the tests he needed and return home.

He had done it all before, he'd do it again.

It was an October day. A Saturday. Karen and Barbara had gone to the football game in town. They were walking home.

"Great game . . . wasn't it?"

"Sure was, Karen."

And then they looked up the road as they walked and there was Elizabeth Anne driving toward them in the family car.

"That Mom?"

"Mom?"

"Get in."

She was upset. What were they doing running off to the high-school football game when their father was in the hospital? "You should be visiting him," she scolded. (Barbara later said, laughing, "My mother was always mad at *something*.")

So they all went over to the hospital and sat with Ralph for the day and into the night.

II

The next morning, a ringing phone woke up the house.

It was 6:00 A.M.

Elizabeth Anne answered. Groggy. Still half asleep.

Then she dropped her head and started crying.

"What's wrong, Mom?" Karen asked, rubbing sleep from her eyes.

"Mom, you all right?" Barbara asked.

III

"Devastating" was the word Barbara used to describe what she and Karen went through after they had accepted that their father was dead and that they would never see him again, or hear any of those family stories, or attend church, or enjoy his supple, friendly, warm companionship and company.

Ralph had dropped dead of a heart attack. He'd had one in his early forties, brought on by, doctors said, the "residual effects of polio." But no one expected Ralph to have another one—and then, on top of it, die. Especially while he was in the hospital undergoing routine medical exams and procedures. "It really disrupted the entire dynamics of my family," Barbara said later. "Because, well, he was the center."

The nucleus. Not the man of the house. That's different. So different from what Ralph was to his daughters. He was the guardian. The light.

Within a week of Ralph's death, the kids were told Ralph had left them something, which, during such a fragile time of mourning, seemed to be all too much to take. Apparently, he had left the kids an audio recording. Perhaps he had sensed death was imminent. Maybe he made the tape *just in case*. In any event, not seven days after they had watched mourners sprinkle dirt on their father's coffin six feet below ground, here he was speaking from that grave.

They couldn't do it. They couldn't put the tape in and press PLAY.

No way. "I can't handle this," said Karen.

Me neither, Barbara thought.

How grim. Macabre.

Ralph was one of those guys who had everything in order in his house, on his desk, in his car. Oil changes on the date. Paper clips in their box. Pencils—all sharpened—in one place. Pens, all the blues and the blacks, in another.

So, in retrospect, the tape didn't seem like it was so out of the ordinary when Barbara thought about it later. "I remember," she recalled, "after the funeral, my mother tried to play the tape and it was . . . well, it was awful. Just awful."

It would be weeks before they listened to it.

IV

One day, a few years after Ralph passed away, Karen and Barbara were talking. "I always felt like I had picked up the role of stepping in [and] helping Mom to hold things together," Karen said, "after Dad died."

Two sisters chatting about a father they loved so dearly.

"Huh," said Barbara lovingly, "I thought I had done the same thing."

It wasn't as if they were competing over who had played a larger role. The point was that they both did their part to pick up the slack—such a contemptuous word in this situation— and help Elizabeth Anne understand that she needed to move on. She was distraught. Her love, her world, was gone.

Elizabeth Anne had been a stay-at-home mom her entire life. Now, into her forties, she was forced to join the work-force like so many of her generation. *The Honeymooners* way of life was a memory . . . no more waiting for Ralph to walk through the door after a hard day's work, toss his fedora on the chair, and sit down to a hot meal.

The routine of life was over.

The fact was, Elizabeth Anne would have to go out and punch a clock.

Which was exactly what she did.

34

I

Karen was a bit more of a "free spirit," Barbara said, than she had ever been. And Elizabeth Anne certainly didn't appreciate it. What she meant was, Karen would do stupid things. Like one night, for example, she took off from the house and didn't come back. It wasn't, however, that she was rebellious or sticking it to Mom; she had just forgotten, she later told her mother, to come home before dark.

Karen would often horse around and get herself into what we'll call minor dilemmas. She once got her leg caught in a cinder block and the cops had to come in and help get her out. Then she got her hand stuck in an animal trap she and Barbara had run into in the woods while walking home from school one day.

Karen was one of those kids her peers could push into doing something and they knew, with enough "Come on, Karen, you chicken," she'd ultimately give in.

Peer pressure—the adolescent web that the world spun around teenagers.

"She'd be the one to forget to hand in [homework], and at

the last minute, you know," said Barbara, "be scurrying around, looking for it."

II

With the end of high school near, Karen began reaching out to friends, the undergrads, making those connections she'd hoped would last into adulthood and maybe a lifetime, while giving them all a bit of advice she'd hoped they could take with them into their final years. To several of her undergrad friends and peers, she wrote a special letter she handed out.

For the past few years the roads of our lives have run to-gether and now mine has turned away. But I am confident that our paths shall cross again. Until then, live your life to the fullest. Never be happy with second best. Work for what you want. Don't be lazy. Face your challenges head on, confident. Don't give up. I hope your life will always be filled with love, hopes, happiness, joy, and all that good stuff.

Before leaving school, Karen gave out gifts to those from her "gang," a group of kids with whom she hung. Ellen Miller, one of Karen's friends from that time, later said, "Somehow during September, she managed to get the locker combinations of all our lockers. Then, at each holiday, we would receive presents from 'the Great Pumpkin,' 'Santa,' 'the Easter Bunny,' et cetera. She was also careful to give a present to herself. As each holiday rolled around, we all anticipated the arrival of these gifts, never knowing who was giving them. It wasn't until graduation we discovered who our 'elf' was."

The greatest gift Karen had given anyone before she left for college was, of course, her love and friendship. Those around her adored Karen and all she had taught them about life through high school. She was, many later agreed, truly one of a kind. And now she was heading into the rest of her life, set to go to a fine college.

35

I

Some say that pride is a rejection of God's grace—that it is such a depleting, emotionally draining characteristic of the ego, that it can bring any good man to his knees and make him beg for mercy. Ned Snelgrove was leaving home and heading south from Connecticut into New Jersey to attend Cook College (a subschool of Rutgers University) in 1978. It might have been only one hundred miles away, but for Ned, it was the beginning of a new life away from home and, for the first time, a departure from the comforting surroundings of family and friends. Perhaps this had been one of the reasons why Ned was able to keep his feelings of violence against women pretty much in check throughout his early years.

Part of Ned moving to another state involved him getting away from the parental grip he had been wrapped around for most of his life. *He wanted to make his own decisions,* his father, Edwin Sr., later wrote. Ned wanted to be able to make choices without the nagging parents telling him what to do.

Independence.

Adulthood.

Solitude.

Ned had never known any of it, but here he was, heading into the beginning of his own life.

His own dream.

II

Ned and his dad, Edwin Sr., always had a "close father/son relationship," the elder Snelgrove noted. But now it was gone. Lost. Left somewhere along Interstate 95 as Ned made his way south into New Jersey during that fall of 1978. Back at home, before college, Ned had led a fairly quiet, ordinary life—at least according to family members and former schoolteachers and friends. *He used to watch football . . . sleep,* even work on projects he brought home from his job, . . . *and spend time with some old high school friends,* his younger brother later wrote. Ned seemed *happy and contented.*

Ned's brother, a navy guy, had always looked up to him. *He was a person,* he wrote, *that I thought people should emulate.*

Like many who knew him back then, Ned's brother viewed him as *ambitious, successful, intelligent, confident, capable and athletic.*

Above normal. Above average. One who was expected to go on and become somebody, do something.

Then there was that side of Ned that reminded people of their next-door neighbor. The guy you'd least likely suspect to see in the newspaper with his hands cuffed behind his back facing accusations of murder, attempted murder, sexual assault, and a host of other charges.

His brother used the word "malice" to describe a trait, a characteristic, a behavior that Ned *never . . . ever displayed.* He wrote about Ned not having one *hateful bone in his body.*

But Ned did. He hated himself. He hated who he was.

He hated women.

And yet he chose—and it was a choice, because he knew damn well that monster was inside him—to ignore those impulses and try to sail through life without complication. For Ned, murder wasn't about hate. Or a burning detestation he had for himself and that other *person* percolating inside him. It wasn't about one person—him—allowing a festering, burning resentment to turn into violence. A sort of "give in" to that twisted grandiose image of women he held so deeply. Nor was it about Ned thinking of this person night and day and developing a revulsion for him.

It wasn't about revenge.

Or money.

Or even lust.

No, none of these.

Contrary to what any of his family and friends had failed to see—and, in truth, how could they?—in his youth, it was about one thing for Ned Snelgrove.

Control.

Well, maybe two: control and restraint.

But not necessarily that control most of us might attribute to a killer. In Ned's case, it was a different type of control. One of which Ned had somewhat mastered through high school. One of which he learned then to keep at bay. A desire to do violence on women that Ned could manage.

That was it: For Ned, it was about mind management. Don't act out.

Fight off those urges.

And for years—at least we think—it worked.

But now Ned was on his way south, out into the open world. No more would his life be contained within the confines of his childhood stomping grounds, his own little bubble. At Rutgers, there would be new people.

New situations.

New challenges for an unstable mind to overcome.

And, most dangerously, new females to encounter.

36

I

Ned was heading into his final year at Rutgers. He hadn't returned home much during the past three years, but he decided that a trip was in order. In between the time he had left for school and now, 1982, as he entered his twenties, one could argue that Ned had matured. It was here, in fact, where Ned had changed, his father believed. He was now "arrogant" and "very self-assured," the elder Snelgrove later described.

The center of his own design.

Ned the narcissist. Ned the perfect man. Ned the future business star.

The new Ned, if you will, was obvious to his parents from the moment he stepped foot in their graces. Mr. and Mrs. Snelgrove were, of course, excited to see their son. But to Ned, returning home was more of a duty, it seemed, than something he had wanted to do out of longing. *I was not really comfortable in his company . . . ,* Mr. Snelgrove wrote, speaking about this day. The son he had loved, had adored, and had so many ambitions for, was alien to him—a different person altogether.

Moreover, several people would later report that Ned was

emotionally abusive toward his parents. Controlling and domineering. Talking to them on the telephone once, said a source, Ned "would not ask them to do something for him— he would demand it. And not take no for an answer, often belittling them and emotionally abusing them."

Ned had gone through the motions of *Hi, how you doin'? How's things going?* But he wasn't at all *interested,* Mr. Snelgrove wrote of his son, *in anything we had to say.*

Condescending, in other words. Patronizing.

Mr. "I Could Care Less About You."

While at home, Ned held his head high and went through the motions of being the good son, back in Berlin doing what sons were supposed to do: visit, eat dinner with Mom and Dad, lie about how much he loved being home, tell them what they wanted to hear about his life strategy after graduation.

Plans. As if he even had them.

Ned wasn't fooling anyone—especially his Yale-educated father. *I didn't like him as much,* his father later wrote, obviously not mincing words, *as my instincts told me I should. . . .* Standing, looking at this shell of a man in his kitchen, this man who was once a happy-go-lucky boy with curly blond hair and a Hollywood smile, the elder Snelgrove couldn't believe his son and this "man" were one in the same person. Flashes of the days when Ned, as a kid, used to be "outgoing and gregarious," Edwin Sr. described, enveloped Mr. Snelgrove. It was a time when Ned had friends. When he always laughed.

Joked.

Played the piano.

Excelled in sports and became a three-letter varsity athlete in high school.

He was on his way to the top, Mr. Snelgrove wrote.

The other two Snelgrove children were more like the old man, Mr. Snelgrove admitted: bookish, cerebral, introverted, "not particularly athletic." When he was a youth running around the Yale campus, Mr. Snelgrove considered himself "a follower," he explained rather humbly, "not a leader."

But Ned . . . Neddy Snelgrove was different—the family member who had broken the mold, so to speak, and carved out a life for himself. A niche. At least that's what everyone thought when Ned left for Rutgers.

So much potential. So much opportunity ahead of him.

So much promise.

But now, his entire demeanor had changed. When Ned left for college, Dad was proud. Ned was a "brain," as dad had told it, but also a popular kid doing cannonballs in the town pool as everyone stood around and marveled. There's Neddy: smart, tough as nails, and popular.

But that person, Mr. Snelgrove could see easily as Ned stood in the kitchen years later, ready to graduate from college, cocky and altered, heading into his final few semesters, was different from the child that had left home some four years earlier—but not in a way that parents wished. Here was this shallow man. Someone so very much different from the child he had been. Someone so very full of himself. An inconsiderate human being who seemingly cared little for anyone but himself.

Cold. Unfeeling.

Ned talked of traveling to Mexico and the Caribbean after graduation.

Edwin Sr. and wife Norma looked at each other. *Huh?*

Skiing in Colorado.

Ned, come on? That's not you was the common reaction.

But who knew Ned, really? Ned was already working for Hewlett by 1983, on his way to becoming one of its top executives. He was excelling in his job. But it did little to challenge his intellect, and instead turned him into an arrogant, self-centered undergrad, with a head too big to fit through the doorway.

What threw off Mr. and Mrs. Snelgrove was that Ned had

never been one to spend money. He was always tight. Mr. Scrooge. Liked to hoard it and pack it away in the bank. His father was blown away by the mention that this same kid who had stowed away for college every penny he had ever earned, this same young man who never, ever took a vacation from *any* job he'd ever had, and generally brought work home with him on the weekends and kept to himself, was standing here, in this kitchen, talking about traveling the world. Was it the same child?

It was a "shock," Mr. Snelgrove later observed, to see such a "self-assertive, me-first" person.

Ned Snelgrove. The new man. The new son. The new exec. Confident. Poised. Egotistic.

Who the heck are you? The senior Snelgroves wondered.

I always loved Ned, his father went on to write, *but . . . I [felt] somewhat distanced from him (that winter he came home), as if I [were] seeing this whole situation through the wrong end of a telescope.*

Mr. Snelgrove concluded by writing how the new Ned was *someone I know, but he is not really my son.*

II

This sudden change Ned exhibited while visiting home could be attributed to many different factors. In a sense, all kids "grow up" while in college. All kids "find themselves," to some extent. All boys leave home and return—dare we say it—men. For Ned, however, this idiosyncratic change in his demeanor at home during this trip was likely brought on by the unstableness of his relationship with Karen Osmun, a classmate he had recently proclaimed his enduring, undying love for. There was no other woman in Ned's life that matched Karen's beauty, pleasurable company, or "let's live life to the fullest" attitude. Ned had fallen for Karen.

Deeply. Entirely. Maybe even obsessively.

But Karen was talking about her future lately—which did not include Ned Snelgrove. Slowly, casually, Ned was beginning to figure out that he was Karen's college lover. A boyfriend. Some dude she dated and had a good time with, but also someone she did *not* want to spend her postcollege days hanging around.

Ned didn't like that so much.

Ned had told people he loved Karen. That there could be no other woman like her.

Karen saw an end to the relationship; it had run its course. Certainly. But she also saw a beginning to her own life.

Ned saw the opposite—and it tore him apart.

37

I

Back in the day when it worked, Social Security helped people. Because their father had died at such a young age, Barbara and Karen Osmun were afforded the opportunity to pick, basically, any college they wanted to attend and the government would foot the bill.

Not a bad deal for a couple of well-groomed, smart kids who would one day make productive members of society and great contributions to the world.

II

Two years after their father died, their mother remarried. Why not? The woman couldn't wallow in sorrow all her life. She was attractive and eager to please a man. For Karen and Barbara, both now in college, the new man took a bit of the worry off their plates and allowed them to focus on school. Through the years of 1978 to 1979, Karen had volunteered at a local animal shelter. Through that close and personal relationship with the animals, she decided to make it her future.

Her vocation.

Her purpose.

"She just adored all kinds of animals," Barbara said.

III

When Karen's mother remarried, she and her new husband sold their homes and purchased a beach house on the Jersey Shore. It was a beautiful place that ebbed and flowed with people throughout the summer like a living, breathing thing. The salty taste of the beach air, the sand on the wooden floors brought in from the beach, the subtle crashing of the waves as you lay on a blanket and collected the sun's rays, were all part of the nuance of a New Jersey summer.

As a unit, the Osmuns were not "overly impressed" with Karen's boyfriend, Ned Snelgrove. She had brought him to the house for the weekend one summer. He was not what they had expected—and maybe no man Karen brought home would have been. But Ned seemed quiet and—innocently, perhaps—mysterious. That boyish charm that had impressed so many others failed to work on the Osmuns, who were, in many ways, tough people, and yet all-around *average* people.

What was clear to everyone, however, was that Ned adored Karen.

It was Ned's "vibe," Barbara said later. There was just something about him that was off—no one could quite put a finger on what it was exactly.

A dark cloud followed Ned. Something was "different" about him.

"He was our friend," a former college buddy said, "so it was easy to brush it away. Ned was just 'weird.' But he was Ned, you know."

Still, as time moved forward, Karen "tried moving away from him" in a romantic sense, but she expressed an interest to remain friends. So for a year, on and off, Ned and Karen dated and separated. They'd be an item, and then they wouldn't.

Karen was cool with it. But, according to former friends and even Ned's own family, it ate him up inside. His first real girlfriend and she wasn't really his girlfriend at all. Just a part-time lover.

"It wasn't like, 'I don't even want to see you again,'" Barbara said. "Karen never said anything like that to Ned. But it was more of, 'I'm moving on—in a new direction.'"

IV

After that weekend Ned spent at the cottage, Elizabeth Anne and Barbara got to talking. Just about things in general. A mother and her daughter shooting the breeze.

It was nice.

Then Ned came up.

"He's not quite right," Elizabeth Anne told Barbara.

Barbara understood. It wasn't any one *thing* Ned had said or anything he had done, but more of a feeling. A sixth sense.

Ned was strange.

Part of it was that Karen and Ned didn't seem like a "hot and heavy" couple. They were dating, yes. But when they were together, it seemed the word "couple" didn't fit. It was like an energy around them.

Bad karma.

There was no chemistry.

"Ned had a strange way about him around women," said one college friend. "He liked to invade their space and get in their face. He'd get physical with women all the time." Not in a fun way. But bothersome. Touchy-feely. Hugging too long. Too close. Embracing females intimately he had just met. It was extremely uncomfortable for those around him.

"And yes, before he met Karen," that same college friend agreed, "Ned was a virgin. No doubt about it."

V

Heading into the year 1983, Karen rented an apartment in New Brunswick. She had been the maid of honor at Barbara's wedding—a dream come true for both—and was beginning to decide on which road to take in life. In the interim, near commencement, Karen had made it perfectly clear to Ned that he had been, more or less, a college boyfriend. She had no intention of seeing him in a romantic way after college. But she didn't want to stop talking or even seeing him. But back in August 1982 she broke it off with him.

"Friends."

The one word no man in love ever wanted to hear.

"Let's be friends, Ned."

Devastation. Rejection. *What's wrong with me? What have I done?*

"I love you, but I'm not in love. . . ."

Ned had confided in his sister near this time that he "loved Karen" more than any other woman he had met. Ned was confident he *would never feel that way about any other girl,* Mr. Snelgrove wrote.

Never, ever. It just wasn't possible. Karen was the first and the last.

Ned's everything.

So, when Karen said, "I cannot see you anymore," Ned saw the end of the road. His one chance at love gone and forgotten. He had never been in love before. Heck, he had never even had a girlfriend before.

But now the free spirit, the girl who had grown into a woman herself and wanted to see the world, was out of Ned's life.

Forever.

Ned crashed and burned. Reality check.

What do I do now? Ned must have pondered.

VI

After Barbara got married, the Osmuns began getting to-gether again: cookouts, holidays, birthday parties. It was a great time in their lives, Barbara said later. Mom was remar-ried. Barbara was just married and talking about kids, and Karen was beginning her life after college, Ned Snelgrove completely in the past. Karen was once again the bubbly little girl she had been before college, before her dad had died, before her entire life changed. What a difference time made. She saw the future. She relished what she had, not what the family had lost. God was good. He was blessing her again. She was traveling. Europe and the Caribbean. Talking about helping animals. Being a veterinarian.

Life couldn't have been any better.

VII

Karen and her mother were talking one night. The conver-sation somehow turned toward Ned. There was almost a silent agreement between them that it was best Karen had broken it off. But, "Ned wants to resume the relationship," Karen said, adding that he was calling her, pleading with her to give it one more try.

"And you said?"

"I discouraged it."

A polite way to say that she wanted nothing to do with Ned.

"He's been persisting," Karen added. "It's somewhat of an annoyance."

38

I

It was late summer. Barbara was down at the shore staying at the house with her husband. Karen had come down for the weekend. They all decided to go out to eat. Their mom and stepdad had gone away on a trip and hadn't been around for a few weeks.

"So, sis, how's it going?" Karen and Barbara were sitting, waiting for their dinner. They finally had a chance to catch up.

"Good . . . ," Barbara said. She was smiling. It was great to see Karen again.

"What is it?"

Barbara's husband was smiling, too. A coy sort of "I know something you don't" smirk.

"I'm pregnant," Barbara blurted out.

"Oh, my goodness . . . how wonderful." Karen beamed.

Auntie Karen. It sounded . . . great!

Images ran through Karen's mind: buying toys for her niece—it was certainly going to be a girl—and, of course, taking her to the zoo. Images beyond just watching her grow up. She couldn't wait to spoil the child.

"Don't tell, Mom, though," Barbara said.

"You want to tell her, I understand."

II

Christmas 1983 was quickly approaching. Barbara and Karen decided to buy their mom and stepdad a gas grill. Seven months pregnant, Barbara was starting to show. That nice little bundle of joy had pasted a brilliant glow over her that only pregnant women can pull off. Christmas, both Karen and Barbara knew, was going to be special this year. A wondrous time to share in the joy of new life and love and family.

What else could they ask for?

A baby was coming.

Karen was busy. Shopping and planning things and just being a young, single woman out enjoying her life.

"We have to pick up the grill," Barbara had told Karen that week.

"I'll do it."

"Great. We'll see you at Mom's, then?"

The family had plans to get together on Christmas Eve.

"Yes," Karen said. "I'll see all of you then."

III

December 23, 1983, was a Friday night. There was a party at a Piscataway (a town north of New Brunswick) house on the campus of Rutgers. Some friends of Karen's who had graduated in 1982 were celebrating. Three friends lived in the house. They had invited sixty to seventy people. The party had been planned for a month. Although Karen had been out of school for a year and a half, and attending graduate courses at University College, she decided to go. It was going to be great seeing old friends again, catching up. Seeing who was making it out in the world, who was married with kids already, and what everyone was doing for the holiday season.

IV

According to Ned, he and Karen had broken up in August 1982. Since then, Karen had been dating several different men. Her latest boyfriend, Philip Costanzo, was a strong young man who lived across the hall from Karen in the same apartment building. Philip was slated, in fact, to spend the holidays with Karen and her family. Elizabeth Anne and Arthur Bilger (Karen and Barbara's stepfather) liked Phillip, as did sister Barbara.

Philip wanted to attend the party with Karen, but had to work. It was no biggie. Karen would go, give her best to everyone, have a couple of drinks, get home, and then meet Philip later that night.

It had been sixteen months since Ned and Karen had actually seen each other on a boyfriend-girlfriend basis. In a letter, Ned later referred to Karen as a "girl I dated." But Karen, of course, was much more than that.

V

There was one girl Ned knew in college. "He asked me out every Thursday night," she later told me, scared to even come forward some twenty-five years later and talk about it. "But I always said, 'No.' I do remember being alone with him (during the fall of 1983). I went to a party he was throwing down in New Brunswick. My friend and I had an argument about staying. I stayed and she left. Ned gallantly offered to drive me back to [my apartment, which was two hours away]. No one saw us leave. It makes me sick now to remember that we 'made out' in his car, in my parents' driveway."

The one thing that saved her life, the woman was later convinced, "Thank God I lived with my parents."

VI

Even if she had known beforehand that Ned was going to be at the house party, Karen would have still gone. It wasn't as if she and Ned were enemies or at odds. In fact, they were still somewhat friendly. They lived right around the corner from each other in New Brunswick. Ned was calling, but Karen kept casually blowing him off. It wasn't even hot and cold anymore. It was over. Karen had moved on.

"I wish he would leave me alone," she'd tell friends.

Ned had arrived at the party at nine o'clock. It was just starting to heat up. Pot smoke filled the air. Kegs of beer. Spiked punch. Loud music.

Karen rolled in by herself around eleven. When she spotted Ned, she walked up to him. "Ned?"

"Hi, Karen."

"What's going on?"

"I'm here just trying to pick up girls," Ned said, half kidding, of course, trying to relieve the tension he felt between them.

Ned looked good: yellow V-neck sweater, lime green golf shirt, brown shoes, Docksiders, and rust-colored jeans. Karen wore a "tight sweater" with stripes, and jeans.

As the party wound down somewhere near 1:30 to 2:30 A.M., Karen decided to leave. She had to get up early and do some Christmas shopping, call the family and prepare for the next few days of holiday celebration. And then Philip would be calling later and maybe stopping by, depending on what time he got out of work.

Ned later said that he and Karen happened to leave at the same time. But others beg to differ. Most reported that Ned watched Karen walk out the door and followed her.

Later, Ned said, "[We] were leaving [the party] at about the same time, but we were not actually 'leaving together.'"

Half of this was true.

They had—again by happenstance—parked rather close together. We know this because Karen pulled in *after* Ned.

Ned walked behind Karen as she approached her car. People were walking to and from the house. It was still loud, that thumping sound coming from inside the house as the stereo blasted. Even though it was late, the campus was also still bustling.

Looking at Karen, Ned could undoubtedly feel *it* coming on.

But now was not the right time.

Fight it off.

As they both got into their cars, Ned followed Karen. After all, he said, they had to go the same way home, seeing that they lived nearly next door to each other.

Lie.

And then, as they drove to their homes, Ned claimed later in a letter, at the last minute he decided to *stop at [Karen's] house instead of going home.*

Lie again.

That urge, no doubt, had been boiling in Ned as he followed Karen home. That irrepressible fascination with the flesh that led Ned down a road of thinking that the only way to curb it was to render the woman, whoever she may be, into unconsciousness and then gratify himself. It didn't matter that he knew her. Or had supposedly loved her. In fact, all the better. It would be easier to trick her. To fool her into thinking that all he wanted to do was "talk."

39

I

So Ned took a right into Karen's parking lot. He parked his car. "Hey," he said as Karen got out of her car, no doubt unnerved by his presence.

"Hey," she said. Karen was startled. She wanted nothing to do with Ned. Philip was going to be calling and/or coming over at any moment. It would be awkward, the two of them. Ned and Philip.

According to what Ned later said—an authority we should probably not take too seriously—Karen walked up to his vehicle and said, "Can you come in?"

She was not, he later insisted, surprised to see him.

"Sure," Ned said.

II

Walking into Karen's apartment, Ned had to think that whatever was going to happen next was not going to turn out positively. He understood those feelings of violence he was having and knew the triggers. Going into Karen's apartment was an episode waiting to happen. There could be no two ways about it.

It was possible that Karen invited Ned in that night. There was never a sign that he had forced his way into her apartment. Maybe Karen thought that she *could* be friends with Ned. Maybe introducing Philip to him would finally cut the cord? But whatever the reason, she had known Ned for about three years and dated him for half that time.

He was certainly no stranger.

And Ned, of course, used this vulnerability to his advantage—something he would become an expert at in the coming years.

When they got inside, Ned said, Karen was the aggressor—again, something Ned would later associate with the women he met and the violence he perpetrated. "We started kissing," Ned explained. Then Karen, Ned insisted, took off her shirt and bra, and that was when Ned saw Karen's breasts and lost all control of himself as the sight of her breasts brought out that *other* person in Ned.

Seeing Karen topless set off a series of receptors. Once that happened, there was no turning back.

Ned's heart raced.

Then "these scenes in my mind began to take over," as they had so many times before, Ned said. He and Karen "rolled" around sexily on Karen's bed, he claimed.

Then they fell off.

At first, it was funny. A roll in the hay had taken them for a ride over the edge of the bed and onto the carpet.

How romantic. He claimed they laughed about it.

Ned, though, in his own way—comparable to no one, I should note—explained away his actions, claiming that when they landed on the carpet, his hands just *happened*—it's worth repeating: *his hands just happened*—to end up on the side of Karen's face.

When Ned found himself with his hands so close to Karen's neck, he said, he couldn't breathe. He couldn't control himself. The power of being so close to taking a life became overwhelming. There was that adrenaline rush again. That drug.

That unmanageable urge to kill.

My hands, he wrote, *just ended up wrapping around her throat.*

His hands just *ended up* wrapping around her throat.

When that happened, Ned said, he just *had* to begin squeezing. What else could he do? It was almost as if it were in slow motion. Karen's feet weren't even off the bed at this point.

And Ned began to choke her.

Without one bit of compassion.

Without a second thought.

Without any sense of remorse.

He knew what he was doing. He knew Karen's life would be over. And he knew that he could—if he really wanted—stop himself. But all he thought at that exact moment, he later admitted, that exact moment when he held the power of life and death in his hands, was *I'm actually doing it this time.*

To Ned, it was no longer a fantasy. He had crossed the threshold into reality.

40

I

Ned was not a drug user. He drank, sure, but he wasn't a guy who liked to get bombed and stumble all over the place. Ned's highs in life came from those moments when he held a female's life in his delicate hands and chose her time to die. Thus, as he choked Karen, that "dizziness" and shortness of breath, which he would describe in the years to come, was a sense of empowerment, a euphoria like no other he had ever experienced.

"Something inside me likes these feelings," he later said.

Moreover, he wanted those feelings to increase. To never end. In fact, there was no drug or drink in the world that could replace this high of taking a life. The feeling of losing grip with reality and taking the breath from another human being was enormously stimulating for Ned.

He was God.

How liberating.

Glorifying.

II

At some point, Karen began to realize what was happening. That Ned was killing her. She was no match at five feet three inches, 115 pounds, even if Ned was no giant himself. *I held Karen's throat,* Ned wrote later, *pressing down with my thumbs . . . but she was still sputtering. . . .*

Karen's eyes were closed, Ned described. *Her tongue stuck out of her mouth.*

As she struggled for breath, Ned explained, Karen began to make terrible, animal-like noises.

And it bothered him. He was having trouble strangling Karen to death, he recalled. As he squeezed harder and harder, he began to realize that, for him, killing a human being was much harder than it looked.

At this point, Karen's life had come down to a psychopath comparing it to that of a scene in a horror film. Karen was twisting and turning, Ned explained. He was looking at her. *Naked from the waist up,* he later wrote, it was "driving" him crazy, allowing him to continue the torture, creating an erection like that of which he had never experienced.

And then, without warning, there was that adrenaline rush: seeing Karen bare-breasted, struggling for life. There came a point, Ned said, as she thrashed like a fish out of water, when Karen just stopped moving, like a machine that had run out of gas.

One minute she was kicking and straining for air . . . and the next, nothing.

No movement whatsoever.

The problem for Ned, however, was that Karen was still alive.

Staring at her, Ned thought, *She's going to wake up and call the police.*

And there was no way he could allow that to happen.

III

With Karen unconscious, on the floor of her bedroom, Ned had to think fast. If she woke up, she'd realize he'd tried to kill her and immediately phone police.

Ned was no stranger. She could identify him.

He panicked, he later said. And ran into Karen's kitchen. *Where are they . . . where are they?* He silently questioned.

Opening drawers and rifling through cabinets . . . he couldn't find one.

But then, there it was: a steak knife.

He ran back into the bedroom and, according to what Ned later wrote, he *stabbed her in the abdomen.*

Karen had once again began "making those noises," Ned described. She wasn't conscious or moving, but she was obviously still alive.

This, he said, made him "so scared."

Imagine this: Karen was dying and Ned Snelgrove was *scared.* Still, even more revolting in its reflection, what scared Ned more than anything, more than anything that had taken place that entire night in Karen's bedroom, what had totally turned him off by the entire ordeal, he later explained, was a "yellow mucus" drooling from Karen's mouth and the blood now vigorously flowing from her abdomen.

All that blood.

All that mucus.

It wasn't, Ned said, supposed to happen this way. It wasn't part of the scene he had envisioned for all those years. No, he wrote, it was *never part of my sexual fantasies.*

For Ned, seeing all the blood "ruined it" for him.

It had drained the sexual drive from him.

IV

Ned needed to get the heck out of Karen Osmun's apartment. Not that the murder had been loud—but it was Christmas.

People would be looking for Karen. Her phone would be ringing.

And Philip . . .

Ned grabbed Karen's keys and the steak knife that he later said he used to stab her to death and ran from the apartment. Within a few moments, he was at home cleaning himself up, preparing to leave for Connecticut to spend the holidays at home.

41

I

By 3:30 P.M. on Saturday, December 24, 1983, Christmas Eve day, Elizabeth Anne, Arthur Bilger, and Karen's boyfriend, Philip, had not heard from Karen. It was so unlike her. Here it was Christmas Eve day and she was nowhere to be found.

Maybe she went out shopping?

No one was panicking yet.

But when Christmas Eve came and went, and it was getting late into the night and early Christmas Day morning, the family became frighteningly concerned. Barbara, pregnant, spent the previous night at her in-laws, and Arthur and Elizabeth Anne agreed not to tell her what was going on, for fear that she didn't need any of the stress. At some point, Barbara called home, however. "We'll be there tomorrow, Mom," she said with holiday cheer in her voice.

Elizabeth Anne was somber. "OK" was all she said. Barbara didn't recognize that her mother was overly worried about anything. ("You know, in retrospect," Barbara said, "who is really looking for that?")

II

Late into Christmas Day, the family was still in a frenzy: *Where in the world is Karen?* They kept calling her apartment. "Frantically," one of them later said.

No answer.

They called several of Karen's friends—anyone who might know where she was, but no one had seen or heard from her.

Elizabeth Anne's intuition told her that something was terribly wrong. Karen was in trouble. She had said she'd be there by "late afternoon" on Christmas Eve day. They hadn't heard from her in almost forty-eight hours.

Elizabeth Anne wasn't waiting any longer. She picked up the phone and called the New Brunswick Police Department (NBPD). "Can you send a car over to my daughter's apartment and check in on her? She was supposed to be here this afternoon and hasn't arrived yet."

"Ma'am," she was told, "your daughter's an adult. We can only check outside her apartment."

III

At Karen's apartment some time later, two officers rang Karen's doorbell and knocked on her door.

No answer.

They tried again.

"Miss Osmun," one of them yelled into the window, "you home?"

Nothing.

It was now close to 10:00 P.M. "Nothing happening here," one of the officers called in and told dispatch. "Seems to be no foul play or anything."

IV

Elizabeth Anne and Karen's stepfather, Arthur, called Karen's boyfriend, Philip, who was at his parents' house. "Can you go over there and check on her?"

Philip said he would.

Arthur said he'd meet him there.

V

Elizabeth Anne knew. She had been worried sick by this point, as were other members of Karen's immediate family. There was no way Karen had run off anywhere on her own. It was Christmastime. She wouldn't have missed the celebration with family for anything.

Philip met Arthur at Karen's door sometime after the police left.

They both knocked and rang the buzzer, yelling for Karen. Not a peep.

It was snowing by this point. Cold and wet. Visibility was dim. The streets were getting slick. Philip had an idea. "I'll be back," he said.

There was a way to hop up onto the roof and look into Karen's window to see if maybe she was in there or things looked odd. Philip didn't know exactly what he was looking for, but he figured, what the heck, it couldn't hurt.

Philip pulled himself up onto the roof and shimmied his way down so he could manage a glimpse into the window. It was slippery, but he was able to make it. There were curtains, however, blocking his view.

Shoot.

"I'll get a screwdriver," Arthur said. He went to his car and dug through the trunk.

According to a detailed police report, based on interviews with Arthur and Philip, it took a few minutes, but they were able to jimmy the door open and walk in.

Philip entered first.

After looking around, he went into the bedroom, where, he later told police, "I saw a green sleeping bag spread on the floor with what appeared to be a body lying underneath it."

He walked over and lifted the end of the sleeping bag up, quickly seeing the feet of a female. Yet, he didn't know for certain that it was Karen's feet, so he lifted the upper portion of the sleeping bag off her face.

My God!

There she was.

Dead.

Philip stood. Tears. Shaking. Disbelief.

"In here . . ."

There were tiny puncture wounds to her chest. Blood all over the floor underneath her body. Light purple-and-blue-and-red bruises around her neck.

After the shock of seeing Karen just lying there dead, with dried blood all over her, Philip and Arthur put the sleeping bag back the way Philip said he had found it and "did not," they explained later, "touch anything else in the apartment."

42

I

Karen's apartment was soon overcome with detectives and EMTs and cops asking questions of neighbors and flashing lights of blue and red—all that comes with the discovery of a bloodied body, a murder victim.

What was evident from the moment detectives started to study the crime scene was that Ned had posed Karen's body. The way Ned described the murder years later didn't necessarily gel with the scene that cops came upon. Maybe it was selective memory on Ned's part. Or perhaps he saw it in his mind another way altogether. But Karen had been propped up with her back against the bed, stabbed upward of about fifteen times in the chest and abdomen (someone even later reported the stab wounds having a distinctive circular pattern to them), and that green sleeping bag had been placed over her corpse, not haphazardly, in haste, but as if it were a shroud.

"Even when murderers confess," an investigator working Ned's case later told me, "they pick and choose what they want to remember to downplay their role, their evil."

II

Detective Dennis Watson, from second assistant prosecutor Thomas Kapsak's Middlesex County Detective Bureau (MCDB), had arrived at Karen's near sunup. Watson was in charge of the investigation. His notes and reports were clear and concise. Direct and very detailed.

It was extremely cold outside ("single digits") when Watson arrived and met with Detective Joe Smith in the parking lot of Karen's building. There were several other detectives from different bureaus on hand and Watson nodded to each that indelible "hello" cops give one another without having to say anything.

When they got inside, Watson noted that Karen was wearing blue jeans "which were zipped up and snapped" with a "belt tied." She had blue socks on. Her panties had not been removed. Karen's attacker was obviously only interested in her upper torso.

From the waist up, Karen was totally naked.

Watson knelt down and took a closer look at the injuries. There were six stab wounds, he counted, in the center of her chest area alone; several more—"puncture-type wounds"—near her lower front neck region. There were bruises on Karen's neck, consistent with strangulation.

After the medical examiner cleared the scene, Watson and his colleagues headed back to the NBPD, where the arduous task of interviewing everyone Karen had come in contact with throughout the past few days, maybe even weeks, began.

This, no less, during the Christmas holiday season.

III

Barbara had called the house that morning. "We'll be there this afternoon, Mom," she said.

Elizabeth Anne was solemn.

"Mom?"

"OK, Barbara."

Nothing more was said. How does a mother tell a daughter that her only sister is dead?

When Barbara and her husband left, Arthur Bilger called back and told Barbara's in-laws what had happened. They didn't want to worry Barbara now. Not with the baby and all. They would tell her in person when she arrived.

IV

A guy named Frank, along with his three roommates, hosted the party Karen and Ned had attended. Beyond describing how packed the house was, Frank offered investigators very little information regarding whom Karen spoke to or with whom she left. After that, detectives spoke with Elizabeth Anne, who was obviously broken up and totally overwhelmed by the loss. Karen was dead. One minute, her daughter was talking about the baby her sister was going to have, and the next moment, she was lying in the morgue.

It wasn't fair.

Cops weren't going to get much out of Elizabeth Anne—but they were extremely interested in speaking with Philip Costanzo. Philip was about to celebrate his twenty-fourth birthday. He had been going to Livingston College in Piscataway and worked part-time at a retail store, Shoppers World, in Elizabeth, New Jersey. He and Karen had been dating for about three months, he explained. "I last saw Karen, let me see, Friday, December twenty-third," Philip said. "It was approximately one-fifteen A.M." Karen had just returned home, he said, from a night out with friends. Karen was tired and wanted to go to sleep. She came in for a while and then went across the hall to hit the sack.

Detectives asked Philip what he did the previous day. If he had seen Karen? Spent any time with her? Philip said he spent December 22 with Karen in her apartment drinking champagne and celebrating the end of the college semester. She was happy. Ready to face the holidays and have fun with her family. She said something about going to a party on campus that night, and Philip said he couldn't go because of work and possibly traveling to his parents' house after work.

Philip was visibly distraught. Poor Karen. Did he have to see her like that? There was an image now in his mind, etched like a nightmare, that would be there forever. A lasting memory of his girlfriend.

The sleeping bag.

The blood.

Her tiny feet.

Her face.

Those soulless, foggy eyes.

The stab wounds.

Philip had an ironclad alibi: he was working. There was no way he'd had anything to do with Karen's death. After a thorough check, Detective Watson and his colleagues were sure of it. In truth, as they started talking to people, dragging friends of Karen's into the station house and shining a light in their face, they quickly began to feel that Karen's killer had attended the house party. Someone had perhaps met Karen and followed her home.

Stalked her.

But who? And how were they going to narrow it down from sixty party guests to one person?

V

Within a day, the MCDB had a list of house party guests. One after the other was brought in for questioning. The most plausible suspect was a guy who lived above Karen. He had gone to Cook College and knew Karen from class. He had last seen her on Friday morning, December 23, as he was leaving for work at People's Express Airlines in Newark. He worked all day, he said, and then went shopping. When he returned home at about eleven that night, he knocked on Karen's door before retiring upstairs.

"Why?" asked one of the detectives.

"Well," he said, "I must have seen her car"—it was there in the parking lot outside—"because I wouldn't have knocked if I knew she wasn't home. But I got no answer."

"You know Philip?"

"Yeah, we all hang out together."

The guy explained that Philip was supposed to go down to his parents' home that night, but he called and said he wasn't going.

It sounded strange.

"It was snowing," he added. "Phil didn't want to drive in the snow."

He then explained that he and his roommate had watched a television movie, *Cotton Candy,* but his roommate left halfway into it. After the movie, he played his guitar, recorded some music until about 3:30 A.M., and went to bed.

The detectives asked him for permission to search his apartment.

"Sure."

After a "brief search," Watson noted, nothing was found.

Detectives going through Karen's apartment found several names and numbers of what they presumed to be friends, but were now, of course, suspects.

All checked out.

And then, after speaking to nearly everyone at the party, detectives came to Ned Snelgrove. His name was in Karen's address book.

"Yeah," someone at the party said, "Ned was here. I saw him talking to Karen."

43

I

That afternoon, Barbara made it to the shore house with her husband. Walking in, she took one look at everyone and knew, she recalled later, that *something* had happened. "It's one of those moments in your life you never, ever forget," Barbara told me. "I get chest pains just thinking about it now. I can feel the pain welling up when I think about it."

II

There was no answer at Ned's apartment when detectives, after finding his name and number in Karen's address book, first called on him. One of his roommates—he lived with two friends from college—said that Ned had left for Connecticut to go spend the holidays with his parents.

After some checking around, they came up with Ned's parents' number. Detective Watson spoke to Ned. He sounded somewhat unfazed, but also jumpy, twitchy. Watson mentioned that the MCDB had heard Ned had been at the same party. "I went to the party alone," Ned said. "It was approximately nine

P.M. I saw Karen a couple of hours later and spoke to her briefly about what we were both doing with our lives."

It sounded as though Ned had rehearsed the conversation in his head.

"Were you dating her?" Watson wanted to know.

"In college, I did. But we broke up in August 1982."

"What time did you leave the party?"

"About two A.M.—with Karen."

"You left with her?"

"Not *with* her. I walked her out to her car, a little economy car. It was parked up the street from the party."

"What next?"

"She went her way and I drove directly to my apartment alone."

As they talked, Ned sounded more scripted than ever. Each little detail perfectly fit into the scheme of things. It was the way Ned added words—"alone," "with Karen," "August 1982"—as if he had gone over the conversation in his head all the way to Connecticut.

"When will you be back in town?" Watson asked.

"The day after Christmas."

III

During the afternoon hours of December 26, detectives tracked down ten more potential suspects and questioned each regarding his whereabouts that night. All were men. All had known Karen in some capacity.

None, however, were taken seriously as suspects.

Whenever a suspect seemed promising, his alibi checked out. That was the thing about investigating a murder during the Christmas holiday: nearly everyone had someone who could vouch for them.

Everyone, that is, except Ned Snelgrove.

44

Whenever Ned found himself in a jam, he reacted. On his way back from Connecticut to New Jersey, after spending the holidays with his parents, Ned must have—I say "must have" because even though Ned would admit to a lot of things in the coming years, this is something he routinely denies—believed that by taking his own life he could escape the embarrassment of showing his true self to those who would now see that he was a failure and murderer. He later wrote that he was *always the prime suspect* in Karen's homicide. The police, however, didn't have one piece of substantial evidence to tie Ned to Karen's murder.

As he made his way back to New Jersey, Ned began to "feel terrible from then on." Killing Karen like that, he insisted, was not part of his plan. As evil or bizarre as it sounded, strangling Karen was part of the fantasy, but knifing her—at least according to Ned—wasn't. Stabbing Karen and making a mess of things was never supposed to happen.

Murder as a contingency. How charming.

Back at his apartment, Ned was stewing, trying to figure

out how in the heck he was going to get out of this one. How should he act? Should he call Karen's family? Show up at her funeral? Run into the police station and throw himself on their mercy? Which was appropriate?

Tears, Ned believed. Tears were the answer. Yes, lots of crocodile tears.

Instead of facing it all, however, Ned decided to take the coward's way out: disappear. So he swallowed *a whole package of sixteen sleeping pills,* he later wrote, a*nd a bottle of iodine,* believe it or not.

It didn't work, though.

I didn't die, he penned.

II

At 7:20 P.M., on December 26, 1983, twenty-three-year-old Ned Snelgrove—looking so much his age and, strikingly, bearing an uncanny resemblance to his later mentor, Ted Bundy—was sitting at the MCDB going over things with Detective Watson and several of his colleagues, all of whom by now had a gut "feeling," an instinct, about Ned.

Ned had swallowed the pills and taken the iodine and was treated and released from the hospital. He was alive. He said he would "get help."

Ned seemed calm and cool for a guy who had just tried to take his own life. He explained where he worked and where he lived, how he knew Karen, when they dated and when they broke up, how he helped her move into her apartment, and that he had just received a Christmas card from her three weeks before her death.

"I bumped into her a couple times since the breakup," Ned explained.

It was important for Ned to place himself inside Karen's apartment, which would account for his fingerprints and any possible hair or clothing fibers they might come up with.

After Ned went through and answered some of the same questions he had over the telephone the week before, he gave detectives consent—after they asked—to search his apartment. Ned had said he left for Connecticut on December 24, at about 1:30 or 2:00 P.M.

Watson's report read: [Snelgrove] *was advised of his Constitutional rights and he signed and dated a rights card—a search was conducted [of his apartment] with negative results.*

III

Karen's mother, Elizabeth Anne, her sister, Barbara, and stepfather, Arthur, of course, were dreading the process of burying Karen. What family wanted to bury their twenty-three-year-old child, a woman with so much promise and virtue and love to shower on the world? It was almost as if there were no words to describe how they felt. For Elizabeth Anne, her heart ached, literally. She was having trouble breathing. Talking. Sleeping. Eating.

Karen was special. She had played the flute, the guitar, the piano. She enjoyed photography and magic, which she learned from "the Great Oz," her father, whom she was now standing with at the gates of heaven, Elizabeth Anne believed.

And yet, during a day that couldn't seemingly get any worse, here came Ned Snelgrove, a man the family firmly believed had had something to do with their daughter's death, sauntering into the funeral home to pay his respects to the woman he had killed.

No one truly knew, but what gall the guy had!

There were hundreds of family members and Karen's friends on hand at the wake to say good-bye. The news media had called "relentlessly," looking to interview anyone, Barbara later said, as the story of Karen's murder was headline news and on the front page of the *New York Times,* but the family shooed them all away.

A college girl—no, a *Rutgers* girl—had been murdered in her apartment.

Big news story.

As the wake proceeded, Ned made his way up to Karen's casket as all those around sobbed and shook their heads.

"What's he doing here?" someone whispered.

"Can you believe this guy?"

Ned, Barbara later said, was "the person crying the loudest."

Ned walked up. Knelt in front of the coffin of the woman he had murdered.

Bowed his head.

Cried.

And then stepped up, leaned inside the coffin, and kissed Karen good-bye.

Kissed her.

A peck.

"He made a spectacle of it all and made sure everyone knew he was grieving," Barbara said. Detectives were there watching Ned. "But they could not do anything."

IV

Detectives had several mitigating factors to look at, or, rather, as they like to say, "go on." For one, Karen lived in a three-story tenement in a section of town that was not at all known for a history of high crime. The house she lived in was four blocks from the downtown district. To get into the building, you needed a key. There were no signs of forced entry into Karen's building or her apartment.

Ned.

Detectives were confident that Karen knew her murderer.

Ned.

They were confident her murderer had been in her apartment before the murder.

Ned.

And had anger issues with Karen.
Ned. Ned. Ned.
No matter how they looked at it.

V

Detective Watson telephoned Ned on December 31. "We need you to come in," Watson explained.

"For what?" Ned asked.

"Answer some questions, you know, and discuss maybe taking a polygraph."

Ned's stomach turned. "When?"

"How 'bout January third, say, um, nine A.M.?"

"That'll work."

Over the course of the next three days, the MCDB brought in several of Karen's college friends—all males—who were at the house party. All agreed to take a polygraph.

None failed.

When Ned hung up with Detective Watson, he immediately phoned his parents and, together, hired a lawyer. On January 3, 1984, Ned and his attorney, Clifford Kuhn, showed up on schedule to speak with detectives investigating Karen's murder. Kuhn said he wanted to read his client's previous statements to the police before allowing him to take a polygraph.

They didn't stick around. Kuhn said he'd call after having a look at the statements.

Six days later, Kuhn called Watson. "I advised my client not to take a polygraph."

"OK," Watson said.

45

I

The MCDB continued interviewing suspects and dragging former college friends of Karen's in for questioning and polygraph testing. And for weeks into the new year, everything kept pointing to one person.

Finally, by January 20, 1984, detectives were able to get a court order forcing Ned to give up exemplars: hair, blood, saliva, fingerprints. If nothing else, they could place Ned in Karen's apartment. His story was that the last time he saw Karen was after the party out on the street as she wiped snow off the back of her window.

It was a lie, of course.

And the cops knew it.

The goal was to catch Ned lying, which would invite probable cause and, with any luck, force Ned into a corner.

But Ned was sticking to his story.

With Ned's attorney present, Watson and his colleagues began asking Ned a series of questions after he gave up the exemplars. It was important to keep asking the same repetitive questions to see how accurate Ned was over a period of time. Lies are hard to keep track of, no matter how smart you are—whereas the truth is a cinch.

Ned gave up a few more names of men he had seen talking to Karen, he claimed, at the party. Then one of the detectives asked him if Karen had any foibles, any characteristics that could potentially cause her trouble. Like, for example, would she talk to strangers? Would she hitchhike or accept a ride from someone she didn't know?

"Look," Ned said rather defensively, "she was friendly toward strangers, but was not a tease," as if they had insinuated such.

"OK . . . and your point is . . ."

"But she was not a Girl Scout, either." Literally, she had been; figuratively, though, Ned was saying that Karen had a reputation for being promiscuous. Several other men they had interviewed had said the same thing. But the truth was, Karen liked to act like she was wild, when she was nothing more than an innocent young girl.

"But then," Ned asked out loud, "was she a whore?"

Detectives wondered what the heck he was talking about.

"Did she hang around with any [other] people?" one of the detectives asked, changing the subject, trying to keep Ned focused.

"There were no black people at the party, nor did she know any that I know of."

They cut Ned loose.

II

A friend of Karen's, who along with several others had been asked to provide exemplars, called Detective Watson on March 2, 1984, to tell him he had found something he believed was important.

"What is it?"

III

There was a guy who liked Karen. He had a thing for her, you could say. He watched out for her. He had wanted to "take it to another level," a friend later said, "but Karen wasn't interested."

The guy felt in his heart that Ned had killed Karen. No one could tell him different. So as time went forward, the guy became fixed on tripping Ned up and catching him in a lie. He'd send Ned letters from Karen. Cards from her, too.

Taunting him. Making him think.

As the second anniversary of Karen's death came up, the guy placed a wreath on the house where Karen had attended that party before her murder. It was nothing more than a memorial.

IV

Watson asked his caller, again, "What is it?"

"A wreath."

"Where?"

Someone had also placed a wreath in another location.

"It's from an unknown person. It was placed [on Karen's grave] between January twenty-second and January twenty-ninth. I spoke to Elizabeth Anne and she contacted every single family member, and no one they knew had placed the wreath. . . ."

The twist to it all was that Karen's headstone or name had not yet been placed where she was buried.

Watson called the cemetery. They had collected the wreath and discarded it. "Has anyone been in lately to ask where Karen Osmun is buried?" he asked.

The cemetery worker said no.

V

That December, Elizabeth Anne, with help from a local newspaper, the *Home News,* invited Dorothy Allison, a well-known, veteran psychic, to travel to New Brunswick, take a ride around town, and see what she could come up with. Middlesex County prosecutor Alan Rockoff, whose office was now driving the investigation, gave the *Home News* the most gratifying quote one could offer when dealing with psychics and murder investigations. He equated Dorothy Allison with "chicken soup," saying her input "couldn't hurt."

As she drove around town with a reporter and detective, Allison made several broad statements regarding Karen's killer, at one time saying that he had "very small ears, with pointed features like a mouse."

One thing she did nail—yet it could have been the sheer chiseling down of facts and applying Karen's lifestyle to the prediction—turned out to be that Karen's killer, and she was adamant, traveled through the campus, which she called a "path the murderer took all the time." She then said that she saw Karen leaving the party and being followed by a black-and-yellow car "driven by the murderer, who had been at the party with her."

When she was asked to point out where the house party was, an address that hadn't been publicized, Dorothy didn't fare so well.

Bringing in the psychic did not advance the investigation. Still, it gave Elizabeth Anne a bit of solace in the fact she could at least, for that one day, grasp onto *something*— something that might lead her to her daughter's killer, which was her only focus in life by this point. Barbara's firstborn daughter, Lauren, who arrived that March, helped Elizabeth cope, but the impact of Karen's death kept dragging her failing health down. She felt tired all the time. Quite sickly. Her heart was thick, tight in her chest, as if something was *always* wrong.

VI

"The police and friends of ours kept a close eye on Ned," Barbara Delaney later said, "following his whereabouts. But no evidence surfaced."

The case grew frigid.

Months turned into years.

Soon, two years had gone by and no arrest had been made.

Frustration.

For Barbara. For Arthur.

For Elizabeth Anne.

Then, out of nowhere, it happened.

Elizabeth Anne dropped to her knees one day and suffered a major heart attack. All that emotional pain had manifested into physical trauma.

46

I

According to Barbara, her mother was "living a life of constant agony." She had suffered a heart attack solely because of Karen's murder and the fact that Ned Snelgrove was out and about walking the streets. By now, it was almost a given among a small group of friends and family—and several investigators—that Ned had murdered Karen; but no one could do anything about it. Barbara had another child, Caitlin, and spending time with her grandchildren helped Elizabeth Anne to recover and heal. She soon joined Parents of Murdered Children and became extremely active in fighting for victims' rights. "She tirelessly went to meetings, signed petitions, and talked to other parents of murdered children," Barbara said. "It was her catharsis."

A pacifier. A cause to help her bridge the gap between losing a child and understanding that there was nothing she could have done to protect her. That maternal instinct. That bond. The mother-daughter connection. Inseparable.

"By doing good for others," Barbara said, "she was able to draw strength and maintain a purpose to go on."

Barbara joined a group, too: Voices for Victims. A group

that fought for legislature to ensure that victims of crime were entitled to the same rights as criminals.

II

The pressure was off Ned for now. He had escaped justice. Later, in a letter to the court, in which he explained what was happening in his mind after the Osmun murder and before the attack on Mary Ellen Renard, Ned spoke of this period when he was in between attacks, if you will. He wrote that he couldn't *eat or sleep,* that he *promised [him]self [he] would never do anything like that again;* at the same time rationalizing Karen's murder, talking about the feelings he had toward females which were "so strong" he couldn't help it.

Karen didn't die, Ned insisted, because she was his ex-girlfriend. It had nothing to do with her breaking up with him. It wasn't an act of revenge.

Instead, it was as simple as Karen being in the wrong place at the wrong time. His other side had come out and Karen was there. There was nothing he could have done to stop it.

Yes, according to Ned's twisted way of analyzing his sick behavior, Karen was killed because she knew him and he had acted out on those stuffed feelings of violence against females.

For no other reason.

According to law enforcement, however, the strangest part of this time in Ned's life is the lull in attacks. As most profilers will say, a person like Ned just doesn't stop for four years and then pick up again. "No way," said one profiler who had Ned on radar for twenty years regarding a murder in Essex County, New Jersey—a female with large breasts who was murdered shortly after Karen Osmun. "There's no way a guy like Snelgrove could just stop for that long a period of time."

He was incapable of it.

III

During this period, between the attacks, Ned and several friends were invited down to West Virginia for a wedding. They rented a van. Drove all night.

As one friend there that day later explained it, Ned was anything but touched by Karen's death, as he would later write to the judge. In fact, having murdered Karen didn't even seem to bother Ned one bit.

At the wedding, Ned drank and laughed and joked and had a ball. He even enjoyed a belt or two of moonshine that a relative of the groom had brought.

By then, Ned had grown a mustache. Put on some weight. He was making 40K a year at HP, traveling, and enjoying the fruits of his labor. And yet here he was, partying it up with friends, having recently murdered someone. To look back, that friend later told me, it was almost remarkable to think how Ned acted. How cold. To be able to socialize like that after killing someone. "I wouldn't have been able to live with myself," that same friend added.

There came a point during the wedding when no one could find Ned—or one of the bridesmaids.

"Where the heck is he?" someone asked.

The wedding reception ceased. Everyone was now looking for Ned and the bridesmaid.

About a half hour later, someone spotted them in the boiler room. ("Ned was [having sex with] her right there. The girl's brother wanted to kill him.")

They left the wedding to avoid any trouble.

"The all-American boy," that same former friend described Ned during this time. "You don't look at your friend and see a killer. You reflect later and say, 'Oh yeah, that makes sense now.'"

Ned was obnoxious in his college days. Intense. Physical. He'd grab kids in the hallway of the dorm around the neck and wrestle them to the ground, for no reason. "He liked to cause pain. He'd pick guys who he knew he could beat up, and guys who he knew would beat him up."

Ned would do odd, quirky things. Quite strangely, it struck his dorm mates, Ned had an old fishbowl in his room. Inside the bowl were pieces of paper with the names of his old high-school friends. Once a week, Ned would pick a name and write that person a letter. "He did that religiously. . . . We found it very weird. We'd ask, 'Ned, why are you writing a letter every week?'"

He never answered.

In college, this was something Ned took great delight in: being different. Making people wonder about him. Ask questions. It kept the focus, of course, always on Ned—which was what he truly craved more than anything.

All the attention.

IV

During his college years, Ned seemed happy, even cheerful: he was a young adult with so much promise of a future in business, a future, essentially, in any profession he chose. He was popular. Went to parties on campus and played sports, debated politics, took part in extracurricular activities, and seemed to display a fitting amount of social skills. Still, Ned was fighting those demons that had plagued him since childhood: those feelings that, according to him later, had emerged and *forced* him to kill Karen Osmun and attack Mary Ellen Renard.

Even after he admitted in 1988 to killing Karen and attacking Mary Ellen Renard, and was sent to prison, those feelings kept pounding in his head. Wherever he went. In the prison yard. In his cell. Violent images. Violent thoughts.

Women. Blondes. Long hair. Curves. Large breasts.

Ned was a pressure cooker.

V

When Ned's attorney had phoned Mr. and Mrs. Snelgrove in Connecticut after Ned had tried to kill himself, Mr. Snelgrove couldn't believe it at first. But then, after Mr. Snelgrove thought about it, he realized Ned had been acting strange over that past year. Yes, it did make sense to him when he sat down and put it all through the mind wringer, he later explained in a letter to the court.

Still, Mr. Snelgrove had to shake his head after hanging up the phone. *Neddy . . .*

I almost wish he had succeeded, Mr. Snelgrove later wrote to the judge Ned was facing for sentencing in 1988, *when I try to imagine his future.*

There were questions Mr. Snelgrove had that, perhaps, nobody had answers to.

Only time would tell.

Wondering if Ned would even survive prison, Mr. Snelgrove pondered, *What will he do when he gets out?*

The best years of his life will have been wasted, he wrote, wondering how in the world Ned would ever *start life over with his record?*

Beyond that, Mr. Snelgrove angrily wrote, Ned had *betrayed all his friends . . . caused terrible disruptions within his family.* The road ahead, he went on to note, would be paved with solitude for Ned.

He will be very much alone, he wrote.

Where would he go?

What would become of him?

If he is some sort of Jekyll/Hyde character, the elder Snelgrove mused, *can he be reformed?*

And the question on everyone's mind, including, of course, Mary Ellen Renard and family members of Karen Osmun, when Ned faced parole, *[would it be] safe to let him back into society?* Mr. Snelgrove penned. A question that, in its sincerity, shocked many when they learned it had come from Ned's own father. The old man admitted that he had many more questions, but *at the moment I don't see any answers,* he wrote.

Where it pertained to Ned, no one did.

47

I

After getting caught for attacking and attempting to murder Mary Ellen Renard in 1987, Ned signed a plea agreement and was sentenced on June 24, 1988, in front of superior court judge James Madden. Most of the sentencing was a structured mass of mandatory motions that everyone in attendance had to suffer through. Each side had its chance to speak, and Ned's attorney, John Bruno, offered a bit of an apology for his client, seeing that Ned, who had numerous opportunities to say how sorry he was, chose not to.

"It is not my function," Bruno told the court, "to apologize to anyone for my client's acts, but I want to publicly indicate to the families of the victims that my heart goes out to all of them."

A collective wince.

"Judge," Bruno continued, getting to the core of what he wanted to put on record, "Mr. Snelgrove has a very, very serious medical problem. He needs help. He did not have to plead guilty to a charge in Middlesex County"—Karen's murder—"because he was smart enough and cunning enough to know that the state had no evidence against him. He kept the secret with him for four-and-a-half years now, but he couldn't live with

himself anymore and that is the only reason he pled guilty. . . .
He couldn't handle the secret anymore and he knows how *desperately* he needs help and he knows how *desperately* he's
needed help all of his life, but never sought it."

Bruno wanted the judge to consider that Ned had people
lined up to back up his character: letters from different family
members. "He had no prior criminal record. And had grown
up in a fine, fine family."

"Come on," someone sitting close by said, "are you serious?"

Bruno continued, adding that Ned was "a person with the
best education money can buy, and a person who does not
even understand the reasons for his own sick acts."

In defense of John Bruno's rhetoric, he did say at one point
that the entire case had "weighed heavily on him." But he was
there doing his job. The best he could.

Addressing the court, Bruno revealed that Ned had cried
uncontrollably while sitting in his office over the past few
weeks. ". . . And it won't bring anybody back or heal any
wounds, but Your Honor's entitled to be aware of the feelings of remorse that Mr. Snelgrove has shown me."

Bruno said Ned did not wish to be heard, but had spoken
through that eleven-page letter he had written to the court—
that narrative of his ailing mind and his obsession with
women. That narcissistic missive of self-pity Ned viewed as
a confession.

II

Prosecutor Thomas Kapsak talked first about how Ned had
killed Karen Osmun, attacked Mary Ellen Renard, then tried
to play cat and mouse with cops, and, to that, enjoyed *every*
minute of it. Indeed, Ned's weak attempt at explaining himself in what had turned out to be such a vile letter had back-
fired. Instead of acting as an apology, the letter proved to the
court who the real Ned Snelgrove was.

Kapsak pointed to Ned's signature: he liked to strip women down to bare breasts after working his way into their lives and viciously and brutally attacking them. He said Mary Ellen survived because she was bigger than Karen and was able to fight back, or she would have been killed, too. "The absolute lack of remorse by the defendant . . . comes," Kapsak spurted with directness, "from the psychiatrist who spoke to him. The pride and pleasure he apparently took in outwitting the authorities. The regret he expressed concerning his choice of victims, and by that, I assume that he felt that the second victim was not a good choice because she lived. The complete absence of excuse or justification in his background. And the physical, psychological, and sexual pleasure he derived while strangling his victims."

Posing them. And, some claimed, pleasuring himself by masturbating into a condom or towel so as not to leave any DNA behind.

The man wasn't sorry for his behavior; he was only sorry he got caught.

"Judge," Kapsak reiterated, ". . . we all try to predict a defendant's future behavior, given various sentencing options. And my conclusion after eighteen years is that we're not really good at it, even though we all tried very hard, but in this case every indication, *every* indication, Judge, that this is a very dangerous man, and that if given the opportunity, he *will*"—allow that word to hang there for a moment—"do again what he has done before."

The judge spoke for a few minutes and laid out the charges and his sentencing guidelines. The bottom line was that Ned had made out: ten to twenty years. It was a slap on the wrist. As a source working for the state of New Jersey later explained to me, "The judge knew it, the prosecution knew it, and, certainly, Mr. Snelgrove and his lawyer knew it."

"It" being the light sentence Ned received for taking a life and torturing another. The way the law was written, considering the commutation credits (good behavior) Ned received on the *day* he took the plea, he was guaranteed to be out in a little over ten years. "Commutation time is an incentive for them to behave—it's the carrot and the stick," a corrections source told me. "With any misbehavior while in prison, then they lose the commutation time."

What's more, another source explained, "corrections apply the credits *ahead* of time as preemptive, or proactive, credit for good behavior, but then would only take them away from you if you misbehaved."

Ned already had jail credits of 150 days heading into sentencing, "good time," in other words, built up from his days in county jail. His commutation time, awarded to him the moment he was sentenced, was a whopping 2,268 days.

Nearly seven years off the top for just agreeing to be a good boy.

"As long as they do their jobs and don't cause any problems, they get that time taken off the front end," a source added. Furthermore, according to another source inside the prison system, a medical staff from corrections examined Ned shortly before his release and found "no problems with his mental health." His file says that he was a "low risk for committing another violent crime."

Huh?

III

And so Edwin "Ned" Snelgrove was off to prison. He was going to spend at least eleven years, perhaps more, behind bars at East Jersey State Prison (EJSP), just plain Rahway to cons, for killing one woman and attempting to kill another. It seemed such a light sentence, so abhorrently wrong, that this man was going to get out of prison one day, walk the streets again, and still be a fairly young guy.

48

I

Elizabeth Anne Osmun Bilger didn't take the sentencing too well. Karen's mother knew what was going to happen beforehand; yet after it was done, it seemed as though the years would pass too quickly and Karen's killer would be out of prison once again and back in her face. Her health weakened as the years passed. She continued to fight for the rights of victims, but the loss kept on coming back to haunt her.

Karen. My poor Karen.

Elizabeth Anne had one wish, she often told Barbara, that Ned Snelgrove would serve those twenty years and not get out a moment sooner.

Arthur Bilger suffered, too. That image of Karen as he found her with Philip plagued the man and sent him spiraling into a deep depression.

And then Elizabeth Anne was in and out of the hospital: congestive heart failure. The loss kept coming back at her. She couldn't seem to shake it.

For Barbara, she said it was one of the toughest times of the entire ordeal. She had two young kids. Her mother's health was failing, and she was still trying to deal with the loss herself. With court dates and the sentencing and Karen's murder as front-page news, it was easy to get lost, easy to push that pain aside and focus on the judicial end of it all. But when it was all over and she had to face her own pain, it became overwhelming.

In a sense, Ned was in prison still victimizing the Osmun family.

II

The incident that took Karen's life, Barbara Delaney has always said, killed two people. *In July 1994,* Barbara wrote to Ned's parole board ten years after he was sentenced, *my mother died of a massive heart attack.* It was Elizabeth Anne's second since Karen's death.

Elizabeth Anne had finally succumbed to her broken heart. She was dead. Karen's mother was, Barbara wrote to the board, *another victim of Edwin Snelgrove.* Oh, how it hurt her to write that name, even ten years after the fact. *My family is gone,* she wrote. *My daughters see pictures of Auntie Karen and know her only from my childhood memories. They are victims, too. Many friends of Karen continue to mourn her untimely passing. She had touched so many lives in her twenty-three years.*

Could it get any worse for Barbara Delaney? She had lost her sister. Then her mother. Now, as Ned sat in prison, could her life, ten years after her sister was murdered, still be affected by Karen's killer?

Barbara didn't think so.

III

Heading into prison, Ned had his own set of problems to contend with—that is, if one is to equate excuses for being locked up with the same gravity as losing a loved one to the hands of a maniac. *I hate myself . . . ,* Ned wrote shortly before entering Rahway. He talked about having it "made" before he found himself facing twenty years, before going through a list of accomplishments in his life that he was giving up in lieu of now being labeled a felon.

Summing up his life in a letter, Ned ended with a few sentences that led everyone to believe there was no possible way he was ever getting out of prison before he served the entire twenty years. He qualified his wonderful words of misguided wisdom by first stating, *This is going to sound ridiculous . . . [but] as long as I am not allowed to be alone with a female, I am not a threat to society.*

The guy was warning the court *and* the public.

Don't let me out of here.

Don't let me be alone with a woman.

Inside these walls, I'm safe.

You're safe.

Outside, well, a time bomb.

BOOK IV

CARMEN

49

I

Outside the walls of East Jersey State Prison in Rahway, the knee-high grass ebbed and flowed with the wind, gently swaying back and forth like sea algae, as Ned went about his daily routine of writing letters, checking stock market quotes in the newspapers, and reading books about his favorite serial killer, Ted Bundy. Ned was just about ten years into his ten-to-twenty-year sentence for the "aggravated manslaughter" of Karen Osmun, back in 1983, and the attempted murder and aggravated sexual assault of Mary Ellen Renard four years later. He was young. Only now heading into his thirties. He knew he'd be out, *without* good time served, at the latest, by the time he was forty-eight, which left him plenty of quality years. *With* good time, well, Ned knew he could hit the streets inside eleven.

As the mid-1990s approached, Ned was thinking about sitting in front of the parole board and pleading his case for early release. One of his first parole hearings was due to come up in 1998. He'd had years to think what to say, how to act. Now, years after writing that eleven-page letter, when he sat down and thought about it, Ned could see himself on the outside again.

Getting a job.

Getting an apartment.

Starting over.

II

Many of Ned's fellow inmates referred to him as "the professor." He was a bookish, smart con, one who was perhaps too intelligent to stay locked up. The other inmates liked Ned. They knew he had gone to Rutgers and studied business, and they knew his advice regarding stocks generally paid off. Still, where was this convicted killer from? What kind of childhood did he have?

Ned grew up in Berlin, Connecticut, a rural town outside Newington, near Cromwell, heading south from Hartford, the state's capital. In the 1970s, when Ned hustled his way around Berlin High School, the town was a suburban refuge on the rise.

They called him "Snedley" in high school. He had brown hair then and a small, geekish frame. He wore thick, "Clark Kent," horn-rimmed glasses that made him look absurdly "nerdy." But Ned was accepted. His unwavering love for the Boston Red Sox, even though the team continued to be held hostage by, some claimed, the Curse of the Bambino, kept Ned's focus on sports. Several of his teachers later claimed that Ned, like most students, hated "running laps," but loved "Ty Cobb and eating at McDonald's." Not that it mattered. Ned was one of only a handful of students at Berlin High to make the honor roll. "He was a good kid," one of his former teachers told me. "Kind of serious, though. I remember the glasses that he wore—and that laugh. Oh, that laugh of Ned's was unmistakable."

Ned's tenth-grade honors English teacher called him

"small, impish, maybe a little sneaky." Ned always sat near the front of the room. One teacher said the glasses he wore made Ned look like the character Piggy in the classic film *Lord of the Flies.* "He was bright and funny, but I cannot remember that he got into any trouble in my class or was ever a behavior problem," she added.

In his Berlin High School yearbook, Ned's peers voted him "Class Headache" his senior year. He was in the service club and on the wrestling team. He was part of Berlin High's National Honor Society. The Honor Society is not something to overlook. Not every student that tries gets in. During Ned's day, there were only fourteen members out of a class of about 275 students. Those who make it are selected for their high academic averages, leadership qualities, extracurricular activities, and service projects.

Ned was active in, and had mastered, all of them.

Ned quoted Benjamin Franklin in his yearbook space underneath his senior photograph: *Dost thou love life? Then do not squander time; for that's the stuff life is made of.* According to Ned, his likes included willpower, Legion Baseball, '75 World Series, A,B,C . . . Z, gaining weight, McDonald's, and "Hey, Big Guy!"

Whatever all of that meant.

His dislikes were easier to understand: 128 lbs., "ninny," running laps.

His ambition was college.

By all accounts, Ned Snelgrove was your average kid.

On the outside, anyway. Inside, Ned was harboring some pretty evil thoughts.

III

Sports kept Ned busy. He wrestled and tried playing baseball, but didn't have the size or the build to excel in either. It was the piano where Ned looked and felt the most comfortable.

Like some sort of savant, he could sit for hours and belt out a tune he had heard only once.

In some ways, Ned *was* the class clown. He soaked up the attention. It made him feel important. But then, there was a serious side to Ned—a formidable aspect of his character that fellow students hardly ever talked about or brought up to him. Ned's intelligence stuck out. Academically speaking, he excelled at whatever he set his mind to. According to its history, Cook College, a subschool of Rutgers University, was conceived between 1967 and 1970 for the purposes of "teaching, research and outreach," with a "theme of 'Man and His Environment.'" How Ned fit into Cook's mainly agricultural curriculum and focus on the environment was never quite clear, but he was accepted into the prestigious school during the fall of 1978 and seemed to embody the prominent status that came with attending, what some believed, was one of America's foremost universities.

Since leaving high school, Ned had grown out of the acne-faced kid he was into a "handsome, polite, and extremely friendly" man. Immediately his classmates and the recruiting officers for Fortune 500 companies with offices on the Rutgers campus noticed Ned's gifts. His GPA was 3.8, far above most. The thing about Ned during those formative college years, so many of his female peers later said, was that he seemed so harmless. He was crass sometimes, liked to use his hands with the girls, sure. But what did that mean? For the most part, he was a pleasant person to be around. No one had any idea that Ned held such ill feelings toward women, or that he was battling thoughts of wanting to strangle females into a coma. And yet, there was always an unknown feeling some women had about the guy who, every once in a while, would act strange and say and do inappropriate things.

IV

One woman came forward to talk about Ned in this regard. It had been over twenty-five years since she'd even set eyes on Ned. They had met in upstate New York before Ned began his first full year at Rutgers. *I'm sorry I opened this can of worms,* she wrote after I had asked for her phone number so I could interview her. She said she didn't want to revisit that time in her life after all. "I'm sorry for contacting you—I didn't hang out with Ned. He was just a guy at a pub who asked me out all the time. Luckily, I said no. Case closed. I don't want to think about what 'might have' been. It also might not have been. I feel bad for the victims of this man. I once thought he was an OK guy."

I asked her if she had any advice for women in general, seeing that she knew Ned personally, even though she refused to talk about her experiences with him. "If there was one thing" she had learned by knowing Ned, it was to "be afraid of everyone. Why? Because Ned seemed 'normal,' like a guy your mom would want you to date."

V

But now, in late 1998, that same lunatic was planning from the prison he had called home for the past ten years to sit in front of the parole board and plead his case. It seemed almost impossible that the state of New Jersey would even consider letting a man out of prison who had, from that same prison, written a letter that expressed a desire once again to pick up where he left off, once he was out.

But here they were. Preparing to consider Ned's freedom.

50

I

Carmen loved to pile her nieces and nephews in her sister Sonia's car and head out to Ron-A-Roll in Vernon, Connecticut, an indoor roller-skating rink about a half hour from Hartford. Skating around, laughing and joking, falling down and scraping her knees, screaming until the blisters on her feet throbbed, Carmen took it all in as if she were a kid herself. There was something about the wind in her hair and the hum of those wheels gliding along the wooden floor—it was freeing and cathartic.

She was born Carmen Rodriguez, the fourth child of ten brothers and sisters. From the oldest down, there was Carlos, Sonia, Petra, Maria, Carmen, Ruben, Rafael, Luis, Luz (pronounced "lose"), and Glendaliz (pronounced "Glenda Leez"). Luz, who was quite lively, spunky, and garrulous herself, later recalled Carmen as the beacon in their rather large family, the one sibling all the others were drawn to, for good or bad.

With her boisterous spirit, Carmen could walk into a room of strangers and walk out of the same room with a posse of friends.

It was her smile.

Her magnetic charm.

Her charisma.

She was, said family and friends, the "life of any party."

There was a bond between Carmen and her mother, Rosa, that went far beyond that of the other siblings, Luz said. Carmen looked to her mother as a source of comfort and dependency. She had gone through the local Hartford public-school system, including Hartford Public High School during the late 1980s, went out on her own, and yet always found herself drifting back to her mom, while the others detached and went about their own lives, some moving to Puerto Rico for good, others sticking around Hartford.

It was that strong-willed attitude Carmen exuded that her siblings—especially Luz and Glendaliz—recalled most vividly. "We were little," said Luz, "Carmen was older. She used to like to take us to Pope Park swimming and roller-skating. She loved Pope Park." Back then, Pope Park was a popular Hartford neighborhood hangout for families in and around the south end. Throughout the decades, however, as Hartford itself showed a "gradual decline" in housing development and crime, drugs and gang violence began to dominate, the park lost part of its beauty and safety. Still, on any given day, one or more of the Rodriguez kids was at the park doing something. Carmen couldn't wait until autumn every year, especially as she grew into her teens. When the apples and pears of Pope Park were ready to be picked, she'd gather her younger siblings and march them all down to the park for a day of fruit picking. "She just loved to do that," Luz remembered. "I don't know what it was."

II

There was one thing about Carmen that all of her siblings later agreed upon: She loved older men. For Carmen, it was, several suggested, an inherent need—and they had no idea where it came from—she absorbed as she grew older to be taken care of by these men. "She didn't want to work," Sonia, Carmen's oldest sister, recalled. "She wanted a man to provide for her."

It started early. *Very* early.

To the family's surprise, Carmen ran off when she was fifteen, in 1983, with a man twenty-five years her senior, and got married. She didn't see a problem with it. She was young. In love. And she wanted to spend her life with the guy. "But she didn't know what she was doing," Luz said. "She was *so* young. How could she?"

Within a few months, Carmen was pregnant and eventually gave birth to her first child—Jacqueline "Jackie" Garcia—when she was only sixteen. The relationship lasted a year. When it was over and Carmen realized that being married and a mother at sixteen was not all that she had expected, she ran back to her own mother, who was living on Benton Street, in Hartford.

Mom was that safety net. Always there to catch Carmen's fall.

51

I

Barbara Delaney had made it her business to write to the parole board anytime she felt compelled to remind them what Ned had done to her sister. Ever since Christmas 1983, Barbara had not spent a holiday season without reliving the nightmare all over again. Karen had been butchered. Ned had admittedly killed her. Her mom was dead. If Barbara and her family had to live with those losses the rest of their lives, how could the parole board even *consider* letting Ned out before he served his sentence?

Not knowing that the letter wasn't going to do any good whatsoever, in September 1998, Barbara sat down at her computer and stared at a blank screen. It would be hard to write out memories. Karen was a bright star, with so much life and energy. She had inspired Barbara, taught her things about herself no one else had. It had been nearly fifteen years, but it seemed like only yesterday.

Edwin Snelgrove will come before you, Barbara tapped out, *to ask for parole.* She paused. It was still hard to write his name. Think about him. Imagine him in her parents' cottage. At the funeral. Kissing the woman he had murdered.

While he pleads to go free, she found the strength to continue, *his victims will never get a second chance to live out their lives. . . .*

She was speaking for Mary Ellen Renard, too.

All *victims,* perhaps.

How could those words—"attempted murder" and "aggravated manslaughter" and "parole"—be considered in the same breath? Here the guy was, not yet eleven years into a twenty-year sentence, preparing to be released from prison. Was there any justice in sentencing laws?

As Barbara wrote, those deep-seated feelings of loss and anger came back. She spoke of Ned's third victim, her mother, relating to the board that Elizabeth Anne, two years after Karen's death, suffered her first heart attack. Then, after a long battle with heart problems, "directly related to my sister's death," died prematurely at the age of sixty-seven.

Barbara took a break. Writing it all out—verbalizing it all over again—was emotionally exhausting. Recalling the horror. The trips to court. Seeing Ned's photograph in the newspapers. Hearing him make excuses.

Tears.

Karen was Barbara's only sister. She couldn't even begin to explain how she'd gotten by. Pacing in her living room, Barbara wondered if the letter would fall on deaf ears. After all, how many of these letters have board members read? How many murderers have they considered for parole? Ned was likely another in a long list of murderers who would serve his time, do the right thing, and see the light of day. They'd pull out that word: "overcrowding."

Barbara had to let them know how she felt—if not for the sake of keeping Ned locked up, then for her own self-assurance. Her own sanity. And so she reminded the board that Ned had attacked again, in 1987, after getting away with killing Karen. She told Mary Ellen's story after detailing how she and her family suffered through the Christmas of 1983.

Five pages of a family's agony. Then another page of Mary Ellen's. That eleven-page letter Ned had written to the judge detailing how "sick" he was and how he could not control those strange, evil, violent thoughts about women. He *needed* to kill, Barbara pointed out. He *needed* to assuage those feelings of sexual violence. It was there in black and white—from his own pen. Had he gotten help for *that?* Could anyone, she wondered, cure such a sickness? Barbara wrote that there was a *substantial likelihood that he will commit another crime if he is released.* She asked the board if a *relatively short sentence [would] deter him from future violence?* If Ned was cut loose now, there was no doubt in her mind that he would hurt other women. That's right: *women.* Plural.

Barbara believed that God would ultimately punish Ned, she wrote. But we, as a society, needed to confine him so he couldn't harm anyone else. *Without repentance . . . he will have to face God's consequence, the wages of sin is death,* she wrote. *I am satisfied with this.*

She asked if they had considered the idea that he would kill again if released. She said he had a reputation for lying and deception. He was smart in those ways. A con man. She said Ned himself had said he was a danger to society. He had even asked for and admitted he needed psychiatric help. *Please heed to his call for help,* she wrote. *I plead with you to scrutinize this case. Examine the* facts *of the past. . . . It is your responsibility to protect us. . . . Deny his parole so we can rest, knowing that someone else will not become another victim. . . . May God help you in your decision.*

She sealed the letter, put a stamp on it, and sent it, not knowing that it wasn't going to do any good whatsoever, because Ned wasn't up for parole—he was due to be released on good behavior. He had served his sentence.

52

I

After splitting up with her first husband, sixteen-year-old Carmen Rodriguez began living with her mom again—but she hadn't learned a lesson, because she couldn't stay away from older men. It was that wandering spirit, always out there looking for a man to carry her off into the sunset. "At that time," Luz recalled, "she really didn't want to do much." Going back to school didn't seem at all interesting to Carmen, neither did working or even joining many of her brothers and sisters in Puerto Rico. She enjoyed motherhood and being a homemaker.

Inside the next few years, Carmen dated another older man and had two more children, Tanaris and Roberto, while Jacqueline, from her failed marriage, grew into a lively toddler. "He treated her very well," said Carmen's niece Kathy Perez, speaking of the new man in her life, "he was a *good* man. She loved him."

Her new man, Roberto, got a job in Springfield, Massachusetts, about a twenty-five minute drive north of Hartford, and Carmen and the kids followed him. Soon they were all living in a small, cozy apartment in downtown Springfield, but Carmen hated it. Almost every day, Luz said, chuckling at the memory, "she was back in Hartford at my mom's house." It was that maternal pull tugging at Carmen, as she lived twenty-five miles away from Mom, that made her drive back to Hartford "almost every day" to be with her mother and sisters. "She'd wake up Roberto," pushing on him first thing in the morning. "'Let's go to Hartford. Take me home.'"

Leaving the unity of the family gave Carmen a sense of disconnect; if she couldn't make it to Hartford for some reason, she was calling to ask what was going on.

The bond between mother and daughter was so strong that Luz and Sonia, after watching Carmen commute back and forth from Springfield to Hartford, found her an apartment next door—connected—to her mother's apartment. But with three kids at home and a man who worked in Springfield, things became difficult for Carmen and Roberto. "They started to have problems," Luz recalled.

Those problems, though, began to affect Carmen's mother, simply because she was living next door. "She (my mother) had to leave. My mother," Luz added, "went to Puerto Rico and left Carmen behind."

It was 1988. Carmen was twenty years old. Now, without warning, her lifeline was gone. Not just a walk across the hallway, but her mom was in another country. Although she had her sisters close by, Carmen still felt alone.

"She was devastated," Luz remembered.

At the time her mother took off, Carmen had been trying to work things out with Roberto. No sooner had her mother left did Carmen drop those reconciliation talks with Roberto and fly to Puerto Rico, too. "Momma is not next to me now," Luz said, speaking for Carmen, "so she's like, 'bye' to Roberto."

It was an easy decision. One of which had little to do with Roberto and more to do with the fact that Carmen didn't feel safe unless she was next to her mother. Still, living in Puerto Rico was not what Carmen had expected. Within three months, she found herself back in Hartford, trying to work things out with Roberto.

A few weeks after she returned to Hartford, Carmen realized she was pregnant again. "The baby wasn't his," one of her sisters later said, speaking of Roberto. Six months after returning from Puerto Rico, Carmen gave birth to Rueben Negron.

Back home now, without her mom to fall back on, Carmen relied on her oldest sister, Sonia, who lived on Capitol Avenue at the time, with her four children and husband. "She came to me," Sonia recalled, "after she tried to make things work with Roberto." Moving in with Sonia, Carmen had Rueben. Her three other kids were still in Puerto Rico with her mother. They were being well taken care of. Carmen didn't have to worry. She knew enough to leave them there until she could get herself situated back in Hartford; then she would send for them.

Sonia was an old-school homemaker. She believed in taking care of her family—to a certain extent. Her own children and husband *had* to come first. Carmen was living in Sonia's apartment with a small child, but now she started to drink heavily. No one knew why. She liked to party, they all said, and it somehow got out of hand for her. "She liked to have a good time," Luz remembered, "and got caught up in it."

II

One day in 1990, Sonia, stressed with taking care of four kids of her own and putting up with Carmen's drinking, called her mother in Puerto Rico. Carmen wasn't drinking every day, she never did. But a few beers on Thursday night, Luz said, turned into a party for her until Sunday or Monday. "And then she'd go two weeks without a drop. But when she partied, she *partied*."

"She got to go," Sonia told her mother over the phone.

Rosa understood. She knew Carmen better than any of them.

Before hanging up, they made a decision. Sonia went out later that day and, unbeknownst to Carmen, bought her a plane ticket and shipped her back to Puerto Rico with Rueben.

Carmen continued to drink while in Puerto Rico, so the family stepped in and took responsibility for the children. For the first time in what seemed to be her entire life, Carmen was childless. She had no one to take care of, but herself. "She was alone, she didn't have kids, no husband," Luz said, "and she was like, 'why not enjoy life, take advantage of the situation.'" Not in a bad way, Luz pointed out. But in a way that allowed Carmen to find herself and deal with the issues she was facing.

While in Puerto Rico, Carmen met that man she had been waiting for. His name was Jesus Ramos, a native Puerto Rican. "A good, *good* man," Sonia and Luz said.

As with all of the men Carmen dated, Jesus was older—yet no one expected how much older. "Sixty-five," Sonia said, wincing. Carmen was twenty-three then. The guy was forty-two years her senior. He could have been her grandfather. "But he was great, a wonderful guy," added Luz and Kathy Perez, Sonia's daughter. "He loved her," Kathy said. "She adored him. What did age matter?"

Carmen needed someone like Jesus, who wanted nothing more than to take care of her. Sensing she had found true love—that unconditional love she had been chasing—Carmen married Jesus, and wound up spending the next six years in Puerto Rico by his side. It wasn't until 1998, when Carmen's mother moved back to Hartford from Puerto Rico, that things changed. She found a cozy apartment on Putnam Street, a block away from Pope Park, inside the Capitol Avenue, Park and Broad Street square the family had lived in and around all their lives. "It was like a rope," Luz lamented. "Where Mommy went, Carmen went with her."

And so, not long after Rosa migrated back to Hartford from Puerto Rico, Carmen followed.

Jesus stayed in Puerto Rico. They were still married, but Carmen was getting bored with the marriage. The change back to the States, she believed, would do her some good. Maybe the time away would reignite that spark of love she had once felt for Jesus.

Carmen was still caught in that spiral of drinking, however; she couldn't seem to get out of it. Sonia once brought her to a local psychiatric hospital, but she left after only two hours. Then she tried working. Luz was involved with a temp service. One day, the service called and needed two workers. Luz called Carmen.

"I don't know," she said. "I'm no good at working."

"Come on," Luz said. "Give it a try."

So she went.

It was a factory job. Luz and Carmen worked on a production line, piecework. The parts on the machine came by, Luz remembered, at lightning speed. "You had to keep up." Once you fell behind, the pieces piled up. Luz had no trouble keeping up with production. "The parts were hot to the touch, but I did my best. Carmen would take one part, and five would go by. She couldn't keep up. She kept leaving the line to go outside and smoke."

By eleven that morning, Carmen said to Luz, "I'm leaving. This working stuff isn't for me."

"Come on, just stay for the day. You'll get paid for a whole day. You need a ride anyway." Luz had driven Carmen to the plant.

Carmen left after suffering through the day. No matter, the foreman had gotten all the girls together after the day ended and announced who was going to be invited back the following day. "You, you, and you," he said, pointing to Luz and a few of the other girls, "come back tomorrow. You," he added, pointing to Carmen, "you don't have a job anymore."

"I didn't [go] back," Luz recalled, laughing at the memory of Carmen's one day of work. "My hands were burned from the parts, it was hot in there. I didn't like. But they had offered me the job and Carmen knew that. It was so funny to see her try to work."

Money wasn't an issue for Carmen. Whenever she needed cash, she'd call her husband, Jesus, back in Puerto Rico, and he'd send her $400, $500, whatever she needed to get by. "This is why she didn't want to work," said Luz. "The men would give her money. She didn't *need* to work."

53

I

Ned had compulsive tendencies. In his teens, he would do certain things that made his mother nervous about a possible condition she believed he had. There was one time, she later detailed, when Ned was at a local public pool and she watched him put on a T-shirt and take it off "six to eight times" in a row, but she didn't think anything of it then. Sometime later, she watched Ned at the dinner table pick up his glass and put it back down in the same spot, over and over again, for several minutes. So she called his doctor.

"I think he should see a psychiatrist," Ned's mother said.

"It's not serious," the family doctor said after asking several questions.

Within a few months, the behavior stopped, and Mrs. Snelgrove said she "never did anything about it" again.

Later, when investigators began to take a closer look into Ned's life, it was easy to see the signs of what might be called obsessive-compulsive disorder (OCD) were prevalent in the way he kept detailed records of his mileage and gas receipts and newspaper articles (and two rather compelling Styrofoam mannequin heads that investigators believed he had doctored up to look like females).

II

Ned hated to be told what to do. He never wanted "advice," a family member later recalled, and would get extremely upset with anyone who ever criticized him. *He was kind of extreme on this score . . . ,* that same family member later wrote, but she believed it was just one more way for Ned to show and *maintain his independence.*

III

On June 27, 1997, the Bergen County Office of the Prosecutor sent a letter to Mary Di Sabato, the chairperson of the New Jersey State Parole Board. In short, the office was sending the letter to officially proclaim its objection to Ned's proposed release or possible parole. Assistant County Prosecutor Fred L. Schwanwede, who had spearheaded the office's case against Ned back in 1988, along with Thomas Kapsak, from Middlesex County, explained to the parole board, just in case there was any misunderstanding, what Ned had done to end up in prison. In graphic detail, Schwanwede narrated both Mary Ellen's vicious attack and survival, and Karen Osmun's painful death. Schwanwede's pain, carried over for the past eleven years, was obvious in every word of every sentence. The anguish for the victim had not left this prosecutor. He was finding it hard to believe he had to actually fight to keep this maniac in prison.

Then Schwanwede went into Ned's eleven-page "explanation" of his crimes, quoting Ned at length. There in Ned's own words was Ned's plan. Could this warped psyche be cured? Could this same person be ready to face society? The Bergen County Office of the Prosecutor didn't think so.

As his letter concluded, Schwanwede, pleading with board members, wrote for them not to be taken in by Ned's *clean-cut, neat, articulate, intelligent . . . sincerity, just as he had [fooled] Mary Ellen Renard on the evening she fought for her life.* Like every other prosecutor and law enforcement official Ned would cross paths with throughout his life, Schwanwede pegged him as the *most dangerous defendant* he had ever dealt with.

Why?

Well, it was pretty darn obvious at this point: he *gives the appearance of being a "regular guy,"* Schwanwede penned.

John Doe.

Bob Smith.

Ned Snelgrove.

The most potent, most sobering words of Schwanwede's letter came at the end, when, in direct and straightforward language, the veteran prosecutor warned the board against the threat of allowing Ned to go free early: *Whenever he is released . . . he will present a grave danger of taking another human life. . . .* He finally asked members *to delay this threat for as long as the board allows.*

Continuing for another paragraph, the prosecutor said Ned could easily dupe anyone he wanted because he was *that* smart and *that* good at what he did. By his own admission, Ned had been harboring these impulses of hurting women since the second and third grade, Schwanwede warned. Now, being *motivated by a thirst for freedom,* Schwanwede astutely wrote, Ned was even more dangerous than he had ever been. *Don't be fooled,* he ended his letter, *someone's life surely depends upon it.*

IV

Despite the warnings and the letters and the pleadings from those who knew Ned Snelgrove best, eleven months after Barbara Delaney wrote with her concerns, and Fred Schwanwede sent his letter, it was clear in August 1999 that the parole board had no choice in the matter. As it turned out, it was up to the New Jersey Department of Corrections (NJDOC). And complicated doesn't even begin to explain the situation. Public information officer and research specialist for the New Jersey State Parole Board Neal Buccino explained to me how Ned got out of prison so soon, saying, "The state parole board was not involved in any way with Mr. Snelgrove's release. By law, he was eligible to be considered for parole, but Mr. Snelgrove requested to serve out the rest of his term in prison without waiting for the state parole board's decision. With that request, the board ended its consideration of his case."

In other words, the parole board never had the opportunity to release Ned. The bottom line was that he had somehow found a way to bypass parole and, as one report claimed, *a mandated psychological evaluation after the court's computer system did not factor credits earned for good behavior into his release date.*

The NJDOC carefully reviewed Ned's records and determined that he was, in fact, eligible for early release—*not* parole—"based on time served and good behavior." Thus, after serving eleven years of a potential twenty-year sentence, thirty-nine-year-old Edwin "Ned" Snelgrove walked out of Rahway on May 26, 1999.

Free to go and do whatever he wanted.

Free to start life over again.

Free to walk the same streets as the victims he had left in his wake.

Free to kill.

54

I

When she wasn't having a good time, going out drinking and dancing, Carmen would take the kids—this time her nieces and nephews and own children—to Pope Park to roller-skate and swim. She helped her mother around the house, cleaning and cooking. She helped the kids with their homework. Even went to the movies from time to time. There was one day, especially, everyone later remembered with warm smiles and belly laughs, when Carmen gathered all the kids together, putting the little ones in an old abandoned shopping cart. They walked down to Crown Palace Theatre on New Park Avenue, which was a good two-mile hike from Putnam Street, just to go to the movies. "She loved to spend time with her nephews and nieces," Luz recalled.

"We were at Pope Park one day, at the carnival," Kathy Perez, Carmen's niece, remembered. "We were having a great time. She was putting all the young kids on the rides and buying them popcorn and cotton candy . . . and then it started to pour." There were about fifteen of them. Carmen flipped open her cell phone, called a friend who had a big truck, and "he came," Kathy added, "and piled us all in the back and took us all home safely."

Whenever one of the boys brought home a stringer of catfish after a day of fishing, Carmen loved to get the fillet knife out and clean the whiskered creatures herself. She craved what Luz, Kathy, and Sonia called *"bacalaito,"* a family recipe Carmen's mother prepared. Catfish, flour, yams, water, salt, and pepper—all mixed together into a dough and then rolled out into round discs and deep-fried (like fried dough).

When it came time to go out dancing, Carmen favored the *bachata,* a form of music and dance that originated in the countryside and rural neighborhoods of the Dominican Republic. What struck a chord with Carmen, no doubt stimulating her fragile soul, were the subjects the music and lyrics often dealt with: romance, especially heartbreak and sadness. The original name of the *bachata* genre was *amargue,* which translated to "bitterness," or "bitter music."

Carmen could get on the dance floor, let her long, flowing dark hair down, and lose herself and possibly her problems in the beat of the music. She could relate to it, having lived a life of failed romances. She knew how it felt to love and lose, as the *bachata* so passionately translated her feelings. In a family video, there was Carmen on the dance floor, moving to the *bachata,* talking to the camera: "Watch me . . . this is the way you do it."

She was perfect.

Happy.

Transfixed by the natural energy of song and dance.

When Carmen went out to the clubs in Hartford to dance the night away, she would pillage Luz's closet for clothes. Luz was the fashionista of the Rodriguez family. She dressed trendy and wasn't afraid to express herself through the garments she spent hours combing store racks for. Luz would be at home on the weekend watching television, her husband sleeping soundly in the next room. Carmen would sneak up to the window, slide the little plastic accordion arm of the air conditioner open like a curtain, and whisper, "Sister, sister?"

Luz would be watching television, rolling her eyes, knowing why Carmen was at the window. "Sister" was a nickname Carmen chose for Luz, in the same fashion as she called their mother, "Mother." It was a term of endearment in Carmen's eyes. ("She never called me by my name," Luz recalled.)

There was that sweet, angelic voice of Carmen's at the window, asking Luz if she could come in and borrow some clothes for a night out.

"What are you doing?" Luz said in a whisper. Carmen was standing at her door by then. "[My husband's] sleeping."

"Come on, Sister, give me a shirt. I'm going out dancing." Carmen would throw her arms in the air and do a little wiggle.

"Be quiet. Come in." Luz would never refuse. Carmen changed right there in the hallway, sometimes on the porch.

"You got a beer for the road, Sister?" she'd ask before leaving.

Luz always gave in. It was Carmen's sincerity. She wanted to have some fun. She didn't want to hurt anybody or cause problems, she just wanted to go out dancing.

"Titi," Luz said, whispering, "I have to go to work tomorrow morning, early. . . . Go ahead, take the beer and go. Go." "Titi" was a nickname given to Carmen by her grandmother. Later, her nieces and nephews called her "Titi, la Loca."

Crazy Auntie.

"There were two 'Titi's in the family," recalled Luz. "So Carmen, later on, became *Titi, la Loca.* It was not in a negative way, nothing ever was with Carmen."

II

During an Easter egg hunt in 1999, Carmen wound up in a spot of trouble. Her daughter Jacqueline's family lived on the opposite side of a two-family house where Carmen had been staying with her mother on Putnam Street. The two families got along, but they weren't necessarily close. "It was a 'hi and bye' type of relationship," Kathy Perez recalled.

On that wonderful early spring afternoon, one of the young girls from Jacqueline's family, who was maybe ten years old, started to give Carmen some trouble, calling her out. There was a dispute over a parking space in the driveway. The little girl got nasty with Carmen as she tried to get someone to move their car.

"I'm not going to hit a little kid," Carmen said, laughing at the gesture.

The girl began provoking her, taunting her to engage.

Carmen laughed. "OK, you want some." She called for her niece Kathy to come out, who was closer in age to the girl. ("I was her baby," Kathy said. "Me and my aunt were always together. She watched out for me. She'd take care of me.")

The girl, nonetheless, wasn't satisfied, according to Kathy. She kept taunting Carmen. So as Kathy was on her way outside to confront the problem, the girl took a swing at Carmen. ("So Carmen grabbed her. She had her by the hair.")

"Kathy, Kathy," Carmen screamed. "Hurry up, come out here." Carmen didn't want to be involved. She was an adult. She didn't want to hurt the little girl.

Against her better judgment, perhaps, Kathy ended up striking the girl. Not hard, just a little poke to the arm. Meanwhile, Carmen fell into the thorny bushes along the side of the driveway as the commotion escalated, and she got scratched all over her upper body. When she got up and brushed herself off, she was livid.

Soon both families were gathered around, throwing insults at one another. Someone called the cops. When they spoke to the young girl, she claimed it was Carmen who hit her.

Sonia bailed Carmen out of jail and the case turned into nothing.

As the next year progressed, Carmen thought long and hard about divorcing her husband. Too much time had elapsed since they had last seen each other. She had been dating other men. She loved Jesus, but she didn't want to string him along, either. She hated taking his money, but he insisted on sending it. Her mother was pushing her to move out on her own with Jacqueline, who was fifteen, and Roberto, now twelve. Tanaris, thirteen, and Rueben, nine, were a handful, but Carmen was able to send them to Puerto Rico for spells of time so they could visit family and learn their culture.

Carmen didn't want to move out, however, until she knew she could provide for her kids. She had applied for state assistance and it was said to be in the works. Once it was OK'd, she promised her mother, the state was going to help her find a place.

III

As the spring of 2001 approached, Carmen seemed to be heading back into a routine of heavy drinking. "She just couldn't stop for long periods of time," said Luz. "We tried to do everything we could to help her, but she didn't want it. What could we do?"

During those periods when Carmen wasn't drinking so much, Luz liked to have her watch her kids. "She was family. We always rely on family."

One afternoon, while Luz and her husband were at work, Carmen was babysitting. On this day, she decided to drink. It wasn't common for Carmen to get drunk while watching the kids. She must have obviously started after Luz left for work. In any event, Carmen and Luz's aunt lived next door. She called Luz at work late into the day and said, "Titi is hitting on your kids." She had heard some commotion next door and went over. She saw Carmen yelling at the kids, acting strangely. ("She was out of control, out of her mind, pushing the kids around," Luz said later. "Carmen was not an abuser. She was drunk and impatient, and the kids got to her. It was all too much." Luz wasn't making excuses for her sister; she was trying to explain how things happened. When Carmen drank for a long period of time, she became a different person, family members said. She wasn't herself.)

"What is she doing?" Luz asked her aunt as they talked on the phone.

"She's hitting on the kids. I'm going to call the cops."

By the time Luz got home, her aunt had already phoned the police. As the police were on their way, Luz and Carmen began arguing.

"What are you doing, Titi? You don't push the kids around!" Luz said. As much as Luz and Carmen got along and loved each other, they also fought more than any of the other siblings. "Calm down, Titi, calm down," Luz said as Carmen screamed at her. Carmen was outside on the porch. They were going back and forth. Luz was trying to keep Carmen cool. Then, at some point, Carmen hit Luz. Pushed her down to the ground and started punching her.

The police arrived. Carmen and Luz were on the ground fighting. But Luz refused to hit back. ("I would never hit my own blood. That's just me. Never. Never. Never. I don't care what she did to me.")

The police took Carmen away and arrested her for domestic violence and child abuse. She ended up spending ninety days at York Correctional Institution, a women's prison in Niantic, Connecticut. When she got out of York during the spring of 2001, she was a changed person. She started to watch her drinking. She was doing great, according to Luz, Sonia, and Kathy. She still liked to go out on the town as a means to blow off steam, but she didn't come home drunk, plus those days of binging were over. Dancing provided an atmosphere for Carmen to let loose and relax. For the most part, she liked to hang out at Portillas's Palace Café, on Park Street, which in Hartford is made up of largely a Spanish community. So Carmen felt at home. "Little San Juan," some called Park

Street. The International, on Capitol Avenue, near Kenney's Restaurant and Bar, was another club Carmen frequented.

IV

One night, while Carmen was dancing at the Portillas's Palace Café, she met Miguel Fraguada, a rather nice-looking, somewhat older man. Miguel fell for Carmen immediately. She liked the way he treated her and her children. He was always putting their needs before his own. A real man, the family called him. Miguel worked hard. He wanted to see Carmen do well. He was good for her.

Carmen had always been rail thin, maybe 110 pounds at any given time. While in prison, however, for just a few months, she had packed on some extra weight and it showed. Miguel didn't mind. He loved Carmen the way she was. "When I saw her the first time [after she got out]," Luz said, "she looked huge, because she had always been so skinny."

The weight didn't seem to bother Carmen. She'd waltz around, laughingly saying, *"Ahora consegui la carne"* ("I got meat now"). She loved the idea of having some "meat on her bones," as she put it. She thought it made her look sexy. By no means was Carmen fat. She was heavier, sure. But it felt good.

In photographs of Carmen with Miguel during this period, she looks content, happy to be with him. Somewhat of a ham whenever a camera was pointed at her, Carmen smiled and stared into the lens, as if she had a connection with whoever was on the opposite end.

V

In July 2001, Carmen finally found an apartment she liked. It was on Grand Street, right off Capitol Avenue, not too far from the safety net of her mother's place on Putnam. Before she and Miguel moved in with the kids, they spent days and nights painting and fixing the place up to make it more homey. In both their minds, they were starting a family together. They wanted everything perfect.

It was funny to Luz, Sonia, and Kathy that they'd come home and see Carmen transporting her personal belongings in a shopping cart from Putnam to Grand. She had no car—not many did in the city. But nothing was going to stop her. That first time Carmen went grocery shopping, Luz and her mother took her. Carmen was like a kid in a candy store. This was the first apartment she'd had on her own. She had never, in all of her years (she was thirty-two then), had a place she could call her own. She either lived with a guy or stayed with family. Ever since she put the deposit on the place and started fixing it up, she had even stepped away from the booze. She still drank, but not to excess.

As they were trolling the aisles of the supermarket a day or two after Carmen officially moved into her apartment, Luz recalled, Carmen was excited about the prices of food. "She'd grab boxes of pasta and say, 'Three for a dollar, I'm getting these.' My mom and I would laugh. We used Goya products for everything. But it didn't matter to Carmen." She'd pick up a bottle of tomato sauce, a different brand that was on sale, and throw it in the cart.

"But we don't use that," her mother would say in Spanish.

"But it's cheap. I'm getting it," Carmen countered.

It was the first time she had ever really been grocery shopping for herself. "It was like two hours in that store," Luz remembered, laughing at the memory.

VI

Carmen had finally cut the cord. She was out on her own with Miguel. She had found her place in the world with a guy who loved her for who she was. As the summer went on, she called her sisters every day, stopped by to see them, or invited them over for dinner. They were a family. A close-knit group living within a few miles of one another. Miguel fit into the mix perfectly. Carmen was proud to call him her boyfriend. She'd even filed papers to divorce Jesus and pledged to marry Miguel as soon as she could.

As fall came, being in the apartment day after day, night after night, began to wear on Carmen. She wanted to go out dancing, maybe have a few drinks. She wasn't going to disrupt what she had with Miguel, she promised. The only way she'd go out was with his absolute blessing. She had stopped at Kenney's, a local restaurant/bar around the corner from the apartment, once in a while to have a drink and play pool. But she hadn't made going out or Kenney's a habit. Luz knew she had stopped at Kenney's, because Carmen had gone to her one day with a check from a Kenney's patron, "Ned something," Carmen called him. The check was for $25. Carmen said she had taken a survey for the guy and he paid her by check. She wanted Luz to cash it—which she did.

VII

On the evening of September 21, 2001, Carmen was at home with Miguel. Things had been going "great" between them, family members said. Because Carmen had been doing so well with her drinking, she had spoken to Miguel about maybe going out that night. Her aunt and uncle were heading to a club to go dancing. Carmen wanted in.

"Can I go with them?" she asked Miguel.

Her uncle and aunt were in the apartment, standing there.

"I'll watch her," said Carmen's uncle. "I bring her home early."

Miguel thought about it. Carmen was standing in front of him. It was almost as if she were saying, *Please, please, please say yes.*

"OK," Miguel said.

Carmen's daughter Jacqueline called her into the other room and helped her put on her makeup and get dressed. Putting on some flashy clothes and sexy makeup was all part of the atmosphere of going out.

Afterward, they piled into Carmen's uncle's car and headed into the north end of Hartford, to the Goravena, a popular nightclub, where Carmen danced, drank, and had fun.

It was around 9:00 P.M. when Carmen's uncle said, "It's time to go. I promised Miguel I'd get you back early."

To his surprise, Carmen didn't bark. "OK," she said.

In the car on the way back, however, Carmen became a little impatient and wanted another drink. They were somewhere near Capitol Avenue, just a few blocks from Carmen's apartment on Grand, when Carmen started arguing with them, saying she said she wanted to stop for "one more." Just one.

"No," her uncle said. "You need to go home."

"I don't want to go home." Carmen kept repeating herself. She was in the backseat. She sounded a bit tipsy.

"Come on, Titi. I gotta take you home."

Carmen opened the door when they pulled up to a stoplight and got out of the car. "No," she said, "I'm not going home."

There was a cop sitting on the corner watching them. Carmen's uncle, family members later said, didn't want to get out of the car and cause a big commotion. The cop would get involved. It would turn ugly.

So her uncle let Carmen go. He figured she'd walk home. She was maybe two blocks from her apartment.

Instead, though, Carmen walked straight down Capitol Avenue and went into Kenney's Restaurant and Bar, which was right around the corner from her apartment, while her uncle drove to her apartment and roused Miguel.

"She took off on me," he said, "when I stopped at a light."

"Let's go looking for her."

By now, it was close to 10:00 P.M. Carmen was sitting

inside Kenney's having a drink, talking to Ned, whom she had met once or twice over the past few weeks. To her, Ned was a harmless white nerd who liked to hang around the bar after work and play pool. She could finagle a few drinks out of him, call it a night, and walk home.

Miguel, Jacqueline, Carmen's uncle, and her aunt drove around the Capitol Avenue area looking for Carmen, never thinking to stop at Kenney's, simply because Kenney's wasn't one of Carmen's preferred hang-outs. They spent hours driving around the city stopping at the bars she liked to dance at. The thing was, no matter where Carmen went, how drunk she got or how late it was, she picked up the phone and called home. "'Mother,'" said Kathy Perez, mimicking what Carmen might call and say when she was out, "'I'm staying at a friend's.'"

After returning home, early the next morning, Miguel and Jacqueline waited, but the call never came. No one could find Carmen.

55

I

After Ned was released from prison, he traveled straight back to Connecticut, settled into a seedy motel on the Berlin Turnpike in Newington (not far from his parents' house) for a few months, and then moved back home. Several things were significant to Ned as he integrated back into society for the first time in over ten years. For one, getting the hell out of New Jersey as fast he could before the Department of Corrections decided to find a reason to keep him behind bars; two, starting over without being pressured from people (the dirty looks, the whispers behind his back); and three, if what Ned had been writing from prison to his former high-school friend George Recck was any indication as to what he had planned postrelease, planting his feet firmly in Connecticut, a fresh location, would provide new faces, new people, and, per Ned's own words, new victims.

Ted Bundy had driven into faraway counties and states to hang out at bars and choose the perfect victims. Ned had even mentioned Bundy's MO in one of the letters he'd written from prison to his old high-school friend George Recck. There's no way to tell for sure—Ned wouldn't admit to it—if he had

chosen Hartford in response to what he learned from studying Bundy, but Ned started hanging out at Kenney's Restaurant and Bar, downtown, after he got settled into his parents'
house and found a salesman's job at American Frozen Foods.
Ned was an expert at what he did; he could sell milk to a cow.
As a "food counselor" for American, he excelled. His job was
to go into customers' homes and pitch frozen foods his company would later deliver.

Kenney's was a popular local restaurant and lounge mostly
populated by blue-collar workers, a few stray Hartford busi-
nessmen and locals, and several hookers working the area. As
Ned's job performance took off, he began showing up at
Kenney's every other day. Not to get drunk, mind you, but
more or less to meet new people, scope out the scene, enjoy
a few beers during happy hour, and maybe catch a Red Sox
game. During the summer of 2001, Ned began asking his new
friends at Kenney's to fill out credit applications for American Frozen Foods. "Ned asked . . . this whole neighborhood
to fill out a credit application or contract," a former Kenney's
regular who knew Ned later said. "He wanted people with
bad credit to fill out a contract to agree to buy frozen foods
based on a credit check. Ned explained that he would put up
a twenty-five-dollar fee (out of his own pocket) for any appli-
cant, who would get a check in the mail."

Carmen had filled one out herself that summer after stopping in Kenney's one night. Luz had cashed the check for her.

For the neighborhood barflies who frequented Kenney's,
Ned's offer was a free night out. For Ned, he would get a
bonus for every contract he signed, whether the credit check
went through successfully or not. Primarily, Ned had asked
only the females. Alice Nevins (pseudonym) had hung around
Kenney's for many years and knew Ned as a traveling salesman, the somewhat taciturn, clean-cut geek with the enormous growth on the side of his neck—a benign tumor Ned
had picked up with age—who liked to sit on the same stool

and make the same stupid sexist jokes. Ned wasn't feeling too good about himself these days. That tumor the size of a grapefruit protruding out of the side of his neck was benign, yet it caused him a great amount of discomfort and, of course, shot down his self-esteem even lower than it was.

II

Alice and her friend Tina were approached by Ned that August. Tina had introduced Ned to Alice. Ned knew all the neighborhood girls. He was even friends with several of the hookers. Tina was quite eccentric. She was thin, had short-cropped hair, with reddish brown highlights, and "very distinct" eyes, Alice later told police, which "seemed sunken in and very dark." She was a chronic drug user, Alice claimed, like many of the prostitutes Ned knew.

On the day Tina introduced Alice to Ned, he asked her if she wanted to help him out with the scam he was running. "I'm paying girls," Ned told her, "to fill out an application. You'll get a twenty-five-dollar check in the mail." So Alice filled out the short application, but failed to put down an address.

"What's your address?" Ned asked, staring at it. "I *need* an address."

"I live at the YMCA, right up the street."

Alice liked to stop in Kenney's every day. As the summer of 2001 wound down, she began to see a lot of Ned. He was always with one of the "girls" hanging out in the bar. Prostitutes were safe companions for Ned. Talking to them made Ned feel superior. Perhaps he could snatch one off the street and no one would notice. No one would care.

Alice's friend Kendra (pseudonym) lived above Kenney's in a small apartment. Kendra and Alice would see Ned several times during the week, sitting at the bar, nursing a beer, trying to charm the girls. There were "several times," Alice later said, when Ned asked her to dress more sexily.

More provocatively.

"Wear a low-cut skirt and boots," Ned would demand.

"Huh?"

"Dress like Carmen," Ned suggested one night, smiling, giving her the "Groucho Marx eyebrow" raise. It was obvious Ned liked Carmen. He hadn't seen her much. But during those few times, according to sources, she had stopped in Kenney's since moving to Grand Street with Miguel, she had run into Ned. At thirty-two (preparing to celebrate her thirty-third birthday that October), Carmen was an attractive woman, with long, flowing, curly brown hair, a shapely, girlish figure, and that Dentyne smile her sisters later spoke of so lovingly. She was five feet three inches tall. Although Latin by heritage, Carmen had a paler complexion—she looked Caucasian.

Beautiful skin. Velvety. Plush. Soft.

She hadn't been partying too much the last few months, ever since getting out of jail. She looked good. Even felt good.

For Ned, it had to be Carmen's voluptuous chest that first drew him to her—Carmen was huge.

With her sixteen-year-old daughter, Carmen and Miguel were happily situated and comfortable two blocks south of Kenney's, one block east, on Grand Street, in that new apartment they had spent weeks cleaning and painting. Carmen talked to everyone. Ned didn't have any other friends to speak of that he hung around or did things with. Ned had settled into his new life after prison as a loner—a man who lived in the basement of his parents' suburban home, worked a professional job all day, and hung out at a city bar talking to prostitutes and locals at night.

Carmen was different from the other women Ned had met. She had a way about her that Ned obviously found attractive. On some nights, Carmen wore her long hair up in a ponytail, like an Egyptian goddess. She strutted into the bar, wearing high-cut black leather boots, sporting bling around her neck, wrists, and ankles, a flashy skirt, and sexy, low-cut, tight blouse. She had likely come from one of the dance clubs in town, and as she had on the night of September 21, 2001, a Friday, when she had stopped at Kenney's for a nightcap.

Ned loved the way she dressed and the simple fact that she paid the slightest amount of attention to him. He never realized for one minute that she was probably just talking to him so she could get a free drink.

When Alice showed up at the bar that night not dressed like Carmen, Ned got mad, Alice said later. ("He would be upset with me when I didn't dress like her.")

Alice had no trouble shunning Ned. And she certainly wasn't going to dress in the manner that a man told her. But the conversations she'd had with Ned made his relationship with Carmen—if it could be called such—stand out. Alice was the first to notice when Carmen and Ned were talking or hanging around together. And also the first to notice when they left together.

56

I

They could always tell when she was in the bar. Her favorite song was "Suavemente," a romantic Latin ballad by Elvis Crespo that took Carmen back to her roots in Puerto Rico. ("That's how we knew she was there," a woman who worked at Kenney's said.) Like a starlet from an old 1950s musical, Carmen would walk into the bar, plunk a quarter into the jukebox, and . . . hit C-4. . . . That's it . . . *click.*

"Suavemente."

Ah, yes.

She would sit at the bar, sipping her drink, whispering the lyrics to herself.

II

The night of September 21 was cool in Hartford. The leaves on the trees in Bushnell Park were still dark green, ready to change any day now. Hartford is a two-and-a-half-hour ride on a bad traffic day from New York City. Only ten days after the worst terrorist attack in American history, the people of Hartford shuffled about the city with a certain amount of fear, uncertainty, and trepidation.

Inside Kenney's on that night, the talk wasn't centered on the recent deaths of over three thousand people in Manhattan and the fact that two national landmarks had crumbled to the ground. Instead, the talk at the bar in Kenney's, at least between Kendra and Alice, was how Ned was schmoozing with Carmen all night long after she had strolled into the bar somewhere around 10:00 P.M. after jumping out of her uncle's car a few blocks away.

As soon as Carmen walked in, she saw Ned sitting in a booth. Unlike a normal night where he'd sit bellied up to the bar, he seemed to be waiting for someone. And according to witnesses, Ned and Carmen hugged when she arrived at his table.

After a while—and a few drinks—they danced.

Played pool.

Janet Rozman, the bartender, even saw them kiss a few times.

Carmen was really tipsy. Well, maybe even drunk.

She and Ned kind of hung around together most of the night. It was loud in Kenney's. Lobsterfest night. More people than usual. Carmen was dressed in those black leather boots, short skirt, and flamboyant blouse that Ned had begged the other girls to wear. Ned had on his typical business attire, but he had loosened his necktie, a red-white-and-blue cheesy sort of homage to the events in New York. At some point during the night, he took his tie off and gave it to Rozman, who put it around her neck, saying, "Check me out. . . ."

Kendra and Alice walked around the bar several times and spotted Ned and Carmen laughing, talking, dancing, both the girls later reported to police. But after going out into the back of the bar late into the night, they lost sight of them. And when the girls returned to the bar area a short time later, Carmen and Ned were gone.

Alice was curious. She knew Ned was weird and could be a bit overwhelming and even violent, but at the same time, she understood why Carmen was hanging out with him: free drinks.

"Anyone seen Carmen?" she asked around the bar.

Several people said the same thing: "Carmen and Ned left together."

III

Carmen's daughter Jackie was pregnant. On the morning of September 22, after a night of looking around the city for her mother with Miguel, Jackie awoke to find that Carmen hadn't returned home—or called. Jackie hadn't gotten much sleep after spending half the night searching for her mother.

It was odd she hadn't called, Jackie thought. Jackie's baby shower was slated for Sunday, September 23. "Carmen had put the shower together," Carmen's niece Kathy Perez later said. "Every month," Luz added, "she used to give me money to hold for the shower. It was at my house. She was so excited about the baby and the shower."

The baby shower had to go on. With Carmen being gone now for nearly a full day, with no word, there wasn't much to celebrate. However, life had to continue as if she was coming home. *Think positive. She'll be home anytime now.*

After the quick shower on Sunday morning, Jackie and the others went back to handing out flyers around the city and calling people. The family got hold of the local newspaper, which happened to be directly across the street from Kenney's, and asked if it would publish a photograph of Carmen with a note. But, like the local television station, editors declined, saying they needed a police report or some sort of acknowledgment from law enforcement that there was an actual problem. After all, Carmen was an adult. She could have taken off.

With no help from the local "English-speaking" media,

family members claimed, Sonia, Carmen's oldest sister, went to Telemundo, the local Spanish TV network, which agreed to immediately air something about Carmen's disappearance.

Kenney's was a quick stop off Interstate 84, a major Connecticut highway cutting a path directly through downtown Hartford. Above all, locals filled Kenney's bar stools. Men and women who called one another by their first names and sat in front of bartenders who knew more about their lives than their own family members did. That afternoon, the family called the HPD. When an officer showed up, Jackie explained that Carmen was happy the previous night. She had gone out with family members and then took off on her own. She drank, sure. She probably hung out at the local bars more than she should have, but Carmen *always* came home at night. Or, Jackie explained, she *always* called. "She'd never miss my baby shower. Never."

Besides a rather artful tattoo on her right leg, Carmen had an *I Love You* tattoo on her left leg, Jackie told the police officer, before describing her features: height, weight, hair, eyes.

"What was she wearing, do you recall?" the officer asked.

"A burgundy blouse," Jackie said. She was sure of it. She'd watched her mother get dressed. Even suggested what to wear and helped her pick it out. "Two gold wrist bracelets, a gold-and-silver necklace, and double gold earrings." Jackie also explained that Carmen had a tattoo on her ankle that said "Tarzan."

On top of that, Carmen also wore those black knee-high "Nancy Sinatra" boots—the ones Ned had been so fond of and demanded the other girls at Kenney's wear.

"Where'd she go last night?" HPD officer Jeffrey Rohan asked next.

Jackie was visibly upset. Something was wrong. She could feel it. "At about nine o'clock," she said, "my mom's uncle dropped her off on Capitol Ave, I think she was going to the El Camerio Bar on Walnut Street." The El Camerio was a bit farther east, on the opposite side of Interstate 84, and Carmen had sometimes stopped in to see friends and have a drink. She never thought about why she had said "dropped her off" when she knew her mother had run from the car when her uncle stopped at a light.

In truth, Carmen could be anywhere. She was a grown woman. She had been known to stay out all night in the past and show up the next afternoon. What made today any different?

Jackie realized something was amiss. She knew her mother was in trouble. She couldn't explain how. She just *knew.* "She always calls home if she stays out all night," Jackie told Officer Rohan.

Rohan asked Jackie for a current photograph, adding, "It'll be filed as a missing persons case today." He didn't want Jackie to worry. Someone would be on it. If Carmen didn't return home by the end of the day, an investigator would be back. ("The Hartford police," family members later said, "were very helpful. They did all they could for us.")

Later that day, Carmen's family posted more missing persons flyers around the Capitol Avenue region near Kenney's and downtown. The Hartford PD had generated the eight-by-ten posters. Carmen's radiant smile and expressive brown eyes—so guarded and yet calm and charming—shined on thousands of Hartford residents as they went about their lives unshaken by this beautiful woman in the poster staring at them. Her image was wrapped around telephone poles, hung up on the bulletin boards of Laundromats, convenience and liquor stores, gas stations and local businesses. Indeed, there was Carmen's beautiful face: now a part of the "Milk Carton Class of 2001."

57

I

As the Hartford PD put together a missing persons file on Carmen, Ned was in Cromwell, Connecticut, just south of Berlin. He had to put on a presentation for a client. The client had arranged for a babysitter so she could dedicate her full attention to Ned and his frozen-food pitch. In actual fact, the woman later said, she had already made up her mind to purchase the service before Ned arrived. She was impressed by Ned during the few times she had spoken to him on the phone.

Ned's client and her husband sat in their dining room while Ned began. He seemed relaxed, ready to make his pitch. "He was dressed casual," the woman later remembered, "but not in jeans. He may have worn a golf shirt. He did not appear hurried or bothered, but his presentation was very pre-rehearsed."

Ned had done the pitch so many times that he could recite the thing while thinking about something else. As he carried on, almost sounding robotic, the woman interrupted, "Do you need a fan?"

Ned was "sweating profusely," the woman later told police. So badly, in fact, that she brought out a fan to "cool him off."

The house wasn't overly warm or cool, the woman noted. It was one of those perfect fall days. "I did not think it was too hot to be sweating so much, but I just thought Ned was a person who sweats a lot."

II

One of the investigators who later studied and interrogated Ned told me that Ned was likely sweating so much because, at that moment, as he gave his frozen-food pitch, Carmen's body was likely inside the trunk of his car out in the driveway. Ned was not known to be someone who sweat a lot. But when he got nervous—extremely nervous, that is—he had a propensity, several people later reported, to perspire like a long-distance runner. Still, although they never confirmed it through forensic evidence, ASA David Zagaja later said, "I believe, as well as my investigators, that Ned Snelgrove had Carmen's dead body in the trunk of his car while he made that sales call."

III

At some point that weekend, Jackie called one of her aunts and said she was worried that Miguel had taken Carmen. There was no motive anyone could decipher, but more or less a feeling Jackie had developed after thinking about the night she and Miguel searched for Carmen. After police told Jackie they believed Carmen had been at Kenney's on the night she disappeared, Jackie thought back to when she, Miguel, and Carmen's uncle had gone out looking for her. Jackie swore they had stopped at Kenney's and Miguel took a walk inside the bar. If he had indeed done something to Carmen, he would have acted as if he had never seen her, especially inside the bar. Beyond that, Jackie reported that Carmen's state card— she was on state assistance, food stamps, and welfare—

was missing. Luz called Carmen's social worker and explained the situation. She soon found out that $300 was missing from Carmen's account and that it had been withdrawn from an ATM that Saturday afternoon, a day after Carmen was reported missing. Moreover, the surveillance video showed a man wearing a ball cap pulled down over his face, a man similar to Miguel's height and weight. ("Miguel always wore hats," Luz and Kathy Perez said.)

At this point, the family was sure Miguel had done something to Carmen. Maybe they didn't know him the way they thought they had? Had they misjudged him?

As Luz and Kathy were driving down Park Street, looking for Carmen later that day, Miguel crossed the street in front of Luz's car. "Miguel, do you have Titi's card?" Luz yelled out the window. Miguel was standing on the sidewalk.

"No, I don't got her card. I don't got her card."

"Miguel, somebody took out her money. She didn't take it out. We want to know who did."

Sometime later, Miguel showed up at the apartment and handed Jackie $300. "Where is she?" Jackie asked, crying. Hysterical. Scared. She started yelling, "You took Mommy's money out. . . . You took Mommy's money out!"

"I didn't take her," Miguel shot back.

"Someone took her money. Was it you?"

Miguel went quiet.

"Miguel?"

"We need the money for the rent," he said brusquely. "I had to get it. We need to pay the rent so we can stay here."

58

I

When Carmen's friend Tina saw the missing persons posters strung up around Kenney's and throughout the city, she became unnerved by something that had been bothering her ever since it happened.

As Tina and Alice sat at the bar one night talking about Carmen, Tina brought up Ned. "He tried to rape me," Tina said. "Look at this." She pointed to her neck.

"I don't see anything," Alice said.

"Look!" It was gone now, but Tina said she'd had bruises around her neck where Ned had tried to strangle her. "I *hate* him."

"Everyone at the bar feels Ned did something to Carmen," Alice told police later that day, "but no one knows for sure."

These reports of Ned getting physical with some of the females who hung around Kenney's began filing in as the Hartford PD started digging. One man who lived across the street from Kenney's had a story to tell that became quite common where Ned and the girls of Kenney's were concerned. "I used to work as a bar back at Kenney's," the man said. "I met a guy named Ned (back in March 2001). Ned was a 'regular' at the bar." Ned showed up always between 9:00 and 11:00 P.M. "[Ned told me] he got up at four-thirty every morning for work." So he had to leave the bar early.

Ned's routine changed, however, during the first week of September. He started closing the bar with the other patrons, the guy said.

The bar back said he knew Tina. "She used to flirt with everyone for a drink."

He kept an eye on Tina because she was a relative. One night, the bar back slipped out into the back alley behind Kenney's to have smoke. Ned was sitting in his car, he recalled, talking to Tina, who was standing by the driver's side door. Ned had his window down. "I could not hear what they were saying," the bar back recalled. "But [Tina] walked away" and began heading for Capitol Avenue. She was obviously upset at something Ned had said. So Ned got out of the car, yelling, "Come back, Tina. Please."

Tina turned and walked back. They talked a little bit more near Ned's car. He was trying to get her into his car, the bar back could easily tell, but she didn't want to go.

"Stop it," Tina said.

Ned grabbed her forcefully by the arm.

The bar back walked toward Ned's car to see if Tina needed help. But she had "quickly" pulled her arm away from Ned and he had taken off hurriedly.

"Hey, you OK?" the bar back asked Tina.

"Yeah." They headed back into the bar.

"Why'd he grab you like that?"

"He wanted me to get into his car and 'go out for a date.' I didn't want to."

II

Luz, Sonia, Kathy Perez, and the rest of the Rodriguez clan were beside themselves with concern and confusion. They had gotten together and talked about the many different scenarios that could have taken place, to see if, perhaps, anyone knew anything. By now, it was clear that Miguel didn't have anything to do with Carmen's disappearance, so they all apologized and he understood. Tempers were fragile. Feelings raw. Miguel was the new kid on the block—it was easy and convenient to accuse him.

Luz had a thought: There was a guy back in 2000 who had been obsessed with Carmen. She had dated him for a few days, realized he was a freak show, and told him never to come near her again. During their last conversation, the man snapped. Raped her repeatedly and then beat her so severely she wound up in the hospital. "She was in bed with the covers over her when I arrived at the hospital," Luz recalled. "I thought she was dead. . . . When she lifted the covers off her face, I gasped." Carmen was covered with welts and bruises and blood. Luz couldn't believe it was her sister.

"My God, Titi," she said.

Carmen was quiet. She didn't speak. Eventually she was released from the hospital and a report was filed. Sometime later, the guy—a serial rapist—was arrested and charged with a host of rapes.

III

Living with the unsettled notion that a loved one is out in the world somewhere in trouble is an ugly feeling, the Rodriguez family explained. There's a part of your spirit dormant, lost. In purgatory. Nothing in your life is quite right. You wake up every day thinking this is it, someone is going to come forward with that tip that will lead you to her. You hang on every word from law enforcement. Your heart races whenever the phone rings.

At one point, after Telemundo ran Carmen's photo and a description, Luz got a call from someone in Willimantic,

Connecticut. "There's a woman hanging around here that fits the description of your sister. She doesn't know her name or where she's from."

It was a Laundromat. *Could it be?* Luz wondered. *Maybe Carmen fell and wandered off and had amnesia?* It happened.

"We'll be right out there," Luz said. Then she called Sonia and Kathy, and they all rushed out to Willimantic, about a thirty-minute trip. ("We got there," Kathy said, "and it was like, 'There's nobody here. Yeah, there's a lady here, but we know who she is. . . .'")

"But we received a phone call from here," Kathy asked, "that you had someone fitting the description."

"No one from here called," the woman said.

Hope was all the Rodriguez family had left, and they weren't about to give up. "The thing was," Luz explained, "and it started to bother me as time went on, that no matter where Carmen was, she had always called one of us. Always, always, always. She called. That was in the back of my mind."

59

I

Ned had been a fixture at Kenney's during the spring, summer and early fall of 2001. During the first three weeks of September, he was at the bar nearly every other night: sitting and drinking, playing pool, talking to the other regulars about baseball, politics, and the terrorist attacks. And yet, since the night Carmen had disappeared, no one at the bar had seen or heard from Ned. He had stopped showing up altogether.

By the end of the first week of looking for Carmen, the family was determined that if Carmen was around Hartford, they were going to find her. Twenty-three-year-old Jeffrey Malave grew up in Hartford. He was a "lifelong friend," he later told police, of the Rodriguez family. Malave's best friend, Hector "Cutie" (pronounced "koo-tee") Velez, was Carmen's nephew. Malave also hung around with Carmen's daughter Jackie. On the Wednesday afternoon after Carmen disappeared, Jackie and Cutie explained to Malave that Carmen had vanished the previous Friday night. No one had seen her since. They were worried about her, he explained, and wanted to help any way they could. Everyone felt the Hartford PD was working on the case, but then, what did they have to go on at this point? Just the other day, an officer had called Jackie and confirmed that the last place Carmen had been seen was at Kenney's, not the El Camerio, as Jackie had initially believed. In the interim, Jackie and Miguel, who had been climbing the walls, calling the HPD, combing the neighborhoods around Kenney's, asking locals if they had seen anything, had not stopped searching. Miguel hadn't slept in what seemed like days. He was prostrated with grief and worry, same as Jackie. Miguel had spoken to a bartender at Kenney's who explained she was certain that Carmen had left the bar at about 2:00 A.M. on September 22 with a regular. ("The bartender told us," Jackie said in a statement to police, "the man's name . . . [and that] he left with my mother that night . . . after drinking and dancing with her.")

Jackie explained this to Malave, who couldn't sit idle. He had to do *something*.

So he walked down to Kenney's to see if anyone "knew what might have happened to Carmen." The first person he ran into was "the guy who watches the cars outside [the bar]."

"The last time I saw Carmen," the guy—whom they all called "John the Security Guard"—told Malave, "was the night she left with that guy Ned."

"Ned?" Malave asked.

"Yeah. I saw Carmen get into Ned's car and they drove down Lawrence Street, away from Capitol Avenue."

"How was Carmen?"

"She seemed really drunk. Ned was kind of holding her up as they walked."

"Who's Ned?"

"He's a regular. Here all the time. The bartender knows him. Ask Paula."

Malave found Paula, who knew Carmen and Jackie. "Ned's a regular," she confirmed. "He comes in almost every day."

"Have you seen him lately?"

"Not since Carmen's been gone."

"Thanks," Malave said as he started for the door. But he stopped just before walking out. "Hey, Paula," he said, "give me or Jackie a call the next time you see Ned."

Paula promised she would.

II

Several days later, Paula called Jackie. It was 8:00 P.M. Malave was with Jackie, consoling her. "Ned's here," Paula said.

"He's there?"

"Yeah."

Jackie hung up, immediately called the Hartford PD, and explained Ned was at Kenney's. They needed to get down there at once and talk to him about Carmen, she insisted. If he was the last person with Carmen, he may be able to tell them where she went. Perhaps he'd given her a ride?

By the time Jackie got off the phone with the Hartford PD, Miguel was leading them to Kenney's, hoping, of course, to talk to Ned. Miguel wasn't giving up—especially since he and Jackie had gotten what could be called a substantial lead in hearing that Ned was the last person to be seen with Carmen. An average-size man, Miguel was not someone many people tangled with. He was calm, quite friendly, and not someone to go around looking for trouble. Still, *I'm going to beat his ass,* Miguel thought as he stomped his way toward Kenney's.

Miguel ran into John the Security Guard, whom Malave had spoken to. He asked him about Carmen. "She left with Ned, a white guy. He hasn't been in here since Carmen turned up missing."

Miguel and John were standing by Kenney's front door. Jackie, Cutie, and Malave were standing by the road, waiting for Miguel to finish. As Miguel talked, John spied Ned inside the bar walking toward them. "That's him right there."

"That's him?" Miguel asked.

"Yup."

Trying to be sly, Ned walked up to Miguel and stuck out his hand.

The nerve of this guy.

Miguel refused.

Ned turned and walked back into the bar hurriedly after seeing Jackie, Malave, and Cutie walking toward him. He sensed some hostility.

John walked down the block a ways, heading toward the side of the building, while Miguel and the others stood by the front door and waited. They didn't want to lose sight of Ned. They kind of had him cornered now: whichever door he came out of, someone would be there. It was clear Ned was trying to get away.

"Miguel . . . ," John yelled, "Ned's leaving. He's running down Lawrence Street."

Ned had walked back into the bar and slipped out the side door before anyone saw him.

But Miguel took off running and caught Ned as he was just about to get into his car. "I want to talk to you," Miguel shouted.

"About *what*?"

"You got my wife," Miguel insisted, although "wife" was more of a term of endearment. "I want her back."

"I'm sorry," Ned said, dropping his head.

"Where is she?" Miguel screamed.

"I dropped her off at the gas station on Capitol and Broad."

"Bullcrap! I know you got her." Miguel was ready to pummel Ned.

Ned began to mumble. He seemed disoriented.

Alarmed.

Scared.

As much as Ned had been involved in violence against

women throughout his life, and felt he could wrestle with the best of his peers, he hated confrontation.

"I . . . I . . . I took her to eat at New Britain [Avenue] and Broad Street," Ned said, changing his story.

Jackie and the others arrived at Ned's car, out of breath. "Where's my mom?" Jackie said quite firmly. There was a tickle of scratchiness in her voice: anger mixed with sadness.

Ned put his head down, Jackie later said. Then, in a low voice, he said, "Oh, *that* was *your* mom? I'm sorry." As he said it, however, Ned took off again toward the side entrance of the bar.

"Hey," Miguel shouted.

They ran after him as Malave screamed, "Hey, we just want to *talk* to you."

Ned quickly slipped back into the bar through a side entrance, saying frantically, "There's some people out there that are going to get me."

The owner walked over. "What are you talking about?"

"There's people out there—"

"Who? Who is going to get you?"

The bar owner went for the door and opened it. He saw Jackie and the others running toward the door. Stopping them, he said, "Whoa, what's the problem here?"

Shouts and mumbles. No one made sense.

"Let's go into the bar and sit down and figure this out," the owner said.

"We want him," Malave said, "to call the police and contact the police about Carmen. He seen her."

After a moment, Cutie, Miguel, Jackie, and Malave rushed into the bar, past the owner. When they got inside, Ned was pacing between two pool tables. He looked nervous. More frightened than ever. He had something in his hand he was holding up—waving—in the air. "I'll pay fifty dollars to anyone who takes these people out of here," Ned shouted.

Newly divorced, 44-year-old Mary Ellen Renard was brutally attacked during the summer of 1987 and nearly died from multiple stab wounds. *(Photo courtesy of Mary Ellen Renard)*

Mary Ellen with her daughters. *(Photo courtesy of Mary Ellen Renard)*

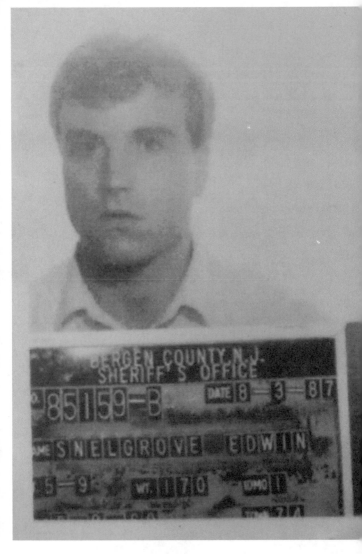

Twenty-six-year-old Rutgers graduate Edwin "Ned" Fales Snelgrove was arrested on August 3, 1987, for attempted murder and aggravated sexual assault. *(Photo courtesy of the Bergen County, New Jersey Sheriff's Office)*

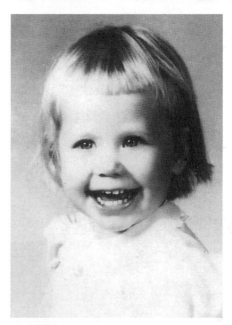

Karen Osmun was a vivacious, happy child. *(Photo courtesy of Barbara Delaney)*

During her senior year in 1982, animal science major Karen Osmun was a popular honors student at Rutgers University. *(Photo courtesy of the Cook College/Rutgers yearbook)*

Karen grew into a beautiful young woman and dreamed of working with animals. *(Photo courtesy of the Cook College/Rutgers yearbook)*

Karen dated Edwin Snelgrove *(below)* while at Rutgers. *(Photo courtesy of the Cook College/Rutgers yearbook)*

Snelgrove, a business science major, was a member of the Alpha Zeta National Honor fraternity at Rutgers. *(Photo courtesy of the Cook College/Rutgers yearbook)*

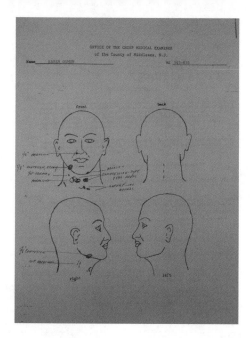

These diagrams by the Office of the Chief Medical Examiner of the County of Middlesex, New Jersey, show the distinctive pattern of knife wounds Karen Osmun sustained during her violent murder. *(Photos courtesy of the Connecticut State Attorney's Office, Hartford, Connecticut)*

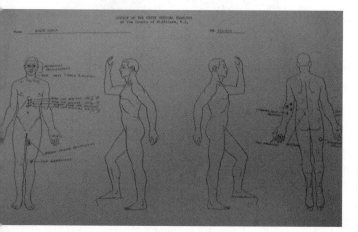

Edwin Snelgrove lived in this modest house in Berlin, Connecticut.
(Photo courtesy of the Connecticut State Attorney's Office, Hartford, Connecticut)

EDWIN F. SNELGROVE JR.
"Ned" "Nedwin" "Snedley"
"Dost thou love life; then do not squander time, for that's the stuff life is made of." — *Benjamin Franklin*
LIKES: Red Sox, will power, Legion Baseball, 75 World Series, A,B,C . . . Z, gaining weight, MacDonald's, "Hey, Big Guy"
DISLIKES: 128 lbs., "ninny", running laps
AMBITION: college
IDOL: Ty Cobb and Edder Klotz

Edwin was known as a "nerdy" honors student in high school.
(Photo courtesy of the Berlin High School yearbook)

Edwin made many friends among his peers during his fours years at Berlin High School. *(Photo courtesy of the Berlin High School yearbook)*

Carmen Rodriguez went to Kenney's Restaurant in Hartford, Connecticut, on September 21, 2001—and was never seen alive again. *(Photo courtesy of the Connecticut State Attorney's Office, Hartford, Connecticut)*

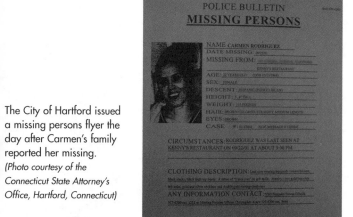

The City of Hartford issued a missing persons flyer the day after Carmen's family reported her missing. *(Photo courtesy of the Connecticut State Attorney's Office, Hartford, Connecticut)*

Carmen was born and raised in downtown Hartford. Since she was a child, she loved to go swimming at the Pope Park swimming pool. *(Photo courtesy of Kathy Perez and the Rodriguez family)*

As a teen, Carmen was an energetic, happy girl, whose smile wasn't easily forgotten. *(Photo courtesy of Kathy Perez and the Rodriguez family)*

In her early twenties, newly married, Carmen began spending time with family in Puerto Rico, where this photo was taken. *(Photo courtesy of Kathy Perez and the Rodriguez family)*

Carmen had nine brothers and sisters. Family members said she was the beacon of the Rodriguez family. *(Photo courtesy of Kathy Perez and the Rodriguez family)*

Family members said Carmen was a ham when it came to posing for photos, as she displayed so beautifully in this photo taken only a few months before she was murdered. *(Photo courtesy of Kathy Perez and the Rodriguez family)*

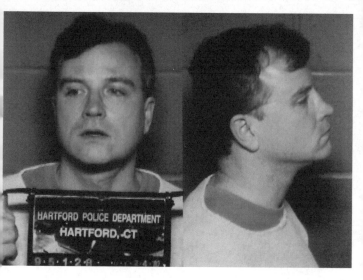

Edwin Fales Snelgrove—the last person seen with Carmen—was arrested on January 24, 2002, three weeks after Carmen's body was discovered. To everyone's surprise, however, Snelgrove was arrested for trying to kidnap a different woman. *(Photo courtesy of the Hartford Police Department)*

Authorities believe Snelgrove used this vehicle to kidnap Carmen Rodriguez and later murder her. *(Photo courtesy of the Connecticut State Attorney's Office, Hartford, Connecticut)*

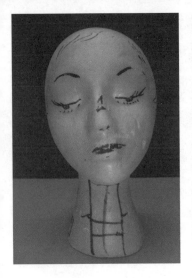

While searching Snelgrove's house, law enforcement uncovered these bizarre Styrofoam heads, which they believe Snelgrove used to practice strangling females and fulfill his sexual fantasies when a live victim wasn't available. *(Author photos)*

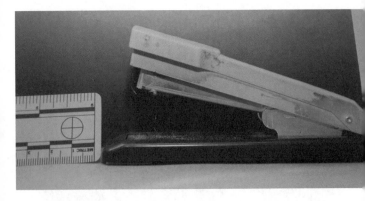

Authorities also found this stapler, which they believe Snelgrove used to staple the garbage bags he put Carmen's body in. Oddly enough, forensic scientists found a pubic hair—not Edwin's or Carmen's—on the stapler. *(Photo courtesy of the Connecticut State Attorney's Office, Hartford, Connecticut)*

We Want Justice

After the Rodriguez family buried Carmen, they made it their mission to see that Snelgrove was brought to justice for her murder. The bottom photo shows a laminated tag the family wore to court every day. *(Photos courtesy of Kathy Perez and the Rodriguez family)*

Many of Carmen Rodriguez's family members got together at her gravesite to celebrate her life on the first Mother's Day without her. *(Photo courtesy of Kathy Perez and the Rodriguez family)*

To this day, a photo of Carmen—with the saying "We will never forget" written in Spanish—hangs in the Rodriguez household in Hartford. From left to right: Kathy Perez (niece); Luz Rodriguez (sister); Rosa Rodriguez (mother); Glendaliz Rodriguez and Sonia Rodriguez (sisters). *(Author photo)*

Panicked, he was sweating, pacing, looking around the bar, hoping someone would take him up on his offer.

According to Jackie, two men "stepped up and blocked us from going into the bar area," where Ned had wandered. "Come on," Jackie said to them, "I need to talk to him," pointing.

The bar owner quickly stepped in between them. This gave Ned a sense of "relief," Malave later explained. The owner wanted to know what was going on.

"We're just trying to ask Ned a few questions," Malave said.

"Ned, sit down over there," the manager explained. "Get him a drink on me," he shouted to the bartender, asking Malave to sit down across from Ned.

Talk it out. No trouble in here, he warned.

Jackie, Cutie, and Miguel stood behind Malave and stared at Ned.

60

I

"Do you know Carmen Rodriguez?" Malave asked Ned as they sat down. Malave sounded unthreatening. Calm. They were looking for Carmen. They were worried about her. They weren't accusing Ned of anything.

Well, maybe they were.

Ned stumbled with his words, appearing not to answer the question. Then he broke into a garbled rant, saying, "The . . . the . . . last time I saw her was the night I gave her a ride home. I . . . drove her up Lawrence to Russ . . . she asked me . . . she . . ." He looked around the bar. He wouldn't look Malave in the eyes. "She asked me for money, twenty dollars, so I told her to get out of my car." According to Ned, when he told Carmen to get out, she asked him to drop her off at her apartment.

Ned looked at Malave. Miguel, Jackie, and Cutie were impatient. Miguel started screaming, so Cutie walked him out of the bar.

"I told her no," Ned said, talking about the point at which Carmen asked him for money. "I told her to get out of my car 'now,'" adding that after Carmen asked him for money, he took a hard left on Russ Street and stopped on the corner of

Broad, about one block away from a Shell gas station. Once there, he told her to "get out."

Police later found this to be suspicious: Carmen lived in the opposite direction, several blocks away. Additionally, Ned had said only moments prior to this that he had taken Carmen to eat at a diner and left her there.

Which was it? Malave was confused. "Do you know where Carmen lives?" he asked.

Ned shook his head no. Then, "She told me she did not want to go home."

At first, Ned had said Carmen asked him for a ride home, but now he was saying she didn't want to go home. Besides, as Ned spoke, Malave noticed his hands: he was shaking like an alcoholic, sweating more and more as the conversation continued.

Jackie, too, was visibly upset. She wouldn't say much.

"I'm sorry Carmen disappeared," Ned said, looking at Jackie, "I'm sorry."

"Give me your telephone number so the detective who's in charge can call you."

Ned took a napkin and wrote a number on it. He slid it across the table toward Malave. "Call Nick (the bar owner) if you need anything more," he said. "He can get hold of me."

Jackie, Malave, and Cutie left.

When Jackie got home, she called one of the detectives and told him what had happened. The following day, the detective called back and told her that the number Ned gave to the bar owner was "not a working number . . . but the bartender knew where Ned works," the detective explained, "which will help us find him."

II

It was clear to members of the Hartford PD that the disappearance of Carmen Rodriguez was more than an adult taking

off and not telling anyone where she had gone. Add Ned Snelgrove into the mix, with his track record of assaulting and
murdering women, and the seeds of a more sinister plot
seemed to emerge. Thus, in light of the new revelation that
Ned was admittedly the last person to see Carmen, a detective
was brought into the case. Luisa St. Pierre was a seasoned cop
with the HPD and had strong ties in the Hispanic community.
She had seen the missing persons file on Carmen and asked
around, but she wasn't able to come up with anything. At the
time Carmen's case crossed paths with St. Pierre, she and several colleagues had been working on an ongoing serial killer
investigation known as the "Asylum Hill Killer." The Asylum
Hill neighborhood, where the murders had been occurring,
was a half mile—maybe ten city blocks—from Kenney's.
More than a dozen prostitutes had been savagely beaten about
the face and body, strangled, and left naked and unrecognizable in different areas of the Asylum Hill section of the city.
All the victims had been placed—it seemed strategically—
inside a small neighborhood. They were brutally savage
crimes.

As St. Pierre began investigating Carmen's disappearance,
the questions in front of her became: Had the "Asylum Hill
Killer" snatched Carmen and, like all of his victims, dumped
her body in an abandoned building, warehouse, alleyway, or
parking lot somewhere? What's more, was Ned the "Asylum
Hill Killer"?

But then the questions turned into: If Carmen was part of
the Asylum victim pool, where was she? All of the Asylum
victims had been left out in the open, their bodies riddled
with the signature marks of his vicious rape and murder tech-
niques. The killer's DNA had been left on many of the victims. To St. Pierre, maybe the Rodriguez missing persons
case was going to finally lead the Hartford PD to catch the
most notorious serial killer the city had ever seen.

III

For most of her adult life, Luisa St. Pierre lived in East Hartford, a small blue-collar city just across the river from the Hartford PD. When St. Pierre took a look at Ned and studied his background in New Jersey, she found it interesting that he had chosen Carmen as his next victim—if, indeed, Ned had had something to do with her disappearance. "Those two victims in New Jersey," St. Pierre told me, reflecting back on Mary Ellen Renard and Karen Osmun, "were professional, working women. Whereas Carmen was a lost soul."

To St. Pierre, there wasn't a connection. The pattern didn't match.

Part of it was that Carmen, although not a prostitute, fit into the MO of the "Asylum Hill Killer," more than Ned's, and could have certainly been confused to be a prostitute by the "Asylum Hill Killer" because of the women she hung around with at times. Of course, St. Pierre had no idea at this point that Ned had spent ten years in prison studying Ted Bundy's behavior, and that Carmen fit into Bundy's choice of "vulnerable" potential victims.

Indeed, Ned had gone from a professional-looking Hewlett-Packard salesman in the 1980s to an ex-con with a massive tumor growth on the side of his neck. In some respects, he fit in with the crowd that hung in the neighborhood around Kenney's: men and women beaten down by the system, tired and poor, living day to day, hand to mouth.

Although he'd never admit it, Ned might have been acting under the pretense that he was now fashioning himself after Bundy, but instead, without realizing it, he had become one of the crowd he had tried to infiltrate.

Save for that one day when Jackie, Cutie, Miguel, and Malave ran into Ned at Kenney's, Ned had stayed clear of the place. If not because he was being suspected of having had something to do with Carmen's disappearance, he was terrified that he was going to be beaten by Miguel if he ever showed his face in the bar again.

IV

By the first week of October, St. Pierre and Detective Harry Garcia, her partner, spoke to a few people at Kenney's and figured out that Ned worked for American Frozen Foods, located in Stratford, Connecticut, an hour's drive south of Hartford, and was basically running American's satellite office in Wethersfield, a town in between Hartford and Berlin. There was still no word from Carmen. Although her body hadn't been found, her disappearance was now an open investigation, a possible homicide.

During the afternoon of October 16, things got interesting for Garcia and St. Pierre. Garcia received a call in the missing persons unit from a guy named Ned, a nervous-sounding man who would not reveal his last name (as if they didn't know who he was): "I'm aware that the police are looking to speak to me about a missing person, Carmen Rodriguez," Ned said. He sounded timid, but also curious. Ned wanted to know what the Hartford PD had on him, or how far along in the investigation they were. Garcia could tell the only reason Ned had called was to fish for information.

"We do want to talk to you," Garcia said.

"What can I do?"

"You can come down here, for one."

They made arrangements for Ned to show up at the Hartford PD to speak with Garcia on October 19, three days later. Ned said he'd be there.

61

I

Ned was forty-one years old—and once again the cops were on his back. After talking to Garcia, Ned sat down in his basement bedroom and decided that he had no future. Being on the road, visiting strangers' houses, Ned had been in some of Connecticut's most expensive homes. He'd pull into the driveway and sit for a moment, staring at mothers and daughters, sons and fathers, swing sets and pools, two cars and a dog and a white picket fence, and hated thinking that none of it would ever be his. He considered himself a huge disappointment to his parents, or "best friends." The six-figure incomes he saw on credit applications his clients filled out turned his stomach. There were people ten years younger than him, he wrote to his parents that October night, living their lives in style and class: this *ate* at him.

Although Ned wasn't an Ivy Leaguer, here he was, a Rutgers grad, making 30K a year, if he was lucky. He lived in the basement of his parents' home. He drove a secondhand car. Dressed in what felt like Goodwill clothing. And felt as though he'd be living at Mom and Dad's in this same set of circumstances for another twenty years. In fact, he wrote, he never saw himself having a *decent career . . . an apartment of [his] own, or a girlfriend.* Never.

Ned saw a sad life for himself. What a disappointment he was to his family. He could never show himself in New Jersey to his old friends. He was a disgrace. It depressed him when he thought about it. Just getting up in the morning, he insisted, and having to struggle through another day was a chore. He saw very little point in living anymore. What for? He had a tough time showing his emotions to anyone besides his parents.

Sitting in his basement room on that Friday night in October, Ned decided to lay it all out in a letter to his parents. They were sleeping upstairs. He was at his desk writing. The television was on in the background, flickering. Pulsating. He paid no attention to it. He had other things on his mind. More important things. Life or death? He had a choice. He could end it right now.

A rope and a rafter.

A razor blade and a bathtub.

A glass of water and a bottle of pills.

The road to death didn't matter. He just needed to get on it and go.

In the letter, Ned said he loved "both" parents. He wrote he *was sorry to do this to you.* Looking at it optimistically, however, he suggested that it might turn out to be the best thing for everyone: *This is the last time I can hurt you or disgrace the family.*

What did it matter? The family hadn't been proud of him, he felt, since his Rutgers years. *And* that *bothers me.* He hated dragging his family through his troubles. They were *his* problems, he insisted. *It's best if I go away . . . ,* he wrote. He couldn't bear the thought, he explained, of being in the house if one of them had died before him. The pain would be too much. If only he could "go" before them.

End it now.

Take the coward's way out.

As far as going through with it, Ned wrote he wasn't *afraid to die*. Eventually it *would happen to everybody*. On top of that, he wrote, he didn't believe in hell, *just sleep*. Anyway, he knew God would *forgive even me* for the life he had lived and the pain he had caused so many. He apologized to his mother first for not playing the piano for her since returning home from prison. She used to like that: Ned sitting at the piano, corduroy jacket, polyester bell-bottom slacks, belting out tunes into the late hours of the night, while she sat nearby drinking tea, tapping her foot, mouthing the words.

For Dad, Ned said he was sorry for playing only one game of golf with him since returning. He knew this disappointed his father.

If it was a suicide note—which it surely seemed to be— Ned didn't have the guts to go through with it on this night. Because instead of putting the barrel of a .45 in his mouth, or slitting his own throat, he went to bed. What seemed odd later was that not once did Ned claim to be innocent of the latest accusations made against him. Quite to the contrary, he seemed to be depressed that he had done it again.

II

Ned's parents went to Applebee's on October 13, 2001, the following night, while he stayed home, stewing, contemplating once again the idea of taking his life. It was a Saturday night. Ned had no date. Never did. Here he was again at home, while his peers and friends were out and about going through their lives with wives and kids. But not Ned. When he wanted companionship, he paid for it. He was a john. A frequent one at that. He struggled with the emotions that came with purchasing prostitutes. For him, it wasn't about the sex or even power; it was more about talking to someone, having a woman there to listen.

Again feeling as if suicide was the answer, Ned paced in his room. He had heard his parents leave the house. He had said good-bye, too. Urged them to enjoy their dinner.

The *real reason,* he wrote, that he could *never* go out to eat in public with anyone ever again, let alone Mom and Dad, was because he knew he could *never hold it together* long enough to get through the night. He'd *fall apart.*

He said it was not feeling comfortable enough to open up to his parents—especially his dad. There were times, Ned explained, when he'd sit in the kitchen across from his father at breakfast or dinner, and the two of them would be at the table with nothing but silence between them. Eating wasn't a social event; it was a chore. Something Ned and his dad had to do.

Sit. Eat. Be quiet.

The not-to-be-discussed elephant wasn't in the Snelgrove living room—it was in every part of the house, wherever Ned and his parents were.

Before bed that night, Ned sat down again and wrote to his mom and dad. A short suicide note was turning into a series of journallike entries, each dated and timed. Ned asked his father if he ever noticed how Ned could never look him in the eyes when they were together. He wondered if his dad had ever really contemplated the reason why. Part of it, Ned explained, was that he felt like a disappointment to them. But it also had to do with guilt and disassociation: Ned felt he had never been able to "tell" his dad "what" he was thinking, or how he felt, because he knew his dad would never understand.

But again, as the night wore on, Ned fell asleep instead of completing a job, one could say, he had started nearly two decades ago when he tried to kill himself after murdering Karen Osmun.

III

Ned woke up late on October 15. He sat in bed for a while, thinking.

Today is the day.

His parents were upstairs, either sitting at the kitchen table reading the morning paper, or lounging around in the living room doing crossword puzzles, watching television. They loved to bury their minds deep into the world of questions and letters. Perhaps it made everything else go away.

It had been a week since Ned had made the decision to kill himself. At 11:00 A.M., he got out of bed and sat down at his desk. By 11:20, he was writing.

He explained that he had "kept calm" because he had made the decision to go through with it. Doing it had given him back a sense of control over his life. He had spent the past several days in bed, covers over his face, curtains on the little box basement windows drawn so what little sun that managed to sneak into the basement was shaded. He liked it that way: dark. He felt he was ready to "go" now. Eternal sleep sounded like a "good idea" to him.

Ned told his parents that if they were to sit down and talk about it as a whole, his legacy could be boiled down to a series of what-ifs and could have beens. And next, for the first time in what had turned into a three-day suicide manifesto, Ned wrote there was a *missing persons case in Hartford* that would be causing him more problems in the coming months and years. He warned his parents that the Hartford PD would *be in touch sooner or later.* He was *supposedly*—a fact that had been indisputably proven by the time he wrote the note— *one of the last people to have seen Carmen something-or-other*—he knew darn well what her last name was—on the night she disappeared. He then launched into details that could arguably be viewed as some sort of alibi he was trying to set in place for himself, making his parents aware of those "facts" he wanted them to know. *I gave her a ride from Kenney's . . . to the Shell Station two blocks from Capitol Avenue,* he mentioned. Carmen, Ned further explained, referring to her as *this girl,* had *reportedly . . . not been seen since.*

He didn't want to *go through this* again, he wrote, no doubt referring to what had happened in New Jersey. Even worse, he didn't want to have to see his parents go through it all again. *It's best,* he wrote, that *I just end it now.* He was *sorry* for leaving the family *holding the bag. . . . I have no answers for the police.*

Ending the letter, he said he appreciated *all the help* his parents had given him since his release from prison. *I do love you both. . . .* And then he took a handful of pills and, comfortably numb, lay down and went to sleep.

62

I

Ed Bouchard had worked for American Frozen Foods for the past six years. He was the regional sales director, working out of an office in Danbury, Connecticut. Besides its main corporate office in Stratford, American had satellite offices in Danbury, Connecticut; Orlando, Florida; Central New Jersey, and Wethersfield, Connecticut, where Ned worked. The Wethersfield office had fallen on hard times and was on the verge of being closed. Because American had leased the building for the year, Bouchard allowed Ned to use the office, giving him a key and total access. "He was one of the better reps," Bouchard said later. "He was willing to travel farther than most reps. And his schedule was a lot more flexible than most reps. So he got more than his share of appointments for those attributes."

All of American's sales reps submitted their billing on a regular basis. They'd put a package together weekly and either mail it into the main office in Stratford, where Bouchard would pick it up, or drop it off at Bouchard's office in Danbury. During the third week of October, Ned had called in sick several days in a row. This was out of the norm for Ned.

He was a loyal employee who took very little time off. Near the end of the week, on or about October 15, Bouchard received Ned's sales report, as he normally did, but something was different about the package. Ned had included what Bouchard interpreted, he later said, as a suicide note. Ned asked him to "make sure all" of his "future" payments for sales got sent to his father. *Please try,* he begged Bouchard, *my parents could use* the money.

The letter shocked Bouchard. It seemed desperate and needy. He called Ned's house to see what was going on.

"Is Ned home?" Bouchard asked Mr. Snelgrove.

"Yeah, he's sleeping." It was almost noon.

"Sleeping?" Bouchard sounded stunned and explained the letter. "You better go check on him."

Mr. Snelgrove went downstairs and returned a few moments later, saying, "I couldn't wake him."

"Get him up. . . . It's important that you wake him up. I'll call you back."

Bouchard waited.

Then called back.

No answer.

He tried again over the next few hours and still couldn't get hold of anyone.

II

The day Ned was supposed to meet Detective Harry Garcia at the Hartford PD came and went. Garcia waited, but Ned failed to show up or call. St. Pierre and Garcia decided it was time to visit American Frozen Foods and begin looking into Ned's professional background to see what they could learn about his movements during the past few months. Maybe get a bead on what he had done in the weeks before and after Carmen went missing. Ned himself seemed to be extremely interested in the investigation—suffice it to say he had called the HPD and told Garcia he would be in to answer some questions. Kenney's patrons were reporting Ned had asked a lot of strange questions after cops started poking around the bar. From experience, curiosity like that told St. Pierre and Garcia that Ned knew something, was maybe hiding something, and wanted to know if the cops had anything on him. Otherwise, why would he even care?

Garcia and St. Pierre took the long drive down to American Frozen Foods in Danbury and hooked up with Bouchard, who explained that Ned was a good employee, who lived in Berlin, about twenty minutes outside Hartford. He'd been working for American for two years. "Hard worker," Bouchard added. "He keeps very detailed appointment books."

"What about his past?"

"The owner," Bouchard explained, "wanted to give Ned a chance after he got out of prison. Ned was a model employee. He had no friends, though, like he was a loner. He complained all the time about not having a girlfriend. He would often speak of 'getting laid.' But he had no sex life. Everyone knew it. But he was obsessed with sex."

Garcia asked if the company knew about Ned's background in New Jersey.

"Yes, we do," he said, explaining what had happened with Ned over the past few days. "Ned called and said he'd send any orders he had taken to the main office. He told me not to call him back until later the next day because he'd had a late night at the casino [in Ledyard, Connecticut, near the Rhode Island border]." But when Bouchard got that package in the mail with the alleged suicide note, he said he called.

St. Pierre was curious. "What happened?"

"His father couldn't wake him up," Bouchard said.

"Did you ever talk to them?" St. Pierre asked.

Bouchard said he finally got through later that night. He said Ned's mother told him what happened: "Ned took an overdose of pills."

But he lived. He was in the hospital.

Garcia and St. Pierre knew from reading Ned's prior record in New Jersey that when he had been accused of killing Karen Osmun in 1983 (before he admitted to it four years later), he had swallowed a bottle of pills and downed a bottle of iodine when cops started asking questions. It seemed whenever Ned Snelgrove got himself into a jam and police put a bit of pressure on him, he curled up into a ball and tried taking a final exit, and yet he couldn't seem to complete the job. Odd that a man who could kill a woman with a knife and attack another—nearly killing her, too—couldn't take his own life.

Bouchard offered to call Ned's mother. "I'll see what I can find out."

"Sure," Garcia said.

Bouchard got Mrs. Snelgrove on the phone. Norma said the hospital was moving Ned to the psychiatric ward any day. Beyond that, she didn't know much else.

St. Pierre and Garcia knew once Ned was moved into the psych ward, he'd be off-limits. They had to get over there immediately.

"What did Ned have for appointments on September twenty-second?" Garcia asked.

"Let me see," Bouchard said, taking out Ned's book. "He had only one appointment that day. Cromwell. One o'clock."

Leaving American Frozen Foods, Garcia and St. Pierre headed to New Britain General Hospital.

III

Ned looked fine, lying in bed, machines buzzing and beeping around him. The pills he had swallowed hadn't done much. St. Pierre noticed the tremendous growth on the side of his neck she had heard so much about over the course of talking to patrons at Kenney's. It was unmistakable; it was like he had swallowed a cantaloupe and had gotten it lodged on the side of his neck.

"I'm getting it removed while I'm here," Ned said of the growth.

St. Pierre explained why she and Garcia were there. Did Ned know Carmen Rodriguez? Had he seen her since she was reported missing? Why had he called the Hartford PD the other day and made an appointment, only to break it? Why had he tried to commit suicide again after the police put a bit of pressure on him?

Ned answered no to all of St. Pierre's initial questions, adding that he had a tendency for depression, was prone to it, and when he felt strained, he considered death to be his only option to take away the pain of being accused of something he *didn't* do.

Right, St. Pierre thought, asking, "You saw Carmen in the bar that night?"

"Yeah," he said, "I saw her. I played a great deal of pool that night. I danced with her a few times."

"You left together?"

"Well, yes. When I explained that I was leaving, she asked me for a ride home."

"Where'd you take her?"

"When we got into the car, she asked me for money. . . . She told me about her new boyfriend."

"That's it?"

"I was upset that she had asked me for money. I kicked her out of my car on the corner of Capitol Avenue and Broad Street at the Shell station."

St. Pierre could sense something odd about Ned. "As smart as he claimed to be, he was fairly stupid," she said later. "He had set up a pattern of behavior with these suicides, which made us that much more suspicious." It was the same scenario—just nearly twenty years later.

"What else can you tell us about that night?"

"Well," Ned said, "I drove her to that gas station and dropped her off."

Which was it? thought St. Pierre. *Did you drop her off at home or the gas station?* Ned had said she asked him for a ride home.

"They are talking about putting me in the psychiatric ward here," Ned said.

After Ned refused to say anything more about that night, St. Pierre and Garcia left, with a promise to return.

63

I

A few days after that first interview with Ned in the hospital, St. Pierre went back with another colleague, Detective Jerry Bilbo. They wanted to find out if Ned had been moved to the psych ward.

The security guard looked it up and said, "No, in fact, he's in the same room."

"Will you speak to us?" St. Pierre asked after entering Ned's room moments later.

"Sure," he said. "Come in."

Ned was eating lunch. He seemed a bit more relaxed. St. Pierre wanted to focus on the "route" Ned had taken when he left Kenney's.

"South on Lawrence Street," Ned said, wiping his mouth with a napkin, "then left (east) on Russ, left (north) again on Broad, where I pushed her out of the car at the corner of Capitol and Broad Streets."

Ned's history came up. "Tell me about your girlfriend in New Jersey?" St. Pierre asked. "What's her name?"

Ned answered immediately, St. Pierre recorded in her report of the conversation. "Karen Osmun. She was killed in

New Brunswick. . . . I served time in jail for Karen's homicide and the rape and assault of another girl." ("His demeanor was very calm," St. Pierre remembered.) It was odd he never said, "I killed her." But instead said, "She was killed."

"Will you sign a consent form allowing us to search your car?"

"Sure," Ned volunteered. (*He appeared very matter-of-fact about the killing,* St. Pierre wrote in her report. That seemed strange to her. She felt the fact that Ned claimed Carmen had asked for a ride home was suspect in and of itself, telling me, "If you're familiar with that area, who in the hell would want a ride for a half a block? It just didn't make any sense to us. On top of that, where Ned said he dropped her off was in the opposite direction of her apartment.")

St. Pierre knew Ned was lying. He was cocky, willing to dish out these stories of that night and allow them to search his car without batting an eye. ("I kept telling myself as he spoke to us," St. Pierre told me, "go ahead, keep on talking, keep on lying. You see, lies are just as good as the truth when you're investigating someone.")

As St. Pierre and Garcia were walking out of Ned's room with a signed consent form to search his car, Ned stopped St. Pierre, saying, "Hey."

"Yeah?" She turned.

"I didn't kill Carmen Rodriguez. I can prove where I was that night."

"Oh, you can," she said, walking back toward him. "How is that?"

"I have all of my mileage receipts from my job. My gas receipts."

If there was one thing about Ned Snelgrove, when it came to keeping mileage records and gas receipts for his job as a traveling salesman, he took on the task as if his life depended on it. He was methodical about keeping records. He had stacks of notebooks at home with all of his mileage written out in chronological order.

"Where are they?" St. Pierre asked.

"I can give it to you," Ned said. He was smiling. It was as if he had pulled one over on everyone. (He was almost gloating, St. Pierre later added.)

"Where can I get it?"

"My dad will give it to you—he made copies. I've already called him."

"OK, then, we'll go and get them."

Several thoughts occurred to St. Pierre as she left the hospital. Driving back to her office, she couldn't help but think, *This guy is either really stupid or* really *smart.* Then again, why would he ring that mileage bell if it didn't mean anything? He wanted the Hartford PD to focus on his mileage. Why would he divulge such information if it wasn't important? St. Pierre was leaving when he had summoned her back into the room. He was offering evidence. Undeniably, she now knew, an important piece of the puzzle.

64

I

Ed Bouchard called Ned in the hospital the day after St. Pierre and Garcia interviewed him. Bouchard had seen the newspapers. He knew of Ned's prior arrest record. He wanted to know what was going on. "How are you? Listen, there were two detectives here—they came to see me about you."

Ned sounded groggy. "Yes, I know," he said. "They were already here."

"What about the girl, Ned? Do you know anything about her?"

Ned paused. "I don't even *know* her," he said. "She's just some girl I gave a ride to."

II

St. Pierre understood that catching killers was a science. There was good luck and persistent gumshoe police work involved as you tracked down new leads and followed up on old ones; but putting away a murderer required essentially patience and tenacity. She was sure Ned had had something to do with Carmen's disappearance. She knew the mileage Ned had mentioned while in the hospital played into that crime somehow, but as ASA David Zagaja later explained, "We were all scratching our heads as to what it meant. The significance of the mileage receipts was that Ned had *offered* them to us. Why was he doing this? It's a troubling clue to us. It tells us that he used his car in some way to take her, deposit her . . . but we don't have any answers."

III

Carmen's family was painfully going through the process of accepting the fact that Carmen was likely never coming home. As much as they didn't want to admit Carmen was dead, there was nothing to convince them otherwise. And with Ned being so evasive, if not cocky and playing games with police, it only made matters worse. Jackie had her baby and slipped into a world of numbing her feelings with alcohol. It was hard for the family to keep track of her anymore. Luz had taken Jackie's child by this point.

As ASA, David Zagaja had worked with St. Pierre on too many homicides to recall. On any given week, Zagaja was up to his neck in violent crimes of all sorts. Yet, having St. Pierre on the job was comforting: "Luisa," Zagaja later said, "is pretty determined. When she locks her focus on something, she follows it."

When St. Pierre got back to her office after speaking with Ned, she called Zagaja, who, after graduating from the University of Connecticut School of Law, had studied Spanish at the University of Valencia, in Spain. If a case was going to be built against Ned, Zagaja would have to get involved. Search warrants were going to have to be written up and signed. In addition, St. Pierre generally ran her theories by Zagaja. They were good friends, colleagues, and supported each other. If Luisa's instinct was wrong, Zagaja wasn't afraid to let her know she was wasting her time.

"This guy killed this girl," St. Pierre came right out and told Zagaja during that first call. She just "had a feeling," she later said.

When St. Pierre heard from Ned's boss at American Frozen Foods that he had killed a female in New Jersey, and then Ned himself admitted to it—seemingly without equivocation—St. Pierre considered the chances to be almost nil that Ned had simply dropped Carmen off at a gas station and she disappeared into thin air. "When we spoke to his boss and he told us, and then Ned said the same thing," St. Pierre said, "I thought, 'Oh, Jesus, this guy is dangerous, he did it.'"

For Zagaja, all he would later say was "Ned's prior history was a clue," adding, with a laugh, "Let's leave it at that."

As St. Pierre spoke to Zagaja, Ned's entire arrest record was just coming off the wire. When they went through it, they couldn't believe, number one, that he was out of prison, and, number two, that he had simply turned his violent behavior off like a switch. Here was a third female in Ned's life who was victimized—a third female, in fact, he had met at a bar or in some social setting. He had been out of prison for two years. It wasn't, *Did he grab Carmen and do something with her?* It became, *How many more were there?*

After reviewing Ned's history, learning of the eleven-page letter he wrote to the judge upon his sentencing in 1988, whereby Ned had described killing Karen Osmun in graphic detail, Zagaja made the determination that probable cause existed. It was time to draft up a search warrant for Ned's car—and maybe even his home.

65

I

Ned and his parents lived in a modest cape—white with dark green shutters—in a rural neighborhood near East Berlin, right off Route 372 and Route 15, which is more commonly known as the Berlin Turnpike. It's a rather busy four-lane roadway, dotted with strip malls, chain restaurants, fuel stations, strip joints, and seedy motels with rooms that rent by the hour, day, week, or month. The area where Ned grew up and now lived, in the basement of the house his parents had purchased a half century ago, was twenty minutes from New Haven and the same from Hartford. The house next door had been abandoned in lieu of being sold. The grass was knee-high and the house looked vacant and lonely. At about 2:00 P.M., on October 22, 2001, Luisa St. Pierre and Jerry Bilbo drove to the Berlin Police Department (BPD) before heading over to the Snelgroves'. Pulling up to Savage Hill Road with that Berlin PD escort sometime later, Luisa saw an older man in the front yard raking leaves. "Must be Snelgrove's father," she said to Bilbo.

Edwin Snelgrove Sr. stopped what he was doing and watched the BPD cruiser pull into his driveway with an unmarked cruiser behind it. He didn't seem too surprised.

After brief introductions, St. Pierre said, "We'd like to look inside your son's car."

"Come with me," Mr. Snelgrove said.

The garage was set back a bit from the house at the end of the driveway. Snelgrove reached down and lifted up the garage door. Then he unlocked the door to Ned's car, a 1998 tan Ford Escort. As St. Pierre, Bilbo, and the Crime Scene Unit (CSU), which had just arrived, began going through Ned's car, his father went into the house and came back out with *an itemized list recording of all [Ned's] appointments and mileage dated from Saturday, August 11, 2001, to Tuesday, October 16, 2001,* St. Pierre later reported. Ned had promised St. Pierre that his father would provide the documents, and here they were. Right on cue.

"Thanks," she said.

What proved interesting to St. Pierre and the other detectives, who had since arrived on scene, was that there were several bundles of rope on the wall, hanging on hooks, yet there was one bundle missing. Inside Ned's car were several interesting pieces of evidence. Among them, what St. Pierre described as *vegetable matter (leaves & seeds),* a set of partial latent prints on the passenger's side of the vehicle from the window, several "stain swabbings" taken from various blotches on the inside of the vehicle, one leaf in the trunk, hair fibers, along with envelopes full of trace evidence that crime scene investigators had sucked up with a vacuum.

II

Andrea Collins (pseudonym) worked as a bartender at Kenney's on Tuesdays, Wednesdays, and Fridays. She was familiar with Ned, who would sit at the bar by himself, she said, and drink Moosehead beer. On several occasions, Collins explained, she noticed how Ned sat in a booth with Carmen, talking. "He would always buy her drinks."

It was about the first week of October, Collins said, when she was working one night and a call came into the bar. Looking back, she said that it seemed "strange."

"It's for you," the bar back said.

"Hello?" Collins answered.

"It's Ned."

"Who?" Collins didn't recognize the name right away.

"Ned—"

"Oh . . . yeah?"

"I heard you spoke to the police," Ned said.

Collins told detectives what everyone else in the bar had: Ned left with Carmen on September 21, or early September 22, and had been dancing with her.

"Yes," she said, "I did."

"You spoke to them about 'the missing girl.'" Another patron, Ned said, had informed him that Collins had talked to the police.

"I did." Collins didn't see the big deal in talking to the police. "Why?"

"I just gave her a ride to Capitol Avenue and Broad."

"OK . . ." *And your point?*

"I'm calling right now"—Ned felt the urge to divulge—"from Rhode Island." It was odd, thought Collins, that he would say where he was, as if she cared.

"I'm busy, Ned, I have to go."

Similar stories came in as detectives continued interviewing Kenney's employees and patrons. Paula Figueroa worked at Kenney's and remembered Ned as the guy who ordered tuna steak salad with extra Russian dressing. "He usually dressed like . . . he had just left work . . . and sat at the bar and made small talk with me."

When she was interviewed by police sometime after Carmen's disappearance, Paula said there was "something about Ned that was really weird—he gave me the chills. He was always polite, but would repeatedly ask me out. He even asked me if I would go away with him. I always refused politely."

III

While all of the forensic evidence was processed—it would take weeks—the search for Carmen continued. As November approached, there was still no word from Carmen. Detectives investigating her disappearance expected the worst, hoped for the best. As Christmas neared, Detective St. Pierre and her colleagues heard that none of the forensic evidence collected in Ned's car yielded any indication that he was involved in Carmen's disappearance. Not one hair matched Carmen's DNA profile—and not one stain was considered suspicious.

Investigators were baffled. Yet, as Christmas and the new year came and went, the investigation was about to take a major turn.

66

I

At about one o'clock in the afternoon, on Sunday, January 6, 2002, thirty-six-year-old Peter Mareck was walking on Grassy Pond Road, a dirt and gravel connector running along his property line. Mareck lived on the corner of Grassy Pond and Route 138 (Rockville Road), in Hopkinton, Rhode Island, a mile or so over the Connecticut border. On certain days, he'd grab his trusty pole with the spike at the end of it, a few trash barrels, and troll the area, picking up the garbage that young kids and litterbugs so rudely dirtied the beautiful landscape with. Mareck hated seeing the trash along the roadside. It took away from the splendor of the pond across the street on Route 138 and the vast wooded area in back of his home.

Picking up other people's garbage came with its share of surprises. On any given day, there was no telling what Mareck would find. "The most unusual thing I came across—until that day in January—was a bag of flounder skeletons," Mareck said later.

Finding the bag, he left it alone and called someone to have a look. It was the large fish vertebrae that piqued his interest.

During the years he has dedicated to picking the garbage, Mareck knew there was nothing people didn't toss out their windows. "I found a dog once," he said. "Someone had put a dog in a bag and just threw it out their car window." That kind of obvious disregard for life disgusted him.

Whenever Mareck found something it was generally on Route 138, which is a fairly busy roadway, being a two-lane state highway. Grassy Pond was more of a byline to another dirt and gravel road and a few private homes out in the woods. As Mareck was walking along Grassy Pond that afternoon, about two-tenths of a mile from Route 138, heading toward Kenney Hill Road, a dirt path that actually led to Hopkinton police chief John Scuncio's home, he noticed a large garbage bag off to the side, approximately three meters into the woods. It was the middle of winter. The foliage on the trees and brush was stripped bare, which made it easy for Mareck to see deep into the woods. He had seen garbage bags this size before. But this one was different. There was something about it. The shape. The way it was sealed up.

The area was known to be a common region of the town for poachers to flash a light in a deer's eyes at night and take a potshot. Some poachers killed the deer, took the meat, and then left the guts and rotting carcasses there in the woods, on the road, or placed them in bags and tossed them as deep as they could into the woods. With this in mind, Mareck walked a bit closer to the bag. Poking at it with his stick, he wanted to see what was inside. As the bag tore open, a putrid smell as potent as a Dumpster in the sun wafted up at him. Unlike the common smell of garbage, however, this aroma was vile and rancid.

And very unfamiliar.

Reaching deeper into the bag with his stick, Mareck opened it so he could see what was inside. *A vertebra? A spine?* he told himself. "It was large," Mareck said later. "It looked human."

He was well aware of what the anatomy of an animal looked like, not to mention large fish. But this spine was a bit larger than Mareck had ever seen. "It didn't look like an animal's." So he ripped the bag open some more. *Clothesline . . . ?*

The clothesline had been wrapped around the bones several times and tied into knots. Mareck stood and thought about it: *This is a little weird. The only two things that would be distinctive are the skull and the pelvic bone.* So he tore at the bag toward the end where he assumed a head would be— and there it was: a human skull. ("It had long hair on it." And maggots, like thousands of Tic Tacs, slithering and sliding throughout.)

Mareck knelt down and went in for a closer look. "The entire torso was decomposed," he said later. "But I could make out the skull. I could see the little cracks and plates that make up a human head."

Once Mareck saw the skull, he lifted the bag from the opposite end and saw the hipbone. He then knew for certain it was a person—a woman.

A flood of emotion washed over Mareck as he stood there. He had lost his sister in 1988. She was one of 243 passengers aboard Pan Am Flight 103, which exploded over Lockerbie, Scotland, on December 21, killing all passengers and sixteen crew members, as well as eleven people on the ground. A total of 270 people perished that day. That pain had never left Mareck. Something like this, seeing a dead body in the woods, all wrapped up in a bag, brought it all back. Standing over the bag, Mareck said aloud, "Sit tight . . . stay right there, you're found now. I know what to do. I know somebody's looking for you." He had no idea why he said it. But he knew there was a family out there somewhere worried sick about the person in the bag. They had lost sleep. Wondered what had happened to this person. All sorts of scenarios were running through their minds. Mareck was familiar with these same feelings. It had been a week or more before his sister was identified, which made the agony of knowing—but not *truly* knowing—even more traumatic. As he stood there over the bag, it hurt him to know that another family was going through the same pain.

Standing up, Mareck told himself, *I need to call someone.* He didn't want to disturb (any more than he already had) what was now a crime scene. So Mareck took off, running. Heading for Kenney Hill Road. His intention was to make it to the police chief's house, whom he had known for years, and tell him. In fact, Mareck had just seen the chief. They'd chitchatted for about ten minutes.

On foot, the chief's house was a haul. So Mareck turned around, ran back by the bag of remains, and headed for his own home. Once there, "John," Mareck said over the phone, out of breath, "I think I found a body—"

"Relax," said the chief. "You sure it's not deer remains or something?"

"That's why I'm calling. I don't want to make a big deal out of nothing. I know you're home. So, I figured, why not. You can take a ride down and check it out for me."

"I'll meet you out there," the chief said.

II

Lieutenant Mike Gilman arrived on scene first. Chief Scuncio used his cell phone to call it in. He advised everyone, at this point, to communicate via cell phone so as not to alert the local press. It was important to make sure it was a human body before news spread.

Scuncio explained to Gilman what Mareck had told him. Then he showed him the bag. Gilman taped off the area and made a few calls, while Chief Scuncio contacted several members of the Rhode Island State Police (RISP) Detective Division and Bureau of Criminal Investigations (BCI) Unit. In about ten minutes, patrolmen were at the scene closing off the road.

III

As Mareck described to patrolman Brian Dufault what he found, Hopkinton Police Department detective Kevin McDonald was at home trying to enjoy a well-deserved day off. It was about ten minutes to two. For McDonald, during the winter months, Sundays weren't scheduled around tending to the horses he and his wife raised on their sprawling spread outside Hopkinton, just south of Providence. Mostly, McDonald liked to sit in front of the television with his college-bound son and watch New England Patriots football. On this day, early into the game, the Patriots were trouncing the Carolina Panthers, on their way to a 38–6 victory.

Growing up in nearby Narragansett, a port town close to the wealthy tidings of Newport, following the Patriots had become a way of life for the somewhat reticent detective. He kept one picture on the wall of his office: a poster of the Patriots.

As a twenty-three-year veteran Rhode Island cop, however, McDonald was aware that any day could turn from the ordinary into the extraordinary with a phone call. And sure enough, about three-quarters of the way into the football game, McDonald's cell phone rang: "We got a situation out there near the Connecticut state line," dispatch explained. "Maybe a body in a garbage bag." The chief was involved, McDonald was told.

So he grabbed his car keys and flew out the door.

When he arrived on scene, Mike Gilman filled McDonald in. After all, it didn't take McDonald long to get out there. He generally drove one of the Hopkinton PD's many confiscated sports cars. For years, McDonald had worked narcotics and drug detail, setting up major buys, busting the big drug dealers. There was always, McDonald said later, a boat or several cars involved in the raid. "I could drive a different car every day of the month if I wanted to." A Hummer. A Porsche. Whatever.

McDonald photographed the scene. As he studied it, he assumed the person who had dumped the body had obviously chosen the area out of necessity and randomness rather than design. There was no reason to believe the woman's killer knew the chief of police lived down the road and wanted to dump the body in, basically, his front yard. ("Son of a gun," the chief said later, quite animated that a killer had left one of his victims in his front yard, "I drove by that body every day for months on my way into work.")

After photographing the scene, McDonald walked up the road and sought out one of the chief's neighbors, John Czerkiewciz. McDonald wanted to know if Czerkiewciz had seen anything suspicious. Although the nights were as dark as used motor oil out there in the woods, someone had obviously drove up Grassy Pond Road to dump a body, which meant someone could have perhaps seen him.

"I saw that bag for the first time about a month ago," Czerkiewciz said. "I remember a friend telling me about a 'foul odor' near the bridge"—there was a small bridge over a small rain creek about twenty yards from where the bag was found—"and I heard about that odor maybe two months ago."

"Thanks," McDonald said. "If you think of anything else, call us."

What the brief interview told McDonald was that identifying the body might prove difficult, especially if it had been out there decomposing for a few months.

IV

By late afternoon, Arthur Kershaw and Diane Dougherty, two members of the RISP–BCI Unit, arrived to assist what had become Detective Kevin McDonald's investigation. McDonald

was happy to have the help. It was going to be tough to identify the body. Besides the lower right leg, from about the top of
the DB's (dead body) shin down, the body was decomposed
to the point of, essentially, a bag of bones. The victim, as Mc-
Donald described the body to the detectives, had been placed
inside several white bags, which were placed inside several
black garbage bags. The person who had placed her—they
knew it was a female—inside the bags had gone to great
lengths to seal the bags. They found no clothing besides a pair
of "medium blue" panties she was wearing. ("There was a rope
(clothesline)," McDonald explained later, "wrapped or tied
around her pelvic bone, which told me that she had been tied
up and bound at some point.")

The coroner arrived, took some photos, searched the area
around the body with McDonald and the others, and ordered
the body to be taken to the medical examiner's (ME) office
for further assessment. When McDonald got back to the Hopkinton PD, he had officers check out the local campgrounds.
"Preference paid to domestic disputes," he suggested. See if
any females had been reported missing within the past six
months. Maybe a husband got drunk, pissed off, and did his
wife in after an argument. While they did that, McDonald
called the Connecticut State Police (CSP) troop closest to
where the body had been found to see if the CSP had any
unresolved missing persons cases that fit the criteria. A
trooper told him they had been investigating a missing prostitute case from a truck stop near Hopkinton. "She worked
that truck stop and vanished at some point last summer." But
there was never a missing person report filed.

Then McDonald called Detective Mike Carrier, from the
Westerly Police Department (WPD). Westerly was beach ter-
ritory. Weekend beachgoers from all over the Northeast
flocked to the popular Misquamicut State Beach Park. There
was always trouble on weekends during the summer. Kids
getting drunk. Drugs. Bar fights.

Burlingame, a campground near the beach, was a common spot Westerly cops were called out to patrol and investigate. The Mashantucket Pequot Casino at Foxwoods in Ledyard, Connecticut, was a twenty-minute drive from the beach. Lots of drugs and trouble flowed from the casino to the beach, back and forth. Maybe a woman had been reported missing from the casino, campground, or somewhere in between.

"I'll search our records, Kevin, and get back to you," Detective Carrier said.

The next morning, McDonald drove out to the CSP barracks in Montville, Connecticut, to see if it had a match of any kind.

No luck.

From there, he stopped at the truck stop to see about the missing hooker. But it was a rumor, he was told. There was no prostitute working the truck stop.

Back at the Hopkinton PD, McDonald sat down with Chief Scuncio. The chief said he remembered something that, in hindsight, might be important to the investigation. "Last November I saw a vehicle—an Explorer or Bronco—in my driveway," he told McDonald. The only way to get to the chief's driveway was to turn left or right from Route 138 onto Grassy Pond and head west toward his house. "I went up to the driver and asked him what he was doing." The vehicle had driven into a gravel bank. The driver seemed confused. When the chief approached and started asking questions, "the guy took off."

So the chief made chase.

Reaching speeds up to 100 mph, the chief lost the guy somewhere over the Connecticut border.

It seemed like nothing, but McDonald said he'd look into it.

McDonald went back to his office and spread out the photographs he had taken at the crime scene. Something was missing. He had recently received several photographs from the coroner, which gave him a fairly good view of the body. What struck him right away was a tattoo on what was one of the only patches of skin that time and the elements hadn't decayed. The coroner described the area as the "lateral aspect" of the "left ankle." McDonald's Jane Doe had a rather unique piece of art there: quite faded, it was an image of flowers, a bird, and several "unreadable words," the coroner noted. Looking closer, however, McDonald noticed something.

Tarzan—written on the woman's ankle.

67

I

At forty, Detective Kevin McDonald was in better shape than half the cadets training at the local academy. Part of it was McDonald's belief in being prepared for any situation. He kept his solid, six-foot two-inch, 210-pound frame in shape by running six miles every morning with Chief Scuncio and other colleagues. For McDonald, growing up in Narragansett, a fishing village, had been a satisfying experience. From an early age, McDonald said, he had always found police work interesting. Out of high school, he started working part-time for the police reserves. "I loved it." By 1984, there was an opening in Hopkinton, and McDonald took the test, scored higher marks than he had ever expected, and immediately went into the academy. From there, he followed the normal route to a gold badge, working several years with the Hopkinton PD's K-9 team.

After a few years as an accident reconstructionist, in 1998, when the Hopkinton PD appointed its current chief, John Scuncio, McDonald made detective. Most of his time had been spent working narcotics. Although Hopkinton, by all accounts, is rural, and its neighbor is Westerly, Beach Town,

USA, crack cocaine has still found its way into the infrastructure of the population. "We did a yearlong case with Westerly once, 'Operation Stateline.' Big case. The FBI was involved. Over the course of a year, we bought about seventy thousand dollars' worth of crack."

McDonald didn't see his Jane Doe as a casualty of the drug war going on in and around Hopkinton, however. The way she had been found just didn't lend itself to being an overdose or drug-related. But before he could begin to think about solving the case, McDonald and his colleagues had to first identify the woman. It was hard to catch a killer without first knowing who his victim was and where she lived.

When McDonald joined the police department back in the 1980s, there were six cops—including him—on the force. A small-town operation by most standards, as he leapt full-throttle into the Jane Doe investigation, the department had grown by ten to make sixteen full-time cops. When the Hopkinton Police Department needed assistance, it turned to the state police. All McDonald had at the moment was a tattoo. *So why not,* he thought, *send a copy of the tattoo around to the local police departments and see if it stirs any interest?* ("We had nothing to lose," McDonald told me later.)

First, McDonald had his friend and colleague from the RISP, Arthur Kershaw, draw a sketch of the tattoo so they could distribute it more easily than a photograph. Then, "After we tried a few prisons," McDonald said, "thinking maybe we could get a match with an inmate or someone who had just been released, I faxed a copy of the tattoo drawing to a majority of the police departments in Connecticut, Rhode Island, and Massachusetts."

McDonald knew it was a long shot, but worth a try. In the interim, several leads were checked. One included following up a tree service worker who had fallen from a tree and died in 1998. By itself, the lead didn't seem significant. But when coupled with the guy's nickname, "Tarzan," the tattoo on Jane

Doe's leg took on new meaning. Was the victim in the garbage bag Tarzan's wife? Girlfriend? Daughter? The key was to locate the family and find out.

After some checking, the tree service worker's wife turned out to be alive and remarried.

II

During the early afternoon hours of January 8, Grassy Pond Road resident Bob Hendricks (pseudonym) came forward and said he had been in the woods off Grassy Pond on November 24, 2001, when he saw something peculiar. It was around 11:00 A.M., Hendricks explained. "I observed a vehicle, a Volkswagen two-door, charcoal in color with a hatchback . . . stopped." Hendricks and McDonald were standing on Grassy Pond. Hendricks pointed to the area where Jane Doe had been found. "Right there," he said, "the car was parked. I was behind a tree."

Hendricks had no idea where the body in the bag had been found.

"What'd you see?"

"Two guys got out of the car. The guy in the front seat was big, had a beard, was wearing a black leather jacket and blue jeans." McDonald was intrigued. "Biker types," Hendricks added.

"What'd they do when they got out of the car?"

"Both walked into the woods and stopped approximately ten to fifteen feet in . . ." The area Hendricks pointed to was _in close proximity,_ McDonald wrote in his report, _to where the body was discovered._

They stood in the woods, Hendricks claimed, for about ten minutes, before returning to the car and tearing off for Kenney Hill Road (not Route 138, the main road). At that moment, Hendricks walked out of the woods—and that's when he saw them pass by, heading in the opposite direction on Grassy Pond (they must have turned around up ahead on Kenney Hill), barreling at 50 mph toward Route 138. Grassy Pond was a road people were afraid to travel more than 20 mph down. Not because of cops, but the road had ruts and bumps.

At this point, with the car turned around, Hendricks saw the driver as they sped past: a white female, brown hair. The license plate was from Connecticut.

III

McDonald and a colleague took a ride to the Troop E Barracks of the CSP on January 9, 2002, with a copy of the tattoo drawing. From there, they were escorted to York Correctional Institution for Women in Niantic, the only women's prison in the state of Connecticut. The idea was to show the tattoo to the guards and have them pass it around to see if anyone recognized it. A quick search of the computer system indicated that an inmate with a similar tattoo had not been released— or if she had been, the tattoo had not been part of her rap sheet. When they returned to Troop E sometime later, one of the sergeants on duty gave McDonald the name of a possible suspect the CSP had termed "extremely dangerous." The guy had been incarcerated for several violent sexual assaults, but he had been paroled late the previous year. "His last known address is in Exeter," the trooper explained. Quite alarmingly, Exeter, Rhode Island, was a twenty-minute drive from where Jane Doe had been found in Hopkinton.

By January 10, four days after the grisly discovery of Jane Doe's decomposed remains, it appeared that every promising lead ran cold. No one at York recognized the tattoo. The Exeter suspect had been out of state since his release. It seemed Jane Doe would end up another body without a name buried in an unmarked grave.

68

I

Medical Examiner Jennifer Swartz released her findings by the end of the second week of January. Jane Doe's body was so badly decomposed it was hard to pin down an exact cause of death, but there was no doubt in Swartz's professional opinion that Jane Doe had been murdered.

Jane Doe became number 040883. She had been found in a fetal position, Swartz wrote, *on her right side with loops of rope tied about the wrists, ankles, and waist.* Jane Doe's killer had hog-tied her, in other words.

Houdini-like.

There was an additional *loop of rope tied around both* of Jane Doe's *forearms and the right knee, a loop of rope tied at the anterior aspect of the left shoulder passing around both knees around the neck, and back to underneath the left arm, and there [was] a loop of rope passing from the ankles up around the neck and through the loops of rope on the wrists and knees and then tied at the neck.*

Whoever had tied the knots knew what he was doing.

Another important piece of evidence Swartz uncovered was that the deceased had been placed inside eleven garbage bags, layered, one inside the other, *that [had] been neatly sta-pled and taped together. [The] ends of the rope looped about the waist protrude[d] exteriorly through the garbage bags.*

The vicim's killer had gone to great lengths in placing her inside the bags and securing them, as if it wasn't the first time he had done such a thing. In addition, there was ninety-four pounds of flesh and bones left to Jane Doe. There were small portions of decomposed tissue on her back, buttocks, lower ex-tremities, feet, right arm, and hands. *Fly larvae measuring 3/16–9/16 of an inch,* Swartz wrote, *in length and unhatched pupae [were] present on the body.* The decedent's underwear wasn't blue, as early reports indicated; her panties were black, size M/6. More graphically speaking, there was also a small portion of Jane's face, the right side, and scalp, still intact; with part of her earlobe—*with two piercings*—hanging beside sev-eral long brown hairs. One finger had red polish on it, as well as several toenails. Jane Doe's skull showed no signs of trauma, a gunshot wound, strike by a club, hammer, or blunt object. There were several *healing fractures* on the side of Jane's nose, which meant she had perhaps broken her nose at some point in her life. A good sign for detectives was that nearly all of Jane's teeth were intact and acutely prepared for comparison once dental records were—with any luck—located. Furthermore, there were *no gross or radiologic evidence of sharp or blunt force trauma to any of the bones.* It was fairly clear, although not entirely impossible, that Jane hadn't been stabbed to death, although her killer could have carefully placed his strikes to pierce only internal organs, missing bones entirely. An experi-enced murderer would be able to pull this off.

Incision of the ankles and wrists underlying the ropes [did not] reveal hemorrhage, meaning that the victim was bound and hog-tied after death.

Swartz listed the cause of death as *homicidal violence.* Manner of death: *homicide.* By all accounts, with the experi-ence of the detectives involved included, it appeared the decedent had been strangled. It was one of the only possibilities beyond poisoning or some other odd way of death—including a perfectly placed stab wound. One of the anomalies Swartz discovered was trauma to the front of the corpse's teeth. It was unclear, however, whether the injuries occurred before or after death. Toxicology indicated nothing beyond nicotine in her system. Moreover, no seminal fluid was found, nor was trauma to any of her ribs, which were checked more thoroughly via X-rays.

One of the most important factors of the examination was that for the first time detectives learned through *measurements and scoring of non-metric traits* that Jane Doe was a *female of European ancestry, aged 30 to 39 at death, with a stature of* five feet three inches. She was Latin or Italian. Swartz was certain of it.

69

I

When Kevin McDonald returned to his desk on January 12, he had a message from the Hartford PD. It appeared Hartford detectives felt confident they could put a name to the Jane Doe that McDonald had been trying to identify for the past week. All those faxes McDonald had sent out to police departments throughout the Northeast paid off. The tattoo on the victim's leg was a mirror image of a tattoo on a missing persons flyer Hartford detectives had posted the previous year.

McDonald was thrilled.

Hanging up with Hartford, McDonald called Arthur Kershaw. "We got us a match."

Kershaw said he'd grab colleague Kevin Hopkins and swing by to pick up McDonald. "Let's head out to Hartford tonight."

II

As McDonald and his colleagues were working to identify Jane Doe, the "Asylum Hill Killer" was arrested. Twenty-eight-year-old Matthew Johnson, a homeless transient and convicted rapist, had been on on HPD's radar for a few years. Johnson was a brute of a man, over six feet tall, three hundred pounds. Some claimed Johnson was severely retarded and couldn't help himself, yet one detective investigating the case later told me that Johnson "was retarded when he *wanted* to be retarded."

There was no doubt that Matthew Johnson committed the crimes he had been later convicted of (three women) and could be responsible for as many as a dozen more murders. Still, the one missing persons case Hartford PD detectives believed without a doubt that Johnson had *nothing* to do with was Carmen Rodriguez. "Johnson's MO," Luisa St. Pierre said, "in no way fit with Carmen's disappearance. If Johnson had murdered Carmen, we would have found her sooner."

III

On the day Peter Mareck found the body, the Rodriguez family, as much as they could, celebrated what was usually, for them, a wild time in the city of Hartford: Three Kings Day. The day, generally celebrated twelve days after Christmas, is known as a time of the Epiphany, when the visit by the Three Wise Men to Jesus is officially noted. With no word regarding Carmen's whereabouts, however, the day had been terribly subdued, especially for Luz, Kathy Perez, and Sonia, who firmly believed by that point that Carmen had met some sort of fatal harm. Knowing that the "Asylum Hill Killer" had been arrested and scratched from the list of suspects in Carmen's disappearance gave the family some comfort, but the inevitable, Luz knew, would be coming any day. When Carmen's birthday passed the previous October, Luz said later, "That's when I knew she was never coming home." Carmen was one of those women who made a big deal out of her birthday. Days before, she would call family and friends and say, "My birthday's coming—what are you get-

ting me?" And she'd laugh her charming giggle. "My grandmother [Carmen's mother] was always cooking," Kathy Perez
added, "and everyone is always around and it's a celebration."
On the day of her birthday, Carmen would go from one family
member to the next, "Are you going to give me my present?
Where is it? Let me see it?" It was a part of her character
everyone lovingly recalled with a noted shade of sadness,
knowing they would never hear those words again. Carmen
was the pulse of the family, true, but also "a headache," Luz
said, "don't get me wrong. She caused our mother a lot of
sleepless nights. But that headache, as the weeks turned into
months, was something we all wanted back."

70

I

Sonia Rodriguez received a call from the Hartford PD during the afternoon of January 13, 2002. "The Rhode Island police found a body."

She knew. She didn't need a "positive" identification. She didn't need dental records. It was there in her heart: that sinking feeling . . . *Titi.*

"Is it her?" she asked the cop as a formality.

"We don't know if it's Carmen or not."

"Is the person alive or dead?" Sonia asked. The cop hadn't mentioned.

No answer. "We'll have someone call you at your mother's later tonight."

When Sonia arrived at her mother's house later that night and explained the phone call, Luz said, "They must know something."

Luz explained to everyone that she'd had a feeling throughout the day. Something was off. When she walked out of the bathroom after taking a shower earlier that day, her husband was standing there. "I got a feeling she's dead," he said.

The hair on her arms stood up. And then when Luz called

Sonia on her way to the house, and she explained that the cops hadn't explained much, she knew. "She's dead," Luz told Sonia over the phone.

Sometime after 5:00 P.M., a detective called Carmen's mother's house. "It's her" was all he said. "We want to meet you somewhere to talk."

Sonia suggested Petra's house, one of Carmen's sisters. Luz lived next door. The family split up and agreed to meet at Petra's.

II

Kevin McDonald and his team stopped at Broad Street in Hartford to obtain Carmen's dental records. From there, one detective drove back to Rhode Island to deliver the records to the ME's office, while McDonald and several detectives and CSP troopers met at Troop H in downtown Hartford to discuss where the investigation was headed. With Carmen's body now found, everyone believed they had enough to serve a search warrant on Ned's house. Ned was the only suspect at this point. There was enough from a prosecutorial standpoint to at least search Ned's home. Quite particularly, McDonald later said, they were looking for any clothing Carmen might have worn, the jewelry she was said to have been wearing that night, rope, plastic bags, a stapler and staples, and adhesive tape—all items that were part of the Rhode Island crime scene.

The judge signed the warrant and a team of investigators from both states raced to Ned's house in Berlin. It was dark out, however, when they arrived, so McDonald suggested they wait until the following morning.

III

Sonia called Luz to tell her they were all next door. Waiting. Luisa St. Pierre was there with her partner. She wanted the entire family together.

Luz's heart started racing.

Everyone was sitting at the table when Luz walked in. When she looked at Sonia and saw the sense of loss in her eyes, Luz didn't need to hear any more. "I was out," she said later. "I don't know nothing else that happened after that."

When she came out of that fog of pain, Luz and her sisters told her father and uncle. Then they drove to her mother's apartment. Rosa Rodriguez had just gotten out of the hospital. She'd had cancer surgery. She was on the couch. Her stomach was stapled. She was taking it easy.

Luz's uncle walked into the living room, where Rosa was resting, while the others waited in the kitchen. "She's dead, right?" Rosa said in Spanish.

Her brother sat down next to her. "Calm down," he said. "It's going to be OK."

"I told you . . . I told you she was dead," Rosa started to scream. "I knew it!"

IV

On January 15, 2002, first thing in the morning, several members of the CSP Major Crimes Unit (MCU), Kevin Mc-Donald and his partner, Arthur Kershaw, in addition to several other officers and Hartford PD detectives, arrived at Ned's home to execute a search and seizure warrant. Entering the house, CSP detective Stavros Mellekas and HPD detective Mike Sheldon walked toward the basement door and opened it.

A figure was standing at the bottom of the stairs. It was dark. The detectives couldn't see anything. Mellekas said Sheldon drew his weapon and pointed it at Ned's head. But when they realized it was Ned and he wasn't doing anything out of the ordinary except wondering what was going on upstairs, Sheldon holstered his weapon.

"You know, you're the first cop to ever point his gun at me," Ned said.

Sheldon and Mellekas told Ned not to move.

V

If one is to believe Ned's version, Arthur Kershaw and Kevin McDonald grabbed him from downstairs and—without allowing him to put his socks on—dragged him up the stairs and placed him in a police cruiser. "What are you doing?" Ned claimed he said as he was wrestled into the backseat of the vehicle. "This is harassment!"

"You haven't seen harassment yet," McDonald snapped at him, according to Ned.

VI

CSP trooper Daniel Crowley was on hand as a liaison between the police and Ned and Ned's parents, Edwin Sr. and Norma, who were home during the execution of the search and seizure. Crowley sat with Edwin and Norma in the living room as other officers began to search the house. It was going to be a long day. As Ned was in the cruiser outside, Edwin Sr. asked Crowley what was going on. "What are you looking for?"

Crowley indicated that they were serving a search warrant.

"I can locate whatever you're looking for," Edwin offered.

"The court issued this warrant, Mr. Snelgrove, we're going to be here most of the day. The items we're interested in are clearly listed on the warrant."

Edwin and Norma were visibly shaken. They were in their late eighties. Ned was worried about them. But sitting outside in the cruiser, alone, he couldn't do much of anything to assuage their trepidation.

As they sat, Crowley mentioned Carmen's name. "We're familiar with her name," Edwin said, speaking for his wife, too. "The Hartford police have been investigating Ned. They suspect he had something to do with her disappearance."

"He told you that?"

"He saw her at a bar, I guess," Edwin explained. "He gave her a ride to a gas station and she asked him for money and he told her to get out of his car."

"What else did he say?" It seemed like a convenient story. Scripted and rehearsed.

"He left her there and hasn't seen her since."

Officers were walking by as they spoke. Static from radios blurred the background. Crowley noticed that as he and Edwin got further along into their conversation, Edwin became "more and more agitated." It was odd, Crowley thought, because Edwin had been "very cooperative at first."

Ned lived in the basement. Ned had always talked about himself as being a meticulous guy, clean-cut, his life in order. He had a bachelor's degree from Rutgers. He believed he was smarter than the average Joe. With the search centered in his room, it wasn't hard to tell that Ned was, for lack of a better term, a slob. There were clothes all over the place, papers, knickknacks, and other personal items all in disarray. Ned lived like a teenager.

While officers were going through everything, Edwin left the living room, where he and Norma had been sitting with Crowley, and walked hurriedly downstairs, saying, "What are you doing? Why are you searching his room?"

"Please go back upstairs, Mr. Snelgrove," a trooper told him. "Leave this area. You're not to interfere with the execution of this warrant."

Edwin said something.

"We're going to arrest you, sir, if you interfere."

When Edwin returned to the living room, Crowley looked out the window and saw several television news crews pulling up to the front of the house. Norma looked panicked.

As the cameramen began to set up their equipment, Norma

began crying. "What have we done to deserve such treatment?"

"Please relax, Mrs. Snelgrove," an officer said.

"Ned could not have done something so wrong to deserve such embarrassment."

"It'll be fine," the officer said. "We'll keep the news crews back."

"Ned had problems in the past," Norma continued, almost talking to herself more than the trooper. "We thought he was finished with his problems."

"What problems?"

"His former girlfriend in New Jersey. Ned was in the wrong place at the wrong time after having a few drinks with her." The way she spun it, Ned killing Karen Osmun didn't sound so bad. Norma was obviously in denial. Protecting her son.

Crowley got both Edwin and Norma to relax a little bit. They were in the back of the house now, talking about Ned. "He's a workaholic," Edwin said, shaking his head. "He works every day."

"What's he do?"

"He's a good salesman."

"He must have a lot of money saved, living at home here with you guys since his release from prison in 1999?"

Edwin laughed. Norma too. "Huh!" said Edwin. "Ned hasn't saved any money—that's why he stays here with us. [He says] that company he works for as a salesman doesn't even pay him for his mileage or expenses."

"He travels a lot?" Crowley asked.

"All throughout the state," Edwin said.

Norma chimed in, adding, "He was fired. He was just fired. The Hartford police detective told Neddy's boss about his 'problems' in New Jersey and that he was being investigated in Connecticut. He then tried to kill himself."

Crowley took it all in. He understood the best thing to do was to allow them the space to talk. Once Norma got going, she didn't stop. Continuing, she said, "Ned had a growth removed while he was in the hospital after his suicide attempt. He even met with a therapist, but refused to continue."

"Is he working now?"

"He just got hired by a promotions company to travel around the state."

71

I

Downstairs in Ned's room, detectives bagged and tagged what they believed would best help them prove Ned had murdered Carmen: staple guns, staples, hair fibers, magazines, videotapes, and several other items that seemed out of place for a grown man living in the basement of his parents' home. Among Ned's personal possessions was an article published in the magazine *Crosstalk*. Written by Joshua Fischman, titled "Arson: A Chemical Fire?" the short piece dealt with the mind and how different chemicals in the brain reacted under various situations. Mainly, the writer argued that arsonists had lower levels of a certain chemical that made starting fires an "uncontrollable urge." But then the article went into the differences between arsonists and violent offenders and how different their brain chemistry was from one another. In red ink, someone—investigators guessed it was Ned—had underlined several sentences relating to murderers. One described a certain chemical found in *abnormally low levels in murderers who killed their sexual partners in a sudden rage*. Further along, someone had underlined a sentence that, in part, said, *researchers believe that low serotonin levels are associated with poor impulse control.*

Another article, in which nothing was underlined, was even more telling. Leslie Lothstein, the director of clinical psychology for the Institute of Living, a mental hospital in Hartford, had written an opinion-editorial for the *Hartford Courant* titled "Changes Must Be Made to Control Sexual Offenders, Reduce Risk." The piece was interesting to investigators in the fact that it dealt with, on some level, the extremely high recidivism rate for sexual offenders. This was not breaking news in itself, but place that article in the home of a guy who has been convicted of two extremely violent sexual attacks and it's worth considering. The main quote of the piece was, at the least, a description of Ned's past life: *"An inmate's contained behavior might be confused with 'good behavior' by prison officials who, under the law, can approve early release."*

By cutting the article out of the newspaper and saving it, was Ned taunting the system? Laughing at it? Was he mocking the Department of Corrections in New Jersey for releasing him from prison nine years early?

And then there was a copy of *The Deliberate Stranger,* the television movie starring Mark Harmon as Ted Bundy. There was Ned's personal copy. Sitting there on his desk, the box tattered and torn as if he'd watched it a hundred times.

II

Detective Thomas Murray had been with the CSP for thirteen years, assigned to the Central Major District Crime Squad in Meriden. As the search continued, Murray walked the site as the search scene officer. His job was to collect the evidence seized from Ned's house and make sure it was processed appropriately. In back of a couch in Ned's room downstairs, Murray found a box of maps. Of particular interest was a detailed map of Rhode Island (which seemed newer than the others, as if Ned had just bought it). On the edge of a large bookcase by Ned's bed was a "coil of line or rope," fashioned into a hangman's noose.

Erotic asphyxiation?

As they continued going through Ned's room, it seemed everything was important. Ned had kept extremely detailed records of all his travels. There were boxes of receipts and notebooks with mileage and fuel fill-ups, along with where and when. Inside a child's toy chest, just to the right of where Ned slept, was perhaps the most bizarre discovery of the day: two Styrofoam mannequin heads with Magic Marker drawings on them. Both female, one was dolled up with a blue marker to look pretty, pleasant, perhaps even lovely. The other, however, was quite eerie looking. Its eyes were wide open—as opposed to its sister, which had its eyes closed, her long lashes perfectly drawn—and bulging, as if she had been frightened by someone or something. Around the Adam's apple area, she had what appeared to be a target marked in a crisscross, gridlike fashion, with a round circle drawn on the money spot—the area someone would, with their two thumbs together, press inward to perform strangulation. In addition, there was an X drawn in the bull's-eye. On the cheeks and forehead and chin were various markings, maybe like scratches or pretend knife wounds. On the forehead was also a large cross or X, marking an obvious sensitive area. David Zagaja later said: "And the Styrofoam heads, the heads . . . do you know what these heads are for? These serve in a pinch when there's no woman available for Ned. This is for sexual gratification. . . . Just look at the [slash] marks on the neck. X marks the spot. . . . [He] is reliving his fantasies . . . he's reliving his past. And, as I said, they serve in a pinch when there's no woman available."

Someone found a manila envelope in a filing cabinet that contained a note Ned had written in 1993 (while in prison). It was clear from the note that he had read an article about how to change one's identity. "It's another piece of consciousness of guilt," David Zagaja added, "that Ned held on to in case he ever became involved in further criminal conduct . . . a way he knows of by changing his identity and avoiding detection."

III

Outside, as the search and seizure wound down, Trooper Daniel Crowley continued talking to Edwin and Norma. "Do you think," Edwin asked Crowley at one point, "that Ned would be stupid enough to bring something back from Rhode Island to tie him to the body of Carmen Rodriguez?"

Crowley was shocked by the question. It wasn't asked for the purpose of an answer; Edwin was more or less mocking the search.

As they talked, Edwin and Norma continued to explain how their Neddy liked to sleep on a couch downstairs in the basement. "It reminds him of the prison cot he got used to sleeping on," Edwin said.

Norma said they refused to answer the phone when it rang, because "it was always for Neddy."

"He had a lot of friends, did he?"

"No," she said, "Neddy did *not* have friends, just coworkers that would call him at home *all* the time."

"Has Ned brought any women home since he's been out of prison?"

Norma said, "Neddy is not interested in women, or men for that matter."

"Have you ever seen him with any pornographic magazines, found any pictures or dirty books in Ned's room or the basement?"

"Neddy would *never*," Edwin said sternly, "bring any of that stuff into *this* house."

"He's not interested in pornography," Norma added.

As the afternoon progressed, those television crews

camped out in front began airing live reports. The search was big news: a former killer involved with the disappearance of a woman. The Rodriguez family had been putting pressure on the news organizations to cover Carmen's disappearance. "Mr. Suburbia" was being investigated—a search was going on in a middle-class neighborhood.

With the news spreading, neighbors began showing up. Friends of the family started calling the house. Crowley stood by as Norma and Edwin received one call after the next and had to explain to friends and family what was happening. At some point, their minister called after seeing a live shot of the house on television. Norma couldn't handle it; she started crying over the phone, saying, "I can't speak anymore."

During each call, Mr. or Mrs. Snelgrove would say: "They're searching the house because they think Neddy had something to do with a body found in Rhode Island." To one family member, Edwin added, "I'm not sure what Neddy knows about the body. But someone may have seen Neddy one of the times that he had lunch at the casino and thought that he may have known something."

Someone called late into the day, just as the search was winding down. Crowley stood by Edwin as he spoke in hushed tones at first, but then just came out with how he felt: "I don't know *what* to think anymore," Ned's father said. He sounded tired. Like he had given up. Confused and upset. "Neddy's a good salesman," Edwin said to the caller, "he can look you right in the face and lie."

72

I

Kevin McDonald had participated in the search and seizure at Ned's. There was some later confusion over whether Ned was driven to Troop H in Hartford by McDonald or another officer, but McDonald and his partner, Arthur Kershaw, were at Troop H after the search, preparing to ask Ned a few questions. McDonald advised Ned of his rights, but it was important to make him aware of the fact that he was *not* under arrest. McDonald had an easy manner about him. It was hard not to feel comfortable around the guy; he spoke softly, with poise and eloquence, and chose his words carefully. However, he seemed to exude an air of cockiness if you didn't know him or his style.

McDonald had to play it cool. One misstep, especially dealing with a suspect as smart as Ned, could be detrimental to the case. Ned wasn't what McDonald had expected. There had been a lot of discussion among detectives about Ned over the past few weeks. "With his background," McDonald told me, "I expected someone different. He didn't look like a monster. He looked, well, he looked like a traveling salesman— quite harmless. Like he wouldn't hurt anybody."

McDonald approached Ned. "You ever been in Rhode Island?"

Ned was sitting, drinking a glass of water. He appeared calm. He was appalled that they had, by his estimation, "dragged" him down to Troop H without charging him.

"You don't have to speak to us if you don't want to," McDonald added. "You can request an attorney, if you like. You can stop talking anytime."

"I'm not going to talk about anything to do with the investigation," Ned said. ("You get to talking to Ned and you understand he fancies himself as someone who is very intelligent," McDonald recalled later. "He likes to put himself over people." It was that pompous arrogance Ned could turn on and off: *I'm smarter than you. . . . You won't get me for this murder.* It was implicit, McDonald said, in his demeanor. "He would try to put his intelligence, in the way he spoke, over us, like we couldn't understand his superior English skills. He looks down on us. The feeling we got was that Ned was saying to himself, 'I did this—and you morons are never going to catch me.'")

McDonald was under the impression that since Ned had "agreed to come down to Troop H" he was willing to talk about the case. Otherwise, why would he agree to get into a police cruiser and ride downtown? He had never called his lawyer from the house.

They talked for approximately two hours, McDonald later testified (and verified with me), and yet Ned revealed nothing about Carmen or the case.

"He was confident," McDonald said. "We talked about the Red Sox."

Arthur Kershaw asked a question about Rhode Island. The Hartford PD had a witness who claimed Ned had called Kenney's one night after Carmen disappeared and said he was in Rhode Island. Kershaw mentioned Rhode Island again. He knew McDonald had already broached the subject with Ned, but he wanted to see how Ned would react.

"You already asked me that," Ned said haughtily. He smiled. "Do you really want me to answer that all over again?"

Near the end of the conversation, Ned said, "Let's do this again sometime, but over lunch, huh?"

II

McDonald and Kershaw left Troop H and walked a block away to a meeting that was going on at State's Attorney James Thomas's office. Within the past week, a woman had come forward and claimed Ned had tried to kidnap her outside Kenney's somewhere around the same timeframe when Carmen disappeared. Christina Mallon said she had fought Ned off and then had thrown an empty beer bottle at his car.

It was just the break they needed: arrest Ned on a kidnapping charge—unrelated to Carmen's disappearance—and get him off the street so they could seriously investigate Carmen's murder without Ned meddling.

Perfect.

With all the detectives working the case sitting in the room, Thomas said, "I suggest you prepare an arrest warrant."

With that settled, McDonald and Kershaw were asked to take a ride to the Berlin Turnpike. The idea was to ask around, show a photograph of Carmen and Ned, and see if maybe Ned had taken Carmen to a motel and killed her there. Ned lived with parents at the end of the Berlin Turnpike.

There was no doubt Carmen was in Ned's car, he had admitted it. Yet, detectives found nothing to prove Ned's own admission. Ned had cleaned his car. If he had killed her in a motel room, evidence would have been almost impossible to gather at this late stage. However, if a motel employee could place Ned in a room with Carmen, it would prove he was not being totally honest. But after an afternoon combing motels and asking about Ned and Carmen, investigators couldn't find anyone who recognized either.

III

When McDonald and Kershaw returned to Troop H, Detective Kevin Hopkins, an RISP investigator who had met up with Kershaw and McDonald in Hartford that day, explained he found something important in the items seized at Ned's.

"The receipts," Hopkins said. "Ned's gas receipts."

McDonald and Kershaw were interested.

"He filled up his gas tank on September twentieth, the day before Carmen went missing." Hopkins had sat and dug through the enormous pile of even more gas and mileage receipts Ned had kept. Ned had written his mileage down on yellow legal pads—every mile carefully accounted for. He logged where he went on a specific day, the times, the mileage, how much fuel he used, and—to investigators' surprise and delight—the time he purchased the fuel. For example, in the days before Carmen disappeared, Ned kept records down to the tenth of a mile and tenth of a tank of gas. *Went to the Miller residence today;* in other words, *filled up at 7:30 A.M., arrived at Miller residence for appointment at 8:15 A.M.* This sort of spotless record keeping went on and on for days and months. Every tank of gas and hour and minute of Ned's life was accounted for. But in going through the records, Hopkins figured out that for a stretch of time when Carmen went missing—an entire day—Ned's record keeping didn't add up.

It seemed he had tried to fudge it.

73

I

CSP sergeant Patrick Gaffney knew he was dealing with a twisted individual in Ned Snelgrove. Ned's past record indicated as much. Beyond that, Gaffney knew the smell of evil, had seen it during his years on the job—but he also understood that the best way to capture a madman was to beat him at his own game. Gaffney was a veteran homicide cop, involved in some of the CSP's most high-profile cases over his fifteen-year career as a member of the MCU, out of Bethany, Connecticut. At the Snelgrove residence during the search, Gaffney hadn't seen or spoken to Ned. "I didn't get a chance to introduce myself to him," Gaffney said later. "Just that there was a bit of commotion and stuff, people in and out. . . ."

Gaffney stayed out of the way and focused on overseeing his investigators and delegating jobs during the search. Back at Troop H now, Ned was in the interview suite sitting alone, stewing, wondering what the CSP was going to do with him.

The CSP couldn't hold him. It was getting late. According to Ned, he had been at Troop H for eleven hours already, confined like a prisoner of war.

("I wanted to make myself known to him," Gaffney said,

recalling that moment before he went in to talk to Ned, "so I introduced myself.") "Were you at the house?" Ned asked when Gaffney, a large man, sat down across from him.

"Yeah, as a matter of fact, I was."

"You were?"

"Hey," Gaffney said, "we're done here. I'm heading to Meriden"—a town just south of Berlin—"you want a ride home?"

Ned smiled. "Sure."

As they headed down Interstate 91 from Hartford, Gaffney began, as he later explained, building a rapport with Ned. "We're about the same age, huh, Ned?"

"Probably." Ned seemed more relaxed.

"You like living at home?"

"Sure. Saves me some money."

While in Ned's house earlier, Gaffney noticed several board games Ned had stored away. Seeing the games brought back memories for Gaffney. "I saw that game," Gaffney said to Ned.

"Oh yeah, you saw that," Ned answered.

After some small talk about childhood memories and sports, Gaffney asked, "What's up with the suicide attempt, your demeanor, you know, why'd you do it?"

Ned winced. "You know about those?"

"Of course," Gaffney said. "We're human beings. I understand tough times."

"It's part of my sickness," Ned said. "Let's change the subject, OK?"

"Sure," Gaffney said.

"Hey, what kind of things did you guys take from my house?" Ned asked. He was more assertive now. It wasn't so much a question as a demand.

"I spoke to your dad about it. I gave him a copy of a receipt for everything."

Ned shook his head. "Thanks."

Pulling into Ned's driveway, Gaffney said, "Take it easy now, huh."

"You too," Ned said, closing the door.

II

Ned and his old high-school classmate George Recck had teamed up together while Ned was in prison and decided they'd someday write a book about Ned's life. Ned didn't want Recck to think in the "*short* term" regarding the commerciality of his story. One of the reasons Ned wanted Recck to wait was that Ned considered his postrelease to be a time to gather more salacious material for the book. *Wouldn't it be a great story when I pick up right where I left off . . . ,* Ned wrote to Recck. Perhaps Ned figured the added body count could help sell his story and also add an additional layer, as Ned put it, of *great characters and anecdotes.* Ned had written the letter on Thursday, August 25, 1988, not long after he was incarcerated.

III

Detective Gaffney grew up (and lived) just north of New Haven, Connecticut, in Hamden. A first-generation Gaffney from ancestors in Ireland, he didn't base his desire to become a cop on a family tradition or an inner calling of some sort. It was, more or less, a challenge. "It basically came down to one night when me and a friend of mine were out discussing our futures and I challenged him to take the naval exam and he challenged me to take the state police exam," Gaffney said. "He scored one of the highest scores ever, but went no further, and I ended up . . . with the Connecticut State Police."

Gaffney spent the early part of his career in Westbrook and Bethany, which he knew well from having grown up in the area. By 1989, he was working for the Major Crimes

Unit. Gaffney learned throughout the years to be open to any situation. Any conclusion. Any possible outcome. And to always think outside the box. Generally, killers don't hang around their crime scenes. Yet, killers with a certain amount of hubris like to be involved. They like to become part of the investigation—part of the story. It feeds the ego, supplying to the killer that additional, after-the-crime high.

From being briefed about Ned by his fellow investigators, Gaffney knew Ned wanted desperately to be involved in the investigation. Gaffney felt there was a part of Ned that wanted to dangle a carrot in front of investigators. Because of that, and the decade or more of experience Gaffney brought to the investigation, he couldn't just allow Ned to sit at home and stew. He had to reach out to him.

IV

It was 2:30 P.M., on January 16, a day after the search, when Gaffney showed up at Ned's. The ruse for Gaffney to stop by was that he said he wanted to drop off a receipt for some items they had seized that might not have been on the original receipt. So Gaffney handed Ned the document, saying, "How are things, Ned?"

"Hey," he said, "why did you guys seize my maps of Rhode Island? I need those back. How can I get them back?"

"Well," Gaffney said, "those are regarded as evidence. Sorry, Ned, but you'll have to get a court order at this point if you want them back."

At one time, Ned's parents had a vacation home in Rhode Island. Gaffney knew Ned had already said he had never been in the state. Yet, he had maps and now wanted them back.

Looking at the list, Ned appeared a bit shaken. "You took a postal receipt. Why?"

"The name 'Carmen' was written on the receipt," Gaffney said.

Ned turned white. His eyes popped open. He looked down and away. ("He didn't want to hear that name," Gaffney commented later. "You could clearly see the wheels turning. That momentary pause, you could see that he was thinking . . . 'How do I explain this?'")

Ned had a revelation to make, however. "No," he said. "That's not the *same* Carmen you guys are investigating."

"No?"

Ned changed the subject. "What about my *maps*—"

"Who is this Carmen on the receipt, then?" Gaffney interrupted.

Ned wouldn't answer. As Gaffney began to ask another question, Ned's parents stepped in and asked what was going on.

"Listen," Gaffney said, trying to avoid, as he later described it, negative contact among the four of them. "I have to get back to the office. If you have any problems, call me." He handed Ned his business card.

74

I

Ned viewed his ten years in prison as "downtime." He wrote this to George Recck on August 25, 1988.

Downtime. A vacation. Some years for Ned to sit back.

Relax.

Reflect.

He sounded cocky and well-situated in his new role as an inmate—rather, a convicted, admitted killer and violent serial attacker of women. In his own words, he couldn't get rid of those obsessive thoughts: seeing women in helpless positions, terribly vulnerable, ready for his ultimate judgment.

George Recck had a tough time adjusting to his new way of life, he wrote to Ned. It was apparent in the way Ned addressed him that Recck had complained about not being able to find a wife. All of his friends, Recck apparently said, were pairing up. But Ned told Recck not to be in such a rush to get married. He wrote he *expected that famous Recck sense of humor to return* in no time.

It was odd, a man who had killed the only girlfriend he'd ever had—a man who had issues with women—was handing out romantic advice.

Recck had asked Ned for real estate advice. Ned agreed that the condo deal Recck had signed "sounds good." As the letter continued, Ned counseled Recck on the advantages of owning property. After a paragraph regarding the state of the American League Eastern Division of Major League Baseball, Ned asked Recck to get hold of a few old schoolmates. They would all play a role in the life Ned was designing for himself postprison, he explained.

Speaking to this relationship, ASA David Zagaja summed up Ned's life quite cogently, making a point that the time Ned spent in prison fueled his desire to kill. That Ned wasn't interested in rehabilitating himself or getting help. Every day he spent behind bars was an opportunity to hone his craft as a manipulator, chauvinist, sadistic serial attacker, and killer. "Does [Ned] have a continued obsession as to what he's doing?" Zagaja asked, explaining Ned's tenure in prison and how he spent *years* thinking about his release. "He most certainly does. Over the years, George Recck established that he wrote, for some ten or eleven years, to him, continually talked about Ted Bundy, continually talked about a possible book deal for his prior crimes, his prior experiences. Continually talked about what went right, what went wrong. . . ."

More than that, Ned's ability to compartmentalize his gloating while writing to Recck stood out most when one had a chance to read the letters in the context of Ned's life. In his eleven-page sentencing letter to the judge, Ned explained how remorseful he was for his crimes. He talked about Karen Osmun being the "first time" anything like "that" had ever happened. He purported to need help. He couldn't stop the thoughts in his mind or seeing women in such a violent manner. In a sense, Ned wanted the judge to believe he was crying out.

Four months after writing that eleven-page letter, however, Ned started writing to George Recck, explaining his desire to *pick up where [he] left off* once he was released.

II

The receipt seized at Ned's house with the name "Carmen" written on the top turned out to be exactly what Ned had said it was: a coincidence. Besides *Carmen,* Ned had scribbled a telephone number and *room # 502* on the same receipt. When the CSP did a reverse search of the number, it turned out to be for a local YMCA in Hartford. At first, detectives thought maybe Carmen Rodriguez had stayed at the YMCA and Ned had been going to visit her. But the housing director explained that the room number was given to a woman by the name of Carmen Carrel (last name pseudonym). The phone number was for a pay phone in the lobby on the fifth floor. Carrel had been renting the room since May 2001.

The situation became even more confusing when the CSP located Carrel later that day. She was at work. "I have a [cousin] named Carmen Rodriguez," Carrel said.

"What?"

"I just saw her a few days ago."

"Huh?"

"I know a Carmen Rodriguez who is missing," Carrel explained.

Upon further talking to Carrel, the CSP learned that she had seen Carmen with Ned at Kenney's on the night she went missing. If there was any reluctance on the CSP's part regarding Carrel's story, she gave spot-on descriptions of both Ned and Carmen, down to the growth on the side of Ned's neck and the long, black "Nancy Sinatra" boots Carmen wore. Like many of the girls from Kenney's, Carrel's name popped up on that receipt of Ned's because she filled out an application for Ned and was paid $25.

The bank, however, refused to cash the check.

"I still have it," Carrel said.

"Great," the detective answered. "I'll need that."

"Ned gave me a ride home one night," Carrel said.

"Anything happen?"

"He tried raping me."

III

On January 23, 2002, Patrick Gaffney was with some of his coworkers discussing Ned's case when he realized that during the search the CSP had ended up with documents of Ned's that had not been part of the warrant. So he phoned Ned.

"Hey, listen. I was just reviewing what was taken at your house during the search and seizure and I realized there was an item here that should not have been taken. I was hoping I could meet you at, maybe, the Olympia Diner and give you back some items we didn't mean to take."

The idea was to get Ned out of the house. Break that bond of him being in his comfort zone. Maybe pull him out of his element and get him on neutral ground. Gaffney figured if he could get Ned alone, he could work on him and possibly get him to open up.

But Ned was "suspicious" of Gaffney's suggestion right away. "I don't know," Ned said. "Sounds . . . why don't you meet me here. I'll make us some coffee."

"OK."

As Gaffney drove to Ned's, he contemplated whether to accept Ned's gesture of coffee. *Everybody knows where I am,* he thought. *It's not like they don't know where I'm going.* Ned's offer seemed subtle and neighborly, but Gaffney knew that for Ned it was a test—an experiment in trust. Gaffney had taken quite a ribbing from his colleagues before leaving the office. "Don't drink that coffee. He's probably gonna spike it." And yet, as funny as it sounded, the situation was more serious. Gaffney knew he had to accept Ned's coffee. ("Ned's actions were one of a person who was guilty," Gaffney explained to me later. "He's exhibiting guilty expressions and mannerisms.

By this time, we were like, 'OK, how do we enforce what we believe—that Ned murdered Carmen?'")

As Gaffney pulled into Ned's driveway, Ned came out of the house and hurriedly walked down the few stairs from the porch onto the driveway. He had two mugs of coffee in his hands.

Gaffney laughed to himself. *He's waiting for me?*

"Sergeant," Ned said, handing Gaffney the mug, "here." There was a car in the driveway. Ned pointed to where the cream and sugar were sitting on the hood.

"Thanks," Gaffney said.

After some small talk, Gaffney handed Ned the documents, asking, "How are you doin'? How are your parents?"

"Good, considering."

"Coffee's not bad, Ned," Gaffney said after taking a sip.

"Hey, you got those maps of Rhode Island—can I get those back?" Ned pressed.

"They're part of the evidence, Ned. I can't give them back. You'll have to make a request by court order."

Ned shook his head. "The Hartford PD never gave me a receipt for the car search."

"You'll have to take that up with them," Gaffney suggested.

Gaffney and Ned stood in the driveway exchanging small talk for a few more moments. The Red Sox (of course). Weather. Family. But Ned kept dragging the conversation back to the HPD and how irritated he was at them for not giving him a receipt. For Ned, he was all about following rules, providing they worked to *his* advantage. He kept an itemized inventory in his head—checks and balances—of the investigation, ready to pounce on the system the moment he saw a violation of his rights.

"Those Rhode Island cops," Ned said next, "they have a lack of credibility with me. They don't know how to deal with people."

Gaffney shrugged. The comment opened up an opportunity. "Why do you feel that way, Ned?"

"Well, when you guys came here for the search warrant on the fifteenth, they were rough. I thought I was being arrested. As soon as I realized I wasn't being arrested, they told me they were going to bring in cadaver dogs and bulldoze my parents' yard."

"It's all part of this," Gaffney said.

"Yeah, but if they had something on me, they *would* have arrested me *that* day, instead of just threatening to dig up my lawn."

"What would they have on you?" Gaffney wondered out loud.

Ned changed the subject. "That Stratford case!" he raged. "My palm prints are being compared."

Since Ned had been under investigation for Carmen's murder and his prior convictions from New Jersey had become part of the case, the Stratford Police Department (SPD) had inquired about Ned's possible role in several missing persons cases and murders it had open. Ned's former employer, American Frozen Foods, had an office in Stratford. It was practical to at least look into the prospect.

This, however, infuriated Ned. There was one particular case the SPD had matched up to Ned's MO and requested a set of his palm prints from the CSP. He was worried about how those comparisons were coming along. "Look," Ned said to Gaffney as they continued talking, "if Stratford had *anything,* if Rhode Island had *anything,* they would have arrested me."

"I can't speak for them, Ned. But they must have good reason for doing what they're doing."

"Do you know anything about those Stratford comparisons?" Ned asked.

For once, Gaffney had an answer. "They came back negative."

Ned looked relieved. Gaffney wanted to maneuver the conversation back into the yard and the idea the CSP had that Ned could have buried evidence or more victims. As they spoke, Gaffney looked toward the backyard. There was a section of the landscape that looked disturbed, which investigators had noticed during the original search. As they talked, Gaffney could see that Ned was stewing over the thought that he could be arrested at any moment. Of course, Ned had no idea an arrest warrant was being prepared for him at that moment, not for Carmen's murder, but for the attempted kidnapping and assault of Christina Mallon.

"Why are you so preoccupied with being arrested, Ned?" Gaffney asked. "Why you so worried about it?"

Ned wouldn't answer. ("He's asking these questions," Gaffney told me later, "because he realizes that once he's arrested, he'll never see the light of day. He's probing. Being evasive. Answering the questions he *wants* to. This tells me that he's hiding something.")

At one point, Gaffney started staring into the neighbor's yard. Ned noticed his interest and became nervous, according to Gaffney.

"How long that house been empty?" Gaffney wondered.

Ned was looking off in the opposite direction when Gaffney posed the question. It was a subject that rattled Ned. He "suddenly turned," Gaffney said. The mention of the neighbor's house put him in a defensive mode.

Pale as paper, Ned asked, "How do you know *that*?"

"The physical appearance of the home," Gaffney said. "It's obvious it's been neglected."

"That woman died some time ago. The family is making arrangements, I guess."

Gaffney immediately began contemplating the notion that Ned had possibly buried a few bodies next door, or hid evidence in the home or yard. Ned was entirely uncomfortable talking about the house. He wanted to change the subject.

Gaffney had struck a nerve.

"Ah, um, I . . . were you present when they searched my parents' house?" Ned asked.

Gaffney looked at his watch. "It's two-thirty, Ned. I need to get going."

"Oh, OK."

"Thanks for the coffee. I appreciate it."

Ned stood by his door as Gaffney drove away.

Gaffney later said Ned was the type of suspect who always thought "two moves down the road." He was "squirrelly, introverted. I understood this. I wanted to put myself in a position where, if he decided, 'OK, if there comes a time when I have to tell somebody something, I want to be comfortable telling this guy.'"

75

I

Ned's phone was ringing. Reporters were knocking on his door. But Ned didn't want anything to do with publicizing what was going on in his life. If not because of the embarrassment, for the sake of his parents. They were old and ailing. And now with Ned's life becoming a major news story, the added weight of constantly being under a microscope was overwhelming. In addition, Ned believed the New Jersey newspapers had made him out to be a monster years ago, up there with the likes of his so-called mentor, Bundy, and although he secretly devoured the attention, he made it clear that he felt betrayed and was being set up by a group of cops out to get him.

In light of it all, however, Ned used the new opportunity to plead his case. As the Stratford story surfaced and a victim's name made it into the newspapers—Shani Baldwin, a twenty-one-year-old woman who had been found stabbed to death in her home in 2001—Ned gave a brief interview to the Associated Press, saying, "I gave them fingerprints . . . but it's important that both sides of the story be printed." Yet, that other "side" Ned referred to never materialized as Ned refused to elaborate or discuss the matter further.

Ned had an eerie sense about him. His enunciation, especially to those who did not know him, might have come across as overconfident and even patronizing. But he couldn't help himself. He drew attention to himself by the things he did—attention, maybe, he enjoyed—albeit good, bad, or indifferent. In every news story published about the search and Carmen's body being found in Rhode Island, those two cases from New Jersey tagged along with Ned's name in the lead paragraph as if they were part of a life's résumé, which, in a certain sense, they were. This made Ned feel as if he were being judged by his prior conduct—crimes for which, he said over and over, he had paid his debt to society. When reporters asked Ned if he knew Carmen, he said he wasn't going to comment on the case. Yet when *Hartford Courant* reporter Ken Byron caught up to Ned one day and asked him if he killed Carmen, Ned replied, "I did not kill her."

There may have been some truth to Ned's statement—because, inside the next few years, one of the many bizarre twists in the murder of Carmen Rodriguez would be that a man—that same man who had been obsessed with Carmen and raped her—would make a deathbed confession that he had killed her.

BOOK V

ELEMENTS OF MURDER

76

I

On the morning of January 24, 2002, Ned was arrested and formally charged with attempted kidnapping and third-degree assault. The arrest stemmed from that night shortly before Carmen went missing when Ned allegedly grabbed Christina Mallon outside Kenney's. When they showed up at his house, detectives didn't tell Ned why they were arresting him. But he assumed it was for Carmen's murder.

Ned didn't put up any resistance, but instead acted as if the CSP—who had taken over control of the investigation by this point—had nothing on him. He laughed and joked with the officers placing him into a squad car.

Back at Troop H in Hartford, Ned sat quietly as detectives entered the room, one of whom said, "You think this is for the murder of Carmen Rodriguez?"

Ned looked at each officer. "Huh?" He was shocked. "What do you mean?"

"You're under arrest for the attempted kidnapping and assault of [Christina Mallon]."

"I'm surprised by that," Ned said, shaking his head. "You've *got* to be kidding."

II

Ned was arraigned the following morning, his bond set at $500,000. And his next court date scheduled for February 5. Later that night, someone from the HPD called Luz Rodriguez. "We brought him in."

Luz sighed. "Thanks for calling."

"You should know, though, that we haven't arrested him for Carmen's murder. We brought him in on another charge."

"I'm confused."

"Don't worry about it," the detective said.

Luz hung up the phone, feeling ambivalent. The end result was that Ned had been arrested. But why wasn't he being charged with Carmen's murder? ("We were told," Luz explained to me later, "that this first arrest was the beginning of the end. We had no idea it would turn out the way it did.")

III

On the day the CSP searched the Snelgrove residence, crime scene investigators submitted several items to the Department of Public Safety, Forensic Science Laboratory, in Meriden, Connecticut, for DNA and forensic analysis. Criminalist Maria Warner was assigned the contents of a trash barrel found in Ned's room. A substance located inside the barrel was suspected to be blood. Warner quickly tested it and determined it to be human blood.

Had Ned made a mistake? None of the other pieces of trash turned up anything useful for David Zagaja. But what about this blood? Whose was it?

IV

There was a sinkhole—a large scallop—in the backyard of the Snelgrove neighbor's house. It appeared to be *consistent with being recently created,* an affidavit accompanying Ned's arrest explained. There was no grass over the divot, which led detectives to believe that someone had (just recently) dug a hole and covered it up.

Detectives got hold of the owner of the house on Tuesday, January 29, 2002, and explained that they needed to get into the yard to conduct a search and, like archaeologists, sift through some of the dirt with screens. Ned was in jail, exactly where they wanted him. The kidnapping and assault charges were going to trial. Ned was not going to plead his case.

"No problem," the owner of the house said. "My mother died years ago. The place has been vacant since 1999."

As crime scene investigators approached the sinkhole, someone noticed a black plastic bag protruding from the ground. "You see that," the investigator said, pointing.

They dug the bag up.

It was empty.

After spending the day searching the yard, nothing else was uncovered. But the bag—that bag had to be significant. What did it explain?

A theory soon developed. Based on the discovery in the neighbor's yard, some detectives began to look at how Carmen's body had been found in Rhode Island. The Hopkinton crime scene showed no signs of being disturbed by animals. If the body had sat in those woods in garbage bags from September 22, 2001, the day Carmen was reported missing, to January 6, 2002, when Peter Mareck found it, many believed wildlife in the area would have at least ripped the bag open or tried getting at it. Furthermore, renowned forensic scientist Dr. Henry Lee made what, at first, appeared to be an important discovery while studying the "secondary" crime scene photographs. (Secondary because investigators believed Ned had killed Carmen in Connecticut and transported her body to Rhode Island.) Analyzing the photographs microscopically, Lee noticed that the leaves around the area where the garbage bag was found were "dry, so it has to be around fall." Moreover, there was no "dated material growth through the bags. . . . If, say, longer than a year [had expired]," Lee said, ". . . usually something can grow through the bags, through the hole, because that area [is] going to be very fertile and you see a lot of new shoots coming out. So that tells me [it] has to be relative, you know, under six months, cannot be over, over a year."

Some believed that as soon as the Hartford PD started sniffing around, asking questions, Ned moved Carmen's body from the neighbor's yard (or another location) to Rhode Island, sensing that a search of his home was imminent.

"You can see little branches *around* the body," Lee explained. "But no branches sticking through the body area. If this body [had] been there . . . usually we see something grow through the body."

For detectives, based on their training and experience, knowing that Ned had spent years in prison studying Bundy's manner of drawing unsuspecting women into his web, realizing he had, upon his release, *improved* on his MO by meticulously wrapping women in various articles of linen and transporting their bodies to various locations, like Bundy, it was their interpretation that *animals will disturb a body left out in the open for an extended period of time,* said the affidavit for Ned's arrest. *Based on this, it is reasonable to assume that Carmen Rodriguez's body may have been moved to the place it was found from another location* after *police contacted Edwin Snelgrove and conducted the first search warrant on his automobile.*

"We did some testing and analysis on the bag found in the neighbor's yard and found nothing," David Zagaja told me. "There was some speculation that maybe he moved her body at a later time. But I don't think he did. I think he placed Carmen's body in Rhode Island on that weekend of September 22 to 23, 2001."

It was easy to figure out that between the end of September

and beginning of January, at least in the Northeast, nothing generally grew wild in the forests. That would explain the bag not being covered with fresh undergrowth. There were dry leaves scattered around the bag and on top of it, which meant that the body had been placed in the Rhode Island woods *before* the month of October when leaves started falling.

Still, how to attest to no animals getting into the bag?

Carmen's killer used nearly one dozen garbage bags to wrap up her body. Stapled and taped them all together so it couldn't—or wouldn't—leak fluids or emit smells. To this, David Zagaja added, "We played around with the possibility that he moved her—put it this way, we're not sure. I think Ned made that trip on that weekend. And remember, the trip being made on *that* weekend matches with the mileage evidence we uncovered."

77

I

Carmen's body was released by the medical examiner's office in late January. The Rodriguez family was getting nervous because Carmen's brothers and sisters in town from Puerto Rico had taken a considerable amount of time off from work to support other family members and be there to bury Carmen. The theme of the burial—if the horror of losing Carmen under such violent means could have one—was *"¿Madre, por qué me dejas?"*

"Mother, why you leave me?"

For the family, telling Jackie, Carmen's daughter, was the most difficult. Luz had called Jackie the day the Hartford PD confirmed they made a positive identification. Jackie, who was still living in the apartment Carmen had rented with Miguel, rushed to her grandmother's house where everyone had gathered. That line *"¿Madre, por qué me dejas?"* was from one of Carmen's favorite songs. After the family had told Jackie what happened, she rushed out of the house, drove home, grabbed the CD, and rushed back. Walking in, she didn't say anything. Instead, she put on the CD.

"It was a bit surprising," Luz remembered, "because if

someone is dead, or murdered, we never play music for like one month. Supposedly, it's bad luck." Respect the deceased. It was a tradition the family valued. Carmen's mother had brought it to America from the old country and the family continued it.

But Carmen's death had changed everything. It was no ordinary celebration of life, as most funerals are.

As the song played, Jackie walked into the kitchen where everyone was standing, sat down at the table, and just let it all out. "Listen," she said, referring to the lyrics, "it's about me and Mommy."

From that day on, the family played the song over and over. At the wake. The funeral. Anytime they visited Carmen's grave site. There were those words: "Mother, why you leave me?"

II

The Rodriguez family was more united than ever. Since Carmen was buried, Luz, Sonia, and Kathy Perez had made T-shirts with a photograph of Carmen on the front. She was smiling her radiant glow. Those eyes. That sincere happiness flushed across her face.

Titi.

On the T-shirt, Carmen was surrounded by a red rose and pearls and baby's breath. In Spanish, the family wrote a message in big block letters on the top: *NUNCA OLVIDAREMOS.*

"Never forget."

A dedication more to the court and Ned Snelgrove than to themselves.

III

On February 5, Ned was scheduled to be back in court. Inside the courtroom, as the day progressed, twenty of Carmen's family and friends sat patiently in the first three rows and waited to see the man they believed had killed Carmen. ("We knew he did it," Luz later told me. "We wanted to show our strength. Our unity. That Ned had picked the wrong victim in choosing to murder Carmen.")

What they learned, however, was that Ned had been released nine years early on a prior sentence of twenty years. ("We were furious," Luz added. "He never should have been out on the street to begin with. But we were united. We were planning on seeing this through until the end—that is, until he was put away for good for the murder of my sister.")

They waited all morning.

No Ned.

Lunchtime came and went.

No Ned.

Finally, near three o'clock . . . there he was: the monster.

During his five minutes in front of the judge, Ned never looked at the Rodriguez family as his case was continued to the end of the month.

Sonia was most troubled by the events. The oldest female of Carmen's siblings, Sonia had not taken her sister's murder well. She'd had her share of problems with Carmen—they butted heads—but the relationship was on the mend when Carmen disappeared. Still, most heartbreaking to the family was that Esmeralda Garcia, a name Carmen had given to Jackie for her first grandchild, was born after Carmen's death. Carmen had never got to see, or hold, or play with, her only grandchild.

78

I

One would only have to assume that Detective Stavros Mellekas, who had been with the CSP since 1994, was feared and hated by the bad guys he went after on any given day. At six feet one inch, 280 pounds, the Rhode Island transplant could be considered massive by any measure, with hands like catcher's mitts, a grip like a vise, and a knack for police work that very few had. Mellekas had been with the Major Crimes Unit since 1999. He had seen his share of death and murder and rape and all things evil. It was Mellekas who had been in the Snelgrove yard one day when a neighbor walked up and lobbed the George Recck lead to him. "Anything you want to know about Ned," said the enthusiastic neighbor, "you talk to George."

The next day, Mellekas and Detective Tom Murray took the drive up to northern Massachusetts, where Recck was now living with his wife. ("Squirrelly guy," Mellekas recalled. "A statistics guy, you know. Nice person, though. Educated.")

Mellekas's intention was to extract from Recck a few details that could help the CSP locate more evidence. Maybe Recck could recall a place where he and Ned used to hang out as kids. The woods. A party spot. Maybe he'd remember places Ned liked to visit. ("We had nothing," Mellekas recalled. "No weapon. Nothing. We were looking for a killing spot. Obviously, it wasn't Hopkinton.")

"So, George, you spoke to Ned on the phone while he was in prison?"

"Yup," Recck said. In the years that Ned was in prison, his only outlet to the outside world was George Recck. "I would send him socks on his birthday."

Mellekas was surprised. He wanted to hear more. If the guy was sending him socks, it was more than just a casual friendship.

"We kept in contact," Recck continued, according to Mellekas's reporting of the conversation. "Underwear too. I sent him shorts."

"What about your conversations?"

It was 2002. The conversations Recck had had with Ned, mainly, took place in 1997 and 1998. He didn't remember—who could blame him?—much of what had been said.

"I have all these letters," Recck said.

What? Letters? Mellekas's interest piqued. "Sure, let's see them."

"You can have them, but I want them back."

II

Inside the car. Heading toward Connecticut. Mellekas. Reading.

I cannot believe this. "Some things were just jumping off the pages of those letters."

There it all was in black and white—rather, blue pen ink—staring at Mellekas as Murray raced down the Massachusetts Turnpike toward Connecticut: *Bundy.*

"He compared himself to Ted Bundy."

Murray shook his head.

It was the first time anyone in law enforcement had been privy to the Bundy connection.

Could we be dealing with a serial? Mellekas wondered. Was Ned like those killers with whom he was fascinated? Was the CSP going to start finding bodies all over New England? As much as the letters didn't reveal, in Mellekas's opinion, they made one important point: Ned Snelgrove harbored sick intentions. Wrote them down. And wasn't afraid to admit his fantasies and impurities. *Can you believe this?*

But then—there it was: that one line. Everyone talked about it later. That one line that sent chills. Made things so real. So evil.

Gooseflesh.

There was Ned writing to George that it would make a much more exciting book if, upon his release from New Jersey, he could *pick up right where I left off.* It was the first time the CSP had heard this.

Mellekas read it again: *pick up right where I left off.*

79

I

Seemingly innocuous letters on a page, put together to make up words, can tell you a lot about a guy. A lot about what is going on inside his head. A lot about how the mind and the hand are connected as the person writes. There's a relationship. Some sort of subconscious id, as Freud might call it, coming out through the process of thinking and writing at the same time. For Ned, the act of writing became his only link, his only connection, to the outside world. Most definitely, it was his only way of feeling a sense of normalcy around what he saw as deplorable, rancid conditions in the New Jersey jail, where he was housed before being sent away to Rahway back in 1988.

For some reason, Ned felt safe talking to George Recck. As the CSP went through what we'll call "the Recck Letters," investigators saw how Ned joked with Recck in one letter, wanting to know if he was "still" Recck's *second-biggest hero besides G. [Gordon] Liddy?* It was June 20, 1988. Ned said he was sorry that it had taken him such a long time to write. He was being shuffled about the system like a file. Finally, though, he had made it into his cell block. It was hot, he explained. Hot and sticky and smelly. He hated it and despised the people around him. Thought he was better than all of them. And struggled to find the survival skills he knew he was going to need. *If it weren't for this . . . fan,* Ned wrote, just outside *his door, [the heat] would be unbearable.*

The electric fan blowing on him all day took Ned back down a nostalgic road as he sat in front of it and dreamed of being back at his apartment *on the front porch . . . enjoying the summer breeze. . . .* He spoke of baseball, giving Recck his predictions for the season. Ned liked the Orioles. Tigers too. He was honest with himself about his favorite team, the Red Sox. He knew they weren't going to have a great season.

While Ned was out on bail the previous winter—1987—he had seen Recck, according to this letter. It was shortly before he cut the deal for the attempted murder of Mary Ellen Renard and manslaughter of Karen Osmun. He wanted to tell Recck his "secret" when he saw him. But it was something, he wrote, *I couldn't tell you [or] my parents* on the outside. But now he wanted to confess and wrote the *incident* with Mary Ellen wasn't the *first time* he lost *control of myself with a girl.*

Investigators were amazed at how easily Ned sugarcoated the entire incident.

Then he warned his friend. Prepare yourself. It's coming. *You'll never believe [it]. . . . I had actually gotten away with murder. . . .*

As Ned continued writing to Recck, he explained how he hoped Recck knew that he had been *doing everybody a favor and postponing a lot of pain* by not admitting to any of his transgressions sooner. Ned had not come clean, he insinuated, for the sake of his friends and family and the turmoil that would ultimately come with his admission. He also said that once the cops had him on radar for the attack against Mary Ellen, he knew it was all over, and that he'd then have

to admit to the *other thing*. He praised his lawyer, John
Bruno, for getting *the damage down to twenty years*.

"Damage": the result of a murder and an attempted
murder.

He explained to Recck he'd be eligible for parole in ten, en-
couraging him to call his parents and talk to them about the
"bomb" he had dropped. He was sure everyone back home
knew, and it was all very humiliating to him.

Not once did Ned apologize for the pain he had caused
his victims and their families. It was all about Ned and his ultimate embarrassment of being caught. It was all about Ned
and how the crimes he had committed would affect him and
his friends and family. It was all about the waste of his life.
He never once, in all the years of causing other people pain,
said he was sorry for what he had done.

II

As he did with everyone else in his life, when Ned wrote
to George Recck there was a thread—no, a certain inherent
charm—of control in the tone of the letters. Ned often told
Recck what to think, when to write, and how to live his life.

Recck must have asked Ned about Bundy, because in the
letters, beginning in 1992, Ned began to talk about Bundy
and the comparisons between his life and the infamous
killer's. Ned had served four years by this point. He was a seasoned con now.

"Whenever Ned went to jail," a CSP investigator explained, "he grew a mustache. We called it his 'bad boy' mustache. Ned was a little guy. He felt small and weak in prison.
He was smarter than just about every other inmate—that
much we gave him. But he didn't have the strength. He grew
the mustache, hoping to look more masculine."

In his 1992 letters, Ned praised Bundy for planning out his
crimes with a methodical sense of awareness of the police.

Ned insisted that the crimes he committed were "impromptu acts." He said on the nights he committed *his* crimes, he simply—his word "simply"—*convinced myself that now was a good time.* Hurting females was never something he had awoken and decided to do on that specific day; although, he was quick to add, *I was always thinking*—his underline—*about it. . . .* Moreover, he wrote, *he never . . . went out* and, prowling around, looking, scoping out bars and eyeing females, tried to *find a situation. . . .* When he did decide to act out on his urges, he wrote it was a matter of *convincing [himself] that now was a good time.* He called getting away—*(temporarily)*—with the homicide of Karen Osmun nothing short of a *miracle.* But still, it was nearly impossible for him to resist Mary Ellen Renard, he explained. Meeting her that night, Ned wrote to Recck, *was the perfect situation.*

III

There is no doubt that Ned Snelgrove got a kick out of toying with law enforcement. Just about every investigator I spoke to said Ned loved the idea of thinking he was smarter than those who were tracking him. He loved the entire catch and release, "I make a move/You counter" aspect of committing crimes and seeing if cops could figure him out. "He and Recck," one investigator told me, "played chess via letters. This is the type of guy Ned is. He had the patience for that."

You make a move.

Now it's my turn.

What tickled Ned's funny bone during the Karen Osmun investigation in 1983 was the fact that he had, at least then, a *squeaky clean reputation,* he wrote to Recck. Ned wrote the cops were *sure [he] did it.* He insisted law enforcement was sending him *anonymous notes, thinking I might "crack."* But little did Ned know that it was actually a friend of Karen's who was sending the notes.

Near the end of this particular letter, Ned talked about how Bundy liked to keep mementoes of his crimes, chiding the famous professional killer for doing so. *This leaves a documented trail for police . . . ,* Ned wrote to Recck, adding that they would know *where you were & where you were headed on any given weekend.*

That one line—the one about leaving a trail of evidence—sent Detective Stavros Mellekas down a path of suspicion. As Mellekas read it, he knew it had been written some ten years prior, but what did it say, actually, about the case Mellekas was investigating now?

Mellekas looked at what the CSP had. Scores of maps found in traveling salesman Ned's basement bedroom. Not in his car, mind you, where one would think the maps might be kept. Additionally, it was the end of that sentence—*where you were headed on any given weekend*—that stuck out to Mellekas.

Carmen disappeared on a Friday night. (Ned chastised Bundy for purchasing gas with credit cards and saving the receipts.)

Hasn't Ned done the same?

80

I

When Ned returned to court in March 2002 after his February date was postponed, the day's proceedings didn't yield much in the form of insight into the case, or even when Ned's trial for attempting kidnapping would begin. And yet the day wasn't devoid of drama.

Carmen's daughter Jackie Garcia was sitting patiently with Luz, Sonia, and the rest of the Rodriguez family, waiting for Ned to be brought in. The family wanted answers. They weren't about to let Ned show up in court without having a presence there to prove to him that Carmen mattered.

She was a person.

They loved her.

Never forget.

As Ned was walked into the room, Jackie stood up quickly and threw a crumpled piece of paper at him as everyone watched.

"What happened? What was that?" someone said out loud.

Then Jackie screamed as she went for Ned's throat, lunging, like a leopard, off the bench into the air. *You bastard.* "You killed my mother!"

Ned turned. "What?"

The marshals covered him and quickly escorted him back to his cell.

The room cleared.

II

By June, the CSP returned to the Savage Hill neighborhood where Ned had lived. David Zagaja had Ned in jail. But the investigation into Carmen's murder was far from over.

Detective Mellekas was at a neighbor's house, again searching the backyard with his colleagues, when he spotted Mr. Snelgrove out in his yard. The old man was looking on. Curious, of course, as to what was going on next door. "Hey, Mr. Snelgrove, how are you today, sir?" Mellekas asked.

Snelgrove nodded.

"Listen," Mellekas continued, "the court signed a search and seizure warrant for Ned's car." Mellekas had it in his hand. It was a second warrant for the car.

The old man shook his head.

"Could we make some room for a tow truck to come in and take it away?" Snelgrove's car was blocking the driveway.

"OK."

"The tow truck should be here shortly."

They stood. Talked. Not like old college friends. But Mellekas was happy with the way in which the old man was beginning to open up. He wanted to say something, Mellekas was sure of it. And within a few moments, they got on the topic of the registration and Mellekas wondered why it had been changed from Ned's name to his father's. It seemed strange. Especially for a guy who had claimed his innocence all along.

"Well," Mr. Snelgrove said (according to Mellekas), "Ned will probably be going away for a long time."

Mellekas thought about it. *What a thing to say.*

"I think Ned killed this girl in Hartford," Mellekas said

casually. Why not toss that bombshell out to the old man and see how he reacts.

Snelgrove looked at ease with the comment, Mellekas wrote in his report, as if it didn't bother him. The senior Snelgrove said, "I would not be surprised if Ned killed her."

"I think Ned has a problem," Mellekas said sincerely, keeping it going. "I think he needs psychiatric help."

Snelgrove shrugged. *Whatever.*

"Ned supposedly," Mr. Snelgrove said, "received treatment in New Jersey, but I guess it didn't work."

Mellekas walked over to the car and stood by it. The tow truck was coming up the road. They could hear its croaky diesel engine, knocking and smoking its way toward the house. Soon the beeping sounds would start as the tow truck backed up and the conversation would be disrupted by the commotion. It was bad timing.

"Why do you think the treatment didn't work? What makes you say that, sir?"

Snelgrove thought about it. He looked toward the truck. "Well, this makes three—and who the hell knows how many more are out there?"

"What do you mean?" Mellekas asked.

"Who the hell knows . . . maybe he thinks he's some sort of goddamn superhero?"

"How so?"

"You know, drubbing out the dregs of society."

Now Carmen was a "dreg." Had Ned told Mr. Snelgrove something about Carmen?

"Why'd you say that just now?" Mellekas asked.

"I don't know. Just thinking out loud, I guess."

III

Ned's pretrial hearing on the charges of attempted kidnapping was continued to May 30, 2002. Then into June. The fall.

Maybe September, someone from the court said. October, the latest.

So Ned sat in prison. Waiting.

No bail.

IV

As everyone waited for the kidnapping trial, Detective Mellekas stepped up his pressure on Ned. During the summer of 2002, Mellekas decided that the way to get Ned to maybe crack under pressure was to stay in his face as much as he could. Play Columbo with him. Ned liked to talk. The CSP's only problem was that Ned liked to talk about everything *except* the investigation. The Red Sox. Stocks. Bonds. Food. Computers.

Ned was being held at the MacDougall-Walker Correctional Institution, in Suffield, Connecticut. Whenever a cop goes into a prison to speak with an inmate, he understands the Department of Corrections has total authority over the prisoner and is in charge of that inmate. The Department of Corrections calls the shots, in other words: paperwork, interview rooms, times, and dates. All prisons require law enforcement of any kind to present the suspect with a waiver that delegates responsibility back to law enforcement for the duration of the interview. By signing the document, the inmate is saying he or she agrees to allow the police to question him or her without a prison official present. If anything happens during the interview, the Department of Corrections is off the hook. Most inmates have no trouble signing the form.

Ned wouldn't sign it, saying, "You know me, Mellekas, I'm willing to talk to you—but I'm not signing any paper."

So Mellekas had a prison official with him anytime he went in. On this day, July 12, 2002, Mellekas decided to try and match Ned at his own game. He knew it bothered Ned that he had disappointed his mother and father. Their feelings mattered to Ned.

Mellekas closed the door. The room was comfortable. Anything other than cement walls and steel bars was a reprieve for a guy locked up.

Mellekas read Ned his rights. Then, "How's it going, Ned?"

Ned was quiet. Yet, there was something, Mellekas noticed, different about him. Prison life was getting to Ned. Mellekas could see it on his face. The guy had done eleven years. Here he was again facing a long bid.

"I believe you killed Carmen Rodriguez," Mellekas came out and said. "I think you did it, Ned."

Ned wouldn't speak on the topic. He shook his head.

"You don't want to stay here the rest of your life," Mellekas suggested. "Come on, Ned. You're sick. You belong in a hospital."

Ned wouldn't budge.

Mellekas stared at him. Ned was tearing up. His eyes welled.

"You did it. You did it. You did it." Mellekas wasn't being pushy or loud or bossy. He was just talking.

But Ned wasn't. He was still teary-eyed. ("Crying?" Mellekas said later. "I wouldn't say crying. . . . He was like a little kid getting caught for something.")

Mellekas needed to keep the pressure on: harder, more firm. Maybe bring in emotion. "Your parents, Ned," he said next, "do want them to have to come *here?* To a jail. They deserve more than that. Wouldn't you rather they visit you in a hospital?"

Nothing.

"They deserve more, Ned."

Head shake. Eyes. Welling up. But no words.

"You've got some serious issues, Ned. Psychological problems. I know. I can help, though. I understand this is why you killed Carmen. You couldn't help it. You belong in a hospital, Ned. I know that. You're sick."

Finally, "They said this before to me."

"Your dad is a Yale grad, Ned." Ned looked up. "Your mom is a PTA type of lady. Do you want them coming up here to the reception area of Walker, a prison, sitting with these common criminals?"

More tears.

Ned Snelgrove never once denied killing Carmen. He'd had every opportunity to slam his hands on the table and scream, *I did not kill that woman!* He had every chance to plead with Mellekas, *You've got the wrong guy. I didn't kill her.*

But he didn't. Instead, he stopped crying and said, "I want to get out of here. This interview is over."

81

I

Mellekas walked out of the prison somewhat disappointed. Not in himself. But in Ned. He believed he could truly help Ned if he only came clean. But Ned wanted nothing to do with remorse or admission.

On July 17, five days later, Mellekas went back to the prison. But Ned refused to even come out of his cell.

Mellekas waited. Soon a prison official took another walk. "That detective is still here, Ned. He wants to talk to you."

Ned shrugged. "No."

Mellekas later said he believed then—and now—that after he interviewed Ned that one time, Ned smartened up. He was scared of being broken. So, in order to avoid being beaten by his own vulnerabilities, he decided he wasn't going to talk at all. But Mellekas wanted another crack. So he went back to the prison a few days later. Prison officials brought Ned down to the interview room. Apparently, they hadn't told him this time who was waiting.

According to Mellekas, Ned took a look into the room through the narrow door window, saying, "No, no, no . . . I don't want to talk to him."

Mellekas stood up. "Come on, Ned." Waving him in. Pulling out a chair.

"No." Ned shook his head.

On August 30, 2002, Mellekas went back for a third time.

"No," Ned said.

II

Christina Mallon had her day in court on October 14, 2002. Christina sat in the witness stand and told her tale of Ned trying to grab her in front of Kenney's during that first week of September 2001. "Get in the car, you bitch," Christina said she heard Ned yell at her before she threw a beer bottle at his car and refused to get in.

Ned still hadn't been arrested on murder charges. David Zagaja was prosecuting the kidnapping case while also leading the murder investigation.

Christina was a tough witness. She had lived a hard life— evident from the way in which she carried herself and spoke. Jurors weren't warming to her.

To Zagaja's dismay, he wasn't able to get any of Ned's prior convictions or crimes into the kidnapping trial. The jury never knew, for example, that Ned had served time for manslaughter and attempted murder and aggravated assault. Nor were they allowed to hear testimony related to any of the letters Ned had written throughout the years, where he had described thoughts of stalking women and hurting them.

Ned sat next to Jack Franckling, his attorney. He knew how to play on the jury's impulses. To every juror hearing the case, Ned was a hardworking salesman from the suburbs who stopped at Kenney's to have a few beers after a long day's work. And here was this woman trying to say that he had tried to grab her off the street. Who was *she* to walk into the courtroom and accuse him of *anything*?

Christina's major problem was that she couldn't pinpoint a

date for the incident. If it had been such a traumatic experience, why couldn't she recall the exact day?

Zagaja didn't look too worried.

Luz Rodriguez and her siblings, however, didn't seem so confident. They sensed—"Especially me," Luz said later— the case slipping out of Zagaja's hands, and, in turn, Ned walking out of the courtroom a free man.

Luz looked at Zagaja: "What's going on?" she whispered when their eyes met.

Zagaja tried explaining with hand gestures—like a cop telling a motorist to slow down near road construction—to chill out, don't worry. *Everything's going to be all right. Trust me.*

Luz was furious. If she and her family couldn't get justice for Carmen with a murder charge, they would accept, at least for now, a kidnapping conviction.

III

David Zagaja later said Ned was cocky and arrogant where it pertained to his crimes. "And it wasn't my opinion," Zagaja added. "It was the psychiatrist's opinion that [Ned] really exhibited a certain pride for his conduct. . . ." A hubris.

Ned could be thinking about killing, in other words, but appear as if he were your friend, someone who would not hurt you.

Poker face.

Ned was an expert at deception.

A pro.

Ned thought like Bundy, Gacy, Dahmer, Ridgway (the "Green River Killer"). "Edwin Snelgrove," Zagaja said later, "sets himself apart from many individuals who commit murder. He has embodied a desire, an obsession, and a purpose to kill. . . ."

This was the real Ned Snelgrove. Not some dude sitting in a courtroom wooing jurors with his smile and plain looks—knowing all the while that his prior crimes were not going to tarnish his reputation.

IV

The jury went back into the deliberations room, had lunch, and then announced its verdict.

Watching them walk into the room, Zagaja and the Rodriguez family knew, then and there, that they were going to— "can you believe it?"—acquit this maniac of the kidnapping charges and allow him to walk out the door a free man. ("Chills," Luz Rodriguez said later. Just the thought that Carmen's killer was going to escape the system was too much to fathom.)

Tears.

Anger.

Zagaja did that thing with his hands again. He was smiling. Well, sort of. Staring at Luz and her family. He seemed confident. "It's OK."

Ned—well, Ned *was* smiling. That much was entirely obvious. There he sat next to his lawyer and realized what everyone else knew: the jury had bought his shtick.

Indeed. "Not guilty," the foreman said a moment later.

A collective gasp.

"Reasonable doubt," Ned's lawyer had argued during his closing. "You cannot believe this witness"—Christina Mallon—"because her stories didn't jibe with her statement to police."

Luz sunk her head into her hands. And cried.

Sonia did the same.

Zagaja looked toward them: *Don't worry about it.*

Ned stood and thanked the jury. Smiling. Nodding his head up and down. *Bless you all. You did the right thing.* "Thank you, thank you," he said out loud. He folded his hands together. *Thanks,* he gestured with a nod, as if bowing.

V

Luz, Sonia, and Carmen's mother, Rosa, were outside the courtroom on the cement sidewalk crying. They couldn't believe it. How could Ned's lies win?

Ned was downstairs signing out, collecting his things.

Zagaja was upstairs in his office.

Detective Mellekas, along with several other investigators working the Carmen Rodriguez case, were also downstairs.

Ned soon spotted them.

They were now smiling.

Smiling?

Right then, Ned knew. Mellekas had an arrest warrant in his hand for the murder of Carmen Rodriguez. Ned wasn't going anywhere, except maybe from one cell to the next.

"You're under arrest for the murder of Carmen Rodriguez," said one of the investigators, "anything you say can and will be . . ."

Ned dropped his head.

High and low. Up and down. One minute smiling. Tasting freedom like a raindrop on your tongue. And the next . . . well, the next . . . handcuffs and processing. Ned was going back to jail—only now he was facing murder charges and a $1 million bond.

In a way, it *was* a game.

If so, checkmate.

"He had to know it was coming," Mellekas told me later. "He saw me and [two other investigators] in the courtroom."

After serving the arrest warrant, Mellekas and his colleagues brought Ned across the street from the courthouse to Troop H, where he was locked up. Mellekas tried talking to him. But Ned didn't want to hear it. ("He'd talk about everything," Mellekas said, "but nothing.")

At one point, Ned went into a diatribe about politics and politicians. He was loath to think about what some politicians got away with. He couldn't comprehend that they were better than him. What an incredible double standard.

"You know, Ned," Mellekas said, "you speak with such eloquence and you're so articulate. You couldn't have been a politician, [though]."

"Politicians," Ned said with a laugh, as if he could in fact be one, "have criminal records."

"Yeah, Ned," Mellekas said, smirking, chuckling a little, "but they never kill anybody."

And then Ned mentioned that one guy, that one Washington politician under investigation . . . what's-his-name? He couldn't think of it.

Gary Condit, Mellekas said.

"Yeah."

Mellekas laughed.

82

I

Ned was sharp. He remembered everything. There was one cop who had seen and spoken to Ned in January and then had to talk to him again three months later. Ned looked at him that second time. Smiled. (Ned liked to smile when he knew something you didn't.) "That suit," Ned had said. "You wore that same suit the last time you were here."

The cop looked down at himself. He couldn't recall. Maybe it was.

The suit comment was, one detective later said, a way for Ned to say, *Hey, I'm smarter than you. I'm watching every move you make and I am the one in charge.*

II

Ned was arraigned the following day. His bail was raised from $1 million to $3 million. There weren't going to be any more Moosehead beers for Ned Snelgrove at Kenney's for quite a while. While in lockup, Ned began to play chess with his cell mates. He talked to them, too. One claimed Ned was beginning to open up. It was apparent that Ned needed a reputation. He was a small man. Protecting himself in prison wouldn't be easy. If he had "a rep," well, that could mean a lot. Maybe save him some trouble.

III

A day before Halloween, Detective Mellekas knocked on the door of a rather attractive young female Ned had tried to get to sign up for his frozen-food sales pitch back in 2001. Mellekas had retrieved the name from Ned's appointment book.

"I had a sales appointment with him back last May," she said, offering Mellekas a seat in her living room.

"Anything strange about him you can relate?"

She "vividly recalled" meeting Ned, Mellekas noted. Ned spent six hours at her house the night he came by for a sales call. "He wouldn't leave," she said. "He was very persistent."

In the end, Ned placed several orders for the woman without her knowledge or consent. She thought that to be both bizarre and unprofessional.

"I later canceled the orders," she said.

"What did he do then?"

"He kept calling and calling." He wouldn't take no for an answer. "He asked me out." She said no way. She had a boyfriend. A big dude. Tough too. But "Ned would call back and say, 'Casino tonight?'"

No, she'd tell him again.

"I love to gamble," Ned had told her. "You're very beautiful."

Don't call me again, she'd command.

He called every day for a week.

Then, near September 21, he stopped.

Mellekas left, thinking, *She is lucky to still be alive.*

83

I

A letter arrived. It was from a man facing murder-for-hire charges. Mark Pascual had initiated the murder of a foe, a man who, he claimed, had been hustling his girlfriend and had burned him on a business deal. "I want to say the reason why I had this guy murdered was partly because of my friend and the way he treated her and her kids, and there were . . . bad deals between me and him," Pascual told police. During a jailhouse interview, Pascual told me, "I made a mistake. I realize what I did was very wrong. I'm sorry for it. I can't change the past. Wish I could, but I can only move on from here and say how sorry I am."

Pascual was "cellies" with Ned for a time. He had written to his lawyer, who passed the letter to the state's attorney's office and told them his client had information about a murder—the murder of "Carmie" Rodriguez.

Carmie.

Yes. It was the first time law enforcement had heard the nickname.

So Detective Mellekas and James Rovella, an investigator for the state's attorney, took a ride out to see Pascual at

MacDougall-Walker Correctional Institution in Suffield, Connecticut.

"I am always very [skeptical] of jailhouse snitches," Rovella said later. "I don't trust them."

The power the state's attorney had over Pascual—and any snitch, for that matter—was that Zagaja and his investigators knew details about Carmen's murder no one else—save for her killer—knew. Important facts they had kept to themselves.

In time, they would see how accurate Pascual was.

II

On the day Ned left his cell for court (the jury in his kidnapping case was being picked that day), Mark Pascual sat down and wrote a second letter. He was nervous, he admitted, the last time he wrote, because "Ned was in the room." But now he had a moment to himself and wanted to talk about a few things.

Ned had met with his lawyer a day before his kidnapping trial started. When he came back from that meeting, he sat with Pascual and talked about it. He had been offered a deal, a lesser charge, in the kidnapping case, Ned explained. But "No way," Ned told Pascual. He wasn't taking any deal. "I'll never admit to anything. . . . They'll have to convict me or let me go."

Pascual thought, *Why not take the deal?*

"You know what I'll do," Ned said, "I can sue them for defamation of character and wrongful incarceration. It's all about a twenty-five-dollar check that she [Christina Mallon] received from American Frozen Foods."

Ned said the scam he was running in Kenney's was designed for him to receive a $100 bonus every month from his employer. For every ten people he could get to fill out an application, whether they were approved or not, he received

$100. Christina Mallon was upset with him after he burned her out of $25.

"That's why it took her so long," Ned told Pascual, "to come forward and report her so-called crime." She wanted to get him back for burning her out of the money.

The point of the story for Zagaja wasn't that Ned had told it to Pascual; it was in the details. Only Ned could have known these details. If nothing else, it told Zagaja that Pascual was maybe telling the truth.

III

Mark Pascual and prison were not a good match. Some guys are born to do time. They accept their sentences with a sense of street pride and content. They have no trouble being confined and being around men for years at a time. While others . . . well, others aren't quite built that way. They have a tough time with just the thought of being corralled like steer and told what to do and when to do it. Not to mention the emotional and physical strength one needs to survive. Pascual was thirty-nine. He had grown up in Torrington, Connecticut, which, like any city, had its rough areas and even rougher people. Pascual ran a garage. He fixed engines: cars, bikes, whatever. In fact, part of his payment to the man he had hired to—as he put it—"whack" his adversary was a snowmobile. "I want five grand," the guy had said when Pascual asked how much it would cost to have someone killed.

"That's too much," Pascual responded.

"Well, what do you suppose, then?"

"Some cash and that snowmobile over there," Pascual said, pointing.

"That'll do," the killer said.

And so, after negotiating the price of death, they made a deal: a couple hundred bucks and a snowmobile for a man's life.

This man now reaching out to the state's attorney's office to say that Ned Snelgrove—the same guy who spoke to no one, the guy who thought he had covered every base, the guy who had claimed he learned things from Bundy, the guy who thought he was always two steps ahead of law enforcement—had, in fact, told him all about the murder of Carmen Rodriguez. On the surface it didn't add up.

The conversations he'd had with Ned, Pascual claimed, had taken place over the course of eight months.

Detective Mellekas and Jim Rovella met with Pascual. "Start at the beginning," Mellekas suggested. "Take your time."

Pascual noted that the two cops weren't offering him anything in return for his statement. No "get out of jail free" cards or reduced sentence deals. It was cut-and-dry: *We'll see what we can do.* No promises. But, of course, if they all sat there and thought this guy was talking to them and wasn't going to want something, they were kidding themselves.

"I got to know Ned and talk to him," Pascual began, "while we were at recreation." They'd be out in the yard, buddying around, playing cards. One day, Pascual said, somebody walked up to him and Ned as they sat and played cards together. And that's when things took a turn from friendly conversation to what each had done to get himself tossed in the can.

"You're the guy who killed them girls in Hartford," an inmate said, referring to rumors that Ned had killed several area woman.

Ned didn't respond. What's a guy to say? Silence beckons power.

"After that," Pascual told Mellekas and Rovella, "there were newspaper articles around."

Inmates started teasing Ned. Drawing cartoons of him with his "girls" and "posting" them up all over. "That's how it all started," Pascual explained.

When Ned found the cartoons, he became angry. Stomping around, he ripped the cartoons down, rushed into the dorm, and flushed them down the toilet.

But it never let up. Then Pascual, Ned, and two other guys were playing cards one afternoon and someone walked up and tossed a newspaper article on the table. It was an article about Ned's case. Pointing, he said, "Look at that!" ("I felt that Ned had to say something to justify it to us," Pascual recalled.)

And so Ned spoke up about his case, according to Pascual, for the first time, saying, "F*** those cops. They got nothing on me. I'm good at what I do. I cover my tracks."

84

I

He was nervous. Rubbing his hands together as if it were a cold winter's day and he was standing by a fire. But it was June. June 1982. Commencement day. Looking around. Fixing his hair. Checking his gown. Ned wore a black robe, white shirt, tartan tie, gray slacks. He was a good-looking kid, with the look of an innocent child with a business degree setting out into a world full of opportunity.

What was going on in his head, however, wasn't how nice the weather was for his graduation day. Or, if those wrinkles in his gown would show up in photographs? Instead, this kid, the one with the golden smile, one of the chosen officers of Alpha Zeta, the honors/service fraternity at Rutgers, the same kid who showed so much promise, was struggling with thoughts of violence against the women around him. He fought—in his own words—just about every day with the tug-of-war between acting out on those thoughts and controlling himself, which, for the most part, he had seemed to do.

Indeed, the Ned Snelgrove of 1982—arguably not yet a killer: *arguably* because no one knows for sure if he had killed *before* Karen Osmun—was quite a different person from the man sitting in jail preparing his case twenty-something years later. Ned would soon stand in front of Hartford superior court judge Carmen Espinosa, a woman he would come to loathe more than perhaps anyone else in the justice system, a woman who would face Ned and say, quite sternly, "Sometimes people are just bad, beyond redemption, and you are one of them."

David Zagaja hoped Mark Pascual could put the final touch on a conviction. Detective Mellekas and Jim Rovella were back at MacDougall-Walker Correctional wondering if Pascual was the real deal as he continued to tell what was turning out to be one heck of a story. Essentially, it was a narrative, as hard as it was to believe, of what actually happened to Carmen Rodriguez on the night she was murdered. It was a story, Pascual insisted, straight from the horse's mouth.

II

"Ned said he covered up what he did real well," Pascual told Mellekas and Rovella. According to Pascual, it was Ned who called Carmen "Carmie," that's why Pascual used the same name.

"What'd he say about how he did it?" Mellekas wanted to know.

"He talked generally about the crime, telling us he was in the bar with her dancing and buying her drinks, saying, 'She was a Puerto Rican girl in her early thirties. I was *really* attracted to her.'" As they partied, Pascual said, Ned asked Carmen to leave.

"Can I get a ride?" Carmen asked. (Odd that she'd ask for a ride—she lived but a few blocks away.)

If you believe Pascual, "Will you have breakfast with me?" Ned supposedly asked Carmen next, before suggesting a diner near his house.

"Sure," Carmen said.

So they left.

"After breakfast," Ned told Pascual, "we went for a ride to get to know each other." Ned drove to an area of his hometown where he used to hang out. The Berlin Fairgrounds. Wooded. Secluded. Dark.

Ned found a spot and pulled over. He "made a move on" Carmen, Pascual said.

After Ned made the sexual advance, Carmen opened the door and got out.

Scared. She stumbled and ran. Fast as she could.

Ned rolled his eyes. That burning he talked about in his letters began: that sexual compulsion, that need to render a woman unconscious and then strip her top off in a fit of sexual confusion and frustration. It was a powerful desire to play with her breasts and then sexually stimulate himself, and if she came to, take out a knife and start poking her with it.

As Carmen ran, it was all too much for Ned. That "feeling" took control of him as he opened his door and started running after Carmen through the woods.

And so the chase was on. Carmen. Drunk. Out of breath. Huffing and puffing. Falling. Slowing down . . .

Ned. On top of his game.

Within a moment, he leapt. Like a cat. Tackled Carmen in the brush. "Knocked her down," Pascual said.

Ned was in his element now. A hunter. That person Mary Ellen Renard had described when Ned walked into the bathroom a nice young man and came out Mr. Hyde was back. He was much more powerful than Carmen, who was running for her life, as though they were in some sort of summer Hollywood slasher flick, and so he took her by the neck and, without speaking a word, squeezed.

Tighter.

Harder.

Yes. That feeling. Here it comes. It was part of the high.

"Her body went limp," Pascual said Ned told him. Ned had

that look in his eye while explaining it. "That gleam," Pascual told me. "That sense of pride that he was a murderer."

"'I strangled her until her body went limp and she passed out,'" Pascual recalled, quoting Ned.

Then Ned walked back to his car. Carmen was on the ground. Ned had a tarp and a bag, he admitted, in his trunk.

Tools of the trade.

He took the tarp out first. The bag—that was where he kept his goodies: rope, scissors, duct tape, flashlight (or lantern, Pascual couldn't recall which, exactly), staple gun, and "other things." And then, after taking his murder instruments out of his trunk, Ned went back and picked Carmen up and carried her to the car, before spreading the tarp out on the backseat. Placing her on the tarp, Carmen "came to and started to fight back."

Wild. Swinging. Screaming. She really didn't know what was going on.

At some point, Ned said, Carmen bit him on the right arm. "[I] thought the police may find something of [me] on her teeth," he explained to Pascual.

Then . . . he "finished her off." According to Pascual, Ned said he took the scissors and stabbed Carmen until she stopped moving.

Stopped breathing.

But for Ned, the thrill—the best part of it all, perhaps— wasn't over. As Carmen lay on the backseat of his car on top of a tarp, Ned pulled off her "top shirt and posed her," Pascual explained. After posing Carmen, as he had reportedly done with Karen Osmun and Mary Ellen Renard, Ned then began to, as Pascual told it, "get off, meaning sexually," by masturbating.

When he was *done,* Ned told Pascual, he "taped her and stapled her and wrapped her in garbage bags."

III

"What'd you do with the body?" Pascual asked Ned after he was finished explaining how he murdered Carmen.

"I got rid of it," Ned said.

The way Pascual told it, Ned chose Rhode Island because he had customers in Jewett City, Plainfield, and Thompson, Connecticut, towns along the Rhode Island border, near Hopkinton. Ned knew the terrain. He knew the land was spread out and woodsy. He knew that at night you were lucky if you found a raccoon hanging around out in the open.

"He would drive in these areas," Pascual told Mellekas and Rovella, "while he was waiting for the customers to get home from work or whatever. Ned said the farther away from Berlin that the body was, the better off he would be about not being a suspect," which was something Ned had bragged about learning from Ted Bundy.

What about evidence? The tarp? The scissors?

"Ned said he drove to Jewett City to a McDonald's," Pascual added, "and dumped the tarp and bag of stuff in a Dumpster. Ned was confident he covered his tracks."

85

I

In jail, Ned was what Pascual called a "pack rat." He saved everything. Condiments. Newspapers. Request slips. Empty bags. Books. Letters. Envelopes.

A real hoarder.

"No one liked him," Pascual told me during one of our many prison interviews. "I was his only friend. He'd get beat up all the time. My mother sent him money because no one else would. He felt he could trust me. He told me everything. He had this gloss over his eyes, a different look altogether, when telling me about the women—several women—he killed. He was certain the cops would never catch him. He got off on retelling me the stories, especially when he spoke about posing their bodies."

Ned would kill a woman, Pascual explained, rip her shirt open, tear off her bra, expose her breasts, and just stop and take it all in. "Looking at the girls all laid out like that, dead and posed," Pascual said, "Ned told me, 'That is the *perfect* woman.'" Ned's idea of the perfect female was a dead woman posed in a compromising position: pants and panties on, no shirt or bra, her large breasts fully exposed. "While he was strangling them or stabbing them," Pascual noted, "looking into their eyes, he told me that the erection he got from this was more powerful than anything he could ever explain. After he posed them, he [gratified] himself sexually, but turned away from the body so he wouldn't leave his DNA at the scene."

II

At home, Ned was the same pack rat. Ropes. Toys. Maps. Notes. Gas receipts. Oil change receipts. Logbooks of his mileage. In saving all of these items—which was perhaps a symptom of a more clinical obsessive-compulsive condition his mother had discovered in his teens—Ned had, essentially, tied his own judicial noose: because all of it (the maps and mileage, especially, those same items Ned had blasted and laughed at Bundy for keeping) was going to come back and hang Ned during his murder trial.

III

A day or so after Ned told his story to Mark Pascual, Pascual and the other inmate were not so sure they could believe him. It seemed far-fetched. Like maybe Ned was using them to plant a seed for trial. The story was too grandiose and Hollywood-like. Ned was bragging. Maybe he was trying to expand on his tough-guy image. He was going to be in jail a long time. Even if he won an acquittal, there was no telling when his trial would start. A few stories of how sick he was, dropped here and there, spread around the prison, would send a message to inmates looking to hassle Ned.

This guy's a wack job. Stay away from him.

Inmates lied—even to one another. Pascual knew this. Ned knew this. In many ways, prison is a fictional world. You can be whatever you want to be.

Feeling that maybe Ned had told them stories, the other

inmate contacted his girlfriend and asked her to do some investigating based on the facts Ned had told them. "Check the Internet," the convict suggested.

About a week later, Pascual said, that friend showed up at his cell. "Hey, check it out." His girlfriend had sent him a long article detailing Ned's history and charges.

"What is it?"

They both sat and read.

"This guy's for real," the convict told Pascual.

Just then, Ned came by the cell. "What's going on? Let me see that."

Pascual handed him the article.

Ned was quiet. He read. Flipping through the pages. Then he abruptly turned and walked away with the article.

A few days later, Ned returned the article to Pascual, but some pages were missing. So the guy asked his girlfriend to send another one.

Matching up the two copies, Pascual was confused. Ned had taken out anything having to do with his crimes in New Jersey. It seemed strange. As if he didn't want anyone to know about his past.

IV

Pascual was moved a few weeks later to another "pod," a unit or cell block in the same prison. That same day, Ned was moved to the same pod. ("He was very suspicious," Pascual explained, "that we were both moved at the same time to the same pod.")

A month later, Ned and Pascual, living in separate cells, went up to one of the corrections officers. "You think we can room together?" Pascual asked.

Sometime after that, they were put into the same cell. Not for a few days, or a month, but 159 days. It was here, during this time, that Pascual began to learn more about Ned and his crimes. And one of the first things Pascual noticed about his new roommate was Ned's paranoia. Ned was the type to worry about *everything.* He wondered if investigators were listening to his every word, reading his mail, and watching him. (In fact, Ned was so paranoid that the prison was opening and reading his mail, when I started to receive letters from Ned in early 2007, he always sent me a subsequent letter in tandem a few days later, aside from his actual response to my particular questions, asking me to describe the way in which his letters had arrived in my mailbox. "Did you notice any tape on the back of the letter?" was a question Ned routinely asked me. In one instance, he even went so far as to send me a one-page letter with three questions and check boxes that he had drawn next to each question. Moreover, in all of his letters, Ned would put a staple in the corner that went through the envelope and his letter. Thus, if a prison official had opened his letter to read it, he or she would have to tear the letter.)

"A month after [Carmen went missing]," Ned said to Pascual one day, sitting in their new cell, "the police came to speak with me. They took my car twice."

This blew Ned's mind—the cops impounding his car. He believed there was a conspiracy, some sort of sneaky little con fleshed out by the cops to track his every move. "They attached a GPS [device] to [my] car to track wherever I drove," Ned explained to Pascual.

"Huh?" Pascual couldn't believe it. The story sounded so full of paranoia. Drama. So James Bond–like. Why go to such trouble when the state police could have just put a tail on the guy? He wasn't *that* important.

"That second time they took the car," Ned explained, "the police took the GPS off."

86

I

The man responsible for putting Assistant State's Attorney David Zagaja's case against Ned in a neat little package and readying it for trial was Jim Rovella, a former Hartford cop with over twenty-five years of investigative experience. A big, hulking man, with white hair and a comforting smile, Rovella was introduced to the missing persons case of Carmen Rodriguez back in May 2003. Carmen's case had been packaged inside a file of other "cold" cases that his new boss at the Cold Case Unit (CCU) of the office of the chief state's attorney wanted him to take a look at.

Rovella's quarter-century law enforcement career dated back to when he started as a patrol officer in Hartford in 1981, a time when there were about thirty-five murders per year in Hartford. When he was transferred to robbery and homicide in 1987, with the crack explosion and gang violence reaching Hartford's North End, the murder rate doubled. It was here that Rovella's people skills were utilized as he seemingly went from one homicide crime scene to the next: an endless disharmony of murder, sexual assaults, rapes, and violent crimes. ("You get a lot of experience in Hartford," Rovella said later.)

In 2002, Rovella retired from the Hartford PD after spending two decades behind the badge, but found himself unable to stay away from the addictive pull of investigating crimes and solving cases. "So I went to work for the state's attorney office."

Part of the work Rovella does for the Cold Case Unit of the state's attorney revolves around sitting and studying files for months. He has the advantage to take all of the police reports and witness statements, along with the evidence, sit down without the constraints of time, and go through the case, piece by piece. He may spend six months, a year, two years. Whatever it takes. It's important to Rovella to try to eliminate a suspect. Take him out of the equation—which stood out to him right away as he started to study Ned in the realm of Carmen's disappearance. "I kept trying to *exclude* Snelgrove from the case, but he kept popping up back in," Rovella said. "The fact that he left the bar with Carmen. That he was a regular at the bar and he *stopped* going once Carmen disappeared, even before HPD started asking questions. These were all important factors to me."

Then there was the gas receipts and the mileage that Rovella's former colleague Luisa St. Pierre had brought into the case. To Rovella, it all added up to one answer.

II

Ned's trial was the most high-profile court case the city of Hartford had seen in years. Not that murder was an uncommon affair in the city. But not for several years had a *potential* serial killer been brought before a Hartford judge. The Rodriguez family was getting most of the press as they stood vigil outside court every morning before proceedings began. For the most part, it was Luz, Sonia, and Kathy Perez leading the charge, with other family members joining them periodically. This first day of the actual trial, however, brought out nearly twenty members of the family.

All united.

All thumping their feet for justice.

For Carmen.

For Karen.

For Mary Ellen.

III

On January 4, 2005, a mildly cold Tuesday morning, Judge Carmen Espinosa addressed the jury. Ned sat wearing a sweater and slacks. He had decided not to wear his large-rimmed "Buddy Holly" glasses. He smirked ever so slightly, as if to say the entire process had been a witch hunt—which would become Ned's mantra throughout the trial.

Pinning the murder of Carmen Rodriguez on him, Ned had convinced himself, was a reaction to his prior convictions in New Jersey. It was convenient. Once a con, always a con.

Regarding his glasses, "He didn't wear them," one investigator who was in the courtroom every day later told me, "because he believed they made him look like the person he was: a vicious serial killer."

Ned tried pulling off the classic "guy next door" look: sweater and slacks, short hair, naïve manner, congenial demeanor. But as the trial commenced, Ned couldn't hide from himself and started right away "stage whispering," one courtroom observer told me. Ned whispered things to his lawyer loud enough so the jury could hear him. "He thought he was smart," Jim Rovella added. "But in the end he disappointed me."

IV

Judge Carmen Espinosa, the first Hispanic sworn in as a superior court judge in the state of Connecticut, a judge many who worked in her courtroom every day later said was as fair as any judge in the state, would end up being the target of Ned's eventual anger and outbursts. Espinosa was a rather good-looking, middle-aged Hispanic woman. She had thick black hair, which she kept cut just above her neckline. Her dark eyebrows were cast against her slightly olive complexion. Her smile was radiant and contagious. Even comforting, some might say.

Her tenure on the superior court bench started in 1992. According to her bio, Espinosa was born in Puerto Rico and moved with her family to New Britain, a suburb of Hartford, at the age of three. After attending public schools in New Britain, she graduated from Central Connecticut State University in 1971, with majors in Spanish and secondary education. Continuing her studies, Espinosa received a Master of Arts degree in Hispanic Studies from Brown University and her law degree from George Washington University. What most don't know about the judge is that she was once a special agent for the FBI. She had a brief run as an Assistant United States Attorney in the Office of the United States Attorney for the District of Connecticut, beginning in 1980, and stayed on as a federal prosecutor until she was appointed a superior court judge. If there was one judge in the county who could preside over a trial that was sure to have its share of controversial moments, there was no better than Judge Espinosa.

"She's almost too fair," one man who knows her well told me later.

V

For the Rodriguez family, talking about Carmen, even years later, was difficult. Teary-eyed and choked up, many of Carmen's relatives couldn't handle sitting and sharing memories. But Luz Rodriguez, who, admittedly, had a difficult time with her sister's death, took a step forward, along with

Sonia, and seemed to be the spokeswoman for the family as Ned's trial—and the ensuing media circus—got under way. ("It was hard," Luz recalled, "don't get me wrong, but we *had* to do it.")

Carmen needed a voice. The family knew Ned was going to shoulder the blame on Carmen. Talk as though she didn't matter. Make all sorts of excuses for her leaving the bar with him. So the family had to stick together in support of protecting her memory.

And, like they had during every hearing over the past few years, members of the Rodriguez family wore T-shirts and badges with Carmen's photograph and sat together in back of David Zagaja's table, where Rovella, whose job it was to make sure each witness was ready to testify, also sat.

Ned's money had run out. Either that, or his mother and father weren't about to drain what little savings they had left to pay for yet another defense, as they had in New Jersey twenty years prior. Donald O'Brien was a court-appointed special public defender. Ned was lucky to have him. Although Ned would undoubtedly be driving the bus and telling O'Brien what to do, O'Brien—who refused to talk to me—was a competent and well-prepared public defense attorney. He was in the courtroom every week, said one law enforcement official, defending some of the state's most undesirables. O'Brien knew the ins and outs of murder trials.

87

I

During those first few days of hearings, where both sides argued over which evidence would make it into trial, the talk inside the courtroom wasn't so easy for Sonia Rodriguez, Carmen's oldest sister. "I had to go out," Sonia said. "I had to scream. I had to clench my fists."

Carmen's life—and death—had come down to this one moment. What if, for some reason, Ned was allowed to walk? The Rodriguez family didn't need a trial to convince them that Ned was guilty. They knew it in their hearts, Luz told me later. Jackie, Carmen's daughter, slated to testify (but nowhere to be found), had interrogated Ned with Miguel, Cutie, and Jeffrey Malave at Kenney's that night shortly after Carmen disappeared: "Oh, *that* was your mom? I'm sorry," Ned had asked Jackie. It was a fact of the case the family had a hard time letting go of.

"That *was* your mom. . . ."

For the Rodriguez family, Ned's use of the past tense was a confession. Sonia, like Luz and Kathy Perez, however, got over the anger and sorrow and decided to honor Carmen's life by moving forward and, being the glue, hold the rest of the family—some twenty members at any given time during the trial—together. There had been one tragedy after another for the Rodriguez family. But it didn't stop them from fighting. Jesus Ramos, the older man from Puerto Rico whom Carmen was married to when she went missing, died two weeks after she disappeared. ("He died of a broken heart," Luz said. "Thankfully, Jesus never knew that Carmen's body had been found.")

With Carmen having been the gypsy she was, it helped her mother cope. Because Carmen moved back and forth between the United States and Puerto Rico throughout her life, always in and out of her mother's house, Rosa could always look at Carmen's photo in the house and, knowing she was dead, still be able to tell herself, *She's traveling. She's in Puerto Rico.* She wouldn't have to deal with the immensity of Carmen being gone forever.

"We have a shirt," Luz recalled, "that Carmen wore shortly before she disappeared, that we haven't washed. You can still smell her on it."

These are the people Carmen left behind.

"He had thought he chose the perfect victim," Luz said later, "that no one cared about Carmen. That no one would miss her. We were there in solidarity to show him—and everyone else—that Carmen was part of our world and our lives."

BOOK VI

"PURE EVIL"

88

I

On the morning of January 4, 2005, the *State of Connecticut* v. *Edwin Fales Snelgrove Jr.* was officially on record. Ned sat next to O'Brien on one side of the small room, while Rovella sat next to Zagaja on the other, as Judge Espinosa addressed the court with her usual cheery demeanor. "Good morning. All right. Is there anything we need to consider before the jury comes in?"

David Zagaja said, "Thank you, Your Honor. I did . . . alert the court that the state is putting forward [an] oral motion *in limine. . . .*"

For the layperson, the term "*limine*" probably threw a kink in the proceedings immediately. In Ned's case, it meant that a request had been submitted to the court before trial in an attempt to exclude certain pieces of evidence. In this instance, Zagaja was arguing that a particular witness Ned was going to call, a man who had supposedly taken a deathbed confession of Carmen's murder, needed to be qualified before he could take the stand. There was some controversy surrounding the witness's statement, whether he was credible.

The judge said they'd take it up at the appropriate moment;

right now, she wanted to get on with the day's proceedings. The trial had been held up long enough.

For the next hour or more, the judge went through and gave the jury its instructions and the attorneys talked about witnesses and availability and other tedious issues that would bore the average reader. The entire time, Ned sat with guarded composure. He watched every move and listened to every word as if he were sitting in a business meeting and had been warned not to speak.

Zagaja's first witness, Hartford police officer Jeffrey Rohan, set the stage for Carmen's disappearance, taking jurors through how he answered the call at Carmen's apartment from Jackie (who, incidentally, was dodging Zagaja and could not be found).

Ever since Carmen had been pronounced dead, more than three years ago now, Jackie's life had taken a turn for the worse. "Poor Jackie . . . she could never face Carmen being murdered like that," said a family friend.

"We have to find her," Zagaja had whispered to Rovella more than once as the trial got under way. "We need her."

Janet Rozman, assistant manager, bartender, and Kenney's waitress, who had seen Carmen and Ned together on the night she disappeared, testified next. Rozman's words were powerful and enlightening. It gave the jury an image that they could use for building events around the night in question. It was clear from Rozman that Kenney's was a special place for Carmen. A place out of her normal routine that her family didn't know about, where she could let loose. A hideaway. Zagaja wasn't trying to tell the jury that Carmen was a choir girl; but she was a human being. She liked to party. She liked to drink and dance and meet guys and flirt.

A free spirit.

And yet, what Zagaja proved was that on the night of September 21, 2001, Carmen met the wrong man. The Devil dressed in a businessman's suit. A killer in disguise. A sexual sadist on the prowl for a victim.

After a few opening questions, Zagaja asked Rozman, "And did you see Carmen do anything when she came in?"

"She walked directly over to Ned."

"And could you describe what you observed them doing, if anything?"

"Um, they were playing pool and dancing, drinking, kissing."

"Was this the first time you had seen them interacting that way?"

"Yes."

"Had you ever seen them together in a situation like this previous?"

"No."

II

Paula Figueroa was another Kenney's employee who took the witness stand and established several important factors. For one, Ned was not some sort of customer who showed up once in a while: an interloper who stopped in from time to time. Ned was a regular Kenney's barfly.

The bar had even ordered a case of Moosehead beer especially for Ned, Figuroa said.

By the end of the morning, Zagaja established that Ned and Carmen knew each other. They had danced and kissed and talked and drank together on the night she disappeared. And there was no way, absolutely *no* way, that Ned could deny that he and Carmen left Kenney's together. Too many people had seen them.

III

One of Kenney's owners, Nick Taddei, raised his right hand, swore to tell the truth, and then told his story of coming in between Ned, Jackie, Miguel, Cutie, and Jeffrey Malave that

day when Miguel and Jackie were on the warpath looking to
question Ned.

"The problem was that Ned didn't want to reveal his
whereabouts," Taddei testified, "where he lived, he didn't
want to give them any information. Family members wanted
assurance that he was going to contact the officer, wanted to
make sure that he was going to go and talk to the police. . . ."

Taddei was just one more piece of the puzzle Zagaja was
gluing together with each one of his witnesses—all of whom
O'Brien tried to impeach on cross-examination, but failed.

IV

The following day began with Jeffrey Malave, who backed
up the testimony of the witnesses Zagaja had already presented. On this day, Ned wore a charcoal gray sweater and
black tie. He looked every bit as uptight and on edge as he
had the previous day. If he thought he was going to walk in
and control the room, he had perhaps watched too many
episodes of *Law & Order*. Judge Espinosa was not about to
let anything in her courtroom get out of hand.

What was intriguing to some, while others didn't even
notice, was that Ned was paying a price for not wearing his
glasses. Reading documents became a task. He struggled like
an old man trying to read the fine print of a contract. Ned
would hold a piece of paper up to the edge of his nose and stare
at it, unable to read it, but he refused to put on his glasses.

One of the problems Zagaja ran into early on was that
many of his witnesses had records of their own to contend
with. Felonies from the past or present. Each witness had admitted to his or her crimes. Zagaja was the first to ring that
bell. Miguel Fraguada, for example, Zagaja's next witness,
had two prior felony convictions. "They were a long time
ago," Fraguada explained through an interpreter.

All Zagaja could do, of course, was have each witnesses

point out his or her faults, as well as his or her role in the case. The jury could decide from there who was credible.

Fraguada told the jury exactly what had happened on the night Carmen disappeared and the day he confronted Ned with Jackie, Cutie, and Jeffrey Malave.

Fraguada kept referring to Carmen as his "wife," but, of course, it was a figure of speech. To him, he loved Carmen— and in his eyes and heart, that made her his wife.

Then Zagaja asked him how upset he was about seeing Ned at the bar. "You said you were going to hit him?" Zagaja said.

"Yeah. He . . . I was going to hit him because he ran off on me."

After several more questions, Zagaja handed Fraguada to O'Brien—who went right after him: "Mr. Fraguada, you say that Carmen was your wife?"

"Yes."

"Where did you get married?"

"She lives with me, but we weren't married."

"OK. So she wasn't your wife, she was . . . you were living with her, correct?"

"Yes. She lived with me."

"And how long had you lived with her?"

"From May until she disappeared on September twenty-first."

89

I

As the clock began to nudge its way toward the noon hour on January 5, in walked a crooked old man, a man of great intelligence and absolute dedication to his son: Edwin Fales Snelgrove Sr. Zagaja called Edwin as a witness to discuss, among other things, the suicide note Ned had written shortly after the Hartford PD and CSP began to investigate Ned—before Carmen's body had been found. In Zagaja's view, this was a very important point. It showed a pattern. Ned had fallen right into his old behavior of killing a woman and then, not being able to deal with it, setting it off with a feigned, ill-fated suicide attempt. For a criminal—*any* criminal—the past is a good indication of the future.

When Mr. Snelgrove settled into his seat on the witness stand, the judge excused the jury, saying that the remainder of the day would be taken up by a lengthy discussion regarding the content of the letters Ned had written to his parents.

Then Mr. Snelgrove was asked to step down. And while the lawyers got into the minutia of the letters, Ned kept calling O'Brien back to the table and whispering things in his ear, to the point where Zagaja and Rovella began laughing at him.

("It was funny," Rovella said later. "He looked like he was directing the entire defense—and I guess he was.")

At one point, Zagaja explained to the judge why the letters were important, saying, "Your Honor, regarding . . . relevance. The fact that the defendant contemplated suicide beginning on October 12 and wrote what his thoughts were—that being, shortly thereafter the alleged disappearance of Carmen Rodriguez—*is* relevant. . . . Already the court has heard he kept up a somewhat normal routine at the bar, up until the time of the disappearance. These are inconsistencies that should be presented to the jury for consideration. These are the defendant's words to what state of mind he was at. . . ."

O'Brien, of course, didn't agree.

As they continued, both parties discussed which parts of the letter would be redacted. The main issue was Ned's prior acts. Zagaja was working hard to get in as much information as he could about Ned's prior convictions. "What's your claim on that?" the judge asked Zagaja, regarding trying to sneak in Ned's prior bad acts.

"I don't see—I don't make that leap. That's why I left it in. I don't see it referring to his prior conviction or his prior record."

The judge agreed, adding, "I don't think there's any connection to any prior convictions or record there."

Unable to contain himself any longer, Ned blurted out, "What else *could* it be?"

Everyone turned. O'Brien tried to downplay Ned's outburst by interrupting: "Other than making a reference to this incident, what else could it refer to? I mean, I've spoken to my client, that's *exactly* what the reference is all about, so he, certainly, knows what his own reference is. But to say, 'They'll never know who I truly am. . . .'"

"Because he'll be dead, that's why!" the judge clarified. "Because he won't be around for them to get to know him."

"No," Ned yelled, "the reason . . ." O'Brien tried to speak

over him, but Ned wouldn't let him. "Well . . . ," O'Brien
started to say before Ned interrupted.

"I can't have lifelong friends because I can't tell *them* who
I am," he yelled.

The judge said, "Well, that might be—you know, you can
say it as loud as you want, it's not going to make *any* difference. Whatever he says *now* is of no significance."

O'Brien wanted to keep the discussion professional. "No,"
he said, "but if you read it in context, 'I can never have lifelong friends who will know who I really am.' The court is
looking at it that that's futuristic after he does the deed. But
my point is that the reference is that he will not have friends
who know who he really is."

"Yeah," the judge said, "people don't know *who* he really
is—"

O'Brien interrupted, "Because of the *prior* convictions."

The judge had heard enough. "That's a leap that is not reasonable," she said. "It is to you because you know what his
past is. But the people who don't know what his past is, they
are *not* going to assume that. It's not logical to assume that it
means that he *has* prior convictions. . . . It's just [not] reasonable . . . so the court will allow that."

II

After an ice storm on January 6, the jury was brought back
in on January 7 and the trial resumed. Outside the courtroom,
the ice cast a translucent glaze, giving everything a lucid appearance. Salt and sand were tossed all over the sidewalks
heading into the Hartford Superior Court, and those entering the building tracked it into the foyer area, making things
a bit messy. Inside the courtroom, however, cold feelings and
tension—forever building among Ned, O'Brien, Zagaja, and
Judge Espinosa—were about to make things even messier.
Ned looked rather respectable: blue necktie noosed tight up

to his throat and a light-colored shirt. He smiled, if ever so slightly, while studying the jury.

After O'Brien, Zagaja and the judge had a brief argument over the redacted suicide letter. Ned watched closely as his father, clearly tired and physically weak, walked up to the witness stand. For a few moments, the elder Snelgrove talked about his family, Ned and his siblings, where they lived, his army days, and how the kids had split up and gone their own ways as they grew older. In many ways, it was a familiar American story.

White picket fence. Suburbia. Two cars. Dog. Neighbors. Kids in expensive colleges. Empty nest.

But then, Ned started acting bizarrely, Edwin implied. Not like the son who had left home for college after high school.

"OK," Zagaja asked, "did there come a time when he ended up living at home with you again? [And] could you describe your home?"

"It's a cape on about a third acre—"

"How many bedrooms?"

"Three."

A few questions later, "Did he occupy one of the bedrooms?"

"No. He lived in the . . . he decided he was more comfortable in the—in the recreation room downstairs. He slept on a sofa down there because he had a desk and some other stuff down there."

And then they discussed Ned's employment. Indeed, Edwin testified, Ned traveled around the Northeast. Meeting people. Selling frozen foods. Driving through Massachusetts, New Hampshire, Connecticut, New York, and, well, Rhode Island.

Zagaja was quite shrewd in his questioning. He was setting up his closing argument. Laying the foundation for one of those character-building sections of the trial. Without even possibly knowing it, Edwin was giving Zagaja exactly what he wanted: the details of a man who liked to be alone, a man who forwent a cozy little room upstairs in the house he had grown up in for an old smelly couch downstairs in the basement. The dungeon. The sexual den, as Zagaja put it later.

III

Edwin talked about Ned taking a bottle of sleeping pills in October 2001, and Edwin calling 911 and Ned ending up in the hospital—which, of course, afforded Zagaja the opportunity to introduce the suicide note.

After even more debate, Zagaja was allowed to read the letter into the record—exactly what he had wanted to do from the start. Near the end of his reading, one of the main points he had wanted to make, by getting the note in, was that Ned was setting up a story, his excuse, his reasoning for being investigated. He was acting strange. Bizarre. Odd.

Guilty.

The end of the note was a warning of sorts by Ned to his parents, letting them know that the cops would be calling on them once again to ask questions about a woman—a missing woman. And here we go again . . . "'Last, but not least, there is a missing person's case in Hartford,'" David Zagaja read aloud. Ned squirmed a bit in his chair hearing his words echo into the record. Zagaja read aloud that Ned told his parents that he was "'supposedly one of the last people to see Carmen something-or-other . . .'" *Carmen something or other.* Ned knew her name. Knew it well, in fact. Zagaja continued, ". . . This girl, reportedly, has not been seen since . . . It's best that I just end it now."

The cops were badgering him again, Ned implied. Focusing on him solely because of his record. He was never going to be able to escape that person he had been in New Jersey. It was better to just kill himself.

Zagaja later explained his thoughts regarding Ned "supposedly" committing suicide. Here's a guy who's going to end it all, yet he is writing details, clear details about where he picked up this woman and where he dropped her off. "He was telling his parents what to say to the police," Zagaja suggested. "That's what he was doing."

Anyone who looked hard enough could have figured out that Zagaja was only interested in dropping the letter into the trial to show how, in addition to all the other evidence he was presenting, Ned was a calculated, well-experienced killer who had gone to great lengths to put every duck in a row. When things didn't work out for Ned, when the cops moved in and his mistakes surfaced, he tried to cover himself.

An innocent man, in other words, had no reason to kill himself.

90

I

After a short break, Zagaja showed dozens of photographs the CSP had taken of the Snelgrove property—both inside and out—to the jury, asking Edwin Sr. to describe the inside of his house. For about ten minutes, Edwin outlined it all: the garage, bedrooms, dining room, living room, and kitchen. And then the basement, which Zagaja had Edwin focus on for a moment. The fact that it was in such disorder. Stuff everywhere. That Ned's "office" and "bedroom" were an utter mess. The guy was a slob. Part of that mess, Edwin admitted, was his own fault. He and Norma had owned a sewing shop. Whatever was left over from the shop after they closed it had been put down in the basement for storage. In fact, inside a toy box to the left of the space Ned called his bedroom, Zagaja suggested, were two of Ned's sexual toys he had manipulated and painted. They were there among games and children's plastic dolls. Those two Styrofoam mannequin heads, which looked as if they were props in a horror film. One had been made to look pretty, as pretty as white Styrofoam colored with blue and black markers could be; the other more vile, with graphs and pressure points on the temple, forehead, and throat. Zagaja asked Edwin if he recognized the photo of the items inside the toy box.

"Yeah," Edwin said, "yes."

"And you'd seen them before?"

"Yes."

"Did these items look this way in late 2001 when they were in the toy box?"

"Um," Edwin said, stumbling with his words, "I don't remember, to tell you the truth. I don't . . . I don't know. I assume they did. I don't know."

"OK. But you don't have any firsthand knowledge that these were in this condition in late 2001?"

"No."

"You don't? OK."

"Well, just . . . just the one," Edwin decided to add at the last minute. "My wife . . . these were mannequins in her shop and she used to put knitted caps and so forth on them. They were on a shelf in her shop. And I know that she drew the eyes and mouth and so forth on this one. This . . . thing here, you know, looks to me . . . I think one of my grandchildren did it. It looks like something a kid would do."

Listening, Rovella couldn't believe it. He shook his head, thinking, *We should have him arrested for perjury.*

When you looked at the objects, one thing became too obvious to overlook: Whoever had drawn on one had drawn on the other. They were created by the same hand. ("The thing is," Zagaja said later, "we weren't even going to make a big deal out of these heads until Mr. and Mrs. Snelgrove said they were responsible.")

To pin the artwork on a child was a significant stretch. There are not too many kids who can create such an eerie-looking model. It just didn't make any sense. Kids didn't think like that. Neither head would look so literal. And the running joke among many in the courtroom in the days that followed was that if a child had indeed painted those heads—which was, of course, a possibility—it was clear that the child in question was in need of some serious psychological help. Quickly.

"You had seen both of those mannequins in your house, however?" Zagaja asked.

"Yes. Yes."

"I would offer seven through eighteen and twenty and twenty-one as full exhibits, Your Honor," Zagaja said, referring to photographs of the heads.

"If I might have a moment, Your Honor?" O'Brien queried.

For the jury to see the heads was enough. The value of their presence alone was that they put a scare—a quick jolt—into whoever viewed them. Nothing more. What could Zagaja actually prove in regard to the heads? He hadn't sent them for DNA analysis, which was something several people suggested (for semen, blood, hairs, and, Lord knows, whatever else). He hadn't really decided exactly what Ned had used them for, besides practice pieces. Props. So, in effect, the heads were showpieces: two rather bizarre-looking creatures the jury could look at and be revolted by.

Exactly what Zagaja wanted.

II

There was an arrogance about Ned that seemed to thrive on the celebrity he achieved by being in the spotlight during the days of his trial, even if the proceedings were cast under such an immoral umbrella. Ned lapped it up. He'd never admit it, but he adored every moment of seeing his photograph on the front page of the local newspapers and the lengthy stories about his crimes. This was it—the payoff. Every starstruck killer lived for his moment in the spotlight. Ned believed he had total control. Everyone was there, situated and brought together, by his actions.

Convicted serial killer Michael Ross, who had been begging the state of Connecticut through the court to carry out his death sentence, was on the cover of every newspaper in New England lately demanding the state execute him. The guy *wanted* to die. Pundits were debating his sentence on national television as Ross granted the first interviews in decades.

But when Ned's case began, Ned and his crimes usurped even Michael Ross (who was granted his wish, incidentally, on Friday, May 13, 2005, of all days, when he was executed by lethal injection), and Ned, seeing Ross pushed to the second page of the newspapers, was prouder than a new father, sources inside the jail where he was being held said.

III

As Ned's father continued answering David Zagaja's questions, a piece of rope became the focal point of the trial. It had been found on the top of a bookcase in Ned's room. Investigators had their theories later of what Ned had used it for, but could never pin it down. Erotic asphyxiation fit into the type of psychotic profile investigators had put together on Ned.

Once again, however, just like with those mannequin heads, Edwin claimed responsibility, at least partially, for the rope, saying at one point, "It was just a little piece of clothesline and I . . . um, one day, you know, I guess I didn't have anything to do and I was fooling around and I—I decided to see if I could remember how to tie the knots that I was supposed to learn how to tie when I was in the navy and I practiced a couple, and when I got through, I put it up there."

IV

Before letting Edwin go, Zagaja wanted to talk about the mannequin heads again, maybe to see if Edwin wanted to change his mind, or if he was going to answer in the same manner as he had previously. It was an old trial-attorney trick, actually. End on a note of which you feel your witness might be pushing the truth. If he breaks, you can go after him. If he repeats himself, you haven't really lost much. "And you said, previously," Zagaja said, "regarding the head depicted on the right, you said you don't know who drew that, but you think your granddaughter may have?"

"Yeah. I . . . maybe, yes."

"Did you make any inquiries to determine who had drawn on that right-hand head?"

"Yeah. We called her the other day and asked. She said she didn't remember." Ned dropped his head. O'Brien winced. If a child had constructed something like that, wouldn't she remember it quite easily?

"Objection, Your Honor," O'Brien said, standing up.

Edwin said it again. "She didn't remember doing it."

Even better, thought Zagaja, smiling as the judge spoke up: "Wait a minute. There's an objection. Sustained."

"All you can say, sir," Zagaja advised, "is whether you *called* or not."

"Oh," Edwin uttered, realizing, perhaps, he shouldn't have said anything.

"You did call her?"

"Yes."

"And did you speak with her?"

"Um, my wife spoke to her, I didn't."

"OK. And your wife relayed some information to you?"

"Yes."

V

Public Defender Donald O'Brien didn't have much for Mr. Snelgrove. All he wanted to do was clear up a few misconceptions he believed the jury might have and get the old man the heck off the stand. My goodness, he had said enough already.

After he was finished, the judge asked Zagaja if he wanted a shot at redirect.

Zagaja declined. Edwin had done a fine job for the prosecution already.

Next witness.

91

I

Norma Snelgrove was heading into her late eighties—and it showed. Inside a courtroom, sitting in the witness stand, was the last place on earth the old woman wanted to be. This was clear from her demeanor. There was little doubt that Ned was his mother's son. Most mothers have an inherent need to protect their sons at any cost, no matter what the circumstances (even if it's for a third time). It is a maternal need, some therapists argue, to shelter.

Zagaja was kind as he walked Norma through the same set of questions he shot at Edwin: Ned's work, living conditions in the house, college, skills, life. Everyday stuff. But quickly, Zagaja steered Norma into the mannequin heads, asking, "OK, I'm going to now . . . ask you . . . do you recognize those?"

Norma didn't hesitate. "Yes."

"How do you recognize those items?"

"They're Styrofoam heads that I used in my yarn shop to display hats and scarves."

"You owned a yarn shop?"

"Yes."

Zagaja established the name and that it was located in Ned's hometown. "And did that close at some time?"

"Yes," Norma said.

"When did it close?"

"About ten years ago."

The markings on the heads, however, didn't appear to be smudged or worn by time. They seemed fairly fresh. "And did you end up taking items from the yarn shop home?"

"Oh, yes, many."

"And of those items, those two Styrofoam heads were one of them?"

"Yes."

"Do you see drawings on those two heads?"

"Yes."

"And do you happen to recognize any of the drawings on the heads that you actually did?"

Norma didn't flinch: "Yes. I did the one on the left." *Here we go again,* Jim Rovella thought.

Zagaja couldn't believe what he was hearing. He asked, "The one on the left. Could you describe what you drew on the one on the left?"

"Oh, I just drew a couple of eyebrows and some eyes with eyelashes. I don't know if I ever filled in the lips or not."

"OK. Do you see that there's markings on the left-hand–side of the head, on the neck area?"

"Here?" Norma asked, pointing.

"Yes. Did you draw those?"

"No."

"And regarding the right hand, the head on the right-hand side of the photo, do you know if you recognize any of those drawings to be your own?"

"Not to be my own, no."

"You don't recognize any of the blue drawings on either of those heads to be yours?"

"No, not mine."

"OK. Ma'am, did you make any inquiry in the last few

days to determine who had drawn on the head depicted in the right-hand side of the photo?"

"I talked to my daughter about—" Norma tried to say as Zagaja interrupted her.

"You talked to your daughter?"

"Right."

"And did you speak with anyone else?"

"Her daughter."

"Her . . . which is your granddaughter?"

"Yes."

"Um, was that inquiry made at the request of anyone?"

"No. I was just trying to think who, I seemed to recall a time when I told her she could draw a face on the one that wasn't drawn on." Anyone looking at the photos could tell that the markings were far from being a "face."

"My question is, were these photos presented to you at some time over the past week?"

"Yes."

"And by whom?"

"Well, I believe Mr. O'Brien gave them to my husband."

"And after seeing them, did you take it upon yourself to call your daughter and granddaughter?"

"Yes."

"OK. No one had requested of you to determine who had drawn on the heads?"

"No."

"Thank you, ma'am. Nothing further."

The judge asked O'Brien if he was going to cross-examine Norma. "I have no questions, Your Honor," O'Brien said. He sounded rather morose. Edwin and Norma may have thought they were helping their Neddy, but they had, in fact, slit his throat.

II

Over the course of the next week, Zagaja brought in his team of law enforcement witnesses to outline the search and seizure of Ned's car, the search warrant served at Ned's house, as well as Ned's arrest. The trial's most dramatic moment came when Zagaja questioned Detective Kevin McDonald, the Hopkinton PD detective who had helped the CSP and Hartford PD serve the search warrant at Ned's house. As McDonald testified, describing how Ned was a willing party once they got him down to the barracks and agreed without balking to submit to an interview, Ned showed his aggravation by moving his leg underneath the table a mile a minute. Sources later said Ned was so enraged by what McDonald said on the stand that he couldn't contain himself or maintain his composure. At one point, as McDonald talked about how neither he nor any of his colleagues ever misled Ned while questioning him, Ned let out a laugh.

The judge shot him a look. As did O'Brien.

But Ned felt McDonald was perjuring himself. Ned had never agreed, he had always said, to speak with police. It was a conspiracy. The judge. The cops. The state's attorney. They were all in on it. All against Ned.

After a recess, in which the jury was asked to leave the room, the lawyers and judge discussed whether the testimony was relevant. O'Brien argued that Ned was never in custody and McDonald, nor anyone else in law enforcement, had read Ned his rights. Therefore, anything he said to McDonald or anyone else should not be part of the trial.

The judge thought about it momentarily. "All right," she said, "the court has considered the evidence presented and the arguments of counsel and finds that given the totality of the circumstances, the court finds that the defendant was not in custody at the time he was taken to the—"

But she wasn't allowed to finish. Ned lashed out as loud as he could: "Can I be tried in absentia?" He wanted out of the courtroom. What a fiasco. A darn lynch mob. They were all ganging up on him and he couldn't sit and watch it any longer.

"Certainly!" the judge shouted back.

Ned wasn't finished, however. "If you're . . . it's obvious

you're not going to be neutral," he said, which was enough to garner a collective gasp from the gallery. *Did he just say that?*

"It's obvious you have no respect for the court," the judge lectured back, "when the rulings go against you. So if you want to be tried in absentia, we have facilities to do that, yes. But the court will *not* tolerate disrespect or any outbursts."

Ned ignored the judge and instead focused on his argument. "Detective McDonald said that I was allowed to go home after two hours," he said in a rage. "He doesn't remember *anything* about that day."

Zagaja and Rovella couldn't believe it. They watched, as if it were some sort of political debate, as Ned and the judge went back and forth. They wondered how long it would be before the judge grew tired of arguing.

"There's no . . . ," she started to say and then stopped herself. Zagaja looked up. *Here it comes. . . .* "The hearing is over," Judge Espinosa said firmly. "And when it's over, it's *over*. And when the court rules, the court *rules*. If you don't like the rulings, then there's an appellate procedure, if you're convicted, that you can file."

"If," Ned said with a snicker in his voice.

The judge ignored the remark, saying, "That's correct. The court is *not* going to tolerate outbursts every time rulings go against you." And then she read her ruling again, just in case Ned didn't quite understand it the first time. "The court finds that the defendant was not in custody at the time that he was taken to the police station, he was not handcuffed, and that there is no evidence that at the time . . . which he admitted he was not handcuffed in the car. There's no evidence that at the police station he was restrained beyond what would be necessary to maintain security of the police station. He was driven home after the interview. And the court credits the testimony of Detective McDonald that he was free to leave—in fact, he *did* leave. Even if the defendant was in custody at the time . . . that he went to the police station, the court finds that he was *advised* of his constitutional rights, which he admitted he had the right to remain silent."

But Espinosa wasn't finished. As Ned sat and shook his head, rolled his eyes and said things under his breath, she continued. "The court finds that the statements that he made were voluntarily made. There was no evidence of coercion, threats, or promises made to him. . . . The defendant, in fact, did not make what he thought were incriminating statements about the murder of Carmen Rodriguez. The defendant's credibility was impeached by his prior felony convictions, his admissions to lying to police in the past. . . . The court does not credit that testimony because he only mentioned asking for an attorney in response to the court's questionings. Had he truly asked for an attorney at the time, that would have been an important fact which would have come up on direct examination."

She took a breath. And then let him have it. "The defendant is a veteran of the criminal justice system, having been convicted of three felonies in the past. The court does not credit his testimony that he was told that he was under arrest or he was presented with a waiver form. For all the foregoing reasons, the defendant's motion to suppress is *denied*."

Gavel.

Espinosa looked at Ned, waiting a moment for him to say something so she could toss him out of her courtroom. And then, when Ned silenced himself, she said, "Ready to proceed?"

With a smile, Zagaja answered, "Yes, ma'am."

"All right. Call the jury in please."

If anyone thought that this was the last of the verbal sparring between Ned and the judge, they were wrong. The best was yet to come. But no one could have, of course, predicted the shocker that was about to take place.

Ned wanted to go on record.

92

I

It was easy, especially in the way that Ned was twisting the entire trial to be about him, to overlook the fact that no one would be in the room if a young woman hadn't been brutally murdered. But it always happens during trials: the victim is forgotten, except in graphic crime scene photographs and evidence and witness testimony. For Luz and Sonia, there in court every day, they had sacrificed so much to sit and watch the man who, they believed, murdered their sister be brought to justice. Both worked third shift. That meant they spent the entire day in the courtroom, went home at around 6:00 P.M. to eat and nap, and then woke for work near midnight to begin all over again. Zagaja had kept in close contact with the Rodriguez family. He spoke fluent Spanish, which made communication between them quite clear. One day, he came out before the day's proceedings began and said, "Hey, there's going to be some graphic photos of your sister today. You might not want to stay for it." And they appreciated his honesty and warning.

Carmen's mother, Rosa, had been sitting in on the trial, but she had to leave at certain times. The photos. The talk of

Carmen's corpse. Ned. It was all too much for her. All she did was weep. According to Luz, whenever she sat in the front row in back of Ned's table, Luz claimed O'Brien made it hard for her to see by blocking her view. There were days when Luz just wanted to stare at Ned. Make him think about the people whose lives he had touched by killing Carmen. On those days, Luz insisted, O'Brien would complain that she stared at him and Ned with "devil eyes."

II

The jury was still out. As he sat in the witness stand, Ned didn't seem so comfortable and cocky anymore. O'Brien put him in this position so Ned could, on the record (as opposed to, say, shouting it out in open court), challenge the testimony of Kevin McDonald. Ned was outraged, of course, that he had to explain himself to *anyone*. Better yet the judge.

O'Brien wasted no time getting to the point. "Mr. Snelgrove," he asked, "were you at home on January 15, 2002?"

Mister . . . it sounded so much the polar opposite of who Ned was. So professional. So respectful. Ned didn't deserve it.

"Only in the morning," Ned answered firmly.

"OK. Were you there for the execution of a search warrant on your house?"

Ned said, "The first thing they did was, they grabbed me and took me out."

Zagaja shook his head. Rovella had the reports in front of him. There was no mention of such behavior. Ned had made it sound as if a SWAT team had busted into the house under the direct order of the attorney general. With goggles and rifles and bulletproof vests, they had chased him into a closet and, as if he were Elian Gonzalez, pulled him out, kicking and screaming.

"So you were there at what time in the morning?" O'Brien asked.

"Approximately seven in the morning."

"And when you say, 'they,' who are you referring to?"

"Well, I later found out it was the Connecticut State Police, the Hopkinton [Rhode Island] Police Department, the Rhode Island State Police, members of the Berlin Police Department and Hartford Police Department."

"Did you hear Detective McDonald?"

Ned became red-faced: "He doesn't remember a *thing* about that day."

"Objection," Zagaja said. "I'd ask that that be stricken."

"Sustained."

"Did there come a time . . . that you went from your house to Troop H?"

Pouting, *"Yes."*

"And how did you get there?"

"I was taken from the house by Arthur Kershaw . . . and Kevin McDonald . . . and put in a car. McDonald drove, Kershaw was in the passenger seat."

Details. Ned was a man of point-to-point facts—at least when he wanted to recall them. It made him sound as though he knew exactly what he was talking about.

"So that was a Rhode Island police car. Do you know, or was it—"

Patronizingly, "I would imagine it was a Rhode Island police car, both of them were from Rhode Island."

"And did you have any conversations with Kershaw and McDonald in that car on the way to the police station?"

"The only thing I said as I was placed into the car . . . ," Ned began, and then went into an explanation of the day, saying, "This is harassment," to McDonald as they drove.

According to Ned, McDonald then turned and looked at him. "You haven't *seen* harassment yet."

"And then on the way to the Troop H building, McDonald tried to start a conversation," Ned added. "He says, 'Where you been working, Ned?' I did not answer."

"Did they or either one of them read you your Miranda warnings?" O'Brien asked.

"Not until we got to the Troop H building."

"So prior to getting into the car, did they read you your Miranda warnings?"

"No."

"Did they tell you why you were going to the police station?"

"The first thing Arthur Kershaw said [was] 'You're under arrest.' They wouldn't even let me put my socks on. Kershaw had me by the left shoulder and McDonald had me by the right as they let me put sneakers on with no socks and they marched me up the stairs onto the main floor right past my parents—my parents witnessed all this!—and *forced* me into the car. . . ."

"OK. So when you go to Troop H, what happened when you got there?"

"They took me . . . sat me down in a conference room. They told me who they were. They told me I was under arrest for murder and they read me my rights. I immediately said, 'I want to exercise my right to remain silent and I didn't want to talk to them about anything and they should take me downstairs to book me.' And they said, 'We don't take orders from you. We'll take our time. We'll book you when [we] want.'"

Ned claimed he spent eleven hours at Troop H. He said as the day progressed, different cops came and went, each trying to break him. Not being able to get him to talk, Ned insisted, infuriated the cops. He said they fed him and allowed him to use the restroom. He was careful not to paint them as all bad. It was part of the con: slip in the points you want to make alongside some truths. Jab them here and there. Never use a broad brush. Pick one cop—McDonald—and focus on him. Continuing, Ned added, "As soon as they read me my rights, I said I didn't want to discuss it and they should take me downstairs and book me. And, in fact, I got up out of the chair and I said, 'Come on, let's go to the basement.' And Detective McDonald said, 'No, no, no. Sit down, sit down, sit down.' And, by the way, this is all my—"

"There's no question pending," Zagaja objected. Interestingly enough was that the judge had already ruled on what Ned was now rehashing: she believed McDonald. It didn't matter what Ned had to say.

"Sustained."

O'Brien figured he might as well give Ned what he wanted: "Did you have something to add about that—"

But Ned didn't let him finish, saying, "My version of events is perfectly accurate and it's backed up by my behavior from two months prior to this in November of 2001 when Detective Mike Sheldon and Luisa St. Pierre came to seize the car. . . . Before they showed me the search and seizure warrant for the car, they asked me, would I be willing to get in my car and drive to the Hartford Police Department? And I said, 'No, I will not.' Just as I would have done on January fifteenth . . . I would have said no."

"So they grabbed you, put you in a car, and took you there?"

"Absolutely. We had—my parents witnessed it."

After a few more questions, O'Brien handed Ned off to Zagaja, who asked, "Mr. Snelgrove, you didn't want to discuss anything about the investigation, right?"

"Right."

"And you made that clear to them, right?"

"Very clear. And when I said I didn't want—"

"There's no question," Zagaja reminded Ned.

"I think he's finishing the answer to the question," O'Brien piped in.

"I believe he responded, Your Honor," Zagaja said.

"It called for a yes or no answer," the judge advised. "Sustained."

"Now, back in November, with Detective Mike Sheldon, you didn't want to speak with him, either, correct?"

"Correct," Ned said. "And he asked me, before he showed me—"

But Zagaja interrupted, "There's no question pending."

"Just answer the question," the judge said.

"Sorry," Ned said with a bit of a smirk.

"In fact, you had in your mind that you did not wish to discuss the matter . . . with any police?" Zagaja asked.

"Correct."

"And you've had some police involvement previously, correct?" It was perfect. The ideal way for Zagaja to get Ned to admit on the record that he was a convicted killer. It was the only reason why Zagaja had been so eager to question Ned. Because let's face it: the judge had already ruled.

"Yes," Ned answered defeatedly, without extrapolating at all.

"You have submitted to questioning to other police officers in the past, correct?"

"No," Ned said.

"In fact, you submitted to a deposition before Detective Watson, of the Middlesex County State's Attorney or District Attorney's Office?"

"That was with my attorney present in the room."

"But you did submit to a deposition, correct?"

"With my attorney present."

"With that said, you *submitted* to questioning with a police officer, correct?"

Merry-go-round. "With my attorney present. I'd never do it without an attorney."

"And you provided some information to the police, correct?"

"In New Jersey?" Ned asked.

"Yes!" Zagaja said.

"With my attorney present, yes."

"And you've lied to the police in the past, haven't you?"

There it was: Ned had told lies all his life. To his parents.

His lawyers. The court. The women he interacted with. Those patrons at Kenney's. And the police. Yes, the police. On the record, in fact. But suddenly Ned couldn't remember. "Um, I don't recall. It's possible, but—"

"You don't? OK." Ned's selective memory, in fact, worked to Zagaja's advantage. "Do you recall telling the police," Zagaja asked, "back in New Jersey, that you accompanied Karen Osmun, by coincidence, outside of a party? You walked with her—"

O'Brien had heard enough. "I'm going to object to the purpose of this questioning."

"Credibility," said Zagaja.

"It's impeachment. Overruled."

"You walked with her past her car and left her at her car. Do you remember?"

Ned became incensed: "No! I told the police that I left at the same *time* as Karen."

"Yes," Zagaja cleared up, "and you *walked* with her to her car and then drove—"

"And then," Ned said, interrupting Zagaja, "she got in her car and then I got in my car and drove, and that's the truth. I did not lie when I said that."

"Right. And you never saw her after that point, you told the police also. *Correct?*"

Beaten. "Correct."

"And that's a lie, correct?"

"Right."

"Because you *did* see her?"

"Yes."

"You killed her later that night, correct?"

"Yes."

"You didn't wish to cooperate with the police . . . in New Jersey, did you?" Zagaja asked.

"I don't recall."

"And you said, up front, you told the police you wanted to leave at Troop H?" Zagaja asked.

"Absolutely. I told . . . I told the—"

"There's no question pending, sir." It almost pained Zagaja, it was evident on his face, to call Ned "sir." But it was more sarcasm than respect.

"After they read me my rights, I said, you should take me—"

"There's no question pending, *sir*," Zagaja repeated.

"Just answer the question," the judge piped in. "If it calls for a yes or no, then it's a yes or no."

"You've been convicted of three felonies from New Jersey, correct?"

"Correct."

"You recall speaking with Detective Kershaw and Detective McDonald for about two hours?"

"They tried to get me to talk to them, I did not talk to them."

"And that was for about two hours you said?"

"Yeah. And then I was—"

"There's *no* question *pending*, sir." Zagaja took a breath, perhaps waiting for the judge to chime in again. When she didn't, he kept it going, asking Ned, "Did you make notes of anything that was said?"

"Did I make notes of anything said on that day?"

"Yes. Or anything done?"

"I remember what was said."

"You do? You recall everything that took place for those several hours you were at Troop H?"

Sharply, "Much, much better than McDonald, yes."

"Who transported you back home?"

"Sergeant Patrick Gaffney, of the Connecticut State Police. And in his report, it actually speaks—"

"Objection," Zagaja said, "there's nothing pending." A pause. No one said anything. So Zagaja asked: "Did you speak with Patrick Gaffney from the state police on your way back home?"

"He asked me—"

"Yes or no?" Zagaja said loudly.

"Well, no. He attempted to ask me questions and I didn't answer."

"You didn't say anything?"

"No."

For the next twenty minutes, Ned and Zagaja sparred on many of the issues that had already been covered. Ned stood his ground, Zagaja fired back. But beyond the fact that Ned was adamant regarding how he was (mis)treated by the police, nothing new came out of the verbal exchange.

93

I

Barbara Delaney had been through the worst that life could toss her way. No one could kill her sister again. Yet, that wound was open-ended, she said. Seeing Ned arrested for another murder was like hearing a tape of that day when she found out her sister had been murdered. She had been up late watching the news one night and saw a reporter interviewing Mary Ellen Renard, getting her reaction to Ned's arrest in Connecticut. "Oh, my goodness . . . that's Ned," Barbara said aloud, staring blankly at the television screen.

II

The drive north from New Jersey was tiring. Here was Barbara once again heading into a courtroom as her sister's killer faced a judge and jury. Barbara had thought she'd seen the last of Ned Snelgrove when she wrote that letter to the parole board more than six years earlier, warning its members that if they let him out of prison, well, they'd all be doing exactly what they were doing: trying to put him back. The guy was a murderer, Barbara knew. Nothing was going to stop him.

Since arriving in Hartford, Barbara had met and bonded with the Rodriguez family. Death could do that: create an instant connection and unite by tragedy.

Sitting in the back of the courtroom, watching Ned, she was sickened by his cocky mannerisms and "I'm in control" attitude. Knowing exactly the type of person Ned Snelgrove was, Barbara wanted to stand up and shout, "I'm here representing Karen. She is here in this room, too." *Don't anyone forget about my Karen.*

The fact that Karen had been killed by the same maniac who was now trying to convince a different court that he had been rehabilitated, cured, that he wasn't a menace to society any longer, was unnerving to Barbara as she sat and watched the proceedings. She couldn't stay for the entire trial, nor could she help the prosecution. But she could make her presence known for the sake of Karen's memory. Let Ned know that she was never going away. That she would always be in his face.

III

Jim Rovella was pacing in the state's attorney's office, a spacious piece of real estate located in the same building as the courtroom. Rovella was nervous, as was Zagaja. One of their main witnesses, the one person who could describe Ned's use of the past tense when talking about Carmen, was still missing. No one could find Jackie Garcia.

Jackie had a warrant out for her arrest. She had violated parole. Jackie had strayed since Carmen's death. She had fallen into an abyss of behaviors that were born out of the tragic loss of a loved one. Murder can have such a ripple effect on families. Now she was set to testify and the prosecution couldn't find her.

So Rovella called Luz. "I need your help." He didn't tell

Luz there was a warrant out for Jackie's arrest. "We cannot find Jackie, Luz, and we need her on the stand."

Luz had an idea of where she was. "OK."

"Can you help us?" Rovella asked.

"Yes, of course, of course."

IV

Dr. Jennifer Swartz, the Rhode Island medical examiner who autopsied Carmen's remains, testified on January 10. Through Swartz's testimony, Zagaja showed the jury what were dozens of photographs that O'Brien had objected to—photos that truly depicted the brutality of the final moments of Carmen's life and the result of her remains decomposing for months inside garbage bags.

The ropes.

The plastic bags.

The bones and skin tissue (what was left, anyway).

Carmen was no longer a fun-loving, roaming spirit, whom family members memorialized as the beautiful woman on the front of their T-shirts; to the jury, she was a bag of bones and decomposed tissue rotting in the woods.

Zagaja called Detective Kevin McDonald, who explained how the body was found, where and what transpired afterward. Zagaja was smart to put up large aerial maps of the region. Through those photos, it was apparent that Carmen's killer had dumped her body at the first possible wooded area over the Connecticut–Rhode Island border. From this unique bird's-eye view, jurors could see that if Ned was driving along the road, looking left and right, coming into Rhode Island from Connecticut, there was no other utility road on either side of the main road until this one area near Peter Mareck's house. Through testimony and photos, it was all clear: Ned had crossed the border, trolled along the main thoroughfare, spotted Grassy Pond Road on the left, turned, driven for a few moments, pulled over, dumped Carmen's body into an area twenty or so yards into the woods, and driven back home.

V

Luz made a few calls. Asked around. Jackie had seemingly disappeared. But then she ran into Jackie's boyfriend. "If you see her, or she returns home, call me."

He said he would.

Heading toward the end of the first week of trial, Luz got that call. She was sitting in the courtroom at the time. "Jackie's here," the boyfriend said. "She's taking a shower."

During a break—Zagaja had been questioning Ned's boss at American Frozen Foods—Luz pulled Zagaja aside. "We found her."

"Great. Where?"

"We're heading over to her apartment now to go get her."

Rovella and Zagaja thought for a moment to send a few black-and-whites. After all, there was a warrant out for a parole violation. But then they thought against it. They needed Jackie to testify. They didn't need her to run. (Luz still had no idea that there was a warrant out for Jackie's arrest.)

When she got to the apartment, Jackie was in the shower. Luz sat directly outside the bathroom door and waited. Jackie had no idea she was there.

As soon as Jackie opened the door and saw Luz, she quickly closed the door and locked it. "Jackie," Luz pleaded, "let's sit down and talk. . . . This is for your mother."

Jackie unlocked the door and let her aunt in. She was crying. Luz was gentle, sincere. "I can't go," Jackie said.

"This is to make justice for Carmen, honey, they need you."

"Auntie, Auntie," Jackie said, "but they're going to arrest me."

"You need to tell them about that day you confronted him at Kenney's and what he said to you."

"Auntie," Jackie said through tears. She had just turned twenty. She was a mother herself. She had been running. Not from the law. But from her own demons and feelings about her mother's murder. She missed Carmen. Missed her tenderness and kind touch. Those mother-daughter times they'd shared.

Luz said, "Jackie," putting her arm around her shoulder, "they are not going to arrest you. I promise on my kids' lives." Luz was speaking the truth from her heart. "It's hard for me and Sonia to sit there every day . . . you can help." Jackie started to get dressed. Luz continued, "It's going to be all right."

"You promise?" Jackie asked.

"I promise. Listen, girl, it's not easy for you, it's not easy for us being there every day. Now they need you. *We* need you."

Jackie thought about it.

"Come on, honey," Luz whispered.

VI

Zagaja finished questioning Ned's boss and there was a little break in the day's proceedings. He looked over at Rovella while he was collecting his files and paperwork. "I hope they found Jackie. She's up next."

94

I

When Luz and Jackie arrived at the state's attorney's office, Zagaja looked as though he had been given a shot of adrenaline. They were inside a room at the courthouse: Zagaja, Rovella, and a uniformed cop. Jackie was nervous. Shaking a bit. Crying. Luz didn't know what was going on. "You see, Auntie," Jackie started saying through tears, "you see, you see," adding quickly, "Now they're going to put me in jail."

"What?" Luz said, a belt of confusion whipped across her face.

"I swear to God," Jackie said, "I didn't do nothing. Swear to God."

"Hey," Luz said, "what's going on?" She felt betrayed.

"I don't ever want to see you," Jackie screamed, "Sonia, or anyone else, ever!"

"David, what's going on?" Luz asked, looking toward Zagaja.

"Well," Zagaja said, "she's under arrest for a parole violation. We have a warrant."

"Tell her I didn't know. Tell her. Tell her I didn't know that, David!"

"I will," Zagaja said.

"Jackie," Luz said, "remember when I said on 'my kids' lives,' I meant that. I *didn't* know."

In the end, Jackie was OK with things. Zagaja promised to send her to treatment, instead of jail, and everyone was happy. But she had to testify first.

II

Zagaja and Rovella believed that some of the best evidence they had was Ned's own mileage records. It was that one comment Ned had made to Luisa St. Pierre as he lay in a hospital bed. That bell Ned had rung himself. That one "mistake" he had made in offering up his mileage books. Zagaja and Rovella had spent hundreds of hours studying Ned's mileage records, matching his mileage up against the gas receipts they uncovered in his basement. They'd hired an outside firm, North Eastern Technical Services (NETS), from Fall River, Massachusetts, to sift through the mountain of records and come up with some sort of way to explain it all in layman terms. ("Those records were important," Rovella told me later. "When you looked at them, and studied them, it was *so* obvious.")

Still, you had to know what you were looking for. Zagaja had spent hours creating charts and graphs to illustrate how Ned had tried to cook his books to make it appear as if he couldn't have traveled to Rhode Island on that weekend Carmen went missing. Ned thought he was smart. He believed he had it all covered. And yet, like the maps he kept in his house, and perhaps allowing Mary Ellen Renard to live, he had made another in a series of mistakes: thinking he was smarter than everyone else. His biggest downfall, after all: his ego. It was all coming back to him now—and although he'd soon try, there was very little he could do to stop it.

III

It was safe to say that Jackie was a mess. She had been booked and was now being housed in the women's prison in Niantic, Connecticut, where she would stay until she saw a judge and was given a bed at a hospital. In court, facing Ned, Jackie looked fragile and on edge, as if the slightest mention of her mother was going to make her crumble. Zagaja got her arrest record out of the way first, then had Jackie talk about where she lived with Carmen in Hartford at the time her mom went missing and how she had phoned the Hartford PD the following morning. Then, after some discussion between O'Brien and the judge over the time frame, Zagaja established when Jackie had gone to Kenney's with Miguel, Cutie, and Jeffrey Malave to confront Ned. He had her explain how she was summoned to Kenney's by a call from the bartender. "And did you end up meeting with this person, you said, Edwin?"

"Yeah," Jackie said. So far, so good. Jackie was holding her own. She was getting stronger, apparently, as she talked her way through that day when she was frantically searching for her mother, who had been missing, by then, for almost two weeks. And after establishing how they flushed Ned out of Kenney's and into the side street and, finally, out to his car, Jackie said he ran back into the bar, which seemed awfully suspicious to her. "He took a bill out of his pocket and started running into the bar again and he screamed, 'Whoever [will] stop those people, I'll give fifty dollars.'"

"Where were you when you saw that?"

"After him."

"Were you in the bar, at that point?"

"No. Two people came right away to the door and they block us."

"What ended up happening then?"

"I tell the guys, 'I just want to speak with him 'cause my

mom was the last person they see with . . . it was him. And I just want to ask where he left my mother.'"

"And did they let you in?"

"Yeah."

Jackie described how they sat down with Ned—except Miguel, who was seething and squirrelly and wanted to kick Ned's butt, so they kept him back. "Can you describe what happened once you sat at the table?" Zagaja asked. "Did you ask him any questions?"

Jackie paused. Recoiled a bit. The memory of it all was getting to her. She was back there that day in her mind, and it was hard. She was no longer telling the story—she was reliving it. "I asked him," she said, "where he left my mom."

"And did he respond?"

"He told me in Shell, in the gas station."

"In the Shell gas station? And did he say anything else?"

"No. Oh, and then [he said] my mother asked him for—for twenty dollar—for twenty dollar, and he was like, 'Get out the car.'"

"Did he say anything else after that?"

"No."

"Do you remember if Jeffrey [Malave] said anything about you being her daughter?"

This seemed to spark a memory for Jackie. "That I was pregnant. I was pregnant about that time. [Jeffrey] was like, 'If you got her mother, just let her go, and, you know, or call the cops if you see her.' Something like that. And he told me . . . and he, right there, when Jeffrey tell him that I was her daughter, he looked at me in my eyes"—Jackie started to breathe heavier—"and told me, 'I'm sorry. That *was* your *mom?*'"

It was all in the way she said it. How Ned had said it: "That *was* your *mom?*" Not, *Carmen is your mother?* Or, *I have no idea where Carmen is.* Instead, Ned had used "was." How telling that one past-tense verb had become to Jackie.

"Did you take that to mean anything when he said that?"

"Yeah . . . because he could have say—he could have say, 'I'm sorry, that's your mom.' For me," Jackie added, crying now, "he killed her already when he told me that."

"That's what you understood that to [mean]?"

She couldn't answer. She was crying too hard. Too piercingly. Sniffling and heavily breathing in and out. "Can we get some tissues?" the judge asked, intervening. "All right. I'm going to excuse the jury for a few minutes."

As the jury exited the room, the marshal said, "Jacqueline? Jacqueline?" She was losing it. The judge said, "Just stay right there."

"No, let me go," Jackie said.

"Have a seat," the marshal said. "No, no, have a seat," he said again as Jackie started to get up. "It's OK. Have a seat."

"All right," Judge Espinosa said, "we're going to take a recess."

IV

When Ned handed over his mileage records to the police, investigators were certain he was trying to say, *Go ahead, try to catch me.* "When you looked at the day Carmen Rodriguez disappeared," Jim Rovella commented later, "it's nothing but scribble." The writing itself was vastly different from the other days around that *one* date, September 21, 2001—which was the first red flag. "Our task was to take that mileage, which Ned had written out for a few years, and compare it against his appointment logs."

They had an abundance of material from Ned's hand that showed where he was and what he did for just about every day he had worked for American Frozen Foods. "The mileage, in addition, is very well done—except for that *one* date of September 21." What was strange to Rovella was that Ned had kept all of his gas receipts; he hadn't throw them out or burned them after he killed Carmen. Same as Bundy.

("Didn't he learn anything from Bundy?" Rovella asked, chuckling at the thought.)

With those gas receipts, the state's attorney's office could figure out the gas mileage Ned's car got, match it up against the mileage he traveled for an allotted time period, see if his record keeping was accurate for, say, a six-month period of time (nowhere near the dates Carmen went missing), and then compare those figures—which were Ned's—to the day in question.

Thus, when Rovella reviewed all of the evidence Ned left behind, he came up with a rather shocking revelation for Ned's car: during the week Carmen disappeared, Ned's car got four miles to the gallon on one day and eighty-nine miles to the gallon on another.

"There was no consistency—but only for that time period."

Smoking gun or fuzzy math?

All throughout the course of that year—minus that one week in September—Ned's car got a consistent twenty-nine miles per gallon of gas. Which meant that his record keeping for the week Carmen disappeared had been doctored. Ned thought he had covered himself, but he had, in fact, calculated wrong. In his own hand, he wrote that on September 21, 2001, beginning at 3:43 P.M., he made a 1-800 call from a pay phone. Then, minutes later, he stopped for fuel at a Mobil station and pumped 10.0006 gallons of fuel into his car. An hour later, he was at a client's home giving his frozen-food pitch: a 27.7-mile trip from the fuel station to his appointment (per MapQuest). But Ned marked it as forty-three miles. A difference of more than fifteen miles.

He was then on to another appointment not too far away from the first; he logged eight miles.

The actual trip was five. A difference of three.

Then another call from another pay phone; then he logged his trip to Kenney's in Hartford, which was 18.8 miles from his final appointment of the day, and logged his trip back home to Berlin.

For the entire trip—from his final appointment to Kenney's to home—Ned logged forty-one miles, but the actual distance was 34.1. A difference of nearly seven miles.

According to Ned's figures, his total for the day was ninety-two. The actual distance, however, was sixty-seven. Ned was building an alibi for himself.

Mile by mile.

Why? Because he needed to make room for a trip to Hopkinton, Rhode Island, Zagaja showed with charts and graphs and through testimony. The plan was always to dump the body out of state, Zagaja suggested. That's the one thing Ned had learned from Bundy: dump the body in another jurisdiction because it is almost impossible—if you do it properly—for authorities to track it back to its original location.

95

I

Jackie composed herself, collected her thoughts, and was able to continue. Zagaja asked her a few more questions and then handed his witness over to O'Brien, who proceeded to do the only thing he could: drag out the statements Jackie had given to police and begin to peck away, hoping to catch her on dates, times, names, or certain situations that conflicted with her direct testimony.

But none did.

Jackie had forgotten a few things, but her story had stayed the same for the past four years. She had no reason to lie. She didn't know that much—other than that one word: "was." That *was* your mother?

O'Brien challenged the statement. "And isn't it a fact that Mr. . . . that you explained who you were [to Ned], right? And then Mr. Snelgrove said, 'I'm sorry. Listen, I'm sorry, but I don't know anything, anything I can tell you.' Isn't *that* what he said?"

Jackie wasn't about to be bullied. Not now. Not after what she had been through in life since her mother had been murdered. "He *said,*" Jackie spoke up, "'I'm sorry. That *was* your *mom?*'"

"Did you, um . . . did you tell that to the police—"

"Yeah."

"The next day?"

"Yeah."

After a few more questions, Jackie was excused.

II

On the morning of January 12, Ned stood outside the courtroom in the inmate holding area. Several marshals surrounded him. He was dressed in a state-issued pumpkin-orange jumpsuit. His legs were shackled at the ankles. His hands chained to his waist. He was livid. The jury wasn't going to be in the courtroom today. When the subject of those letters Ned had written to George Recck—and, more to the point of the hearing, the eleven-page sentencing letter Ned had written to the judge in New Jersey back in 1988—came up, O'Brien and Ned argued relevancy. Of course, allowing the letters into trial would alert the jury to Ned's prior crimes and show intent. A pattern. They spoke of what Ned wanted to do upon his release. But that wasn't what made Ned so mad. He wouldn't show himself to the judge until he could change, he said. He didn't want to present himself in court in prison attire. He thought it made him look guilty.

When the judge asked where Ned was, O'Brien said, "Your Honor, apparently Mr. Snelgrove wants to change into the clothing that he's been wearing." Sport jacket, button-down shirt, necktie, slacks. The salesman's uniform.

"He doesn't have to, there's no jury here."

"I know that. But his position is that he would like to. So if the court would accommodate him."

The judge was fed up with Ned, his accusations, demands, and outbursts. This was just one more way for Ned to try and control the proceedings. "We're going to start," Espinosa said. "*What* is the difference?"

"I guess there's a feeling of because he's in a prison uniform that the judge may be swayed by that. Some—I—there's some element of, perhaps, truth to that."

"Well, this court won't be swayed. I've seen hundreds of defendants in prison uniforms." A few laughs rang out.

"But that's his position, Your Honor . . ."

"Well, fine."

". . . that's all I'm doing is reporting it."

The judge paused. Leaned forward. Paused again. "OK. Denied." Gavel.

Bring him in.

III

Zagaja addressed the judge first, explaining his position regarding the letters and how important they were to proving Ned's motive, saying at one point, "It's the state's opinion that there is no better substitute to indicate the defendant's intent than the sentencing letter." That eleven-page manifesto Ned had penned to the judge. "It describes what he wanted to do upon attacking and killing Karen Osmun," Zagaja explained, "and what he wanted to do when he strangled and stabbed Mary Ellen Renard. Oftentimes we are presented in a somewhat routine or normal situation where the state moves to present prior crimes to prove intent or motive. . . . Rather than having the need for an inference, the sentencing letter lays out, in plain terms, what the defendant's *intent* was, what his motive was. . . . He describes, in detail, the engaging in the strangling process—how, by strangling, he had great difficulty in causing the death of both individuals, describing how it's not an easy task to do with your bare hands." For Zagaja, that letter proved Ned had *learned* his lesson in strangulation and went on to other sure means of killing.

As Zagaja read excerpts of the letters into the record, those in the courtroom sat in utter silence—shock and awe, actually—as Ned's pen described, in graphic detail, how he strangled Karen and attempted to kill Mary Ellen by strangulation, and because killing a woman with his bare hands wasn't so easy, he was forced, instead, to stab both women.

The judge wasn't entirely convinced, however. "So you want to," she asked Zagaja, "you want to, like, virtually, try those other two cases?"

O'Brien and Ned brightened up.

"I don't want to *try* the cases. In fact, I believe they become somewhat nonissues because he admits to all the conduct in the sentencing letter. Let me, then, point out specifically what I wish to offer—Mary Ellen Renard coming in, really, just going through her deposition, describing how she met the defendant . . . going home, and describing the incident that took place with her being strangled by him, the actual strangulation, her passing out, being carried to a bed, finding, at that point, when she regained consciousness, that her top was removed and that she had been stabbed. . . . She's not going to testify about the other components of the investigation. As far as Karen Osmun's homicide, what I'm most interested in getting out before the jury is the similarly situated position of Ms. Osmun."

Ned sat in his state-issued jumper, while Zagaja, a man Ned loathed more than any other human being at the present moment, kept pushing his head farther and farther underwater—and Ned wasn't able to do anything to stop him. There wasn't a person in the room who didn't realize what a brutal, evil, woman-hating man Ned was—a man without so much as an ounce of compassion for human life. No conscience whatsoever.

Zagaja argued his case for including the letters, while the judge peppered him with questions. Zagaja explained: "I would ask the court to consider the sentencing letter and consider what the defendant wishes to do, what his pleasure is when he engages in this conduct—and nowhere does his conduct involve having sex or sexual intercourse with his victim.

This is where, in the state's opinion, the situation of Carmen Rodriguez falls in line with the two previous incidents. There were certain analyses done on the vaginal smears and swabs of Ms. Rodriguez, with no semen being found. . . . In the state's opinion, they represent a progression of conduct and that's really where the defendant's letters to George Recck come into play, and they're the utmost relevance, the packaging of the body, the disposal of the body at a remote location."

A collective gasp. For the first time, Ned's previous crimes were aired in vivid practicality. If nothing else, Zagaja was able to get the stories out there for the public to hear.

Zagaja cited case after case where a similar ruling had been made. While he was at it, Zagaja asked if he could get the actual Styrofoam heads in, too. Previous discussion and testimony had been based on photos of the heads. Showing those actual props to the jury would be dramatic. ". . . The state would point, specifically, to the neck areas where a grid formation is actually drawn with an X in the center of the neck, which, in my opinion, is right at the Adam's apple, a perfect space for accomplishing a strangulation. And I think these were actually practice tools for the defendant or tools for his own arousal in the event that a woman was not sought at that time."

Ned turned red-faced. He pulled O'Brien close to him and whispered. Zagaja continued, "Also, Your Honor, although this has not been submitted yet, there was a disclaimer on one exhibit of various serial killers—"

The judge seemed confused. "I'm sorry?"

"Various serial killers being reported upon in the *Hartford Courant*," Zagaja explained, "and the title of the whole story was 'Why They Kill.'" It was research. A killer and his reading list. Zagaja wanted Ned's reading choices made part of the trial, adding, "That was also found in the basement area near the defendant's couch. . . . And there's an additional article, 'Changes Must Be Made to Control Sexual Offenders, Reduce Risk,' found within that package of literature."

"May I see that? Is there a date on this?"

Ned said something to O'Brien.

"What about the movie that you—" the judge started to say.

"Yes," Zagaja said, unable to control his excitement, ". . . I would offer the movie *The Deliberate Stranger,* that of being a story about Ted Bundy. And the reason I'm offering it is because the specific movie is cited by the defendant as he speaks and criticizes or critiques himself and Mr. Bundy for his conduct and whatever, in his opinion, was done right and was done wrong. . . . And that's how it impacted his comments relative to keeping receipts, as Mr. Bundy did, and that he would never do that. . . ."

O'Brien argued that none of it had anything to do with the content of Ned's character. It was a smoke screen. A railroad. A clever way to try Ned for his previous crimes. "Your Honor, I would submit that introducing what Mr. Zagaja would like to offer that we could all go home, at that point, because there would be no need for additional evidence. What it is, in effect, is a substitute for a *lack* of evidence. The introduction of this extremely inflammatory material as to what happened in the '80s in my client's life no doubt would prejudice, severely prejudice, the jury, and they would think, well, of course he must have done *this* crime. If he did that in the '80s he must have—he must have done this. . . ."

"Well," said the judge, "if you say that, then doesn't that mean that the probative value outweighs the prejudice?"

Zagaja liked what he was hearing. "Well," O'Brien said, "in the sense that it's a substitute for lack of evidence. There isn't any evidence other than the fact that Mr. Snelgrove was last seen with Carmen Rodriguez. If that is the case, then every person that Mr. Snelgrove was seen with, given that alone, if that person is murdered, then there's no need to have any evidence in the case."

96

I

Ned and I wrote to each other for about eight months. In some of those letters, Ned goes into great detail while explaining how the state failed to produce the appropriate amount of *evidence* to convict him. To say that Ned is obsessive-compulsive does not truly describe him accurately. One day, he sent me a package. It contained trial transcripts, autopsy reports, police reports, and other documents associated with his case. In between each page of official documentation was a note from Ned to me explaining why certain pieces of evidence submitted during trial were inaccurate, fabricated, or irrelevant. Ned had separated each set of the documents with a vanilla card—with more exposition and instruction—*look here, read this, you won't believe this*—on the cards. He was certain the Connecticut Department of Corrections was *going to make sure,* he wrote, *you don't get my story told.* The key to this line is, "my story."

I had explained to Ned that I wanted to understand his *side* of the Rodriguez matter. Fair and balanced, I promised, stealing that overused phrase.

He told me I had a *blockbuster bestseller* on my hands *if* I was to *expose the dishonest prosecutor [David Zagaja], the flagrantly biased judge [Carmen Espinosa], and the many witness statements that [didn't] make sense when held up to the light.* . . . Everyone, he seemed to suggest, was lying, all brought together by an overzealous, power-hungry prosecutor who had gathered them all together to frame Ned and punish him for his previous crimes in New Jersey. He was certain of it.

In his letters to me, Ned carries on and on about witness statements and lies and the cover-up afterward. He talks about how the state had it in for him from the beginning of his trial, solely because of his prior crimes. He had gotten out of prison early, he seethed many times, and they were making him now pay for that early release. In a letter dated June 13, 2007, Ned talked about the medical examiner's report from Rhode Island and how it failed to explain the many different ways in which Carmen *could have* been murdered. Ned was upset with the fact that his lawyer failed to ask the medical examiner important questions regarding how Carmen *could have* been murdered. According to his letter, Ned is somehow under the impression that medical examiners in the real world are like Cyril Wecht or Michael Baden and each case is a cable news program panel discussion. He believes that the medical examiner, in his or her report, should speculate and talk about the different ways a victim *could have* been killed—if, for example, the manner of death isn't obvious (as in Carmen's case). What's important about this letter is the various ways in which Ned describes to me *how* Carmen could have been murdered. In and of themselves, some of Ned's answers—beyond the norm—are chilling. I had to ask myself: *Is he telling me how he murdered this woman? Is he telling me* how *he killed other females several investigators and profilers I have spoken to claimed he has?*

Ned's list:

- *Electrocution*
- *Drowning*
- *Forced starvation as a result of being held captive*
- *Forced dehydration as a result of being held captive*
- *Hard blow to the temple (no skull damage)*
- *Heart attack brought on by external traumatic event*
- *Hard blow to the chest*
- *Suffocation with pillow*

If I thought this was strange, his next letter was even more shocking.

97

I

When Donald O'Brien returned to his oral argument in front of Judge Espinosa regarding allowing those letters and the Bundy movie, and the Styrofoam heads and the kitchen sink that Zagaja wanted to present to the jury, he said, rather somberly, "In terms of similarities between the crimes, Your Honor, Karen Osmun was the former girlfriend of Mr. Snelgrove. Ms. Renard he met that night at a bar. And Carmen Rodriguez he knew from Kenney's, as he knew other women from Kenney's."

And that was Zagaja's point exactly: Ned had, in fact, honed his craft. He had gotten to *know* his victim. In choosing Carmen, in getting to *know* her personally, Ned thought he was choosing the *perfect* victim. The victim no one would miss. The victim Bundy had taught him to choose. But, of course, Ned had no idea members of Carmen's family would be combing the streets that night, looking for her.

"In Karen Osmun's case," O'Brien argued, "he followed her home. [In] Renard's case, he followed *her* home, and, in this instance, Carmen Rodriguez, she *asked* for a ride."

In truth, that was what *Ned* had claimed. No one knew for

certain if Carmen had asked Ned for a ride, or if Ned forced
her into his car. He had been seen leaving the bar with
Carmen. Beyond that, anything was possible. He'd allegedly
tried to grab Christina Mallon outside Kenney's weeks before
Carmen disappeared. Who's to say Ned didn't convince
Carmen to walk outside with him and when (and if) she refused to get into his car, he forced her.

". . . The medical examiner kind of left it open that you
can't rule out various factors," O'Brien argued. "You can't
rule out strangling, it could have been strangling and stabbing. But you also can't rule out a number of other factors,
electrocution being one, suffocation, those factors, any other
causes of death. . . ." O'Brien then began to lay out how far
apart each murder was, trying to explain that there was no
pattern. "In terms of remoteness, Your Honor, this occurred—
'83 was the killing of Osmun, I believe, '87 was the attempted murder of Renard. So we're . . . we're twenty-two
years post the killing of Osmun, and, at the current time we
are, we're twenty years post, let me see, eighteen, eighteen
years post on Osmun and Renard—"

Sitting, shaking his head, watching his attorney struggle to
do simple addition, Ned couldn't take it. He blurted out:
"Eighteen." *Eighteen years,* for crying out loud.

II

Connecticut case law had a long history regarding the ad-
missibility of prior misconduct evidence. It was "well established," Judge Espinosa explained as she began to hand down
her decision on the morning of January 13. "All right," she
said pleasantly, confidently, "the court has reviewed the arguments of counsel, the relevant case law. . . . The court rules as
follows. . . . Evidence of prior acts of misconduct, because of
its prejudicial nature, is *inadmissible* to show that the defendant is guilty of a subsequent crime. However, evidence of

acts of misconduct are *admissible* for the purpose of proving many things—such as, intent, identity, motive, a common scheme, or a system of criminal activity." And this was Zagaja's main point: Ned had provided a blueprint for future behavior that was relevant to not only the murder of Carmen Rodriguez, but how he had chosen Carmen as his victim. "To be admissible," Espinosa continued, "such evidence must also be relevant and material." She explained that the eleven-page letter written by Ned "is relevant and material to the issues of intent, motive, and knowledge. It is relevant to prove what the defendant's intent was on September 21, 2001, when he left Kenney's restaurant with Carmen Rodriguez. It is also relevant to the issue of the defendant's motive for killing Carmen Rodriguez that night. The defendant admits, in this letter, that he has a longtime compulsion to kill women for sexual gratification by rendering women helpless and posing their bodies in seductive poses. He admits getting pleasure and sexual arousal when he kills rather than by having sex with his victims." Ned shook his head. He couldn't believe what he was hearing as Espinosa continued, saying, "Accordingly, the defendant's letters . . . the court finds that evidence of these two prior acts of misconduct are relevant and material to the issues of intent, motive, common scheme, and identity. All three women were friendly with the defendant and had a speaking relationship with him, they all interacted with him socially." But, ". . . at this time, the court will *not* allow the testimony of Mary Ellen Renard. The court finds that the prejudicial effect of her live testimony, at this time, would outweigh its probative value. . . . The letters to George Recck. The court finds that the letters . . . are relevant to the issues of establishing a course of criminal activity culminating in the murder of Carmen Rodriguez, as well as to the issues of common scheme, intent, and motive."

Zagaja wanted to pump his fist in the air. He wanted to

stand up and say thank you. Yell and scream. But, of course, he sat and took it all in. He hadn't won yet.

On the other hand, Ned looked as though he had been told he had terminal cancer.

"The court further finds . . . that these letters to George Recck describe the defendant's compulsion to kill and were consistent with the statements to the sentencing judge. They are relevant to show the development and progression of his compulsion to kill, how he learned from his mistakes, how he learned from Ted Bundy's mistakes, all of which culminated in the murder of Carmen Rodriguez. . . ."

As for the movie *The Deliberate Stranger,* the judge said she had watched the movie the previous night. She believed— and rightly so—that the "prejudice of showing it to the jury outweighs its probative value."

Nonetheless, Zagaja could not have asked for a better judgment.

Ned's hatred for the process grew as he sat and boiled. He believed without a doubt that the judge was now entirely against him. He kept quiet, but promised himself that before the trial was over, there would come a time when the judge truly got an earful. It was just a matter of when the proper time for such an outburst would present itself.

98

I

The admission of the letters essentially sealed Ned's fate: he was finished. He knew it. O'Brien knew it. And Zagaja knew it. No matter what else the state had, the jury would see, in Ned's own words, the callous sociopath and remorseless killer he had been in the past. They *would* judge him on his previous acts—exactly what he was afraid of. He had killed before and had promised to kill again.

Guilty!

II

And so David Zagaja began his parade of witnesses to talk about the letters and Ned's previous crimes—and the noose, as each witness stood, raised his or her hand, and testified, got tighter and tighter around Ned's neck. No matter what he said or what he did now, he was a convicted murderer. He couldn't escape his past. His past, in effect, had become his future. His present.

Hartford PD detective Timothy Shaw testified how he logged all of the evidence—there wasn't much—from Ned's car. What was significant about Ned's car was not what investigators found, but what they *didn't* find. DNA is ironclad science, some might contend. Finding DNA or trace evidence—a cigarette butt, hair, saliva, anything that can tie or trace back to a person being in one place at some point—inside a car is generally a way for a prosecutor to say, *She was in his car. We have the DNA to prove it.* What does one do, however, when one finds nothing? Not once piece of trace evidence to prove Carmen Rodriguez was in Ned's car. Well, for starters, he points out the most important fact gleaned from such a find: Ned admitted Carmen had taken a ride with him. With her nest of long and flowing hair, it would almost be impossible for her *not* to have left one hair in Ned's car. From Zagaja's perspective, this meant that Ned had swept that car clean. Totally wiped it down from bumper to bumper. "There will be much said about the lack of forensic evidence," Zagaja explained to jurors, "the lack of scientific evidence. And in a very eerie sense, we have to give Ned credit for that. . . . It's not for a lack of testing or a lack of want or a lack of analysis. . . . Based on the state of decomposition of the body, the late time in its detection, this is the *evolution* of a killer. And we, unfortunately, have to give him credit for that. It's a sick statement, because I don't mean 'credit' in the sense of 'you did a good job.'"

III

CSP detective Thomas Murray testified about items the CSP found when they served a search warrant on the Snelgrove property. Addressing the jury under Zagaja's questioning, Murray said he and his colleagues seized maps. Several staple guns. Ropes. Notebooks of Ned's mileage. Gas receipts. And inside the Snelgrove garage were several coils of rope hanging from several hooks, all of which were accounted for—except one.

Next, Maria Warner, a scientist for the State of Connecticut,

Department of Public Safety, Forensic Science Laboratory, was asked about a hair found on one of the staplers in Ned's basement bedroom. Could it be Carmen's? "And on any of the staplers submitted," Zagaja said, "were you able to identify anything attributable to any person?"

"Yes."

"And what was that?"

"On one of the staplers . . . there was . . . a human Caucasian pubic hair."

"And by that point, had you received known samples from Edwin Snelgrove and Carmen Rodriguez?"

"Yes."

"And did you engage in a comparison of those items?"

"Yes. I did a microscopic comparison [and] they were dissimilar to Carmen Rodriguez, and the hair was similar to that sample sent in from Edwin Snelgrove." In other words, one of Ned's pubic hairs was found on his stapler. No one ventured to ask why.

Filling up the rest of the day were more cops and more testimony describing searches and warrants and seizures. And then it was on to the next day, when Warner returned briefly to explain a very important fact for Zagaja: there had been no seminal fluid found on or near Carmen Rodriguez. Sexual intercourse or rape were, apparently, not part of the motivation behind Carmen's murder.

99

I

In preparation for the trial, David Zagaja read many of the books written about Bundy. He didn't expect to find some sort of groundbreaking revelation; but he was hoping for, at the least, a bit of insight, anything that could help him understand Ned more than he already did. He was closing in on the end of his study when, suddenly, he realized something he had overlooked all along. In one of the books, as Zagaja read it, a sheriff, a "good old boy," Zagaja called him, goes in to see Bundy after he is caught. "He starts interviewing Bundy," Zagaja told me, "beginning with something to the effect of, 'Now, who are you again?'" A tactical move, of course. Because "Bundy explodes," Zagaja said. "'How dare you? Don't you know who I am?' The entire country had been on edge because of Bundy and his crimes. His image had been plastered all over the media. And in walks this cocky sheriff asking who he is." The nerve. "It was the biggest deflator for Bundy," Zagaja added. "That this sheriff walks into the jail and tries to say he doesn't know who he is."

While reading that section of the book, Zagaja truly saw Bundy through Ned's eyes, understood the hero worship.

They were alike in what was a common hubristic sense of self. It was all about the individual. Call it narcissism or self-reliance. They both work. But Bundy and Ned had lived lives centered around their crimes. Their crimes defined who they were as human beings—which was to become important to Zagaja as he headed for the homestretch.

II

Ned's past became part of the trial on January 14, when Judge Espinosa addressed the jury, saying, "Ladies and gentlemen, I'm going to say a few words to you now about the evidence you are about to hear"—which alone made the imminent testimony even more powerful than it probably was, but Espinosa had to say it. She explained the law, adding near the end of her speech, "The evidence is not to be used by you as evidence that the defendant had a propensity to commit the crime with which he is charged in this case, or since he did these things, he must have committed the crime alleged in this case. Such evidence is being admitted," the judge warned, "solely to show or establish a common *plan* or *scheme* in the commission of criminal acts, the existence of the intent. . . . "

Yeah, OK.

III

Dennis Watson had been employed by the Middlesex County Prosecutor's Office in New Jersey for the past thirty-two years. He had investigated Karen Osmun's murder. He had been a witness to the tragedy of Ned's handiwork. And it had haunted him ever since.

Zagaja was smart to bring in Watson. He could give the jury an image of what Ned had done to a human being. In a metaphorical sense, the prosecution could say: *That man, the one over there with the necktie and sport coat and slacks and*

*perfectly combed hair, the one who refuses to wear glasses
because he thinks it makes him look like a serial killer, he
strangled a woman, stabbed her, and posed her body. And
then, when faced with committing a similar crime, he admitted to both.*

Watson cut whatever tension was in the room and replaced it
with horrorlike images of a woman who had lost her life to the
man sitting center stage. Karen's name was rarely mentioned—
one would have to imagine by design. And when you sat and
you closed your eyes as Watson spoke, you could almost see
Carmen or Mary Ellen—or God knows who else—struggling
for life. "She was lying on her back," Watson explained. "She
was naked from the waist up. On the lower part of her body, she
had a pair of jeans, which were secured, zippered, snapped, and
there was a belt that was buckled. She had socks and underpants
on. . . . I saw numerous injuries. There were, I believe, six, what
appeared to be stab wounds in the center, lower chest area. I noticed two superficial apparent stab wounds in the lower neck
area. There were abrasions and bruising on her neck and there
were numerous petechial hemorrhages all over her face. . . .
My understanding—and, again, I'm not a medical person—
they're small hemorrhages of the small blood vessels . . . in the
face." The detective paused for effect. Always a brilliant move.
Then the selling point: "They're indicative of asphyxiation." He
didn't need to say anything more.

IV

George Recck walked into the courtroom, and under
Zagaja's questioning, he authenticated the letters he and Ned
had exchanged. This allowed Zagaja to make the letters part
of the court file and available to the jury during deliberations.
Zagaja didn't need any dramatic re-reading of the letters, although he did get as much of them as he could into the
record. The letters, of course, would speak for themselves. In

his own words, Ned explained to jurors what he had done in the past, what he had learned throughout his incarceration, and what he intended to do in the future. Putting Carmen into the context of the letters, one could argue that Ned had fulfilled a promise to himself to kill again.

Recck sustained questioning from both sides throughout the afternoon and into early evening. In the end, he came across as a believable ex-friend of Ned's who, at one time, was talking about writing a book with Ned and producing a movie about Ned's life. Ned listened, perhaps quite alarmed by the words he once wrote—so profoundly eerie and so obviously vile—to a trusted friend, which were now going to be in the hands of a jury deciding his fate.

100

I

When the state's attorney's office called Ned's former psy-chiatrist to ask if he'd participate in the trial as a witness, ex-plaining what they believed Ned had done to Carmen, he dropped the phone. He couldn't believe it. Ned had gotten out of prison and killed again. "I use Ned as a case study for one of my classes," Ned's former psychiatrist said over the phone. He was noticeably distraught. Quite upset, in fact, that Ned could have killed again. Still, he said he couldn't help. He and another psychiatrist who had interviewed Ned when he was in-carcerated in New Jersey couldn't testify for the state. He be-lieved the doctor/patient confidentiality agreement still existed.

But the state had access to those reports. "Ned proclaimed that he was a breast man in those reports," a source who had access to them later told me, "and intercourse had nothing to do with his desires." Ned gloated when he explained this fetish to his doctors. And "he was proud of the fact that he was able to get a twenty-year sentence for his crimes in New Jersey and how he had duped the police all those years."

One of the reasons why Ned was so open and honest with the doctors in New Jersey, my source speculated, was that he knew when he was talking to those psychiatrists, his words would later be protected.

The point was, look at Karen Osmun, look at Mary Ellen Renard, and then look at Carmen Rodriguez: even after they were attacked (or killed), they all had their undergarments on. "[Sexual intercourse] has nothing to do with his motives," my source added. "Mr. Snelgrove wanted to make sure the [victim's] top was off—and that was it."

II

The trial had taken a four-day break. By January 19, Judge Espinosa had her courtroom back on track—and Zagaja made the announcement before the break that his star witness, Mark Pascual, the jailhouse snitch, was next in line.

III

As a prosecutor, Zagaja later explained, you don't take someone like Mark Pascual, when he comes to you, and "run with him. You have to put him through a number of hoops. Because, as far as we're concerned, if *we* don't believe him, a jury's certainly not going to." So Zagaja and Rovella, after Pascual came forward, simply let him talk. "There were certain pieces," Zagaja said, which Pascual brought to the table, "that were never out there."

"He had information that was only known to the killer and the police," Rovella added. "That was what really kicked the jury."

After Pascual came forward, claiming Ned had confessed to him, Rovella sat and listened to hours and hours of telephone conversations Pascual had made from prison to various people. "I listened to find out if he'd ask his girlfriend, 'Hey, can you send me this article or that article?'" It was O'Brien and Ned's contention that Pascual had merely read the newspapers and offered up Ned as a sacrifice so he could, in turn, cut a better deal for himself. "But I never heard any of that from those calls I listened to," Rovella claimed. "Pascual had never asked for any newspaper articles during those calls. Pascual, you see, knew something that could have only come from Ned: taking Carmen to breakfast."

No one had ever known that until Pascual had come forward.

101

I

It was an unseasonably warm autumn afternoon the day I drove up to Suffield, Connecticut, to meet with Mark Pascual for the first time at MacDougall-Walker Correctional Institution. Pascual had answered a letter of mine. I had asked him if there was anything he wanted to add to his testimony and the various statements he had made to police. I didn't think there was. I had a lot of material on Pascual and believed he was, largely, telling the truth about Ned (whether Ned was being honest with Pascual—well, that's another story). I had studied his statements and testimony and put them to the test, matching everything up to the newspaper articles written about Ned's case that Pascual could have had access to. I didn't find any significance to Ned's argument that Pascual had used the newspaper articles as a resource. There were too many variables.

I can tell you more, Pascual wrote in that first letter to me.

Reading, I wondered, *More? What* more *could he possibly add?* Reading further, I found the answer: *More bodies,* Pascual suggested, promising to tell me where, when, and how many.

I was interested, to say the least. So I drove up to the prison and signed in.

102

I

Dr. Henry Lee walked into the courtroom during the afternoon of January 19 to inject a bit of adrenaline and celebrity into a trial that was, honestly, dragging on. For many, Lee was easy to recognize. He'd starred in several shows on Court TV over the years and was a regular pundit on any number of networks when a major crime story broke. He had also testified during several high-profile murder trials throughout his career, O.J. and the like. He was pleasant and kind and walked with authority and confidence.

After going through what was a long list of esteemed credentials, Lee began to talk about his main course of study and present occupation—the reason so many law enforcement agencies around the world seek him: crime scene reconstruction. "Last year around October, November," Lee said, "I receive a request from state's attorney's office to conduct a reconstruction. I received original crime scene photographs, autopsy pictures, and initial crime scene investigative report. Also, I received some evidence, the plastic bags and ropes and tapes. . . ."

Zagaja had Lee go through and identify several secondary

crime-scene photographs. Lee talked about leaves and foliage and the time of the year, working his way into a discussion of Carmen's body. How she was found. What the scene had told him. "When I exam all those materials, first thing I found [was] the body was original had ropes tied to the body. When I examined the rope—it actually have six group of the rope—based on the description provided to me, some are tied on the wrist, some are tied around the ankle, some tied around the body, I was able to measure each piece of rope, look at the knot, look at the ending." As Lee spoke, it was hard to understand him. His English was not so clear. Still, it didn't prevent jurors from understanding the facts as Lee explained them. It just took a little bit more time and patience. Lee talked about the length of the ropes. How Carmen's body was tied up in a fetal position. "When you do that," he suggested, "which means the body rigor haven't set yet. If the person becomes stiffing, very difficult to tie like that," he added, waving his hands in the air to emphasize his point, "which shows the body still fresh, was tied up." Carmen was murdered and tied up almost simultaneously. Very little time had elapsed in between (a subtle, however vital, point Mark Pascual would soon back up).

"Then you have a white plastic bag. The white plastic bag is smaller, the black plastic bag is forty-four inches long, so the white plastic bag was put in first and you staple—staple some of the bag together. I notice a list . . . a dozen of staple holes. Because I wasn't the first one exam, some of the staple already removed from bag for tool mark analysis, but I was able to look at staple hole, it's over a dozen little holes. . . . Then some more ropes was tied and made like a handle, like material so, of course, they have black bags. Five white bags, four black bags. Black bags was put lower the body, top the body, middle, then have three-quarter-inch of plastic tape was taped the bag together."

Methodical. Well-planned.

"Approximately about fourteen inches long, those pieces, put in, joined the bag together. It's a very elaborated long process. Also have a handle of the rope, not bond over rope, it's almost two hundred ninety inches long all wrapped together. So the total length of rope, in this case, approximately sixty feet long. That's a lot of ropes. A lot of—you're marking a lot of knot, cutting. So this case, basically, takes a little while to complete all those tasks."

"Based on [your] observations," Zagaja asked, "do you make any other conclusions as to the extent to which the body was wrapped and stapled and taped?"

Lee's answers were a good foundation upon which Mark Pascual's testimony would stand. Lee was putting a professional spin on it all, thus setting the stage, if you will, for Pascual to come in and tell the jury *how* Carmen was murdered. "Yes," Lee said. "When I look at the material need to complete a task, you need white plastic bag, you need black plastic bag, you need almost sixty feet ropes, you need Scotch tapes, you need some sharp instrument, could be knife or scissor, to cut the rope, [and] then you need staple, you need a vehicle to transport."

Carmen's killer had planned her murder like packing for a vacation.

"And one additional thing," Lee smartly noted, "is the tape and the bag—our fingerprint examiner report to me they did not find *any* fingerprint. . . . There couple reasons. Maybe aging too long? Maybe some other reasons, such as wearing glove without leave any fingerprint? Especially if a Scotch tape, adhesive side, usually if somebody finger touch, we usually see a couple ridges, maybe not enough to compare, but he did not find *anything*. Maybe it's a suggestion somebody wearing a glove or avoid to leave fingerprint. So all of those, in totality, this case, preparation work and the actually manipulation tying the body, putting in the bag, it's a very elaborated activity."

The guy might have been hard to understand, but he was a pro.

II

After several hours of discussion regarding what Mark Pascual could say, and what Mark Pascual couldn't say, he was brought into the courtroom. No doubt Pascual was Zagaja's most explosive witness of the trial, thus far. He looked uncomfortable and nervous while sitting in the witness stand across from his old cellie. It was clear that turning state's evidence wasn't one of Pascual's favorite things to do. He would forever be branded a snitch. Rat. Not necessarily the cloud you wanted hanging over your head when you were spending the rest of your natural life in prison.

Zagaja started with money questions: "You're presently incarcerated?"

"Yes, I am."

Bond? One million. He then had Pascual explain why. "Murder for hire." But Pascual told jurors he wasn't trading testimony for a lighter sentence, but that he, of course, knew it might help him in the long run. Which all sounded good. But the bottom line was: Mark Pascual had cashed in. Why else would he take such a risk but to hope for a lighter sentence?

Zagaja soon worked his way into how he and Ned met. When. Where. What they talked about.

Carmie . . . Ned called her, Pascual said. That's how Pascual referred to Carmen.

"Could you relate . . . what he told you happened?"

"Yeah. He said he was at, um, Kenney's Bar in Hartford. And when he walked in, he saw her sitting there and he went up to her and asked her if he could buy her a drink and she said yes." This statement didn't gel with what other witnesses had reported: they said Ned was sitting in a booth when Carmen walked in and sat down next to him. "And then," Pascual continued, "he asked her if they—if [she] wanted to dance and she said, 'Yes.' So they danced and they drank for the greater part of the night. And then when it was time for them to leave, she said she'd like to have a ride home, and he said, 'How would you like to go to breakfast?' And she said, 'OK.' . . . And they went to have breakfast at a place he said wasn't too far from his home in Cromwell. . . ."

During an interview with police on April 30, 2003, Pascual claimed Ned had explained to him that as he strangled Carmen, Ned had his first orgasm that night. Afterward, because Carmen was still making "noises," Ned told him, he "stapled her mouth shut."

This was likely untrue. Insofar as there was no evidence—other than a newspaper article—of Carmen's mouth ever being stapled shut. But then Carmen's body was decomposed to a point where the medical examiner could not have explored whether her mouth was stapled shut or not.

III

One day in early spring 2007, I checked my PO box and found ten newspaper articles Ned had sent me inside a package of other documents. In his note attached to the package, Ned spoke of Mark Pascual as nothing more than a murderer looking to cut a better deal for himself. Ned said Pascual had "patched together" from newspaper articles the story he told police and, subsequently, the jury. Ned cited several references from those articles, which he believed juxtaposed perfectly with Pascual's "story." He highlighted the most obvious phrases he claimed Pascual had lifted from those articles. Sentences such as: *Stuffed in a plastic bag . . . Kenney's Restaurant on Capitol Avenue . . . Saw Snelgrove dancing with Rodriguez at the bar . . . Strangling girls and carrying the limp body onto a bed.* And so on.

Next to each highlight, Ned had made notes for me. For example, underneath *American Frozen Foods,* Ned wrote, *the meat guy,* quoting Pascual from the witness stand, insinuating that Pascual knew Ned sold meats only because he had read "American Frozen Foods" in the newspaper. Underneath the newspaper quote *preoccupied with sex,* Ned believed this was the passage that sparked Pascual to take a leap from "preoccupied with sex" to "as Snelgrove strangled the girl to death, he related that he had an orgasm."

The newspaper had printed Ned's address. Ned's note to me next to that quote said, *Close to the Berlin Fairgrounds. . . .* He believed Pascual had put together that entire scenario of Ned taking Carmen to the Berlin Fairgrounds based on where Ned lived. Many later told me that Pascual is not that smart. Interviewing him myself, I'd have to agree.

The newspaper read: *He'd stripped her to the waist . . . half-naked. . . .*

From Ned: *[Pascual said I] took off her shirt and posed her. . . .*

The package Ned sent goes on and on with many of these same references. At best, Ned is obsessed with the fact, many close to the case later insisted, that the prosecution *failed* to prove he killed Carmen Rodriguez, but instead they were able to get a conviction based on his prior bad acts. At worst, Ned accused the CSP and David Zagaja of fabricating evidence (and police reports), along with making false claims in order to convict him. At one point, Ned talks to me about the warrants and affidavits prepared against him before his arrest. He asked me why Pascual's name is never mentioned in any of them. Answering himself, he said the statements by Pascual to police were *put together and back-dated by Detective [Stavros] Mellekas. . . .* In other words, Ned wants me to believe Mellekas fabricated reports and notes and put his career on the line to help convict Ned.

Ned fails to mention the simple fact that Mark Pascual was a confidential informant (CI). His information was extremely fragile, sensitive. If inmates knew he was a "rat," Mark Pascual's safety would be jeopardized. Still, in all the pages of

documents Ned sent, along with his letters and notes, not once
does he show me *any* evidence pertaining to his innocence—
instead, he carries on and on about how the prosecution failed
to *prove* he killed Carmen and how Zagaja and his posse of
law enforcement prepped Pascual, wrote reports that were
untrue, and propped Pascual up like a puppet to convict him.

IV

On the witness stand, Mark Pascual continued to tell his
story, relating to the jury what Ned had admitted to him,
saying at one point, "[Ned told me he and Carmen] then had
breakfast and after they had breakfast he asked her if [she]
wanted to take a ride and get to know each other. And she
said, 'OK.' So he took her not far from where the diner was.
He said it was a place where he used to hang out when he was
younger, the back side of Berlin Fairgrounds. And he stopped
the car and he made a move on her and she got out of the car
and ran. So he said that he got out—he stopped—shut the car
off, and ran after her and jumped on her and choked her." At
which time, Carmen stopped breathing. (Luz Rodriguez and
her family members gasped. The courtroom went silent.)
"Her body went limp," Pascual continued. "And, at that point,
he went back to his car and got a tarp, and a bag and went
back to where she was and rolled her body onto the tarp, and
she started to come to, and . . . as she was coming to, she bit
him on the wrist and he got really upset with that, and he
just killed her right there by strangling her."

Which was it? Pascual had said months earlier that Ned
used a pair of scissors and stabbed Carmen to death. (Pascual
told me he was certain that Ned used a pair of scissors. "I
don't [know] how that got all screwed up. He told me scissors. Definitely scissors.")

Zagaja didn't go there, however. Instead, he stuck to Pascual's narrative, asking, "And did he say what he did after he killed her?"

"He said he taped up her arms and her legs and he took her top off and he posed her body in certain sexual positions. . . . After that, he basically stuffed her in some garbage bags and took her to some place in Rhode Island and dumped her off."

"Did he say anything about that area in Rhode Island?"

"All he said was that he had some customers up there, where he worked, and he used to drive around there while he was waiting for them to get home from work, so he knew the area."

"Did he tell you the specific location in Rhode Island?"

"No, he did not."

103

I

Donald O'Brien began his cross-examination of Mark Pascual with a bit of sarcasm, asking Pascual the most obvious question, getting the witness to admit that he faced capital felony murder charges, which could result in a death sentence. Then O'Brien made the assumption that the only reason Pascual had come forward to begin with was to save his own life. "And you went to the police and told them the information about what my client supposedly told you, correct?"

"Correct."

"So you *knew* that if you did that, you could work yourself a deal where you wouldn't get a lethal injection—"

"Correct."

"So you're testifying to save your own life, correct?"

"Yeah, I'm not denying that at all."

"Uh-huh," O'Brien said smartly. Then, with a shudder of cynicism, "You'd admit to the *Kennedy* assassination, too, to save your own life, wouldn't you?"

Zagaja stood: "Objection. Argumentative."

"Overruled."

O'Brien picked up where he left off, asking Pascual, "Right?"

"No."

"No?" A pause. Then more scorn and ridicule: "You'd say that your *brother* killed somebody in order to avoid the death penalty, wouldn't you?"

"No."

"No?"

"Objection," Zagaja said. "I'd ask counsel not to respond to the witness's responses."

"All right. You know that's improper."

"I'm sorry," O'Brien apologized, rolling his eyes.

And it was this type of back-and-forth, cross-fire-like exchange that took place between O'Brien and Pascual throughout the remainder of the afternoon: O'Brien questioned Pascual on everything he had told the police, and Pascual stuck to his story. O'Brien tried confusing Pascual, but Pascual slowed the testimony down, said he didn't understand, and answered all of O'Brien's questions without missing a beat.

Ned kept leaning over and, with his finger, motioning for O'Brien to come to him, whispering in his ear. But O'Brien didn't have much to work with—he was left with what Ned had told him. He went through Pascual's statement to the police, line by line, and asked him to repeat what he had already testified to on direct. In some instances, he'd catch Pascual on minor things—things that, in the grand scheme of how much of an impact Pascual's testimony was going to have on Ned, added up to absolutely nothing.

Pea splitting and bean counting. The jury looked uncomfortable and restless.

"Did he tell you what the lighting conditions were in that open field?" O'Brien asked at one point.

"It was dark."

"It was *dark*?" (Attorneys love to repeat answers.)

"Yeah."

"This was, what, one o'clock in the morning, two o'clock in the morning?"

"I don't know."

"But it's the back side of the Berlin Turnpike—of the Berlin Fairgrounds, correct?"

"Correct."

"Did he have a flashlight?"

"A lantern, he said."

"He had a lantern? Was it a flashlight or a lantern? Do you know?"

"He said a *lantern*." (You could hear the frustration in Pascual's voice.)

"But did you tell the police it was a flashlight *or* a lantern?"

"I believe I said it was a lantern."

"If you can take a look at your statement and see if it refreshes your recollection."

"Yeah, it says 'flashlight' or a '*lantern*.'" (Zagaja shook his head.)

"And that's what you signed, correct?"

"Correct."

The day was long and it was clear Pascual wasn't budging. As early evening approached, O'Brien asked, "Mr. Snelgrove . . . sorry, it's been a long day. I mean, Mr. Pascual, you never—in all your discussions with the police, state's attorney—you never mentioned to them that Mr. Snelgrove had mentioned Ted Bundy, did you?"

"No."

"He didn't?"

"No."

"Nothing further."

104

I

Inside the waiting area of MacDougall-Walker Correctional, the prison that I interviewed Mark Pascual in, I sat and listened as several women argued over whose man was cleaner—yes, cleaner. "My man takes a shower right before every visit with me," said one woman, a heavyset Spanish lady, her head bobbing and weaving, forefinger waving like a wiper blade. "He's been doin' it for twelve years."

Twelve years, I thought. This poor woman, like a half-dozen others there beside her, had been faithfully coming to this godforsaken smelly place to visit "her man."

A dozen years. Three presidential terms. A cycle of schooling.

The visiting room was quite small. Quite vanilla. And rather claustrophobic. Pascual walked in first, a guard said something to him, and then they buzzed me from the waiting area into the visiting area, a large sliding metal door separating the two rooms. This occurred after making me wait, standing by the door, until the obvious personal conversation the two guards were having was over.

Pascual is a short, stocky man. He has long reddish hair flowing halfway down his back, pulled and tied tightly into what looks like a horse's tail. As I approached him, he stared at me as if I have some sort of "get out of jail free" card for him, which, being someone who can connect him with the outside world, I guess I do.

We talked about his case. He expressed his sorrow for the man he had paid two other men to kill. He wished like heck he could do it all over. Take it back. "I'd just walk away from that woman," he said, shaking his head in disgust at himself.

Love triangles. They never end in harmony.

"Tell me about Ned," I said about twenty minutes into our conversation.

Pascual told me to keep my voice down. "The guards," he said, cupping his hands around his mouth, pointing with his thumb, "they hear everything."

He told me the story of how he and Ned met. "We got split up," Pascual noted, "but then after I spoke to the cops, they put us back together again." And this was when Pascual began to work on getting Ned to confess. They played chess. "Ned was a terrible chess player." They watched television and hung around together, watching each other's back. "Ned was scared. He'd gotten pummeled several times by friends and cousins of Carmen's who had ended up in the same jail. Everyone wanted a piece of Ned once they found out how [sick] he was." As Pascual talked, I studied his body language and facial expressions. My instinct told me he was speaking the truth as he knew it. He said Ned had told him about two additional homicides, on top of murdering Carmen. One was a prostitute Pascual claimed Ned said he had picked up off the streets of Hartford one month after he was released from prison, in 1999. "He did one right away"—Pascual was certain—"he had to. He told me that he couldn't help himself. He punched this woman so hard that he thought he broke her jaw. Then he stripped off her top and bra, posed her, and did his thing."

"His *thing*?" I asked.

"Yeah," Pascual said, motioning a masturbation technique with his hand.

The next one, Pascual said, wasn't until a year later. "Ned

said he would always wait a year between them. Something about the planning. He wanted to plan the perfect murder, right down to every detail. It was part of what got him off on it all."

II

"I wouldn't put it past Ned," one inside source told me, "to plant these homicides in Pascual's mind to try to set up an alibi for himself later on. Remember, this stuff with Pascual, it all takes place pretrial, so Ned is perhaps working on Pascual to set up his own defense, knowing that Pascual will later testify." The idea was that Ned planted enough details about several crimes in Pascual's head, in addition to those details about Carmen's murder, for the sake of confusing Pascual so Ned could turn around during his trial and prove that Pascual was a liar. "Ned was *that* smart. And it fits with his wanting to play a game with the law enforcement and the system."

I checked into both of the murders Pascual told me about. He gave names. Dates. Locations. Specific details. All of which matched up with these crimes—crimes, I might add, that were not high-profile enough to garner extensive news coverage. The details Pascual gave me, in other words, matched the details of the crimes, but were not reported in the press in a manner that Pascual could have *studied,* as Ned would argue.

III

Pascual has no pedigree of crime or violence. Before he asked two guys to murder a rival, he had never been arrested for anything serious. It's easy to see how Ned and Pascual formed this friendship, if we can call it such. Pascual has this sort of demeanor that seems honest and forthright. Yet, from Ned's point of view, it's also easy to see how he believed he could manipulate Pascual. With me, Pascual was sincere. I believed most of what he had told me. Our conversations continued, as did our letters. Pascual never asked me for anything.

105

I

Over the course of the next week, Zagaja's case against Ned cruised along on autopilot: witnesses came in, witnesses walked out, each hammering one more nail into Ned's coffin. The focus of the trial went from Ned's admission to Mark Pascual to the mileage Ned had logged. Zagaja brought in his experts and explained how Ned had tried to fudge his record keeping to incorporate enough mileage into his accounting in order to make up for those additional miles he had traveled to Rhode Island to dump Carmen's body. One after the other, the experts explained to the jury in layman's terms how Ned had cooked his own books to try and hide the fact that he traveled an additional 140 miles. Michael O'Shaughnessy, who worked for NETS, which provided analytical services (primarily on vehicles) to a number of different agencies, including police, was asked if a request was made of his firm "to focus in the area of September 21 through September 25, 2001" and match those dates against the records Ned had kept. "On that particular instance, I took the actual reported fuel (from Ned and his receipts) and reported mileage driven and then calculated out," he testified, "basically, how much fuel had to be replaced after those miles were driven. In other words, I got the mileage, again, similar to what I had done on this one. I did run into a problem on this, however."

O'Shaughnessy hadn't run into a problem with the other months Ned had kept records for. It was just this *one* particular period in which Carmen had happened to disappear.

What a coincidence.

"There were two instances where there was more fuel purchased than would appear to fit in the tank." Zagaja encouraged him to explain. "Well, I took the miles driven and then compared the fuel that was put in the tank after those miles were driven and found that the actual fuel that's gone into the tank was higher than what the mileage would indicate would have been used based on the overall average of this particular vehicle."

Ned was caught red-handed—by his own mistake—with information *he* had volunteered and provided. "And you had two overall averages to use in your calculations?"

"Both of them were very, very close, one was twenty-nine, and on the last set of calculations we got, it was in the very low thirties."

"And, specifically, can you draw our attention to what dates you considered and what calculations you used in coming to those conclusions?"

"On the paper that we had on September twenty-first there was ten gallons—well, 10.006 gallons purchased. Then, on September twenty-third, there was 9.131 gallons purchased."

"In between those two purchases, how much mileage was reported to have been driven?"

"We received, after adding it up, we got about one hundred and twenty-six miles."

"And based on your calculations with the determined average mileage to be somewhere between twenty-nine and the low thirties miles per gallon and the hundred and twenty-six miles driven, how many gallons of gas would be used up in that distance?"

"I used twenty-nine flat. I used a lower number, actually. I used below the lower number we received. And there was approximately four gallons more put into the tank than the actual mileage of this vehicle."

"So four gallons—"

"Excess."

"—of gas excess?"

"More than what the tank would have [been able to hold]." (It all came back to that day in the hospital when Ned—after trying to commit suicide—offered his mileage records to Hartford PD detective Luisa St. Pierre. Ned had rung this mileage bell. *Why?* St. Pierre had asked herself as she left the hospital. Because Ned thought he had it all covered. And here it was—in black and white—coming back to sink him. He had calculated wrong. He had fudged his mileage well enough, but he had forgotten to adjust the fuel.)

II

By January 20, Ned and O'Brien were bringing in their own witnesses. Many were former cell mates of Ned's there to explain how Ned never said much about his personal life. He was quiet. Reserved. He never talked about his crimes. Ever. No one understood why he had chosen to open up to Mark Pascual. It was so unlike Ned.

The jury, sitting, listening, had to see that Ned was putting all of his chances for acquittal in Mark Pascual's hands. *If we could just prove Pascual to be a liar . . .*

Not true. Many of the jurors later said that they had tossed out Pascual's testimony right away. They didn't trust him.

Then again, they didn't need him.

O'Brien called a few detectives in to try and prove that

they had made things up about Ned in their reports. But it didn't work.

Then he called Mark Pascual back to try to prove he was a liar. But again, it didn't work.

As the days ticked by, it appeared that Ned had dug himself a hole. He and O'Brien keyed on certain issues that made little sense to anyone sitting in the courtroom, a room that was closing in on everyone as the trial dragged on into its third week.

But then, when things looked grim for Ned, a surprise—a witness with a confession: he knew who had murdered Carmen.

And it wasn't Ned.

106

I

There was an inmate at Connecticut's maximum-security prison who said he had taken a deathbed confession from a friend of his—that this "friend" had, in fact, killed Carmen Rodriguez. The proposed murderer, a convicted rapist many times over, who, the snitch said, "had never used condoms" during his many rapes, had picked Carmen up in his van on the corner of Broad Street and Franklin Avenue. (He could not recall the exact date, nor was this the corner that Ned said he had supposedly dropped Carmen off at.) He raped and murdered her that night, and had recently committed suicide. Before he died, however, at the very moment he was about to hang himself, the inmate said he had whispered across the hallway to his friend's cell and admitted killing Carmen.

He gave no details. He had no particulars of the crime itself. Not even a last name. Only, "I killed her. . . . I cannot live with myself." On top of that, the witness was classified as a psychotic who took a pharmacy of meds for delusional thinking, besides routinely seeing and hearing people who just weren't there.

The judge decided to hear the witness out without the jury

present. It was only three weeks ago that the guy had come
forward. It was clear he wanted something out of it all. And
the admitted killer—well, he was dead.

O'Brien got to work right away and asked, "So the same
day that he committed suicide, he told you that he—"

"Yeah."

Err . . . "—killed Carmen—"

"Yes."

"—Rodriguez?" O'Brien finally finished.

"Exactly."

"Do you remember if he said anything else about Carmen
Rodriguez?"

"No."

"At any point during the time that you were with him?"

"No."

After a few more questions, O'Brien finished and mo-
tioned to Zagaja, who said, "And when the private investigator [the ex-cop that O'Brien had hired to help him with Ned's
defense] spoke with you, did he tell you the last name of—"

"Yes," the witness said, not allowing Zagaja to finish.

"—Carmen?"

"He told me the last name," he said, meaning O'Brien's
investigator.

"Did he tell you when she was killed?" Zagaja asked.

"Yes."

"When did he tell you she was killed?"

"September."

"And did he tell you if her body was found?"

"Yes."

"And where did he tell you her body was found?"

"In another state."

"And you already said that you asked, 'What can you do
for me?'"

"Yes."

"Did he provide you with a response?"

"Yes."

"What did he say to you?"

"He could try to get me out of jail."

In her decision, Judge Espinosa explained what she thought of Ned's star witness: "A statement from a psychotic inmate, if you will," she said, "a statement from a guy who has delusions, who hears voices, who takes at least three medications for psychiatric problems, that leads one to believe that this person was not very reliable if you believe [the witness], which, frankly, the court does not. It's a very self-serving situation on [the witness's] part."

Ned shook his head. His last chance . . . gone. "How is it self-serving, Your Honor?" O'Brien stood and asked.

"Well, it's also interesting that this just came to light a couple of weeks ago. When, in relation to [other] testimony, did this come up? The court's impression is that inmates are trying to jump on the bandwagon of coming in, and everybody has got something now to say about this case."

The jury wasn't going to hear *any* of it.

Gavel.

Next witness.

II

By February 1, the trial was getting *old*. O'Brien was calling witnesses who were adding nothing to the process. Most of the testimony was weak and repetitious, if not totally unbelievable. Most believed Ned was behind it all. At lunchtime, the judge had finally heard that Ned was not going to testify. He had discussed it with O'Brien and came to the conclusion that it wasn't in his best interest.

Smart move. Zagaja would have mopped the floor with him. Still, Espinosa wanted to be 100 percent sure that Ned was making the call, not O'Brien. "Now, let me ask Mr. Snelgrove," she said, ". . . your lawyer has told us that you do not want to testify. And I want to ask you some questions about that decision. Have you used any alcohol, drugs, or medicines of any kind today?"

"No."

"Now, have you had enough time to discuss with your lawyer your decision not to testify?"

"Yes."

For the first time during the trial, Ned was terse and respectful. "And I note that during the entire trial you've been very active in your defense, assisting Mr. O'Brien, so is it correct to say you've discussed with him, fully, the pros and cons of testifying—"

Ned wouldn't let her finish: "Yes."

"—on your behalf?"

"Yes."

"And do you agree with the decision, or, I take it, it is *your* decision that you do not want to testify? Is that correct?"

"That's correct."

"And you understand that you have a right to testify?"

"Yes."

"And you're giving up that right?"

"Yes."

"Are you doing that knowingly?"

"Yes."

"Voluntarily?"

"Yes."

"With understanding of the consequences?"

"Yes."

"Are you satisfied with the representation you've received from your lawyer?"

"Yes."

"All right. Very well. . . ."

Gavel. Time for closing arguments.

107

I

After introducing himself to the jury and thanking them for sticking it out through such a long process, David Zagaja put it as plainly as he could, "What you have here," he said, "what happened to Carmen Rodriguez on September twenty-first—the evening of September 21, 2001—up to the point where her body was found in Rhode Island on January 6, 2002, is a reflection on the evolution of a killer.

"What does all of that packaging speak to?" Zagaja asked the jury halfway through his closing. "It speaks to his reflection on Ted Bundy and it speaks to his intent . . . he planned this. He planned this for the evening of September 21, 2001, he had his goody bag all packed. He had everything that was necessary to kill and dispose of the body ready to go: tape, staplers, one or more rope, two types of bags, a cutting implement to cut the rope. It speaks to the planning, it speaks to a well-laid-out plan to execute a murder. Look at the dumping of the body right over the state line in Rhode Island. What I think was so amazing was the constant questioning about the defendant's familiarity with Rhode Island. That's missing the point. What you need is the familiarity with the eastern border of Connecticut. It was the first possible turn you could take off of Route 138, once you hit the state of Rhode Island, the first possible turn. Not the second, not the third, not a well-plotted-out turn, the first possible turn. There is literally no other turn. And you know what's great about dumping the body in Rhode Island? Connecticut is not going to go help in investigating that matter, Rhode Island is. . . ."

Zagaja went through the entire crime, moment by moment, while Ned sat. Twisted in his chair. Winced at times, smiled at others, and repeatedly frowned.

Zagaja spoke of the letters and how significant they were. "You get down to these writings. Are they the same as Ted Bundy or are they different?" Zagaja allowed a moment. Raising his voice, "I would tend to believe that they are actually the same because what Ned Snelgrove became was . . . Ted Bundy." Then, concluding, "And although he fails to see how he turned into Bundy—he did. In his mind these are things that will actually shift the police attention from him and not allow them to identify him as the true suspect in the killing of Carmen Rodriguez. But when you look at it and you look at his impression as to what Ted Bundy did and the mistakes *he* made, so did Ned Snelgrove. He wrote himself right into a guilty verdict, ladies and gentlemen. The evidence so supports."

II

What could Donald O'Brien say? He hadn't much to work with. He had a client who would have probably given the closing argument himself, if the court allowed. He had a client who had killed one woman and attempted to kill another. He had an ex-con for a client. An admitted liar. An admitted maniac who could not control himself around women. Thus, about the only option O'Brien had was to try and break down Zagaja's arguments and attack each one. "Now, the state wants to say that there's this evolution, that he is becoming a better killer, and that he's not going to do what Ted Bundy did and how Ted

Bundy screwed up. Well, if that's the case . . . if he were trying to do better than Ted Bundy, would he go to Kenney's and would he be seen leaving with an individual—and everybody saw him leaving—a woman that he knew, as Mr. Zagaja points out, somebody he signed up for his frozen-food contract?"

Great points. But again: O'Brien was asking the jury to throw away the facts and insert opinion and speculation. Who said Ned had planned to kill Carmen on *that* night? Maybe the opportunity presented itself and, as he had with Mary Ellen, he seized the moment. "Is that improving on Ted Bundy?" O'Brien asked. "Ted Bundy screwed up because he had a credit card and he had all of these receipts they can trace . . . a paper trail for Mr. Bundy, and that was his mistake. But what does Ned have? Ned has gas receipts. He has mileage that goes back to 2000. . . . He's keeping a paper record, he's keeping gas receipts. Do you think, for a moment, that if he was trying to evolve as a killer, as the state says, that he would keep those receipts?"

He kept those receipts, Zagaja had said throughout the trial, because he was going to use them to clear himself if the murder ever came back in his face. Those receipts were Ned's alibi.

In the end, O'Brien concluded: "The state is relying on you people focusing on that very powerful evidence of his past crimes. They're counting on you to use that to mask the lack of evidence they have in this case. . . . The evidence of the present crime, what he's here for, must be proved beyond a reasonable doubt. Please consider the evidence very carefully and we're confident that you'll return a verdict of not guilty. Thank you."

III

After Zagaja and O'Brien rebutted each other, on February 2, 2005, Judge Espinosa put the trial into the jury's hands. On February 3, the jury asked for several calculators and an easel. They were obviously adding up the mileage.

Bad news for Ned.

IV

Midway through the afternoon of the following day, the jury foreperson, Michael Silva, stood and read the jury's verdict: "'Guilty.'"

James Rovella and David Zagaja jumped up and down and hugged.

Was there ever really any doubt?

Still, although several might have predicted Ned would be found guilty, no one could have forecast what he was about to say.

108

I

On April 14, 2005, Ned was back in court to face the judge for sentencing. First the judge ruled on two motions O'Brien had filed on Ned's behalf: one for acquittal and another for a new trial. Quite direct in her ruling, she kept it short and simple: "Both of these claims—or all of these claims—have previously been made to the court during the course of the trial. The court considered all of the arguments and the circumstances surrounding the arguments, and the court found that they were without merit then and the court finds that they are without merit today. So for the reasons previously stated, both motions are denied."

Ned looked as though he had expected it. He sat and he trembled with anger and resentment, both of which clearly washed over his face.

For the next hour, members of the Rodriguez family—including Carmen's sisters Luz and Petra—read statements through an interpreter. When Barbara Delaney spoke, she placed a photograph of Karen on the desk in front of the lectern she stood behind. The bottom line for all was that Ned had destroyed their lives, but not their will and their memories. He could *never* take those away.

As Barbara spoke, Ned cried.

After O'Brien went through and cleared up a few things members of Carmen's family had said about him, he turned it back over to the judge, who asked if Ned was ready to say anything for himself—and, boy, was he ever.

"I would like it stated, on the record, Your Honor," Ned said after standing, "for today, that I believe that I'm entitled to a copy of everything in discovery pertaining to this case for purpose of preparing my appeal." Ned paused. Then began again: "I *believe,*" he said rather loudly, "I'm *entitled* to that material and I should *not* be subject to fees or delays. Whoever is responsible for making sure I get a copy of everything in the discovery . . . I want it on the record today that I have made that request and I will not allow stalling, on anybody's part, to go without becoming part of the appeal."

Zagaja sat back. Rovella, sitting next to him, listening intently, smiling at times, shook his head. *How pathetic is this guy?*

"One of the most memorable aspects of this trial," Ned explained, "was at the end when the verdict was announced when David Zagaja and Jim Rovella jumped up and down and congratulated themselves as if they had really accomplished something significant. . . . For cryin' out loud, a twelve-year-old could have prosecuted this case with all the help the judge provided them throughout this trial." Espinosa raised her eyes, nodded her head casually, but allowed Ned to continue. "As a matter of fact," he said, "there was *no* judge in this trial. Carmen Espinosa was the lead prosecutor and Mr. Zagaja was just a little apprentice prosecutor taking instructions from his mentor every time the jury was excused and benefiting from every significant ruling regarding what may or may not be mentioned to the jury as evidence." The courtroom sat stunned. Ned didn't get his way. And here he was, once again, blaming everyone around him. Speaking of the judge in the third person: how insulting. "This conviction will *never* stand and I think everyone knows it," Ned added. "Whoever heard of a trial where a parade of detectives and one death penalty inmate just takes—lines up to take the witness stand and put words in the defendant's mouth. Just as Mr. Zagaja said, on Wednesday, January nineteenth, that an acquittal by a jury is not probative that the defendant is innocent of a crime. While using Zagaja's own logic, we can acknowledge here, in this case, that a conviction by a jury is not probative that the defendant is guilty of a crime. And those are David Zagaja's words, *not* mine. . . ."

Ned turned and invited all the reporters in the room "to get a copy of the transcript to confirm . . . that a prisoner, who never met me, took the stand and gave a detailed account of how his cell mate, now deceased, had confessed this murder to him." He poked his index finger into the table: "His testimony was just as reliable and much more believable than Mark Pascual's. But, true to form, the chief prosecutor, *Carmen Espinosa,* made *sure* the jury never knew about someone actually confessing to this crime. I wonder what the jurors on the case now think of this judicial process after learning about this minor detail? Please, members of the media, get a copy of the transcript from January 28, see if I know what I'm talking about. The integrity of the Hartford Police Department . . . is not exactly above reproach. The newspaper writers here know very well that every month or so a Hartford police officer is arrested for stealing or lying. . . . The Hartford Police Department itself [is] full of criminals and liars. As for the jurors, I hope they didn't base their decision too heavily on the testimony of Mark Pascual. His story did not come from him or me—did it, Inspector Rovella?"

At that moment, Ned turned and stared at Rovella. The judge

leaned forward, quickly saying, "Address your comments to the court—and no one else!"

"I can't prove it now," Ned raged, ignoring her, "but give me two years, members of the media, and I will be able to *show* you, *unequivocally,* that Mark Pascual's testimony and police statements were provided to him to memorize, they did not come from him or me. So, please, whatever news organizations are represented here today . . . wherever I am in April 2007, two years from now, please locate me and contact me and I will put you on my visitors list."

II

I made contact with Ned, per his suggestion. Over and over, I begged him to put me on his visitors list. I begged him to put me on his telephone list; so this way he could call me and explain this. I begged for this *proof.* He'd had his two years. He'd had time to come up with the evidence to prove his claims. Instead, though, Ned sent me a package of meaningless documents and never put me on his visitors list.

III

The gallery could not believe that Ned was carrying on and on. His speech seemed born in the cynicism one assumes a defeated man might spew. Ned was a sore loser, with hatred in his voice, saying, "Now, Judge Espinosa, this is the part where you gather yourself together and tell everyone here that the evidence against me was overwhelming. 'Overwhelming,' that's a word judges like to use. In my case, however, there was *no* evidence. As a matter of fact, there was exculpatory evidence at the crime scene on the body of Carmen Rodriguez that actually belonged to somebody else. (Author's note: This was untrue.) But, not to worry, you and your apprentice, David Zagaja, simply used my past convictions as a substitute for no evidence. Problem solved. Things that happened more than seventeen years ago totally unrelated to Carmen Rodriguez." (Karen and Mary Ellen were now *things*.)

"The judge in this trial made sure, early on," Ned said, speaking of Espinosa as if she weren't present, "that the defendant would have no chance to be vindicated by conducting a trial in this fashion. You could easily charge me with any unsolved crime in Connecticut in the last six years. A clever court-assisted substitute for no evidence. That is one reason, among many, why the appellate court, any appellate court, will erase this conviction and force Judge Espinosa to conduct a fair trial. . . . This conviction will never stand. Mr. Zagaja is in no position to take credit for it, and I'll see you in a few years, after the appeal. . . . I also know that you're going to sentence me to the maximum penalty, for the time being, but you, of course, decided that *before* the trial even started. . . . So go ahead and sentence me to life and I'll see you after the appeal in two or three years." Ned began to sit down, then stopped, adding, "Don't forget to tell everyone how overwhelming the evidence was."

Judge Espinosa could have done a lot of things, but she said, "Thank you." Paused, then, "State?"

Zagaja brought up a great point: "The court will note that the defendant did not indicate he *didn't* kill Carmen Rodriguez."

With that, Ned screamed: "I did *not* kill Carmen Rodriguez."

"Thank you," Judge Espinosa said. Then, "Tell me, Mr. Snelgrove, I noticed that when Mrs. [Barbara] Delaney was speaking, you were crying. Why was that?"

"Because I . . . ," Ned started to say while sitting down, but the marshal ordered him to stand. "Because I *did* kill Karen Osmun."

"You did kill Karen Osmun. So you were crying because you're a murderer?"

"I was crying because of the hurt I have caused to the family of Karen Osmun."

Judge Espinosa paused. Sat back. She had a few words for Ned before she sentenced him. "Well, we've just seen a prime example of who Mr. Snelgrove is. Everybody else is bad, everybody else is wrong, and he is the only one who is right. Psychiatrists have examined him, and I'm not a psychiatrist, but those professionals have described him to be an extremely dangerous individual who requires professional psychotherapeutic treatment in a secure setting. Unfortunately, those were the words of a psychiatrist who examined him *before* the sentencing for the murders of Karen Osmun and the attempted murder of Renard. We've just seen a display of the personality that is Mr. Snelgrove.

"Self-centered.

"Manipulative.

"Psychopathic.

"Detached.

"A braggart.

". . . Those are the words of even his own family, his family members who wanted nothing to do with him because they were afraid of him," Judge Espinosa said, "who would not allow their children to be near him, alone with him. *That* is Edwin Snelgrove. As the probation officer stated, Mr. Snelgrove has been plagued by lifelong, persistent, violent, deviant, sexual fantasies—despite his level of education, intelligence, and self-reports acknowledging these fantasies were problematic, he never sought treatment for them. To the contrary, he appeared to get pleasure from the fantasies. The central theme of his fantasies were focused on the degradation and humiliation of females, both during and following their murders." (Members of the Rodriguez family began sobbing.) "As evidenced by his criminal record," Judge Espinosa said with sincerity and professionalism, "the offender turns these fantasies into actions for the sole purpose of fulfilling sexual gratification. By his own admission, Mr. Snelgrove is a murderer and he will always *be* a murderer. You talk about the evidence in this case—well, that's why we have appellate courts and you're going to have a long time to work on your appeal and consider all of the legal avenues available to you and all of the assistance that the system will give you . . . to pursue those appeals and to seek to overturn your conviction. . . . Sometimes psychiatrists and psychologists spend a lot of time trying to figure people out, but sometimes people are just bad. Sometimes people don't have redemption, there's no recourse. The only thing that the criminal justice system can do is warehouse them, separate them from society so that no one else is murdered, no other female is murdered by Edwin Snelgrove."

Then, after a break to catch her breath, Judge Espinosa shuffled a few pieces of paper in front of her and proceeded to say what everyone but Ned was thinking: "The court is convinced that if he *ever* gets out on the street, he *will* kill again. Accordingly," she said, then stopped and addressed Ned directly, saying, "please stand." Ned stood without emotion. "It is the sentence of the court that you be committed to the custody of the commissioner of [the Department of] Correction for life and that is, in Connecticut, sixty years."

The courtroom exploded with applause. Whistles. Cheers.

"All right," Judge Carmen Espinosa said, slapping her gavel. "That's enough."

But they wouldn't stop. "That's enough," she said again, over the roars. "That's *enough*."

109

I

"Pure evil," David Zagaja said. "I see nothing but pure evil." Later, "Edwin Snelgrove sets himself apart from many individuals who commit murder. He has embodied a desire, an *obsession,* and a *purpose* to kill, and that is really what we saw through the trial."

II

Ned could not allow the prosecutor he now loathed more than anyone—except maybe the judge—to have the last word. He had to say *something.* On October 31, 2005, the state's attorney's office received a letter that sparked a shakedown of Ned's cell. Ned's new cell mate wrote to say he'd had a bizarre conversation with Ned recently. The new cell mate said Ned had admitted to him "that he killed Carmen Rodriguez [and] that he had committed other crimes in Connecticut and Bergen County, New Jersey, and that he would never get caught" for those additional crimes.

But he didn't stop there.

The cell mate was intrigued, to say the least. After describing how he had killed Carmen, he said Ned came right out with it: "[I'm] going to kill superior court judge Carmen Espinosa because she allowed [my] prior New Jersey convictions to be part of [my] Connecticut trial."

Ned said he knew where Espinosa lived. He had the right address.

The cop interviewing the cell mate asked him if there was anything else he knew about Ned. He thought about it. "He keeps his personal papers and violent pornography hidden in an envelope among his personal possessions."

Ned must have smelled something, because when they shook down his cell sometime after receiving the tip, prison officials found nothing.

110

I

One of the last times I heard from Ned, he started to do to me what he had done to just about everyone else: play the control game. In one letter, he proceeded to tell me how to write my book: whom to interview, whom *not* to interview; which documents to explore and which *not* to pay any attention to. He questioned my integrity. He questioned how I was going about (re)investigating his case. He accused me of using his past—big surprise—to prove he killed Carmen Rodriguez.

I had contacted Ned's former attorney from New Jersey, John Bruno. Bruno and I talked. He had many informative things to say. But what he made clear from the very start was that he would *not* discuss Ned and his prior case without Ned's consent.

I respected that.

"Get Ned to OK it, and I'll visit him with you," Bruno said over the phone. And that was about the end of our communication.

I wrote to Ned and told him. I asked Ned to put Bruno and myself on his visitors list. This upset Ned. Riled him. I was breaking a golden rule: looking into his past. Bruno, he wrote back, *doesn't have anything to do with me being convicted of something I didn't do (the Rodriguez murder).* . . . From there, he went on to crush Zagaja and his "theories." It was the same rhetoric Ned rattled off during his sentencing: everyone that doesn't agree with him is wrong. *I did not kill Carmen Rodriguez,* I began to see, was turning into, as I had been warned, *They didn't prove I killed Carmen Rodriguez.*

He then began to make the claim that I was in cahoots with Bruno—that we were writing this book together and I was paying him.

Ned knew I worked alone and paid no one. I had explained this to him.

He then wrote I had a *blockbuster bestseller* on my hands. But without him, I had nothing. No one would buy my book because it would be all lies. *When your book is done,* he wrote to me on September 14, 2007, *I would be very anxious to have you tell me if you've ever seen such clear-cut instances of prosecutors lying. Not "cutting corners" or "shading the facts a little." Lying.*

It was things like that, that made me wonder, *What in the world is he talking about?* I had found no such thing.

My bestseller, Ned suggested, would be based on a *dishonest prosecutor,* a *flagrantly biased judge,* on top of the *many witness statements that don't make sense.* He encouraged me to *expose Connecticut's judicial system for what it is: arrogant, incompetent and dishonest.* He said this type of book would make me a household name. I'd be a true investigative reporter then—and only then, he said.

I sent Ned a blistering letter back, telling him, primarily, that I wouldn't be bullied. That he could take a hike if he thought that I was going to jump aboard the Snelgrove train of lying and cheating and manipulation. I opened that letter, writing, *Your last missive disturbs me. I thought we had an agreement. I thought you understood that I have a job to do and*

*part of that job includes digging into every single aspect of
your case in order to present the facts as I uncover them. . . .*

But it wouldn't be the last time we spoke.

II

The bottom line regarding Ned Snelgrove is that he *will*
kill again if he is ever released. The jury knew it. The judge
understood it. And everyone in that courtroom applauding on
the day he was sentenced experienced it. Heck, even Ned
Snelgrove—at forty-six years old, writing to me during the
winter, spring, and summer of 2007, telling me that the state
of Connecticut never proved he killed Carmen Rodriguez—
knew it.

I keep thinking back to his letters from Rahway during
the 1990s when he warned everyone that he would kill
again—a promise he, in fact, had kept.

111

I

The thing about Ned is, just when you think he's done, he invites you back into his sandbox, hoping you'll continue to play. He had exhibited this aspect of his character throughout his trial. In the fall of 2007, as I was beginning to think about finishing my book, after not hearing from Ned for well over a month, I received a letter, which was once again written on Ned's preferred stationery: the back side of a "religious articles" prison order form. Was he exposing his stinginess by not purchasing plain paper from the prison commissary? A bit of irony, however, had always been one of Ned's trademarks. Was this Ned's subtle idea of turning his nose to organized religion, or just a way to save a few bucks? Who knows? The guy is as unpredictable as a storm.

In a short note I had sent to Ned two weeks prior, I had asked him, *Are you done talking to me?* I knew that my last letter, where I had prodded him a bit, made Ned salivate with fury. His gargantuan ego wouldn't allow him to answer me right away. He had to give in, of course, because whether he admitted it, the book I was writing was something Ned had wanted for the past fifteen years.

Ned wrote he still wanted to talk, but he had been busy working *laboriously* on his appeal, which was *taking up all of [his] time.* While reading this, I couldn't help but think: *What is there for Ned to do?* Besides driving his new lawyer crazy, no doubt controlling every aspect of the appellate process, was there any work for him?

The answer is no. His lawyer handled it all.

He also said he was working on a chronology of his life that I had suggested in my first letter the previous winter.

And so I waited.

Ned's history finally came in, which allowed me to add some minor detail throughout the book, beyond what I had found out on my own. Detail that makes little difference, mind you, to the grand scheme of his life. Ned spent ten pages, for example, outlining his work history, his love for the Boston Red Sox, and the most memorable baseball game he had ever watched on television. I was hoping he would come clean. You know, tell me what every law enforcement official I had spoken to about him suspects: there are unsolved murders with his name attached. I was looking to offer several families some closure. But Ned never extended me—or them—that courtesy.

And really, why should he? Part of knowing he is the only person who can close the book on those cases must feed Ned's ego, and certainly falls in line with what Ned's so-called mentor, Ted Bundy, believed: if you tell law enforcement *anything,* lie just enough to throw off the scent.

112

I

I received a letter from Ned in late September 2007, which sparked a rather straightforward, finger-in-the-chest response from me. This latest letter from Ned was four pages long; but was accompanied by a half-inch-thick "stack of notes," to which Ned titled: "Common Sense Replies to the State's Brief as Was Submitted by Harry Weller [the state's attorney handling the appeal]."

Common sense. Perhaps an ode to Thomas Paine, but more likely Ned's sarcastic, belligerent way of once again addressing his grounds for appeal.

Back to square one: *I didn't kill Carmen Rodriguez.*

Some of it, or maybe a majority of it, Ned wrote to me, *will illuminate some new points if you consistently refer to the specific transcript pages I cite throughout. . . .* Ned opens his "Common Sense" rebuttal with: *[T]he "packaging," as described here [in the state's brief], has nothing to do with anything Ted Bundy ever did.* By "packaging," Ned is referring to how Carmen Rodriguez's body was bound and found. *Somehow, however,* he continues, *the State still maintains that the Carmen Rodriguez homicide is a manifestation of a Ted*

Bundy "wannabe." Ned then asks the justices, those appellate judges reviewing his case, to have a look at the actual dummy heads, those two Styrofoam heads Ned had dolled up, according to Zagaja, and used in a pinch when a real victim wasn't available. Ned wrote to me, *Not only did the police make sure not to test the mannequin heads for fingerprints (finding fingerprints of someone other than the Defendant would have ruined this opportunity to use them for their melodramatic effect), but there is nothing in the Defendant's previous convictions, nor is there anything in his writings . . . that involves this ridiculous idea of rehearsing with props or using mannequins as a substitute for an actual woman.*

This is an important statement from Ned. He likes to use his previous convictions and behavior as a means to prove how different his previous crimes were from the Rodriguez homicide. But when the state uses those *same* cases to prove its case, to show intent and a developing serial killer in action, Ned claims it's all irrelevant.

In his rebuttal, Ned goes on for page after page, describing each of his points where he believes the state's experts either lied during his trial or the prosecutor failed to prove his case with evidence. The problem Ned runs into, however, is that he doesn't offer an antidote, any refuting evidence, other than his opinion, to back up his claims.

Reading this, I thought, *As if I hadn't heard all* this *BS before.* Like Ned hadn't told me—time and again—that the plot against him was all there in the trial transcripts. As if he hadn't told me ten times already that all the lies law enforcement and the prosecution had told stood out, if only I could see them through the sociopathic lens he had been looking through himself for the past twenty-five years. Regarding the state's argument on appeal, for example, Ned asked me: *I would really be interested to know if you are as* dumbfounded *as I am that the prosecutor who wrote it* (Harry Weller) *can so easily lie about what was said at the trial, and/or simply*

*go against the prosecution's own witnesses? Obviously,
David Zagaja is no longer Ned's target; now it's Weller. Am I
just imagining all of this? Ned asked me. Am I just stamping
my foot, crying "foul" for no good reason? Please tell me
what you think.*

People who know me will agree that I rarely hold back
when the conversation pertains to certain issues—that I
sometimes say *too* much. In any event, with Ned asking me
for my direct opinion, I couldn't resist. So I read his comments two or three times, over the course of a few hours on
the night I received the letter. I sat and thought about things
before sleeping on it (something my manager and my father
have always encouraged me to do). The next morning, I sat
down to finish up work on this book and began writing Ned
a letter. I'd had it with his back-and-forth, "beating around the
bush," "blame everyone else for his crimes" diatribes and
rants. His arguments were weak and unsubstantiated. He had
been convicted of Carmen Rodriguez's murder. The state
proved its case. This *fact* was *never* in dispute. Calling the
case against him a conspiracy (my word, Ned never went that
far) was, at least to me, the same as calling Ted Bundy a considerate human being for sitting down and explaining (lying,
actually) some of the details behind his crimes before he was
executed. Like so many other serial killers, Ned Snelgrove
thinks the world revolves around him. That by telling a lie
long enough, it becomes a truth.

I'd had it.

With all this in mind, I began to write a final letter to Ned,
thinking, *It is about damn time he faces the truth.* At least the
truth as I had uncovered it throughout my research.

113

I

Today, Ned is in what they call PC (protective custody), housed at the Cheshire Correctional Institution, on a segregated floor away from the general population. He is in an area of the prison that corrals some of the state's most perverted, violent sexual predators, only because there are inmates throughout the prison system, I'm told, that want to see Ned pay for what he did to Carmen. In fact, one story I heard actually proves how small a community prison can be—especially for a guy with a target on his back. Ned was in Hartford for a court appearance. He was being held at a local prison that houses men coming and going through the system. Ned and several inmates were sitting around a common area watching television. Ned's case was all the buzz around town. Top story on all the local television news stations. At some point, a story detailing Ned's case popped up on the overhead television. There was a Puerto Rican guy, a large man, young, facing some serious time for a nonviolent crime, sitting next to Ned. At one point the guy looked at the television, then at Ned, and said, "That's you!"

Ned's eyes bulged. He didn't say anything.

"You killed my cousin Carmen," the guy raged.

Ned froze. Everyone backed away. And the inmate proceeded to "pummel" Ned into a bloody pulp. "Lumped him up pretty good," said a source of mine who saw Ned later that day.

"Kicked his ass *real* good," said an inmate with whom I spoke. "He f***ing deserved it, too, what he did to that poor Rodriguez girl."

Among Ned's jailhouse peers, there is no doubt that he murdered Carmen Rodriguez. In prison, it's a given that Ned is a hideous serial killer with scores of "kills" under his belt. Indeed, Ned's aloof bravado gets him nowhere behind bars.

II

I must admit that it felt good to write a serious letter to Ned. To sit down and say what I needed to say, without having to pander, so to speak, to his ego with the hope that he would open up to me. The time for all of that nonsense was behind us. I've interviewed many murderers throughout my career. I've sat in front of the most despicable human beings whom, I'm convinced, the Devil himself has put on this planet. I've been forced to refrain from sharing my personal feelings. I had done this with Ned throughout our correspondence. I needed to stay objective. I needed to play the role of the reporter. And I needed to allow Ned to speak his truth, whatever it might be. But there came a point when I needed to also stop playing devil's advocate—literally speaking—and hit Ned with the facts of his case, along with those questions no one else would ask him.

In his letter accompanying his "Common Sense" document, Ned had given me a ridiculous explanation regarding several lines he had written to George Recck. For example, Ned told me that *"when I pick up right where I left off"* quote he had written to Recck *refers to [him] returning to the sales career [he] had at Hewlett-Packard before being arrested in 1987.*

Ned expected me to believe that the quote had nothing to do with him besting Ted Bundy, or returning to a life of murder so he and Recck could, as Ned himself said and Recck testified to, have more fodder for a book they would someday write together. Instead, Ned expected me to believe that it had to do with him going *back* to New Jersey and once again returning to work at Hewlett.

The fact of the matter is, Ned didn't do that. Leaving prison, he ran up to Connecticut and moved into a seedy motel room on the Berlin Turnpike, one of those weekly (or hourly) fleabags, next to drug dealers, prostitutes, pimps, and addicts—and, according to one of my sources, he murdered a prostitute not a month after he was released.

In any event, I began my letter to Ned by stating the obvious: *Well, Ned, since you asked for my opinion, it's time, perhaps, that we stop this game between us. There's a theme to your letters,* I wrote, *that I need to point out: I find that you say the same things over and over without offering much proof-positive evidence to support your claims. Just rhetoric, in other words. No substantial* evidence. *Calling someone a liar does not make that person a liar—evidence does. I have yet to see any* evidence *that proves* any *of your claims. I have studied police reports and trials for my entire career (tens of thousands of pages, dozens of cases). . . . In none of the papers you've sent have I seen any* evidence—*just your "interpretation" of the facts.*

Ned's contention to me had always been that the state never proved its case. That he was convicted on evidence of his past crimes. In Ned's view, every witness lied, while every piece of evidence was tainted in some respect. In his stack of notes, he goes on and on about Carmen's murder being totally different from those "two cases" in New Jersey. He is fixated on the notion that he left Karen and Mary Ellen dressed from the waist down, but Carmen's killer left her panties on, and this alone proves that he could not have been involved. *Carmen Rodriguez,* Ned wrote to me, *is not "naked from the waist up"! She is* completely naked, *except for underwear! How many times throughout the [state's] brief will the state claim that Carmen Rodriguez's "circumstances of undress" are identical to the defendant's New Jersey convictions?*

You see, Ned misses a major point here, one that, with a little help, a five-year-old could see clearly. He gives no explanation for the simple fact that most serial killers—himself included—change their behavior, if ever so slightly, each time they kill. Not to mention that Ned admitted he was studying—and learning from—one of the most famous, prolific serial killers of his time. Thus, *to ask me to buy into your idea that there is no pattern, no "signature,"* I wrote in my letter to Ned, *surrounding the three victims . . . is quite a stretch on your part. This has always been, however, another theme of yours: that Carmen's murder was "different" from those in NJ. The theory is . . . that, after studying Ted Bundy, you* changed *your signature. . . .* (I often wondered why this was so hard for Ned to see. He had always given me the impression that he was an intelligent guy. Was he patronizing me?) *Furthermore, to claim that the "pick up right where I left off" quote from the letters you wrote to Recck pertains to you going back to Hewlett is, to use your own term, "laughable." Come on, Ned, do you expect me to believe that? Do you expect* anyone *to believe that after eleven years in prison . . . your goal, your dream, was to return to HP? And you didn't move in with your parents right away (as you told me). You moved into a seedy Berlin Turnpike motel and, according to a source of mine, started killing again right away. You never went back to HP.*

I explained to Ned that I needed to ask him several questions in order to give him the opportunity to respond, adding, *I think it's only fair, since I've been interviewing you (through our correspondence) now for several months.*

My questions: 1.) Explain what you mean by "responding to questions" posed by George Recck? . . . Certainly you don't expect me to believe that everything you wrote to Recck was a response to a question he asked. I feel your were gloating, bragging, etc. 2.) Where do you think your thoughts of harming women and posing their bodies come from? You said it was there since the second and third grade. Explain that for me a bit more. 3.) One of my . . . sources tells me that you told him/her that you're a breast man—which makes sense, seeing how your victims were attacked and left exposed from the waist up. How do [you] explain this behavior? Where is it rooted? Were you ever sexually abused? Why is it, you think, that in your mind you equate this type of violence with sexual gratification? 4.) How many other women—if any—have you murdered or harmed? Sources I've spoken to (many different sources, mind you) claim the number could be five, six, even ten more? Would you like to go on record as being one of the most prolific serial killers in the Northeast? Or do you deny all of this? 5.) A final statement from you: what is it you'd like to say? Give me a direct quote that you want printed—a sort of statement from Ned Snelgrove to all of his critics. 6.) Why did you never put me on your visitors or phone list?

In closing, I asked Ned not to *take offense to any of these questions. As a journalist I needed to ask them.* I was obligated. *Finally, you asked if I am "dumbfounded" that a prosecutor (in your words, the prosecutor in your case) could lie? No prosecutor lied in this case, Ned. I've studied all the data. I've spent a long time reviewing all of the documents and statements and interviewed scores of people connected to the case. Don't kid yourself into thinking that you're going to get someone to believe that there was a conspiracy against you. It's simply not true. . . . If I don't hear from you [within two weeks], I'll consider your silence a refusal to respond to my questions.*

III

I heard from Ned on October 29, 2007, a short while after the two weeks I had given him to respond. He was in rare form. I had put it all on the table and, to be honest, never expected to hear from Ned again. But he is a control freak and has to, of course, have the last word. His trial proved that.

In any event, Ned went on for twelve pages, explaining to me why I was wrong and he was right. He accused me of not reading any of his previous letters or notes. He said I had "rambled." He called me "angry." He claimed to have answered all of my questions at some point or another throughout our correspondence. *Thank you for your bizarre, disturbing, not-supported-by-the-facts letter!* he wrote. *C'mon now, admit [it]! As a professional writer, that's got to be the most Hunter S. Thompson-like piece you've ever put together, am I right?*

He carries on, never once addressing my questions directly, nor dismissing the idea that he killed other women. Instead, he pigeonholes me into the same box he put Judge Espinosa, David Zagaja, and anyone else who doesn't agree with him: we're all liars and cheaters out to get him.

In my previous letter, I asked Ned for a direct quote. *I will give you,* he wrote back, *the "direct quote that you want printed." . . . However, the quote makes your research look pretty shoddy*—funny that Ned thinks he knows, without reading my book, what type of research I put into it—*so I think I know what to expect—two things I can easily predict: 1) You will print it neither accurately nor in its entirety, and 2) you will never acknowledge that I caught you in a trap of your own words.*

Whatever the heck that all means is beyond me. What I can and will do is offer this final quote from Ned up to you—the reader—here on its own page in Ned's own handwriting.

BEGINNING
OF QUOTE

"M. William Phelps's own logic
discredits the theory that he claims
'profilers' have formulated. Case in point,
if I were guilty of unsolved crimes,
then, according to Mr. Phelps's prior
reasoning, George Recck would have
produced written boasts and critiques
pertaining to them, comparing them
to the misdeeds of Ted Bundy. As it
turns out, Mr. Recck, Mr. Phelps and all
his 'sources' and 'experts' come up
completely empty on this point, a main
pillar upon which Mr. Phelps attempts
to build his thesis." END OF QUOTE

Note the little boxes: "Beginning of quote, end of quote."
Pure Ned. Here he is with his irrational theories at work. To
say that because he never shared any information about unsolved crimes with George Recck makes him innocent of any
additional murders is, in and of itself, impractical and narcissistic. Bundy would have never done anything like that—and
neither would Ned. Still, here is but a brief glimpse into the
mind of a killer who actually believes he can wipe away a
lifetime of psychological issues with women in a few words.

EPILOGUE

I

There's no doubt that we learn something new from each book. We gain an understanding of yet another layer of society that, thankfully so, not too many of us come in contact with on a daily basis. In authoring eight true-crime books now, I had gotten to a rather complacent point in my career: where I thought I had seen and heard everything.

Not true. I had yet to meet a killer like Edwin Fales Snelgrove. I firmly believe that there are at least four more bodies in Ned's past—bodies of women killed in the same manner as Karen Osmun and Carmen Rodriguez, left in towns where Ned had been on a business trip, a business call, or, like Hartford and Kenney's, he had traveled to in order to exclusively seek out new murder victims. These are open cases that should not be made public right now.

"Ned is one of the scariest killers in recent history"—I heard this time and again. From cops. From lawyers. From profilers. Even from people who were close to Ned. And here's the thing: no one has heard of the guy outside of the law enforcement community and those in Connecticut who followed the case. It's not as though Edwin Snelgrove is a household name, like Manson, Dahmer, and especially Ned's mentor, Bundy.

Part of Ned, I feel, relishes the fact that he's killed more women, and those family members of the missing go through misery each day, unable to put their loved ones to rest. Another part of Ned, I am convinced, believes that he is an innocent man who was framed for killing Carmen Rodriguez, sick to his stomach that Zagaja and his crew did not *prove* their case.

Either way, Ned is where he belongs.

II

The scores of recorded interviews, thousands of pages of documents, police reports, witness statements, depositions, trial testimony, autopsy reports, and other documents, along with anonymous sources inside and outside the system, and letters from the killer and his cell mates and several others involved personally in this case, allowed me to add a depth of reporting to this book I rarely get a chance to explore.

ACKNOWLEDGMENTS

I

It was a rainy Saturday morning when I met the Rodriguez family at Rosa's home (Carmen's mother) in Hartford, Connecticut. Luz and Sonia and Petra and several of Carmen's brothers and friends and her son and grandchild and Kathy Perez, Carmen's niece, were there to greet me. I sat on a comfortable couch in the living room, with a large photograph of Carmen hanging on the wall in back of me, as if she were there, too, watching over all of us. Talking for hours, I asked Luz at one point about Carmen's favorite meal. She called it *"bacalaito"* and explained. Then she yelled in Spanish to her mother, who was in the kitchen cooking. It seemed Rosa was cooking from the time I arrived to the time I left.

A moment later, Rosa came out with a plate of *bacalaito;* she had just happened to be cooking it that day. "My mother," Luz said, "says you can't know what Carmen loved until you've eaten it yourself."

I'll never forget that day and the subsequent interviews I conducted with this smart, lovely, and loving family, who had accepted me (and trusted me with Carmen's story) as if I were one of their own. I especially wanted to say thank you to Luz for being so outspoken and honest and always willing to answer my questions. Luz and her family are tremendous people.

II

Mary Ellen Renard is one of the most courageous women I've met. What she went through at the hands of Ned Snelgrove would have led most into a life of hell—especially considering the road Mary Ellen traveled before she met Ned. But Mary Ellen was able to pull herself out of it all, stay positive, and get the help she needed. I commend her for opening up to me about her life and telling me her incredible story of survival. In addition, Diana Jansen, Mary Ellen's daughter, was equally helpful. I appreciate her honesty, integrity, and guts to speak out about her past. Likewise, the discussions I had with Barbara Delaney about her family and sister Karen Osmun were incredibly useful. I thank Barbara for her candor and sincerity—not to mention all the documents she willingly handed over.

David Zagaja was as helpful as any prosecutor with a case on appeal could have been. He was always kind and generous with his time. I thank Mr. Zagaja for the interviews and direction. In addition, all of the detectives and investigators involved in the case that I spoke to were always open and willing. Hartford Superior Court clerk Anthony D'Addeo was extremely considerate with his time and helpful with documents and photographs.

Everyone in Hopkinton, Rhode Island, was courteous and kind to me as I asked tough questions, especially Detective McDonald and Hopkinton police chief John Scuncio. Also, Mr. McDonald's secretary, Lorraine Serio, was accommodating in collecting documents connected to the case and getting them to me.

Whenever you do a book like this, with so many people involved, it's hard to thank each and every person. There were dozens, literally, who helped me create this work of nonfiction. And each and every person that helped has my utmost respect and praise.

Lastly, the usual suspects: my family, my editor, Michaela Hamilton, and my business manager. Thank you for all you do. Also, copy editor Stephanie Finnegan's work was exceptional on this project.

III

This book is dedicated to my readers because I have come to learn throughout the years that they are the most important part of what I do—and I am grateful and humbled by having so many. My deepest appreciation goes out to every reader.

Truly.

IV

Curtain.